ANTHROPOLOGY OF THE
MIDDLE EAST AND NORTH AFRICA

PUBLIC CULTURES OF THE MIDDLE EAST AND NORTH AFRICA
Paul Silverstein, Susan Slyomovics, and Ted Swedenburg, editors

ANTHROPOLOGY OF THE
MIDDLE EAST AND NORTH AFRICA

Into the New Millennium

Edited by Sherine Hafez

and

Susan Slyomovics

INDIANA UNIVERSITY PRESS

BLOOMINGTON AND INDIANAPOLIS

This book is a publication of

Indiana University Press
Office of Scholarly Publishing
Herman B Wells Library 350
1320 East 10th Street
Bloomington, Indiana 47405 USA

iupress.indiana.edu

Telephone orders   800-842-6796
Fax orders   812-855-7931

Manufactured in the United States of America

Library of Congress Cataloging-in-Publication Data

Anthropology of the Middle East and North Africa : into the new millennium /
edited by Sherine Hafez and Susan Slyomovics.
p. cm. — (Public cultures of the Middle East and North Africa)
Includes bibliographical references and index.
ISBN 978-0-253-00746-9 (cl : alk. paper) — ISBN 978-0-253-00753-7 (pb :
alk. paper) — ISBN 978-0-253-00761-2 (eb) 1. Anthropology—Fieldwork—
Middle East. 2. Anthropology—Fieldwork—Africa, North. 3. Middle East—
Social life and customs. 4. Africa, North—Social life and customs.
I. Hafez, Sherine. II. Slyomovics, Susan.
GN635.N42A6 2013
306.0956—dc23
2012037380

1 2 3 4 5 18 17 16 15 14 13

Dedicated to our fathers, Mounir Hafez (1927–2009) and
Josef Slyomovics (1913–2011)

CONTENTS

PART 2.
SUBJECTIVITIES: YOUTH, GENDER, FAMILY, AND TRIBE IN THE MIDDLE EASTERN AND NORTH AFRICAN NATION-STATE

PART 3.
ANTHROPOLOGY OF RELIGION AND SECULARISM IN THE MIDDLE EAST AND NORTH AFRICA

PART 4.

ANTHROPOLOGY AND NEW MEDIA IN THE VIRTUAL MIDDLE EAST AND
NORTH AFRICA

ACKNOWLEDGMENTS

This volume had its origins in a two-day conference organized by Sherine Hafez and Susan Slyomovics in April 2010 at the Gustav E. von Grunebaum Center for Near Eastern Studies (CNES) of the University of California, Los Angeles (UCLA), when a group of scholars convened to tap into the recent contributions to the field of the anthropology of the MENA. We thank the staff of the Center, Mona Ramezani, Warren Berkey, and Hanno Petro, for expertly helping to organize the conference. The conference attempted to provide comprehensive and comparative coverage of Middle East and North African countries; however, our edited volume essays do not fully reflect conference participation, so our thanks to participants in the conference whose papers are not in this volume: Alan Fromherz, Stephen Russo-Shilling, Camila Pastor y Flores, and Sofian Mrabet as well as to Professors Barbara Aswad, Jessica Cattelino, Saloni Mathur, and Aamir Mufti who ably served as panel chairs and discussants. Funding for the conference came from the Department of Education Title VI awards to CNES. For close readings of the manuscript and expert comments and editing, we thank Thomas Mertes. Funding for this volume is from UCLA's Committee on Research (COR) Faculty Grant for 2010–2011 to Susan Slyomovics and a grant from the Department of Women's Studies of the University of California, Riverside, to Sherine Hafez.

INTRODUCTION

POWER AND KNOWLEDGE IN THE ANTHROPOLOGY OF THE MIDDLE EAST AND NORTH AFRICA

Sherine Hafez and Susan Slyomovics

The third millennium opened to a decade of transformation in the Middle East and North Africa (MENA). From Tunisia to Egypt to Iran, to Libya and Syria and beyond, riveting images of revolutionary Tunisians, Egyptians, Iranians, and others captured the world's attention, as young and old, women and men, changed forever the course of their countries' history. Revolts calling for the end of authoritarian governments gave witness to more than just history in the making. Dubbed by many the advent of a new "Arab Spring," the events sweeping the region emerge from the depths of a recent history of oppression and silence. They call attention to an incredible will, an underlying determination and a burgeoning social and cultural movement that has challenged postindependence myths of failure and incompetence in the region. The sociocultural dynamics of this recent past are evolving into an unknown future, filled with possibilities, that are captured in this volume by anthropologists working in the region on issues that range from human rights, empowerment, memory, youth, and media, to governance, gender and sexuality, religion, and secularism.

The region of the Middle East and North Africa (hereafter the MENA) has played a prominent if not central role in the development of human civilization. The twenty-one countries in this region that extends from Morocco to Iran are home to approximately 381 million people. Agriculture, systems of writing, codified law, and social and political structures were developed and honed in this region. Mathematics, literature, philosophy, and astronomy from the MENA—all shaped the modern sciences around the world today. And, lest we all forget, the Middle East was the cradle of the contemporary world's major monotheistic traditions.

Despite and perhaps because of this historical importance, the area that we call the MENA has been at the core of political and militaristic upheaval since the turn of the century. From Western colonialist occupation in the nineteenth century to wars of independence in the following decade, the area has been enmeshed in world political events to this day. Contemporary struggles include the Israeli–Palestinian conflict, the wars in Iraq and Afghanistan, and growing problems over natural resources such as oil, water, and land.

Anthropologists who have dedicated what is now an overwhelming corpus of work to understanding the MENA have been faced with the very challenging task not only of conducting fieldwork in a region that is commonly linked to war and terrorism but also of contending with the need to constantly work against the grain of constructed and now normative knowledge. Since the beginning of anthropological interest in the region, such knowledge has been linked to the exercise of Western power and Orientalist representations of the region's peoples. So while anthropologists of the MENA produced a plethora of works on kinship, gender, tribal and urban social organization, religion, and ritual, this scholarly work continues to engage with hegemonic power, whether by rejecting or normalizing it. Processes of knowledge construction grew more complicated after the 9/11 terrorist attack on the United States, when media images of the peoples of the region began to evoke suspicion, fear, and a reductionist demonization of MENA peoples.

This volume contains selected anthropological studies of the MENA that represent a trend in opposition to the historical pattern of Orientalizing the peoples of the region. It seeks to redress an imbalance in modes of representation that decontextualize knowledge about the region and reduce the complexity and heterogeneity of its cultures to serve political and imperialistic aims. At a time when the MENA is witnessing waves of change that challenge the historical roots of oppression and free the voices of its peoples, it seems appropriate to publish a volume that foregrounds the contributions of contemporary anthropology.

The waves of change sweeping the MENA compel social scientists, and anthropologists in particular, to move beyond local specificities and images of "untouched" communities or Middle East exceptionalism to consider wider patterns of social and cultural change. The region is poised at the intersection of global and local discourses that have an immense impact on the ways in which scholars depict, delineate, and map historical and sociocultural processes. A vast body of literature constituting the field of the anthropology of the MENA addresses the tensions between national or global aspirations of empire and the aspirations of the local populations and communities that empire encounters. Scholarship, research, and fieldwork produced since the 1990s have faced the challenges of accounting for war, terrorist attacks, and economic and political disruptions specific to the region, as well as global historical and political changes. What insights do anthropologists and anthropology bring to local uprisings, or to transnational and international conflicts? What methodological and theoretical approaches do anthropologists use that might provide perspectives not available through dominant paradigms, especially those that pit "the West" against "the rest"? How do the complicated legacies of anthropology's past continue to shape research questions and even choice of fieldwork sites?

Focusing upon processes of power characterized by a dynamic location in the world, this volume highlights collaborative academic research that demonstrates the potential of ethnographic methodologies to serve as a catalyst for theoretical debate. Although predominantly anthropological, the essays draw on approaches from several other disciplines to explore theoretical paradigms and methodological approaches that have emerged when scholarship meets the larger analytics of power. The overarching goals of this volume are to address contemporary theoretical debates about modernity, postcoloniality, and nation-state building projects within the field of Middle East and North Africa anthropology. The contributions to this volume reflect a growing concern with issues of representation in relation to close ethnographic research and writing. They deal with topics such as transnational identities, civil versus state definitions of Islam, and the binaries that shape interpretations of religious subjects. These essays point to a pressing need in the scholarship of the MENA to challenge anachronistic tendencies and to re-evaluate the creative ways local populations restructure their normative worlds and their place in it. This work cannot be done without grounding ethnographic research within trajectories of power that are interwoven in local and global historical and social processes.

To do so, four important themes form the organizing framework for the book: *part 1:* Knowledge Production in Middle East and North Africa Anthropology; *part 2:* Subjectivities: Youth, Gender, Family, and Tribe in the Middle Eastern and North African Nation-state; *part 3:* Anthropology of Religion and Secularism in the Middle East and North Africa; *part 4:* Anthropology and New Media in the Virtual Middle East and North Africa. Our first section highlights the changing boundaries between those who study and those who are studied, as anthropologists have come to realize that our production of knowledge about the region is historically situated. The subjects of our studies increasingly revise and contest our works to add their perspectives, answering back through a multiplicity of new venues in which we all now participate. Ethnographic knowledge about others ("the West versus the rest") demonstrates the possibilities of real power over the lives and futures of those who were objects of our knowledge production, because inevitably social science representations of the Middle East and North Africa have historically produced consequences for the inhabitants of the region. Our second section documents changing relations between the observer and the observed framed by America's wars in and on the region and the West's reliance on Middle Eastern and North African oil and gas reserves as they continue to have an impact on the terms of anthropology's classic categorizations, such as the tribe, youth, and the family. Our third section demonstrates the ways in which individual essays in this volume maintain an uneasy equilibrium of providing theoretical frameworks for religion and secularism without eliding or privileging local experiential social realities. Our fourth section elaborates on new methods and new topics that have forced anthropologists to open up to actual, positive knowledge creation from the region, while we face the issue of how we present and represent the boundary-destroying properties of new media according to the constraints of an academic essay within an edited volume.

Knowledge Production in Middle East and North Africa Anthropology

Susan Slyomovics's opening essay presents definitions of "state of the art" in both everyday and academic discourse, and specifically its uses as a noun or adjective to mean "incorporating the newest ideas and most up-to-date features." A "state of the art" review is a past-oriented comprehensive survey of what has been accomplished and what is missing, frequently used to assess the originality of future projects. Slyomovics focuses on discourses about the state of the art that have been organized around the oppositional figure of antithesis, while considering the implications of a Janus-faced methodology that looks backward to look forward. Exploring the state of the art as a productive category of social science criticism with a specific set of conventions, she teases out relations between power and ideology that inhabit the classic review of the anthropology of the MENA.

More than twenty years have elapsed since the last review essay on the Middle East appeared in the *Annual Review of Anthropology* (Abu Lughod 1989) and over thirty years since one specifically focused on ethnicity and difference in the region (Cohen 1977). Although there have been many advances in the anthropological literature that speak to issues of identity construction and the articulation and mediation of difference in Middle Eastern societies, on core issues concerning constructions of ethnic difference, inter-group relations, ethnic and sectarian conflict, and relations between states and minorities, the social science literature is dominated by work in political science and security studies, fields that generally lack an ethnographic perspective on the dynamics that they seek to interpret. Seteney Shami and Nefissa Neguib's co-authored essay in this volume considers anthropological works produced over the past two decades to address how identity and difference are to be theoretically conceptualized and empirically investigated. Their essay presents a critical overview of seminal works about nation, gender, and religion (mainly Islam). They also address the academic literature about difference that analyzes ethnicity, religion, and race in order to call into question the predominant and central categories of state and nation.

What made anthropology possible in the Middle East? asks Jon W. Anderson in his essay. He notes that for a generation the answer has been complicity with power: anthropologists have focused on power and the powerless according to a paradigm of interdisciplinary area studies in decline since the passing of the Cold War. Anderson returns to the ways in which modern anthropology arrived in the Middle East—not on the coattails of power, as did other disciplines, but through archaeology, which provided legitimacy, local contacts, connections, fieldwork bases, and overseas institutional support. To demonstrate his thesis that fieldwork begins before the anthropologist reaches the field, Anderson engages with the entry of modernist anthropology into Iran and Afghanistan in the 1970s, for a fuller ethnography of the state of the art and resistance to the appropriation of knowledge by hegemonic powers.

Moving away from U.S.-based spheres of anthropological activity, Paul Silverstein discusses the experiences of anthropologists conducting fieldwork in the MENA who rub ethnographic shoulders with a variety of development professionals and local cultural experts. Grassroots cultural entrepreneurs in particular have been committed to pursuing areas of traditional anthropological knowledge production: collecting genealogies, transcribing oral narratives, recording rituals, and preserving material artifacts. Silverstein's essay engages with the case of Berber/Amazigh activists with whom he has worked for over a decade in rural

Morocco and the diaspora. Mindful of their concern with the survival of an endangered language and culture, he describes complex outcomes when activists return to the colonial ethnological and philological archive in order to establish a baseline for Berber language and culture before Arabization. Silverstein presents recent fieldwork in the southeastern Ghéris Valley, Morocco, while discussing dilemmas for both activists and anthropologists in appropriating each others' research, the practical opportunities and limitations such appropriation entails, and the conflicts that can arise when the ideological commitments of the two parties prove to be incompatible. Such tensions and negotiations point to the ways in which ethnographies of the Middle East, North Africa, and beyond are ultimately collective productions and challenge the conceit of the anthropologist as an autonomous researcher.

Lara Deeb and Jessica Winegar's co-authored essay presents an ethnography of a particular generation of Middle East anthropologists in order to shed light on the contemporary state of the discipline. Anthropology, they argue, situated in the intertwined domains of anthropological, academic, national, and global politics, was profoundly affected by the aftermath of September 11, 2001—an event they describe as a "trigger action" or "crystallizing agent" for the formation of a self-identified cohort of Middle East anthropologists. Using ethnographic, textual, and statistical data, they analyze the intellectual and political contours of generational consciousness; these include scholars' encounters with academic politics at multiple career stages (graduate school, job market, and early job experiences) and scholars' understandings of and encounters with the American Anthropological Association.

Subjectivities: Youth, Gender, Family, and Tribe
in the MENA Nation-state

According to Suad Joseph, since World War II, when most states in the region gained independence, the story of state-making and nation-building in the Middle East has been a story of failure. Nationalist and pan-Arab nationalist projects are characterized as stalled, never started, or unsuccessful. Wars and civic violence have wracked the region: the Arab–Israeli war, the Lebanese Civil War, wars in Yemen, civic turmoil in Algeria, and more recently, the U.S.-led wars in Iraq in 1990 and 2003. Large populations of children and youth in the Arab world have grown up in situations of instability and high risk, and with a rather bleak sense of their future. Many try to leave their natal countries, but increasingly the doors of migration are closing. Some are mobilized into militias, or into movements, be they nationalist, resistance, or sectarian/religious. Islamist movements, which have swept through the region since the 1980s, are among a variety of alternatives that are attractive for some youth who try to make claims to a vision of the future. Children and youth constitute 65–75 percent of the populations of almost all Arab nations. In an area of the world that produces a critical source of global wealth, the rates of poverty, illiteracy, unemployment and underemployment, and health problems among the majority of the population are staggering. Joseph's essay examines fifteen years of ethnographic research on children and youth in Lebanon in the aftermath of the Lebanese Civil War as an example of the work that anthropologists can and need to do in order to understand both the contemporary dilemmas of the Arab world and the prospects for its future. She considers the problems and limitations in interviewing and observing children and youth, the nexus of family that shapes the conditions of research, and the conundrums of ethics and practice in research on children, youth, and projections for the future.

In various Middle Eastern and North African conflict zones, not only do different ethnic groups and people with differing modes of economy remember their pasts differently, so do women and men. Men may claim to remember the "homeland" through the bodies of women, a process that can lead to gender-based violence in conflicts. Theorizing this process is the goal of Sondra Hale's research in Sudan. Since few anthropological approaches are more theoretically generative in analyzing conflict than the politics of memory, Hale draws on the memory work of anthropologists, understood as an epistemological, theoretical, and political force for the future of the discipline: memory work is at the heart of ethnography, where people confront each other with the past and refute each other's tellings of the past. In conflicts, people not only kill each other, but they try to kill memory and their adversary's ideas of this contested past, or alternatively attempt to colonize each other's pasts. Hale investigates various strategies for killing and colonizing memory, annihilating culture, forcing one group's practices on another, exterminating intellectuals, dislocating people from their homeland or forcing them to live among different ethnic groups. Hale's essay is a review of strategies of violent conflicts aimed at forced forgettings that are hard to forget.

Dawn Chatty's long-term ethnographic fieldwork has been among the Harasiis, a nomadic pastoral tribe who, for centuries, were the sole human inhabitants of the central desert of Oman, named the Jiddat il-Harasiis in the 1930s by the reigning sovereign. This remote tribe, one of six in the region who continue to speak South Arabian languages predating Arabic, is organized around a sub-sistence economy based on the raising of camels and goats. Mobility over the vast and largely inhospitable rock and gravel plain of the Jiddat il-Harasiis has been the principal feature of their livelihood, focused on camel transport and more recently on truck transportation. For Chatty, the authenticity of their attachment to their region is intimately tied to the traditional distinction in Islamic histori-ography between *bedu* people in the deserts and *hadar* people in the towns and cities. Her essay deals with recent decades in the Sultanate of Oman, character-ized by increasing pressure from the central government, international conserva-tion agencies, and multinational corporations engaged in extractive industries that threaten tribal peoples' claims of belonging to the landscapes of the desert. Efforts to settle such groups, to turn them into day laborers and to assimilate them into a broadly homogenized Omani identity all contribute to the same trend. Chatty's work examines developmental processes, both national and in-ternational, and explores the ways in which the Harasiis have responded by both voicing their dismay and voting with their feet. A small element of the Harasiis as well as other tribal groups in southeastern Arabia have begun to trickle across international borders to the United Arab Emirates, where they are well received, well treated, and recognized as possessing the authenticity of *bedu*.

Christine Hegel-Cantarella analyzes legal subjectivity and transactional practices in Egypt, describing new technologies with which Egyptian locals secure contractual agreements and delayed transactions (such as retail credit). Using ethnographic and historical material, she reflects on the constitution of and interplay between economic and social obligations. Many aspects of Egyptian commercial law retain a measure of continuity despite radical legal reforms since the early twentieth century. In tandem, she considers legal and socioeconomic transformations that inflect contemporary practices of private law and the de-ployment of trust receipts. She begins with the year 1974, a time when Port Said, officially decreed a Duty Free Zone, began to experience a trade boom along with significant population increase as Egyptians from other regions migrated to the city to make their fortunes in the commercial sector. She describes ruptures in local business practices, both as a break from the past in which "old" Port Saidians had a monopoly on the local market, and as the dawn of an uncertain future. To analyze the significance of credit relationships in the Free Zone era and the roles they play discursively and through practice in constituting meanings of morality, social distance, and social networks, she focuses on one ubiquitous commercial document known as a trust receipt, a documentary technology that extends the capacity of law to enforce agreements because a breach constitutes a criminal misdemeanor; hence, they are viewed as uniquely capable of putting pressure (*daght*) on parties to fulfill obligations. She then raises questions about how "pressure" might be related not only to the document's legal capacity to stretch or constrict the temporality of negotiated agreements by delaying while invoking future legal consequences, but also to questions concerning materiality and silences that documentation invokes.

The Anthropology of Religion and Secularism in the Middle East and North Africa

Modernity is the defining characteristic of liberal Western thought, which remains the building block of secular nation-states around the world today. Western modernity was based on assumptions about universal significance and lent itself to projects to transform societies and reconceptualize the intricacies of their ways of life into simplistic readings of history, thus paving the way for colonization. A core component of the state-building project in Europe was the notion of secularism, which emphasized the power of the state in contrast to religious institutions. As religion was gradually relegated to the private sphere, secularism was expected to claim control over the public sphere. But as a number of scholars in this volume argue, the distinction between the secular and the religious is not so clearly demarcated "on the ground." Not only is there diversity in the practice of secularism among contemporary nation-states, but, despite claims to the contrary, the secular continuously produces the religious. Others suggest that liberal modernity merges seamlessly with local cultures and politics to produce an ever-mutating set of identity markers that draw upon intersecting historical trajectories.

In her contribution to the volume, Sherine Hafez critiques scholarship on the Middle East that depicts religiously motivated subjects as the antithesis of modern subjects. The binary representations that emerge from this construct posit that those who engage in Islamic activism, for instance, are emotional, irrational, and violent subjects, while those who participate in secular activism are the epitome of rationality, responsibility, and freedom. These constructs rest on the common Western view that distinguishes religion from other forms of public and political life, hence ascribing a religious subjectivity to individuals who engage with Islamic movements. The essay explores practices that the author observed while conducting fieldwork among a women's Islamic activist organization in Cairo, Egypt.

Kim Shively examines Islam in Turkey, contending that several forces in power compete over the authority to define Islam and its role in public life. The state defines Islam as a private practice and constrains its public forms following a western conceptualization of religion, thereby producing a "Turkish-style laicism." Shively draws on extensive ethnographic material gathered from her research on women's Qur'an courses to draw out the points of contention between Turkish citizens and their state over the space and practice of Islamic faith. This essay highlights a trend in anthropological studies of the MENA region through an examination of the ways in which local populations claim individual paths to define Islam within larger transnational contexts. She sheds light on new discursive formations of Islam that are locally specific as they are simultaneously mainstreamed by new transnational networks. In a similar vein, Susanne Dahlgren explores emerging forms of *shari'a* law that are disseminated through satellite and cable television and the internet. She reflects on the impact of these new interpretive forms of Islamic law and argues that they have assumed hegemonic forms that have questionable affects on women's issues and human rights discourse. By looking back into the colonial archives of the India Office in London, and ethnographic fieldwork in Aden, Southern Yemen from the late 1980s, her work historically contextualizes recent changes in the global platform of Islamic interpretation. Dahlgren weaves these various historical strands into what can be described as a corpus of legal debates on *shari'a* that have been largely ignored by anthropologists of the region in the larger field of Anglo-Muhammadan legal practice.

Examining another facet of creative processes with which local populations in the MENA engage across national boundaries is Cortney Hughes' essay on contraceptive practices in Morocco. She demonstrates that national borders do not limit the perspectives of citizens of MENA countries to the extent that one might think. Taking Morocco as an example, she argues that urban, working-class female research participants constructed an alternative space to remove themselves conceptually from "conservative" Middle Eastern states such as Saudi Arabia and move toward what was to them a "liberal" Europe, specifically France. Focusing on contraception, Hughes reveals how Moroccan women forge an identity that transcends the regions of Africa, the Middle East, and Europe. In light of the fact that women are a central trope of nationalism in Morocco, Hughes highlights the importance of such negotiations as key to understanding Morocco's social and cultural processes.

Anthropology and New Media in the Virtual MENA

The theme of media and new theoretical spaces that virtual worlds offer their inhabitants today characterize the fourth section, dealing with the virtual Middle East.

In his essay on Morocco, Emilio Spadola argues that the "technologized call," or the mobilization of the masses through virtual communication, is a phenomenon that deserves deeper examination by anthropologists of the MENA. Spadola explores the call for the 1975 Green March by King Hassan II in Morocco and the enormous popular response, a bewildering development mediated by modern mass communications. These events, argues Spadola, open up new possibilities for understanding how power operates.

Sebastian Maisel examines blogs run by two tribal groups in Saudi Arabia and notes novel affiliations similarly forged in virtual space. He observes that the introduction of the internet to rural Saudi Arabia has encouraged uncensored interaction among individuals, thereby giving voice to communities that have not had access to public forums of this nature. He explores the impact of the IT revolution and asks whether new media truly represent a profound change in identity politics or a challenge to the state's monopoly on control of information, as is so often assumed.

Charlotte Karagueuzian and Pamela Chrabieh Badine explore cyberspace and youth in their chapter, which is based on a study of the Arab and Iranian blogosphere and also touches on their use of a variety of new media. They describe how young people reach across sectarian and political divides to connect in cyberspace, and suggest that youth-created counter-cultures that operate in virtual space offer mutual support and understanding, possibly enabling resistance, despite profoundly differing religious and political affiliations.

While chapters in this volume consider a variety of topics, all reflect a commitment to ethnographic research informed by current discussions about the field of Middle East and North Africa anthropology. All attempt to take stock of what anthropologists have and have not accomplished in their endeavors to understand this region. Fieldwork in the region remains the bedrock foundation of MENA anthropology. Fluency and literacy in the languages of the region are increasingly important prerequisites. Embedded knowledge of concrete ways of living, then, is informed by the history of anthropology of the Middle East and North Africa but never ignores the position of the observing anthropologist, who in turn is changed by her presence and role among fellow culture-making human beings.

ANTHROPOLOGY OF THE
MIDDLE EAST AND NORTH AFRICA

PART 1.

KNOWLEDGE PRODUCTION IN THE ANTHROPOLOGY OF
THE MIDDLE EAST AND NORTH AFRICA

1.

STATE OF THE STATE OF THE ART STUDIES: AN INTRODUCTION TO THE ANTHROPOLOGY OF THE MIDDLE EAST AND NORTH AFRICA

Susan Slyomovics

In the present state of the art, this is all that can be done.

—H. H. Suplee, *Gas Turbine*

In both everyday and academic discourse, as noun or adjective, the phrase "state of the art" has come to mean "incorporating the newest ideas and most up-to-date features" (*Oxford English Dictionary* online). The first usage, dated to 1910 according to the *Oxford English Dictionary*, was recorded in *Gas Turbine*, an engineering manual authored by H. H. Suplee, who issued this laconic observation: "In the present state of the art, this is all that can be done." Wikipedia's definition is:

> The state of the art is the highest level of development, as of a device, technique, or scientific field, achieved at a particular time. It also applies to the level of development (as of a device, procedure, process, technique, or science) reached at any particular time usually as a result of modern methods. (Wikipedia, 1 October 2011)

At least in legal parlance, the semantic range of the phrase extends beyond the implication of a definitive overview of what came before toward something new in order to establish the originality of an invention in patent law. Similarly, in state-of-the-art surveys in the social sciences, the understanding has been that the disciplinary terrain is to be surveyed primarily for the purpose of relegating known and disseminated research to the past in order to ask what's new. My version of the "state-of-the-art" definition, by contrast with this forward-looking focus, is a past-oriented survey of what's been accomplished and what's missing. It must be excellent and comprehensive, publicly available for scrutiny, and used to assess the originality of future projects; these were the three goals of a 2010 UCLA conference titled "State of the Art: The Anthropology of the Middle East and North Africa," and of this volume which it inspired.

Critically reviewing critical reviews enables me to engage shamelessly and explicitly with issues of hindsight bias, or roads taken and not taken. This is because decades of essays about the state of the art are characterized by negative assessments of the anthropology of the Middle East and North Africa (MENA). Discourses about the state of the art have been organized around the oppositional figure of antithesis, a Janus-faced methodology that looks backward then forward, not only echoing and presaging the underlying shared enterprise of hindsight bias but inevitably embedding the particular biases of the author and his times (most authors were male). We could go so far as to label the "state of the art" as a genre, meaning a productive category of social science criticism with a specific set of conventions alluded to above, notably negative assessment, hindsight bias, and a dialectic of proposition and counter-propositions. Timothy Mitchell, in his 2003 state-of-the-art review, "The Middle East in the Past and Future of Social Science" provides examples of hindsight bias, the trope endemic to state-of-the-art studies. In so doing, he underscores the ways in which the genre of the state of the art begins by and depends on reciting a litany of failures attributed to Middle East studies and the social science of the region. Mitchell's prime example is Leonard Binder's sweeping condemnation of the field in his 1973 article, "Area Studies: A Critical Reassessment": "The fact is that Middle East studies are beset by subjective projection, displacements of affect, ideological distortion, romantic mystification, and religious bias, as well as a great deal of incompetent scholarship" (Binder 1976, 16). Another example is an essay by anthropologist John Gulick (1969), "State of the Art III: The Anthropology of the Middle East," which depicted the Janus-like face of Middle East anthropology poised between the negative and the positive, faced with two potential opposing directions:

The state of art of anthropology in the Middle East is a state of growth like Topsy.[1] We continue to be faced with the dilemma of either filling subregional gaps in descriptive knowledge (so that we can make generalizations more confidently) or of focusing much research on a few sub-regions (so that we can generate more sophisticated hypotheses). Unable to resolve the dilemma, some of us continue to make hypotheses and generalizations which are always subject to summary rejection, while others of us appear to remain either very narrowly focused or inarticulate, or both. Whether the anthropology of the Middle East will develop into a cumulative discipline or a congeries of mostly unreliable parts is difficult to say. The potentialities for development in either direction are definitely present. (Gulick 1969, 13)

Evidently a retelling of past regressive academic practices is insufficient, although necessary, to the genre. Mitchell warns that if, as he claims, the state-of-the-art formula must begin retrospectively with "regular statements of failure," then we must also beware of its polar opposite, which is the countervailing upswing of upbeat optimism that touts the latest novel combinations of social science and Middle East area studies (Mitchell 2004, 71). In the spirit of Mitchell's caveat, but oscillating like a pendulum gone berserk between negative and positive reviews, I now resurrect a range of prior state-of-the-art writings about anthropology of the MENA as a systematic review to introduce this volume. In this chapter, I emphasize the 1949 American Council of Learned Societies' (ACLS) *A Program for Near Eastern Studies* report; Louise Sweet's surveys (1969–1971); Morroe Berger's 1967 article, "Middle Eastern and North African Studies: Development and Needs," published in the first issue of the *Middle East Studies Association Bulletin;* the 1976 article by Leonard Binder, "Area Studies: A Critical Reassessment"; three *Annual Review of Anthropology* articles (Robert Fernea and James Malarkey in 1975; Abdul Hamid el-Zein and Erik Cohen in 1977; and Lila Abu-Lughod in 1989); Richard Antoun's 1976 chapter on "Anthropology" in *The Study of the Middle East: Research and Scholarship in the Humanities and Social Sciences;* R. Bayly Winder's 1987 "Four Decades of Middle Eastern Study" in the *Middle East Journal;* and finally Timothy Mitchell's 2002 "The Middle East in the Past and Future of Social Science." One conclusion from all of this is to be foreshadowed: the fact that any statement about the state of the art is not about the past, but how to recreate the future. We are all pursuing the retrospective in search of the prospective.

Coon, began study of MENA?

Carleton Coon (1904–1981):
MENA's First American Anthropologist?

It is remarkable now to read the early 1949 state-of-the-art report entitled *A Program for Near Eastern Studies* issued by the Committee on Near Eastern Studies of the ACLS in which it was noted in passing that "*only one anthropologist is known to have begun to concentrate on the area*" (emphasis added). Almost forty years later, R. Bayly Winder's 1987 state-of-the-art report covering Middle East studies 1947–1987 speculates that this sole American anthropologist was Carleton Stevens Coon (Winder 1987, 45 cited in Mitchell 2004, 6). The figure of Coon lurks throughout this chapter, popping up as a foil and a cautionary tale, a progenitor and precursor, in unexpected ways. Coon, who completed his Harvard doctorate in anthropology with fieldwork in northern Morocco, belonged to the swashbuckler school of intrepid fieldworkers, archeologists, and undercover agents. Frequently inhabiting the contradictory roles of spy, scholar, and adventurer simultaneously, he lived among and wrote extensively about Berbers, Albanians, and other hardy mountain people. Coon's *A North Africa Story: The Anthropologist as OSS Agent, 1941–1943* recounts the effective deployment of his anthropological and archeological skills on behalf of the North Africa station of the Office of Strategic Services (the OSS was the precursor to the CIA). He writes as if fully prepared to raise up armies of his beloved Rifian Berber tribes against Hitler's Afrika Corps during World War II, especially since such an uprising could do double duty by confounding the resident French and Spanish colonial powers. Coon was by no means anti-colonialist; he wholeheartedly assimilated the French colonial "Kabyle myth" that pitted Berber against Arab to the latter's perennial disadvantage.[2] Berbers were white folks, or so Coon averred:

> The lightest pigmentation recorded is that of the Rifians, the most European-looking Berbers. They have a 65 percent incidence of pinkish-white unexposed skin color. This goes as high as 86 percent in some tribes. Twenty-three percent are freckled. Ten percent have light brown or blond hair; in some tribes, 25 percent do. In beard color, 45 percent of Rifians are reddish, light brown, or blond bearded; in some tribes the figure rises to 57 percent, with 24 percent completely blond. (Coon 1965, 177)

Coon's racial theories have been largely discredited. He held that five primordial species preceded the evolution of *Homo sapiens,* with each race evolving separately and at different speeds. Coon's subsequent physical anthropology battles were as much about turf disputes with his rivals, whom he called the "Boasinine" Columbia school of anthropology, as they were disagreements over scientific authority. In 2001, an article in the *Journal of the History of Biology* revisited the controversy surrounding his 1962 book, *The Origin of Races*, demonstrating the ways in which Coon's theories had been transformed by others into a political weapon. The article concluded:

> Coon's thesis was used by segregationists in the United States as proof that African Americans were "junior" to white Americans, and hence unfit for full participation in American society. . . . The paper concludes that Coon actively aided the segregationist cause in violation of his own standards for scientific objectivity. (Jackson 2001, 247)

Coon's additional claim to anthropological fame is as the precursor case of our discipline's current imperative to grapple with militarized anthropology and the "embedded anthropologist,"[3] activities that seemed benign during World War II but are topics of intense debate as they continue to play out today in Middle Eastern and North African crisis and war zones such as Iraq and Afghanistan. Moreover, Coon exemplifies for me successive generations of misguided American foreign policies that willfully failed to engage major political movements then and now. Read (and weep over) Coon's assessment of the Moroccan nationalist movement that successfully led the country to independence from France by 1956. In his 1980 memoir, Coon restated his wartime predictions:

> I came to the conclusion that the Nationalists, however honorable they might be and however worthy their ambitions and ideals, were not men of action. They were great talkers and mystics, hard to pin down to facts. They had had enough European education to make them restless, but not enough to let them know how to act in either a native or a modern sense. Since we were interested only in action, we would do much better to confine our attention to the men from the hills, the men who knew how to handle not the inkpot but the rifle. Therefore we concentrated on our friends in the North and left the dreamers alone. (Coon 1980, 23)[4]

Coon may have been America's first practicing Middle East sociocultural anthropologist in the field, but it is worth noting a fascinating earlier example of

America's imperative to understand the Arabic and Berber-speaking world, one cited by Morroe Berger, professor of sociology at Princeton University and the Middle East Studies Association's first president. Berger's state-of-the-art article, "Middle Eastern and North African Studies: Development and Needs," published at the Association's founding in 1967, opens with the case of William Brown Hodgson (1801–1871), dispatched by President John Quincy Adams to Algiers and the Barbary States of North Africa for language training. Adams' diary entry was dated 16 January 1830, a mere six months before the French army invasion of Algeria, and illustrates linguistic lacunae still evident during America's twenty-first century war in Iraq: "We were in this country [Barbary States] so destitute of persons versed in the Oriental languages that we could not even procure a translation of any paper which occasionally came to us in Arabic" (Berger 1967, 1–2, citing Adams vol. 3, 1877, 412–413). Earlier, when Hodgson was America's first consul in Tunis, in the 1840s, he authored *Notes on Northern Africa, the Sahara, and Soudan: In Relation to the Ethnography, Languages, History, Political, and Social Condition of the Nations of those Countries.* Like Coon, Hodgson remained fascinated by the language and people known as Berber, who in contrast to the Arabs were recognized even in Roman times as a race "unconquerable in war" (*genus insuperabile bello*). His thesis is familiar, reprising Samuel Huntington's "clash of civilizations" model, with presuppositions that simply update old wine in new political science bottles:

> On the Mediterranean coast of Africa, there are in progress, at this moment, great political and commercial revolutions. There exists in that region, a sanguinary and unceasing conflict of Christianity and Mohammedanism, of civilization with semi-barbarism. . . . The result of a conflict, between undisciplined hordes, and the science of European warfare, cannot be doubtful. (Hodgson 1844, 2)

I have embraced Coon for his originary role as Middle East anthropology's early ethnographer, but anthropologist Louise Sweet, author of a handbook and reader in the anthropology of the Middle East, proposes a different choice for the first "classic" and "watershed" publication of Middle East ethnology. In her 1969 state-of-the-art review entitled "A Survey of Recent Middle Eastern Ethnology," Sweet opines:

Up to-date anthropological research in the Middle East began with the publication in 1949 of E. E. Evans-Pritchard's *The Sanusi of Cyrenaica*. This account of the rise of the Sanusiyyah order and its structural relation to the Cyrenaican Bedouin tribal system, its political changes and decline over a century (1843–1943), was a major step away from folklorism and trait distribution surveys of a more naïve anthropology. It is, I think, the watershed of modern Middle East ethnology. It rests upon, in part, foundations laid by such distinguished predecessors as the French students of Moroccan and Algerian Arabs (in particular, the works of Robert Montagne) and on the Italian ethnographers. It rests also on informed knowledge of Islamic religious history and movements. But, independently of these, it rests upon Evans-Pritchard's own deep experience in field research among African "tribal" peoples, seen in their ecological contexts, and viewed "holistically," i.e. as whole cultural systems in adaptation to their geographical, and cultural environments over time, in economy, social and political dynamics and ideology. (Sweet 1969, 222)

former – ME oriental studies, etc

Nonetheless, since Evans-Pritchard was British, Carleton Coon's status as America's unique Middle East anthropologist in wartime North Africa is secure. He was replaced not by another lone researcher abroad but by the phenomenal postwar growth of United States–based Middle East area studies in American universities. Formerly, the subjects of Middle East studies had been couched academically as oriental studies, biblical studies, and Semitic philology. In 1958, a new financial powerhouse for the academy was launched by the government passage of the National Defense Education Act along with the associated Fulbright-Hays programs in 1961. The Title VI section of the NDEA plowed federal funds into "language development" of less commonly taught languages, targeting in the first phase Urdu-Hindi, Arabic, Chinese, Russian, Japanese, and Portuguese. Avowed goals were to educate and send scholars from what John F. Kennedy called in 1961 the "first anti-colonial nation" to the "third world's" newly independent countries. UCLA's Center for Near Eastern Studies, founded in 1956, was among the original nineteen centers established during that first year (Hines 2001, 6–11).[5] But how were the students in the burgeoning network of Middle East university language classes speaking to anthropology's pursuits? Characteristic of the 1970s state-of-the-art genre was the lament voiced by anthropologists Robert Fernea and James Malarkey (then Fernea's student) in their *Annual Review of Anthropology* assessment: "[Not only has there been no] appreciable development of a fruitful

1958 – language funding to third world

dialogue between MENA anthropologists and Orientalists . . . [but,] in addition, anthropological studies from the MENA have largely failed to attract an audience of scholars beyond those devoted to the undertaking of such studies themselves" (Fernea and Malarkey 1975, 183). Despite large numbers of available bibliographies, ethnographies, and reviews of the field, by 1975 the authors deemed Anglo-American anthropology of the region parochial and without vitality, a field that discouraged debate and critical reflection; in their own words, "a set of speakers without listeners" (201).[6] Consequently, Fernea and Malarkey, joining many others including Louise Sweet in her 1969 survey, proposed a radical practical solution: Anglo-American anthropologists should read French. They cited the francophone ethnographic literature of the 1960s and 70s written by Franz Fanon, Jacques Berque, Pierre Bourdieu, and Jean Duvignaud, all researchers profoundly marked by the experience of French colonialism in the Maghrib, and included Claude Levi-Strauss and the French *Annales* School of social history, specifically Marc Bloch and Lucien Lefevre:

> But why in the writings of French and Arab intellectuals, do we hear consistently the words *authenticité, specificité,* and *identité collective?* Why do we hear from these Orientalists, ethnologists, and other concerned commentators the admonitions that researchers look to the past, that only speaking to the past and understanding MENA culture historically (its language, poetry, art, law, etc.) can progress be pursued rationally? Is this mere French mysticism? (Fernea and Malarkey 1975, 192)

A year after the Fernea and Malarkey overview, Richard Antoun, who fits his own definition of "native anthropologist," or the Western-trained Middle Eastern researcher conducting fieldwork at home in the Middle East, contributed a lengthy chapter on anthropology that appeared in the 1976 edited volume by Leonard Binder, *The Study of the Middle East: Research and Scholarship in the Humanities and Social Sciences.* Antoun's conclusion resembled many of the state-of-the-art reviews that preceded his own in that "those who have entered Middle Eastern anthropology are primarily interested in the area and only secondarily interested in the discipline" (Antoun 1976, 169):

> The state of the art of Middle Eastern anthropology is related mainly to things Middle Eastern rather than things anthropological. That is, it is the Middle Eastern anthropologist's preoccupation with the unique, esoteric,

[handwritten marginalia: state of art related to Middle East anthropology vs US anthropology / things]

and the romantic aspects of the culture and the negative popular image of a hostile Islam that accounts for the state of the art. It could also be argued that the cultural antiquity of the region requires a relatively greater commitment to the study of history and language and, consequently, a lesser commitment to the study of anthropological theory and method. (Antoun 1976, 169)

Additional fascinating data can be gleaned from a questionnaire that Antoun sent to some 300 Middle East anthropologists in the mid-1970s. He reported that anthropologists were engaging in lengthy fieldwork to produce ethnographies and that the majority of our course titles employed the word "ethnography," surely the mark of a redundant hermeneutical circuit. More facts emerge from these reports. There was only one reported course on Islam according to Antoun (1976, 153). Paradoxically, our foremost titles for publication were about religion; few, though, were on Islam (unless by native anthropologists), and more concerned witchcraft, shamanism, Judaism, and Christianity in the region, followed by topics on ethnicity, nomads, village studies, and on FBD—father's brother's daughter marriage, and its endogamous extensions—which accounted for an extraordinary preponderance of research, as noted also by Fernea and Malarkey. Antoun, seconded by Erik Cohen's 1977 state-of-the-art review, calculated that half the research in the region between Morocco and Afghanistan was about Israel, with three separate review essays published by 1976 and devoted to anthropology in Israel (Cohen 1977; cf. Goldberg 1976; Handelman and Deshen 1975; and Marx 1975).

By 1977, the date I call my watershed year, how did anthropologists of the Middle East envision future directions? A state-of-the-art review by Abdul Hamid el-Zein in 1977 on the anthropology of Islam considered primarily three American anthropologists and their work on religion and Islam in Morocco, namely Clifford Geertz, Dale Eickelman, and Vincent Crapanzano (El-Zein 1977). Antoun pointed to new works about the emerging field of ethnicity, while deploring the erasure of a key work, *Caravan* by Carleton Coon, a readable bestseller (so rare for our field) that provided a popular introduction to Middle Eastern anthropology in the 1950s—in fact, a book purchased by my parents and, therefore, the first anthropology book I encountered as a teenager. *Caravan* was published in 1951, revised in 1958, with a last second edition in 1967, and, its bestseller status leading to a circumstance equally unusual, was translated into Arabic as *al-Qafila*, published in Beirut in 1959. *Caravan* famously proposed the metaphor of the "mosaic"— as in Coon's oft-quoted statement, "The most conspicuous fact about Middle

Eastern civilization is that in each country the population consists of a mosaic of peoples" (1951, 2)—while Islam and the *suq*, or marketplace, were respectively the cultural and economic "cement." Antoun deemed Coon's mosaic model an effective and overarching theoretical superstructure, a way out of particularistic, ethnocentric, microscopic studies of a single village or a lone linguistic group and a much-needed step toward framing interactions among groups: "Coon's metaphorical model becomes not merely a basis for the description of isolated social units but rather a means of analyzing important processes of a society in transition" (1976, 179). Reading *Caravan* almost sixty years later resembles a nostalgic voyage back to a time when the multiethnic, pre-nationalistic worlds of the Hapsburg and Ottoman empires ruled, with your guide Carleton Coon, dubbed by Earnest Albert Hooten, his Harvard anthropology professor and mentor, "An Untamed Anthropologist among the Wilder Whites."[7]

1977: My Watershed Year

In 1977, the year I began graduate school at UC Berkeley, there were two publishing landmarks, more accurately bombshells, that dealt with the relationship between knowledge and power—each in its own widely disparate disciplinary mode, neither explicitly including gender (here, my own hindsight bias is evident). Both interrogated the ways in which representation, including anthropological representation, is so often informed by the particular circumstances of asymmetrical power, whether in the international arena between the U.S. and the Muslim world, or at the micro-level of the individual anthropologist's engagement and positioning in the Arab world. The first was an early chapter excerpted from Edward Said's as-yet unpublished *Orientalism* that appeared in *The Georgia Review* in the spring of 1977. Said's questions over thirty years ago implicitly interrogated then prevalent theories of the Middle Eastern mosaic and Janus-faced state-of-the-art surveys that haunt our discipline:

> Can one divide human reality, as indeed human reality seems genuinely divided, into clearly different cultures, histories, traditions, societies, even races, and survive the consequences humanly? By surviving the consequences humanly, I mean to ask whether there is any way of avoiding the hostility expressed by the division, say of men into "us" [Westerners] and "they" [Orientals]. (Said 1979, 45)

I recall the negative reaction to Said's *Orientalism* by my first Berkeley thesis advisor, Ariel Bloch, a German-born Israeli professor of Arabic dialectology whose parents barely escaped to Palestine before World War II. Bloch belonged to the last generation of scholars trained at the University of Münster, Germany by Hans Wehr, the great lexicographer of the eponymous *Arabic-English Dictionary,* an indispensable companion for American students of the Arabic language. Bloch's dismissal of Said's book stemmed from the latter's exclusion of the countervailing case of German Orientalists, scholars who did not fit the paradigm Said was critiquing, the French and British colonialist-Orientalist approach to scholastic empire-building projects. I regret that I never dared ask Bloch about Wehr's own life and research context, surely more heinous than the ravages of colonialism. What could we students then make of these disconcertingly cryptic sentences in Wehr's introduction to the 1979 *Dictionary of Modern Written Arabic,* which placed him in the heart of Nazi Germany?

> The major portion of this book was collected between 1940 and 1944 with the co-operation of several German orientalists. The entire work was set in type, but only one set of galleys survived the war.... The author is indebted to Dr. Andreas Jacobi and Mr. Heinrich Becker who, until they were called up for military service in 1943, rendered valuable assistance in collecting and collating the vast materials of the German edition and in preparing the manuscript. (Wehr 1976, x–xi)

In a wide-ranging, much-quoted exploration titled "On Orientalism" published in his *The Predicament of Culture,* James Clifford replied to critiques about overlooked German scholarship by reflecting on what Said had accomplished.[8] Said's aim, Clifford maintained, was not to produce an intellectual history of Orientalism or a history of Western ideas of the Orient. Although he noted that Said's "narrowing and rather tendentious shaping of the field could be taken as a fatal flaw" (1988, 267), nonetheless Said's definition of Orientalism as a pervasive and coercive discourse was persuasive:

> Orientalism—"enormously systematic," cosmological in scope, incestuously self-referential—emerges as much more than a mere intellectual or ideological tradition. Said at one point calls it "a considerable dimension of modern political-intellectual culture." As such it "has less to do with the Orient than it does with 'our' world." (Clifford 1988, 260–261)

Orientalism
divided perception of
Arab culture
vs us

While my professor's dislike of the book rested on the exclusion of his own category of German Orientalists, Clifford referenced Said's genuinely serious genealogical omissions. For example, Said emphasized the Arab Middle East, the Mashriq, and omitted the Maghreb, the region explicated by modern French Orientalists who conformed to the pattern of anthropology's incestuous relationship with power, so evident for French colonial domination in North Africa. In Morocco, the French had created the Mission Scientifique au Maroc in 1904, and another institute in Cairo in 1909, in addition to the journals, institutes, and scholarly organizations they had established in Algeria within days of their 1830 conquest. Anglo-American institutional development lagged behind France's long-term academic infrastructure resulting from colonial rule over the region, while the lengthy Algerian struggle for independence ensured, according to Clifford, that the MENA countries were not mere data providers for social scientists:

> In a French context the kinds of critical questions posed by Said have been familiar since the Algerian war and may be found strongly expressed well before 1950. It would simply not be possible to castigate recent French "Orientalism" in the way that he does the discourse of the American Middle East "experts," which is still shaped by Cold War patterns and by the polarized Arab-Israeli conflict. (Clifford 1988, 267)

marginalized?

Despite Clifford Geertz, Vincent Crapanzano, and other American anthropologists studying French North Africa, and although Said was fluent in French culture, another concentric circle of marginalization is to be traced: Middle East anthropologists are marginal to anthropology and anthropologists of North Africa are marginal to Middle East anthropology. So vital is the genealogical distribution of marginalization (or perhaps anthropologists always imagine the discursive action is elsewhere) that on the occasion of the twenty-fifth anniversary in 2009 of the founding of the American Institute of Maghrib Studies (AIMS), Jerry Bookin-Weiner, Director of Study Abroad and Outreach at America-Mideast Educational and Training Services in Washington, D.C. emailed the AIMS membership this inspiring account of marginalized Maghrib-oriented researchers organizing in order to flourish academically:

> In the late 1970s and early 1980s North Africanists weren't entirely sure where they fit into the academic universe. Most saw themselves as part of the MESA [Middle East Studies Association] universe while others gravitated

to the African Studies Association. In any case we were quite peripheral to both spheres. Neither organization's annual meeting had more than one or two sessions on the Maghrib and it was not unusual for the panelists to outnumber or be barely outnumbered by the audience. Many of us remember sessions scheduled in the last time slot of the conference when most of the participants had already left for home or very early in the morning on the last day.

And so, with that as background, a small group of North Africanists came together in 1982–1983 to try to coordinate our activities and increase our presence in the conferences. Ken Perkins and I took the lead and were dubbed "co-presidents" of what the group decided to call the "Maghrib Studies Group." Because I was also head of the Office of International Programs at Old Dominion University and had an early model desktop computer (Radio Shack TRS80 Model 3, with no hard drive and a dual floppy disk drive in the days when floppy disks were really floppy) in my office, I maintained the mailing list of a few dozen and Ken edited our newsletter. The newsletter, which was pretty informal, came out a couple of times a year. That and attempts to make sure there were more North African–oriented sessions and papers proposed for the MESA Annual Meeting were our main activities.

The Maghrib Studies Group ceded to AIMS as it emerged beginning in 1985 under the leadership of Bill Zartman and George Sabbagh. We turned over our mailing list, our "executive committee" was absorbed into the initial AIMS Board of Directors, and a vibrant era in Maghrib studies began. (Bookin-Weiner 2009)

Out of Morocco in my watershed year of 1977 emerged my second example of a path-breaking work, *Reflections on Fieldwork in Morocco* by Paul Rabinow, then a recent addition to Berkeley's Anthropology Department. As an experiment in ethnographic writing, it contributed to fissures in the persona of the anthropologist unassailably conveying truth in his text, what James Clifford aptly subsumed under the rubric of anthropology's claim to "ethnographic authority" (1988, 25). *Reflections* is a key example of reflexive anthropology, especially when paired with the publication in 1975 of Rabinow's *Symbolic Domination: Cultural Form and Historical Change in Morocco,* a standard sober fieldwork ethnography under the direction of Clifford Geertz. Thirty years later, focusing on fieldwork itself as a practice,[9] Rabinow would dismissively describe reflexive ethnography as "morpho-clastic moves [that] have tended to be carried out as ends-in-themselves. They have been aligned in poorly thought through ways with the hope of more or less radical, political, aesthetic, or ethical transformation. That horizon has rarely included scientific advance as an explicit goal."[10]

Nonetheless, reading, rereading, and teaching *Reflections* since 1977, I remain astonished, amused, and yes, moved. It seemed to me that Rabinow had attempted a narratological and sexual climax, one in which the narrative arc of his ethnography managed to achieve a fleeting anthropological epiphany about the researcher in relation to his informants. It was not through the intimate meeting of the American male and Berber female bodies, nor through a baring of the ethnographer's soul, but through a baring of his mind. It helped that Rabinow was one of my teachers. He and James Clifford co-taught for some three years a remarkable semester-long course, "The History of Social Thought," physically shuttling students between Berkeley and UC Santa Cruz and pedagogically presenting us with Michel Leiris, Marcel Griaule, Georges Bataille, Alfred Métraux, and Michel Foucault: we were reading French. I can assure readers that bliss it was in that dawn to be alive, but to be young was very heaven (*pace* William Wordsworth), far from my Montreal hometown, driving a convertible packed with impoverished fellow graduate students under the warm California sun to a forested, magnificent beachfront campus. When I can separate the happiness of discovering California from any pleasure I might have derived from combining Berkeley's graduate school programs in anthropology, folklore, and Near Eastern studies, I must admit, with hindsight bias infused with nostalgia for my youth, that I rarely succeeded in bringing together my distinct disciplinary domains and intellectually antagonistic departments. Fortunately, having imbibed James Clifford's approach, I was able to sustain my belief that bipolarity in the academy could be productive, if the methodology embraced were a collage, but never a mosaic:

> My topic, and method, is collage, a mechanism described by Max Ernst as the "coupling of two realities, irreconcilable in appearance, upon a plane which apparently does not suit them." I take this mechanism to be intrinsic to both surrealism and ethnography, discourses enmeshed in a constant play of familiar and unfamiliar realities, of relative orders, of interrupted wholes. To juxtapose ethnography and surrealism is to reinterpret—or better, to reshuffle—invention of culture from its comprehension. (Clifford 1984, 282)

Parenthetically, it must be recalled that in 1977, a third book appeared with great impact, namely, Elizabeth Warnock Fernea and Basima Qattan Bezirgan's edited volume entitled *Middle Eastern Muslim Women Speak.* Exemplifying the power of anthologies to set themselves off from their predecessors, their selected translations helped shape English-language academic representations of women from the Middle East. Due to the thematic reach and regional focus in addition to the scope and variety of women's "voices" not previously available in English, some state-of-the-art reviews on women and Middle East studies have dated the "first corpus of materials" for this area to Fernea and Bezirgan (along with Beck and Keddie's *Women in the Muslim World,* cf. Baron 1996, 172; Sharoni 1997; Abu-Lughod 2001, 113).[11] If I pursue important research avenues about gender made possible by Said, and include what the Fernea & Bezirgan anthology accomplished, I ask myself the following question: If it is the case that Orientalism powerfully constructs the object it speaks about to produce the "truth" of the object it speaks about, then how do these translations of women's writings from the region intervene in Western scholarly projects about gender and the "other"? Scholars who focus on these kinds of questions about representation and translation have illuminated the ways in which the concerns and questions of fieldwork and ethnography were not neutral, objective enterprises, but projects susceptible to producing and reproducing representations of the "Orient" as inferior, exotic, tyrannical, exceptional, gendered, and sexualized, the consummate Other and "them" to our "us." Certainly, Said and Rabinow contributed to disseminating French poststructuralist thought via Foucault into the American academy, while the emergence of women's studies about the Middle East opened up new avenues to explore the ethnocentric American self allied to the relationship between power and knowledge. *power & knowledge*

Therefore, for the purposes of this essay, I consider Said's *Orientalism* as the magnum opus, the best and most wide-ranging, spectacular state-of-the-art review of Western scholarship with a direct bearing on the social sciences and area studies of the MENA. If so, Said's goals are clear:

> My aim . . . was not so much to dissipate difference itself—for who can deny the constitutive role of national as well as cultural differences in the relations between human beings—but to challenge the notion that that difference implies hostility, a frozen reified set of opposed essences, and a whole adversarial knowledge built out of those things. What I called for in *Orientalism* was a new way of conceiving the separations and conflicts that had stimulated generations of hostility, war, and imperial control. (Said 1994, 350)

difference implies hostility

Moreover, Said too, hews to the paradigm of the state of the art by balancing trenchant critiques with chronicles of positive changes, emergent voices, and theoretical openings in the academy. For the twenty-fifth year re-edition of *Orientalism,* Said's 1994 "Afterword" veers optimistically toward scholarly transformations and institutional trends influenced by his own writings:

> A leading motif has been the consistent critique of Eurocentrism and patriarchy. Across US and European campuses in the 1980s students and faculty worked assiduously to expand the academic focus of so-called core curricula to include writing by women, non-European artists and thinkers, and subalterns. This was accompanied by important changes in the approach to area studies, long in the hands of classical Orientalists and their equivalents. Anthropology, political science, literature, sociology, and above all history felt the effects of a wide-ranging critique of sources, the introduction of theory, and the dislodgement of the Eurocentric perspective. (Said 1994, 350)

Middle East Anthropology and the Conundrum of "Localized Questions"

Framed by Said's challenge to anthropology to reshape the "politics of scholarship by . . . Western-oriented scholars of the region" and by the school of reflexive anthropology, Lila Abu-Lughod's 1989 review, "Zones of Theory in the Anthropology of the Arab World," reads qualitatively as a different kind of state-of-the-art critique, one that she labels "situated—a reading and writing from a particular place, from an individual who is personally, intellectually, politically and historically situated" (Abu-Lughod 1989, 268). She also reminds readers that Talal Asad's edited volume, *Anthropology and the Colonial Encounter,* had already taken up the issue of anthropology as the discipline that reinforces inequities between researchers traveling from the West and their subjects in the Third World. Asad made these connections with great clarity in his 1973 "Introduction":

> We are today become increasingly aware of the fact that information and understanding produced by bourgeois disciplines like anthropology are acquired and used most readily by those with the greatest capacity for exploitation. This follows partly from the structure of research, but more especially from the way in which these disciplines objectify their knowledge.

It is because the powerful who support research expect the kind of under-standing that will ultimately confirm them in their world that anthropology has not very easily turned to the production of radically subversive forms of understanding. . . . We then need to ask ourselves how this relationship has affected the practical pre-conditions of social anthropology; the uses to which its knowledge was put; the theoretical treatment of particular topics; the mode of perceiving and objectifying alien societies; and the anthropolo-gist's claim of political neutrality. (Asad 1973, 16–17)

Previous reviews I have discussed shared these features: they included sober, annotated, quasi-bibliographical essays with selective lists of works surveyed. They came both to mourn poor scholarship and praise new scholars. They con-curred that Middle East anthropology remained theoretically irrelevant to the discipline of anthropology, merely addressing the marginalized group of isolated Middle East area specialists and even smaller numbers of North Africa specialists. In contrast, by 1989 as Abu-Lughod calls on the works of Crapanzano, Bourdieu, Geertz, and others, she allows for the importance of Middle East anthropology and its theoretical contributions to anthropology:

If it can no longer be said that there are no theorists in Middle East an-thropology whose work is read outside the field, even if this theorizing is limited to a certain set of questions and slanted away from history and global politics, it is still true that most theorizing in the anthropology of the Arab world concerns more localized questions. (Abu-Lughod 1989, 278)[12]

While "localized" theoretical writings concerned with segmentation, seg-mentary lineage, and tribalism have abated since 1989 when Abu-Lughod identi-fied the "prestigious and enduring zone of anthropological theorizing about the Arab world," it is now worth asking whether the state-of-the-art article as an ex-amination of many scientific studies, is an actual scientific study itself. Literature reviews and systematic studies rely on quantitative analytical tools that may work well at the level of generalizations about a topic, approach, or even a geographical region, while ethnographers work in a tradition that is susceptible to, and there-fore often recycles, commonly held opinions and stock themes masquerading as knowledge. We are long past Carleton Coon's "mosaic" theories in which a raft of discrete assembled vignettes posing as facts are glued together to form patterns according to the prejudices of the writer-ethnographer. Yet, new and tendentious topics that function as metonyms for the Arab world have come to the forefront to be identified by ethnographic surveys mapped onto this region. Examples are the status of Muslim women, issues of human rights abuses in the MENA, the relationship between democracy and Arab culture, and more. A state-of-the-art review holds at bay the cumulative numbing effects of too much detail and information overload, ensuring that we shift the emphasis from anthropology's single ethnographic study to synthesizing multiple studies that may even include the ways in which people of the region think and express their own futures. Once again, multiple and contradictory questions about Middle Eastern and North African exceptionalism in the social sciences loom large and, therefore, will have to be balanced, or at least contextualized, politically and historically, not merely regionally, as a result of the dramatic events in the region termed the "Arab Spring." Certainly, for several decades, sociocultural anthropologists have taken on research that charts the movements of populations, while deploying the terminology of diaspora, transnational, and globalization studies in order to discuss Muslims in Europe; sub-Saharans in North Africa, the Arab North, and South American communities; South Asians in the Arab Gulf region; and so on. As languages, the religion and practices of Islam, and diverse cultures move around the globe, they appear to contribute to anthropology's disengagement from the discipline's emphasis on the local. Nonetheless, and especially when thinking about the uprisings that swept across the MENA in 2010–2011, a meta-analysis is imperative if only to search for common themes that have contributed to the distinctive cultural and political tipping points, yet all the while not sidelining the local specificities that anthropological analysis is adept at producing. The Arab Spring—that began in December 2010 in Tunisia, then spread to Egypt, and by the time of this writing, Libya, Bahrain, Syria, and Yemen, and that remains ongoing—has taught the world that despite widespread and global transnationalizations of the uprisings, it is the history and specificity of each nation-state of the Middle East and North Africa that should be paramount. The possibility that a people may radically change the conditions they live in owes much to discarding hopelessness in favor of human rights, but each country has accomplished it differently and with ongoing and wildly varying outcomes. For a Middle East and North Africa anthropology of the future, my questions are about where claims about human rights begin—in the prison cell, at home, on the street, via social media, from youthful peers, arriving through exiles of a neighboring country?—and how to document intimate and emergent human rights processes ethnographically (Slyomovics 2012).

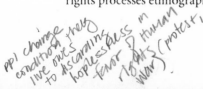

NOTES

The epigraph is from H. H. Suplee, *Gas Turbine,* 1910 (cited in the Oxford English Dictionary 2011, and en.wikipedia.org/wiki/State_of_the_art, as accessed 1 October 2011)

1. A young black slave girl in the novel *Uncle Tom's Cabin* by Harriet Beecher Stowe, Topsy has no parents and, when asked to explain this, she answers, "I 'spect I grow'd." People often mention Topsy when they are talking about something that seems to have grown quickly without being noticed. (Oxford Advanced Learner's Dictionary online, accessed 15 June 2012.)

2. On the ramifications of the French-inspired colonial "Kabyle Myth," see Lorcin (1995).

3. See Price (2009) and the section on Coon in Price (2008, 248–255).

4. Between Coon and half a century later lies the establishment, in 1998, of the Middle East Section of the American Anthropological Association, whose bylaws recount the modest and sober goal of "encouraging anthropological research in and of the Middle East" (http://www.aaames.net/about/bylaws.html).

5. See also Hajjar and Niva (1997):

> Middle East area studies began in 1946 with the establishment of a training program in international administration at Columbia University, and Army Specialized Training Programs for languages at Princeton and the Universities of Indiana, Michigan and Pennsylvania. In 1947, Princeton founded the first interdisciplinary program specializing in the modern and contemporary Middle East.

6. Reviews available by 1975 were Sweet, Gulick, and Antoun, as well as bibliographies in the *Annual Review of Anthropology.*

7. This was the title of his report for the *Harvard Alumni Bulletin. Carleton Stevens Coon, 1904–1981: A Biographical Memoir* by W. W. Howells is available for download at books.nap.edu/html/biomems/ccoon.pdf.

8. For a review of the reception of Said's *Orientalism,* see Lockman (2004, 182–214).

9. Other notable reflexive ethnographies of the 1970s were also set in Morocco: Vincent Crapanzano's *Tuhami* and Kevin Dwyer's *Moroccan Dialogues* plus two 1986 collections, Michael M. J. Fischer and George Marcus's *Anthropology as Cultural Critique* and James Clifford and Marcus's *Writing Culture: The Poetics and Politics of Ethnography.*

10. Paul Rabinow, "Steps Toward an Anthropological Laboratory," Discussion Paper, 2 February 2007, available as a pdf under "Working Papers" on the website of Anthropological Research on the Contemporary: http://anthropos-lab.net/working_papers.

11. Margot Badran challenges this 1970s American origin, proposing that "a genera-tion earlier, foreshadowing the creation of the new field, Zahiyya Dughan, a Lebanese delegate to the Arab Women's Conference in Cairo in 1944, called upon Arab universities to accord the intellectual and literary heritage of Arab women a place in the curriculum by creating chairs for the study of women's writing" (Badran 1988, 7).

12. A more recent example of systematic reviews of Middle East anthropology are found in anthropologist Dale F. Eickelman's *The Middle East and Central Asia: An Anthropological Approach* (4th ed., 2001), conceived as a synthesis of important research in the form of both a textbook and an extended interpretative essay.

2.

OCCLUDING DIFFERENCE: ETHNIC IDENTITY AND THE SHIFTING ZONES OF THEORY ON THE MIDDLE EAST AND NORTH AFRICA

Seteney Shami and Nefissa Naguib

Not so long ago, in the late 1970s, the Middle East was in an oil boom, on the brink of the Islamic revolution in Iran, the Russian invasion of Afghanistan, and a decisive military coup in Turkey. Ruling regimes were facing powerful new challenges in consolidating their power bases and boundaries. The wars in Lebanon had destroyed Beirut as the financial center of the Middle East and labor migration within the region was at its height. On the eve of Egyptian president Sadat's historic visit to Israel, this is how societies of the Middle East were represented in the *Annual Review of Anthropology* (ARA):

> The winds of change have by now penetrated even the more outlying, isolated communities. The process blurs the traditional boundaries between the component pieces of the Middle Eastern "mosaic of people," but the mosaic does not disappear: new and larger pieces are formed and imposed upon the older ones as new boundaries are forged and older ones reassert themselves in new disguises. (Cohen 1977, 385)

What are the notions of identity and difference on the one hand, and of change and modernity on the other, in this 1977 review of anthropology? And what do they reveal about presuppositions that long configured the ethnography of the region? Exploring these questions and tracing trajectories to contemporary anthropology reveals some long-occluded issues as well as potentials and strategies for a new ethnography of identity and difference in the Middle East and North Africa (MENA). This intellectual project takes on renewed urgency with the dynamics unleashed by the uprisings in the Arab region starting in late 2010. New forms of knowledge about identity and difference in this region are central to the new social imaginaries that are emerging and being contested in city squares and streets every day.

A Surfeit of Difference

The notion of the "mosaic" became a pervasive metaphor of the "essential" Middle East once Carleton Coon deployed it as an organizing principle of his widely read book *Caravan: The Story of the Middle East,* first published in 1951. He argued that the Middle East was characterized by a diversity of social, ethnic, linguistic, occupational, and ecological groups, whose identities mapped a division of labor that perpetuated the differences between groups while linking them through the marketplace. The fundamentally religious fabric of society, especially Islam, provided a cementing factor, as did the various imperial, colonial, and post-independence authoritarian states that held these groups, the pieces of the "mosaic" together.

More than twenty years after, in the quote above, Cohen redeploys the "mosaic" and represents the MENA as ahistorical, stagnant and unable to experience real social transformation or to accommodate changing, fluid, or multiple identities. "Change" arrives from the outside ("the winds of") and shifts the pieces of the "mosaic" around, but the "groups" themselves are historical givens, always represent communities, and change only their "disguises." Underscoring the continuity in intellectual genealogy, Coon wrote the introduction to the ARA volume in which Cohen's review appeared. Coon and Cohen share a notion of change as a "blur" and even an inconvenience for scholarship. For Coon, change is a chimera that obscures the essential qualities of society but does not transform them and in fact detracts from the task of the ethnographer, for

> a culture in transition is hard to describe and harder to understand; we must find some period of history when the culture was, relatively speaking, at rest. Then when we know the background we can bring in the automobiles

and the movies and the parliaments and the radio broadcasts; and the presence of these bits of plastic and broken glass in our mosaic will no longer obscure the plan of the picture. (Coon 1951, 8)

The production of modernity and processes of circulation, representation, negotiation, and communication, which today form the focus of the most exciting anthropological literature on the region, are here prefigured as inauthentic "bits of plastic and broken glass" obscuring the deeper inlay of the static *objet d'art* that is society. From the standpoint of contemporary ethnography, therefore, we could simply and comfortably relegate the "mosaic" and its implications to a bygone era of anthropology that has been superseded. To what, however, would we point as the new frameworks for researching ethnic identity? What interpretations of social and cultural difference would we find that are inclusive of minority populations? What studies of shifting and hybrid ethnic and linguistic identities would we cite? Instead of ethnography and instead of theory, we find a puzzling silence.

The mosaic was not generative of theory. Nor, it turns out, of ethnography. The mosaic generally falls into benign acceptance in anthropology, its premises and implications rarely unpacked and elaborated. We have now learnt to be suspicious of metaphors and representations masquerading as neutral or innocuous, seeing them rather as central and politically powerful in the construction of the objects of scholarship. After all, the "mosaic" metaphor caricatures not only the region but also the discipline. An uncritical acceptance helps perpetuate a perspective of the region, which goes back to colonial writings, as characterized by a pervasive and enduring fragmentation into ethnic, linguistic, religious, sectarian, and other groups, usually described in overview works with the tentative, and unhelpful, phrase "diversity and unity."

It is important to note that the mix in the mosaic, in addition to ethnic, linguistic, and religious groups, also includes occupational groups (e.g., merchant elites, craft guilds), kinship units (tribes), urban neighborhoods (quarters), and economic/ecological distinctions (nomads, peasants, urbanites). The poverty of this descriptor "mosaic" is apparent in the lumping together of identities constructed on completely different bases, while also designating as separate "groups" identities that are overlapping, coterminous, and interpolated. Interestingly, while the decades following the introduction of the mosaic saw an ethnographic focus on the latter types of difference (kinship, urban neighborhoods, nomadic tribes), in contrast ethnic, linguistic, and religious identities did not become sustained objects of research.

When difference is everywhere and everything, it is also nowhere and nothing. How else do we explain the occlusion of ethnic identity and difference and of minority populations in the literature on a region supposedly suffering from a surfeit difference? How is it that Lila Abu-Lughod's review article, which appears in ARA (1989) a decade after Cohen's, identifies the "zones of theory" for the Arab world as focused on "tribe," "women," and "Islam," without mention of ethnographies that might emerge from a "mosaic" perspective? As intimated above, it is seductive to think that, with the critique of Orientalism and other theoretical advances in the late 1970s, anthropologists rejected and deconstructed the static notion of the mosaic. However, this road to nowhere was both more complex and more significant. As the zones of theory shift from "tribe" to "nation," from "women" to "gender," and from "Islam" to "religion," the explosion of recent ethnography and the significant theoretical advances still seem incapable of accommodating some basic and important structural and cultural features of identity and difference in the MENA region. This requires explanation.

Anthropology at a Crossroads

The late 1970s / early 1980s represent a crossroads in the fortunes of the mosaic. There is a brief but rather interesting debate that reveals a great deal about roads not taken in the anthropology of the region. Richard Antoun in his 1976 comprehensive review of the field quotes the same paragraph above from Coon but does so ruing the fact that anthropologists, diverted by the study of plastic and glass, had abandoned the mosaic. Combining the notion of the mosaic with the works of Fredrik Barth and Abner Cohen on ethnic groups and interethnic relations, Antoun asserts that the future of anthropology of the Middle East belongs to the study of "ethnicity, class and the mosaic." Antoun's attempt to theorize the "mosaic" by emphasizing the role of religion and of the market in ensuring the cohesion of the parts remains unconvincing, and he himself admits that the problem may emanate from the inadequacies of the "mosaic" concept itself (among which is the impossibility of factoring in class relations and processes). Moreover, Antoun is pessimistic about the possibilities of a focus on interethnic relations given that "one of the most alarming discoveries of the empirical review of research cited above is the tiny number of anthropologists who have done work in geographical areas representing more than one linguistic tradition or more than one social type" (1976, 178). This is an important observation, which to a large extent still holds true, including in the small literature on ethnic groups and minorities.

Nevertheless, the framing concept taking shape in this period, inspired by the work of Fredrik Barth as well as the anthropology of other regions, is that of "interethnic relations" (1969). For Barth and his associates, "ethnic boundaries," including individual movement across such boundaries, were the focus of research. Ethnic identities and groups were seen to be fluid: to appear, undergo transformation, and disappear in response to changing distributions of resources and other conditions. In the meantime individuals move back and forth. Building upon these ideas, Jon Anderson, based on his research in Afghanistan, contested the concept of the mosaic and argued that identities are constantly changing, flexible, multiple, and negotiable (1978). Richard Tapper picks up the argument a decade later, reviewing ethnic identities and "social categories" in Iran and Afghanistan (1989). Like Antoun, Tapper evokes the work of Barth and Abner Cohen

> that inspired a generation of anthropological research on ethnicity. They were slow to affect research on the Middle East, however, where social and political scientists, as well as ethnographers, continued until recently, with few exceptions, to accept Coon's classic "mosaic" model (1958) of a "diversity of peoples and cultures," with its implicit assumption that ethnic groups were biological units of fixed membership. (Tapper 1989, 232)

Tapper goes on to advocate juxtaposing authoritative and subaltern conceptualizations of ethnic difference. Thus,

> whereas official and academic categories are simple and clear-cut, being used for administrative and comparative purposes, the identities and categories of popular discourse, having to cope with everyday, face-to-face political and social realities, are complex and essentially flexible and ambiguous. (1989, 232)

Additionally, he makes the important distinction that while in the literature on Iran the stress is on economic, political, and class characteristics, in Afghanistan cultural criteria (kinship, descent, language, and religion) have been more prominent.

It is interesting to note that this critique emerges from work on Iran, Afghanistan, and Pakistan. In a similar vein, Suad Joseph's work on Muslim–Christian relations in Lebanon questions prevailing notions of sectarian conflict (1983). Significantly, all the countries in which the questioning of hegemonic and subaltern identities was raised during this period later succumbed to civil conflict and/or to war.[1] Elsewhere post-independence states took on a renewed authoritarian turn accompanied by a "second wave" of nationalism. Add the continued threats of Israeli and foreign intervention in the states of the region, and we have a region that closed its doors on critical inquiry concerning diversity, pluralism, and difference, and, in many cases, on research and outside academia as a whole.

Thus, one would like to think that anthropology has rejected the Coonian legacy and simply chooses not to "beat a dead horse," but, unfortunately, that which remains unexamined and untheorized also remains powerful, even if occluded. Furthermore, the horse is alive and kicking in the real world of *realpolitik* as well as in other academic literatures, less reticent than anthropology to "other."[2] For example,

> political space in the Middle East is more intimate than nation-states, most of them recently built on ancient ethnic and religious foundations. All three main areas of warfare in the Middle East today—Arab–Israeli, the Gulf, and Lebanon—provide the same lessons in the limits of national coercive action, chiefly in the form of military power, in conflicts among local communities. In each case local and indigenous pathologies resist outside intervention, either from a nation-state or from foreign powers, much as certain strains of disease become resistant to medication designed to curb them. (Pranger 1991, 33–34)

In much of the public and political discourse on the region, democracy, peace, and war, one can hear the sedimented traces of longstanding ideas about "age-old" (and pathological) identities, enmities, and conflicts, whether in characterizations of Iraq as composed of "Kurds in the North and Shi'ites in the South," or in discussions of "Arabs and Jews" and the Palestinian–Israeli conflict, or, in a somewhat more subdued fashion, in evoking relations between "Arabs and Berbers." Concerning constructions of ethnic difference, inter-group relations, sectarian conflict, and relations between states and minorities, the literature is dominated by the fields of political science, international relations, and security studies (as well as journalism), which sorely lack an ethnographic perspective on the dynamics they interpret.

The persistence of the image of the "Middle Eastern Mosaic" in the academic and public sphere is important to explore not simply because of its continued essentializing function but rather because of what it reveals and inspires concerning questions of modernity, societal integration, and forces of change in societies supposedly made up of fragmentary pieces kept together only by repression and authoritarian regimes. The issue of ethnic diversity is particularly linked to political fears of fragmentation, as is clear in the literature from the region which posits these identities as a creation and legacy of colonialism and then dismisses them as "fabricated" for the same reason (for critiques, see Ali and Hanna 2002; Farsakh 1994). The legacies of colonial ethnography are particularly powerful and threatening in North Africa but resonate throughout the region (Goodman 2002, 2003; Goodman and Silverstein 2009). The fear of political, social, and cultural fragmentation translates into a negative perception of ethnic identity itself and those who would appropriate, cultivate, or even study and write about such identity constructions.

Thus in anthropology today, despite important advances in the study of many topics and issues and understandings of the region, the issues of ethnic identity and difference are remarkable for their absence. The study of dynamic social, political, and cultural constructions of nations and nationalism, of gender relations, and of religious beliefs and practices all address, in their different ways, processes of identity construction. Yet the rejection of static notions of culture and group identity does not seem to lead to more nuanced, more useful and interesting approaches to the study of ethnic identity and minority groups but rather to silences. This ethnographic silence is not simply a product of neglect but emerges out of a coincidence, or perhaps collusion, between disciplinary legacies and political exigencies—it is a silence born out of a particular conjunction of knowledge and power.

Shifting Zones of Theory

Naturally, the silence is not all-enveloping or unbroken. In addition to the small number of works dealing specifically with ethnic and (more recently) racial difference, there is a large body of works that focus on different types of identity in the region (national, gender, global, urban, etc.) and thus touch upon or help conceptualize ethnic identity. A number of conferences and special-issue journals over the past five years or so have also been turning attention specifically to the topic of minority identities.[3] Where, therefore, lies the potential for generating a more inclusive theory and ethnography of identity and difference?

Abu-Lughod's review essay in *ARA*, written just over a decade after Cohen's, illustrates the important moves, theoretical and topical, that anthropology had made in the interim as well as the ways in which a critical reading could recon-figure the legacies of past scholarship (1989). Her three "zones of theory" in the anthropology of the Arab World (note: not Middle East) identified the domi-nant topics of the day to be tribe, women, and Islam. While she made clear the basis for these preoccupations in Orientalism as well as disciplinary "prestige zones," she also identified the important advances that had begun to unmake these legacies.

Similarly, but not identically, we examine seminal works produced in the last two decades under three main categories: nation, gender, and religion.[4] These categories represent important types of identity and difference in any society and have seen the most growth in writing on the region in recent years. While these literatures are often silent about ethnic difference and minority status, and may collude in erasing them, they are necessary frameworks as well as building blocks for a more inclusive anthropology, one that is attentive to a varied and nuanced range of identity and difference.

Nation

The ways in which national identity has been constructed in different parts of the region has been explored mainly in Turkey, Egypt, and Israel/Palestine, with some substantial work developing on North Africa. It is important to empha-size that work on the nation and nationalism, largely inspired by the work of Benedict Anderson, is fairly new to anthropology, whether in this region or else-where (1983). This focus thus represents more a disjuncture than a shift from "tribe" (as a metonym for all "bounded" and "local" groups) to "nation," and the transition between literatures has not been smooth. While rightly dismissing evolutionary paradigms ("from tribe to nation"), the new literature has largely not been able to address how the structures of the state are constructed by the production of locality and localism (but see Crawford 2005; Layne 1994; Shryock 1997; Stokes 1998). More attention to how the nation is imbricated in the local (and vice versa) would reveal the coexistence of alternative identities as well as differing readings of the nation by various social groups and communities.

Ethnographic work does focus, and in highly interesting ways, on his-tory and memory (Bruinessen 2000; Dresch 1989; Özyürek 2006; Sawalha 2010; Swedenburg 1995), constructions of social categories such as the peas-antry (Swedenburg 1995), notions of secularism and modernity (Fischer 1980, 2003; Meeker 2002), and the role of knowledge production and "science" in the consolidation of nations (Abu El-Haj 1998, 2001). Also of interest are works on the past and present strategies of elites, roles of intellectuals and various occupational groups (Dominguez 1989; Messick 1993; Vom Bruck 2005), the mobilization of different population groups (Fábos 2002), and the role of the media and other modes of communication in the construction of nationalism and of the national public sphere (Abu-Lughod 2005; Armbrust 1996; Wheeler 2006). The work on expressive culture, distinction (in Pierre Bourdieu's sense), and representation is also growing (Beal 1999; Goodman 2005; Stein 1998; Swedenburg and Stein 2005). Social historical works, such as Beth Baron (2005), Eve Trout Powell (2003), and Elizabeth Thompson (2000), also contribute greatly to anthropological discussions on these issues, and the history of Arab nationalism presents a particularly interesting case, given that it is simultaneously produced in different locations such that inhabitants of twenty-two countries identify themselves as Arab in addition to identifying as Syrian, Egyptian, Moroccan, or Saudi (see *International Journal of Middle East Studies* 2011). Arab nationalism is particularly illustrative of the transnational processes underpinning the production of nation, as well as the tensions produced by overlapping, and even competing, nationalisms.

Anthropological arguments about the nation in the Middle East have been especially interesting where they concern the intersection of the individual and the national, the private and the public selves. In Aleppo, Annika Rabo shows how traders and shopkeepers see state regulations as unclear and subject to frequent change (2005). They attempt to mediate these uncertainties of the state while balancing considerations of respectability and individuality. Also significant here is the literature on the politics of memory and the ways in which the stories people recall transform individual memory to something more public and *national.*

For example, Yael Navaro-Yashin's *Faces of the State* explores what the state means in people's lives and how people endorse and cultivate the nation in their public life (2002). She goes beyond deconstructing the state–society dichotomy to argue that the political and the state survive deconstruction and are recreated and maintained through public life and the "fantasies" people have of the state. By locating the political and the state in the context of the dialectic between secularism and Islamism in Turkey, Navaro-Yashin explains the meaning of secularism in Turkey and how it has been transformed into a hegemonic public discourse, a calcified state ideology upheld by a significant constituency.

Ethnographic narratives also contribute to the understanding of the role of the arts and media in the construction of nationalism. The instrumental cultural and political roles of television melodrama in the production of national culture and the molding of individuals into modern national citizens is the focus of *Dramas of Nationhood* (Abu-Lughod 2005). It explains how serials, especially during the holy month of Ramadan, encapsulate and disseminate devotion to the Egyptian nation and help define the role of all decent and patriotic citizens.

While the literature on nation focuses on the construction of a national and collective identity, especially in the ways that body, self, family, sociability, and citizenship/participation are transformed (Joseph 2000; Ali and Hanna 2002; Kanaaneh 2002), less explored are the political and discursive processes of foregrounding certain identities and erasing others that lie at the heart of any national project. National identity is premised on the existence of a "majority" with varying degrees of tolerance for those who would then be cast or cast themselves as a "minority" (see Shami 2009). Those who embody the non-majoritarian identity are often left understudied, making ethnographers complicit with the nations that they study in unproblematically imagining that a majority exists and is fashioned out of a collectivity that is premodern. In other words, ethnic identity and minority populations, if noted, are seen as vestiges of the premodern, and thus displaced and out of place in the nation.

It is in places where the contradictions between past and present are too sharp to ignore, and where the politics of recognition throws up powerful competing claims, that national projects can be best deconstructed through critical research. The palimpsest that is Palestine is the prime example. In the story of Ein Houd/Ein Hod, Susan Slyomovics gives an account of two peoples, Palestinian Arabs and Jewish Israelis, who cultivate the link between memory and place, and the sense of loss permeates the narrative at every level (1998). Her *The Object of Memory* is about dispossession but also about active remembrance. Throughout the book we are reminded of the man who points his finger to the ground where his family once lived. Slyomovics situates Palestinian memory in the larger genre of memorial books produced by those who have suffered war, dispersion, and traumatic loss as they strive to construct a nation, a community, through the links between memory and place. An obvious constraint in the use of such powerful biographical accounts is that they are based on remembering and forgetting with all the irregularity and fragility of human memory and the apparent obligation to edit disordered human life (see Naguib 2009). Other works on Palestine/Israel, whether focusing on places or people, begin to unpack the overlapping and contradictory processes of nation-making and the inclusions/exclusions and fashioning/erasures that are at work (Rabinowitz 1997, 2001; Kanaaneh and Nusair 2010).

The literature on Turkey is similarly fascinating in both erasing and celebrating Kurdishness depending upon context, thus echoing political positions often taken by progressive secular elites. Many of the excellent works on Turkish nationalism which focus on state projects of remaking gender, family, domesticity, and citizenship somehow elide the issue of ethnic differences, although this becomes manifestly the object of research when studying how Kurdishness is constructed against an imagined Turkishness (but see Kirişci 1998; Gambetti 2009).

Works on Sudan (Doornbos 1988; Manger 1999; Fábos 2002, 2007, 2008; Jok 2001), on the Gulf (Anscombe 2005; Leinhardt and Al-Shahi 2001; Limbert 2010), on Syria (Rabo 1999), and on Cyprus (Calotychos 1998) all begin to explore the fluidity of identities and the politics of ethnicity and nationalism, making clear the urgency of such processes. While Lila Abu-Lughod (1989) rued the focus in anthropology on "peripheral" places (such as Yemen and Morocco), the power of the margins in unmaking hegemonic discourses (including academic discourses) is never clearer than when looking for traces of occluded identities (for unique ethnographic insight into South Yemen see Dahlgren 2010).

Gender

The literature on gender roles and relations has perhaps witnessed the most robust growth and generated interesting discussions on the region. Starting in the 1970s, particularly following Cynthia Nelson's 1974 article in which she challenged the stereotyped images of women succumbing to patriarchal rule with docility and passivity, the theme of women as victims of patriarchy and Islam has been replaced by narratives of women as agents who negotiate their own survival. This survival takes place, in part, by "bargaining with patriarchy" (Kandiyoti 1996). A burst of work on women appeared in the 1980s, as covered in Lila Abu-Lughod's 1989 ARA review, which aimed at moving beyond simply debunking stereotypes to constructing theory. Contemporary trends in the literature further move from a focus on women to the study of gender, including the construction of gender identity and notions of femininity and masculinity; the fashioning of the body through economic power, political participation, violence, and war; and women's enmeshment in national and transnational processes (Wikan 1991; White 1994; Moors 1995; Shami 1996; Hoodfar 1997; Chatty and Rabo 1997; Jennings 2009; Abusharaf 2009; Dahlgren 2010). This work has yielded insight not only into how male and female persons are culturally constructed, but also into female contributions to the construction of larger social identities. Interestingly, recent work focuses mostly on the Arab "Mashreq" region, with a heavy focus on Egypt, and there are astonishingly few ethnographies of gender in Turkey (but see Delaney 1991). Anthropological research on Iran remains difficult under current political conditions, and the work on gender is often through the lens of "youth" (Khosravi 2009) or takes cultural production, and especially film works, as its main ethnographic texts (Varzi 2008). However, Homa Hoodfar has several works on gender in relation to Islam, citizenship, and reproduction in Iran (2000, 2001).

Thus, a number of anthropologists have examined the lived experience of gender subordination in a hierarchical system. Janice Boddy's work on the zar cult in rural northern Sudan explores how female gender identity is created through the practice of zar possessions, which allow women to explore subjectivity (1989). She also describes circumcision as a cultural practice that creates both male and female persons by removing the part of the anatomy identified with the opposite sex. Anne Meneley demonstrates how elite women's socializing practices in a Yemeni town create social status for families and communal identity (1996). In contrast with the predominant focus on homosocial spaces and social worlds, Kapchan examines the construction of gender through discourse and performance in "heterogeneous" spaces, primarily the space of the public market in Morocco, where women construct gendered identities in the presence of men (1996).

Gender relations and gender identity have also been a central focus of medical anthropology in the region in the past twenty years, largely on Egypt. Soheir Morsy examined the relationship between gender differentiation and ideas of sickness and health in rural Egypt (1993). Reproduction and motherhood are major practices through which women create their gender identity, impacted by other vectors of identity such as class and religion (Inhorn 1994, 1996). Fertility and reproduction articulates with national identities and state policies for shaping citizens (Kanaaneh 2002).

Several works in medical anthropology have included a focus on maleness and the body and bring in regional, transnational, and global processes as well. Thus, Kamran Ali (2002) looks at international development programs as well as how national family planning produces new bodies and selves of citizens, both male and female roles. Following on two earlier works on women and infertility (1994, 1996), Marcia Inhorn extended her research to the gendered consequences of male infertility for men in both Egypt and Lebanon (2004), and their responses to new reproductive technologies (2006), bringing in a "local in the global" perspective on the practice of in vitro fertilization (IVF). Morgan Clarke's recent study on the changing ideas of kinship, religious practice, and religious authorities in Lebanon provides insight into the diversity of Islamic debate on reproductive technology and "new kinship" (2009).

These examples point to the fact that the study of gender in relation to men specifically and the construction of masculinity has greatly expanded in recent ethnographies. Studies include men's roles in systems of hierarchy and domination, whether within communities of study, in a national context, or in contexts of national or global conflict and inequality. Julie Peteet examines the violence of detention and torture as a rite of passage for Palestinian men in the Occupied Territories during the First Intifada (1994), and Rhoda Kanaaneh examines the experience of Palestinian men serving the Israeli military (2008).

There has also been a trend toward studying male and female roles in gender relations concurrently, particularly within the family. Suad Joseph and Susan Slyomovics highlight the central role of the family in their introduction to *Women and Power in the Middle East* (Joseph and Slyomovics 2001). Joseph looks at the brother–sister relationship from the perspective of both power and emotional relations within patriarchy in the Lebanese context (Joseph 1994). Iris Jean-Klein also examines how young men and their sisters and mothers challenge patriarchy during the First Intifada in Occupied Palestine (2000).

Women's political activism and participation, particularly under conditions of conflict, has formed the focus of a number of noteworthy monographs. Studying the connection between political participation and changing gender relations in a Palestinian refugee camp in Lebanon in the early 1980s, Peteet looks at how crisis impacts the relationship between political economy, practice, and cultural ideologies in the context of a national liberation movement (1991). Sondra Hale studies both Islamist and secularist trends within the state targeting women in political integration and mobilization in a highly multiethnic context (1996). Nadje Al-Ali provides a thorough ethnographic examination of secular women's movements in Egypt (2000).

As can be discerned, an important theme in much of the above-mentioned work attends to the ways in which gender identity articulates with communal and national identities on the one hand, and global processes on the other hand. Homa Hoodfar's research on the economics of marriage examines the impact of structural adjustment and international migration on gendered strategies in marriage and labor force participation in Cairo (1997). Also in Cairo, Farha Ghannam focuses on women's identity in connection with urban neighborhoods in the context of state projects and national images of urban modernity (1998).

The creation of modern subjects in Lebanon is also a central focus for Lara Deeb (2006). She and other authors found that one of the central concerns of her research community, pious Shi'i Muslims in a Beirut suburb, was how they see themselves as being modern and how their community responds to women being the target of Western control and domination (see also Kanaaneh 2002).

From the perspective of the study of ethnic identity and how it intersects with gender issues, the two most disappointing aspects of this otherwise exciting literature are, first, its almost exclusive focus on Muslim women, and, furthermore that, in the exploration of family, nation, body, etc., various types of difference other than gender differences are erased. This makes the work of Anita Fábos on the Sudanese in Cairo quite unique (2008), with its focus on *adab* or propriety and practices such as female circumcision in the context of the cultivation of Sudanese identity in the particularly ambiguous zone of Egyptian–Sudanese relations. Also revealing is the work on female migrant domestic workers of Southeast Asian origin working in Arab families (Moors et. al. 2009; Nagy 1998). The analysis of how the incorporation of "foreign" women into the intimate domestic sphere brings into question national, racial, and religious identities is promising for exploring a new challenge to ethnic boundaries, those within the home itself and in the "private" sphere. While hitherto the focus in this regard has been on religious dimensions, especially when differing practices of Islam come face-to-face within the domestic sphere, the same perspective can be applied to other aspects of gender relations and roles.

It has long been recognized that gender relations and gender identities are central to constructing and perpetuating collective identities, including national, ethnic, and minority identities (see Shami 1993). For the MENA region, this has been often explored through visual culture, for example in the excellent works by Viola Shafik (2007a, 2007b) on Egyptian cinema. One looks forward to a more robust ethnography of gender dynamics as they intersect and interact with different types of collective identities on the one hand and local contexts on the other.

Religion

The works on gender and religion intersect in important ways, as a major trend in the past twenty years has been a focus on women and Islam, with a growing recent interest in Shi'a women. Both Ziba Mir-Hosseini and Deeb examine the construction of religious discourse and women's participation in constructing discourse about themselves. Mir-Hosseini ethnographically examines "how cultural notions of 'gender in Islam' are produced" through the dialogues she engages in among clerics in Qom, Iran and the texts she examines (1999). While Mir-Hosseini focuses on the construction of religious discourse *about* women, Deeb considers how women themselves participate in authentication, or actively defining faith in daily life and discursively establishing religious authority not only about women but about Islam. The ideal for women in the religiously observant Shi'i community she studied was that of public piety (Deeb 2006).

Several major interventions on Islam have influenced much of the anthropological literature of the past twenty years, for example Talal Asad (1986, 1993), Sami Zubaida (1995), and Daniel Varisco (2005). Unsurprisingly, there is particular ethnographic attention to Islamism or fundamentalist Islamic movements. From Turkey, Jenny White tells us that the key to the Islamists' success lies in their ability to engage in a "vernacular politics" which is "value-centered" (2002, 27). With vernacular politics, Islamists tap into communities and their networks, creating bonds and linkages based on mutual trust and understanding. Saba Mahmood offers a critique of much previous work on women and Islam in the region through examining women's piety movements in Egypt. She questions ethnographic depictions of women's agency and feminist goals and argues that there is a tendency to look for resistance and challenges to male domination even when they are difficult to locate (Mahmoud 2001, 2005). Agency is thus understood as "the capacity to realize one's own interests against the weight of custom, tradition, transcendental will, or other obstacles (whether individual or collective)" (2005, 8), taking for granted a desire for liberation from relations of subordination and male domination. Based on studies within an Islamic women's organization in Egypt, she calls for a notion of agency that can account for women's active pursuit of ideals considered illiberal and regressive within a Western feminist discourse, such as certain Islamic ideals of female piety and modesty. Her ethnographic study exposes assumptions of both feminist theory and "secular–liberal thought" about the nature of the self, agency, and politics, as well as assumptions about the relationship between interiority and performance.

In spite of this literature, in comparison to other topics, there are fewer monographs focusing on religious identity than the prominence of religious revival movements in the region since the 1970s would seem to warrant. While much of the literature neglects the question of how different groups in society may articulate their Islamic identity and piety in ways that vary significantly from one another, a small group of recent writings are beginning to address this; Asad (1993), Fadwa El Guindi (2008), Charles Hirshkind (2001), Lawrence Rosen

(2002), and Ayse Saktanber (2002) research Islamic identities and the ways in which these identities express other local, national, and transnational identities. An emerging and productive area of research concerns piety and issues of religiosity in everyday life, mainly that of women, through public participation (Deeb 2006) but also in the domestic sphere (Meneley 1996). This leads to questions about how religiosity in everyday life shapes Muslim subjects where religion is part of an urban sensory environment, whether through religious practices (Mahmood 2005), the consumption of religious commodities (Starrett 1995), or listening to sermons on cassette tapes (Hirschkind 2006). Similarly, the subject of El Guindi's book *By Noon Prayer* is rhythm and aesthetics in Islam. She argues for an approach that captures the "pulse," "feel," and visualization of devotional practices in order to better understand how the religion "manifests itself in the social life consistently with cultural notions of time and space" (2008, xiii).

From the other end, state responses to Islamist movements and governments' attempts to shape a particular type of Islamic identity are also the focus of study. For example, Gregory Starrett examines the process of how the Egyptian state attempts to inculcate Islamic identity in opposition to Islamist trends as part of national government attempts to counteract what he calls the "Islamic trend" (1998). Abu-Lughod attends to how portrayals of state-supported "good" Islam and sectarian harmony in television serials are perceived to combat extremism and sectarian violence. As part of religion's reemergence into contemporary public spheres in the region, Abu-Lughod argues that its objectification in the Egyptian media is conducted in relation to the nation (2005, 163–191).

Of particular interest in the context of this discussion are studies of religious identity in relation to national identity and also social class and other categories. Gabriele Vom Bruck's ethnography of a religiously ascribed identity of *sadah* (descendants of the Prophet) in Yemen demonstrates how this Sayyid identity gains meaning in people's lives in a post-revolutionary national context. In this fascinating study on status identity and difference, Vom Bruck details how hereditary elites whose identity is religiously defined cope with the stigmatization of that identity in the context of a recently secular state and the elimination of privileges enjoyed under the previous social hierarchy (2005). Hirschkind's ethnography focuses on lower-middle-and lower-class subjects, though he does not elaborate on how class stratification in Egypt impacts the "technologies of the senses" that he studies (2006). The most thorough work to consider religion and politics in a multi-sectarian environment is Joseph's (2000) research in Lebanon examining how sect endogamy and the "civic myth" of sectarian pluralism obscures the working of kin endogamy and patriarchy encoded in personal status law and sanctioned by the state. Hale's work on women's participation in both secular and Islamist politics in Sudan is exceptional in its scope. Rather than focusing her gaze on one or the other, Hale productively examines how both secular (Communist) and religious (Islamist) national parties objectify women (Hale 1996). Also, Abu-Lughod's work on television dramas draws attention to convergences between secularist and Islamist points of view both originating in twentieth century modernizing discourses (1998, 248).

Even works supported by rich and valuable ethnographic detail sometimes seem to treat "Islam" and the "Islamic Revival" as monolithic categories and processes. A neglected topic within the study of the resurgence of both political and personal Islam is how changing perceptions and practices of Islam intersect with other identity factors, including ethnic and linguistic identities. It is important to note that Islamic identity may act as a unifier across ethnic and other differences in some contexts, while in others it can conversely exacerbate such differences as well as fuel competing sectarian identities. The lack of studies on interreligious interaction or in-depth ethnographies of communities with mixed religious populations is almost inexplicable. Thus Christian and Jewish communities, when studied, are usually dealt with as though separate and contained—a continuing vestige of the mosaic model.

Identities and Differences

While the literature on nation, gender, and religion (Islam) examines important major categories of difference and identity construction in society, there is a general tendency in interpretations to collude with the "national order of things." The "nation" is discussed as the property of the majority with little attention to minority groups, or how notions of "majority" and "minority" are constructed in the first place. While the literature on gender identities, roles, and relations is rich and nuanced, the social and cultural context is almost always an "unmarked" Muslim national grouping. When religion is the focus, Islam clearly dominates work on the region and remains mostly on the majority religious group (Sunni or Shi'a) to the occlusion of other Muslim and non-Muslim groups in the country or region.

The *relational* quality of identity construction and the structuring (and even *classificatory*) impulse produced by the construction of difference are usually mentioned cursorily if at all. Religious minorities for the most part are only seriously discussed if they are the specific group under study. Thus, ethnographies that do discuss non-Muslims, mainly Christians, tend to treat them almost incidentally as part of the broader society. For example, there has been no ethnographic work on gender and religious practice, or indeed religious practice at all, among Christians in the MENA. There are no cultural analyses of how nationalism is perceived and reproduced (or resisted) among non-Muslim groups.

How is this ethnographic silence to be filled? What can we make of the literature, small as it is, that specifically does focus on particular ethnic, religious, and linguistic groups? We find this literature clustered around quite specific geographies and groups. As noted above, in the work on Iran and Afghanistan, there is a literature on various ethnic and linguistic groups (Hopkins 2003; Beck 1980, 1986, 1991, 1992; Oveson 1983; Tapper and Tapper 1988, 1986; Tapper 1989). The fact that many of these constitute quite distinct pastoral nomadic groups constitutes both a problem and an interesting trajectory of research. As an illustration, while nomad–settler relations constitute an important focus in ecological and economic research on various hinterlands, few such studies take into account the often different ethnic and linguistic identities of the nomads and settlers involved. In contrast, earlier work on Iraq, such as by Amal Rassam-Vinogradov showed great promise in focusing on the mutual brokering of economic and ethnic relations and social hierarchies in rural settings (Vinogradov 1974, Rassam 1977). Current work on Kurds and Kurdistan, including historical works (Fuccaro 1999) similarly show promise despite being few in number (Allison 2001; cf. Bruinessen 2000; Hassanpour 1996; Meiselas 1997; Mojab and Gorman 2007; O'Shea 2004).

Another location, namely the literature on ethnicity and ethnic relations in Israel, could be the focus of a paper on its own. There was a robust literature in the 1970s and early 80s (though much of it from a sociological rather than ethnographic perspective) that looked at the "integration" and "assimilation" of Jewish groups from various lands into Israeli society. Much of this mimicked the "melting pot" literature on the United States. However, the period also saw a few good ethnographies on Jewish communities in Arab lands, mainly in North Africa (see Goldberg 1972, 1977, 1985; Shokeid and Deshen 1982). On the other hand, Palestinian Arabs were completely erased in this literature, an issue (among others) that Virginia Dominguez took up and interrogated in her penetrating ethnography of Israeli "Selfhood and Peoplehood" (1989). Over the last twenty years, the literature diminishes in quantity but gains in quality and also begins to consider different groups. Works such as by Andre Levy (1997, 1999, 2001, 2003) and by Joelle Bahloul (1996) go back to Jewish communities in North

Africa but study them in context and interaction. As described above, works that examine Palestine/Israel and Palestinians in Israel go a long way to interrogating earlier narratives of ethnicity and nationhood (Slyomovics 1998; Rabinowitz 1997, 2001; Kanaaneh and Nusair 2010).

Another focus of research is on Sudan and Egypt. Again, a story of roads not taken lies in the flurry of research that was carried out in the 1960s by anthropologists at the American University in Cairo on Nubians of the Aswan region, in response to the massive relocations taking place in the wake of the construction of the Aswan Dam (see Burton 1987; Fahim 1983; Fernea and Gerster 1973; Geiser 1973, 1986; Kennedy 1978). The categories of "Nubian" and "Arab" remained unexamined in that literature (but see Salem-Murdock 1989). The recent work by Carolyn Fluehr-Lobban and Kharyssa Rhodes (2004), Sondra Hale (1996), Anne Jennings (1995), and Elizabeth Smith (2006) begins to interrogate Nubian identity and its expressions in various settings, rural and urban. This opens up a brand new avenue of research in the region that can usefully intersect with research on ethnicity, namely "race." Thus works by Stephanie Beswick (2004), Gunnar Haaland (2006), Jok M. Jok (2001), and Roman Poeschke (1996) on Sudan; Mandana Limbert (2010) on Oman; and Anita Fábos (2002) on Sudanese in Egypt; as well as social-historical works such as by Troutt Powell (2003), all point the way to nuanced cultural analyses of the intersections of race, ethnicity, and nation in historical and contemporary contexts (see also Greenberg 1997; Walters 1987; Silverstein 2004).

Similarly, work on the cultural politics of Berber identity focuses attention particularly on linguistic and symbolic aspects of Berber–Arab interactions (Battenburg 1999; Goodman 2005; Hoffman and Crawford 2000; Sadiqi 1996; Silverstein 2003). In the way that the literature on Egypt/Sudan leads us to race, the North African literature alerts us to the topics of migration and diaspora (also see Peteet 2007). Here, in addition to North African migrations and the politics of identity in Europe (Salih 2003; Al-Ali and Koser 2002; Silverstein 1996), the ethnographic gaze shifts to the Arabian Peninsula and the Indian Ocean. A most exciting literature that looks at history, diaspora, and identity should inspire generations of students (Ho 2004, 2006; Limbert 2005, 2010; Longva 1997; Manger 2010; Nagy 1998). Questions concerning displacement, deportation, and their intersections with nationalism on the one hand and locality on the other are beginning to produce interesting ethnographic work (Davis 2010; Fábos 2007; Ghannam 1998; Lavie and Swedenburg 1996; Naguib 2008; Parla 2003; Peteet 1996, 2005; Sayad 2000; Shami 2000). We can add to this the study of groups and communities originating from the Middle East and living in the West (Al-Rasheed 1998; Naficy 1993, 1995; Samhan 1999; Silverstein 2004).

The unity of the transnational community is sustained by the desire to belong to a "people" through a process of nominal appropriation of its actions and discourses, a sense of participation in its "destiny." This desire constructs new subjectivities that accompany the imagined geography of the "transnational nation." In the emerging literature from the Middle East on diaspora we see two strands of research: one that connects to the ethnographies which draw on the politics of memory in contested places, the second belonging to studies connecting history and anthropology. In both approaches writings illuminate everyday life and tell us more about how history, memory, and events impact people's everyday life. These works are examples of how personal, familial, or local memories may explicitly or silently challenge official versions of national history.

Drawing inspiration from works on memory, anthropologists working on contested sites and particular social or cultural groups are exploring the "politics of memory" and the significance of memorializing practices to the politics of the nation and the state (Slyomovics 1998; Naguib 2008; Sawalha 2010). Such explorations have been fruitful in understanding the role of commemorative practice in producing or reinforcing political ideologies of ethnic or religious group solidarity. Anthropologists have shown the myriad linkages between communal rituals and state policies in their historical unfolding. Connections are made between works of memory, colonial history, and political dislocation, demonstrating the centrality of political autonomy to the possibility of performing commemorative acts in postcolonial contexts or under repressive state regimes (Silverstein 2003; Slyomovics 2005).

Ways Forward

The study of identity creation is, and continues to be, part of anthropology's longstanding commitment to human relationships. This is what makes Barth's work on ethnicity as an ongoing process, created through continuous interaction between people, still a touchstone. Anthropologists have built upon this notion to examine issues of power and hegemony, and anthropological interest in ethnicity developed concurrently with the interest in nationalism. Questions are asked about how public expressions of ethnic identity and minority status are part of state projects of constructing national identities. Anthropology has also been attentive to counter–public expressions, that is, what is left out of official narratives and can be reclaimed through anthropological recourse to specified "ethnic locations" above-or underground.

These are significant questions as yet not explored in Middle Eastern and North African settings. Promising trends in the literature reviewed above point to new geographies and new perspectives in the construction of ethnic, racial, linguistic, and religious identities. However, we continue to be vague on questions of expressions of ethnic identity in everyday life, on socialization (which seems to be treated as a passive process of reception rather than an active appropriation), and on the symbolic reproduction of these types of identities. In another vein, in this era of globalization, the boundary lines between local, regional, and global affairs are not easily drawn, and the study of ethnicity is now intimately related not only to the study of minority groups but also to dispossessed and displaced populations (Chatty 2010). To indicate that the complex forms of ethnicity take place both inside and outside the arenas normally designated as political, economic, or social is to draw attention to controversy, hegemony, resistance, and conflicts of interest that underlie both the structuring of ethnicity and structuring of public agendas. But this also implies taking steps to elaborate how ethnicity is both a structured and structuring force, how it is entrenched in relationships of subordination, governance, and domination.

Difference involves history and an intangible future. Although abstract, the power of difference lies in the structuring of human relationships and the life-worlds that individuals carry with them and represent. When it comes to the study of ethnic difference, the focus has been too little on relationships or on life-worlds and too much on (presupposed) culture (in the monolithic sense), continuity, and immutability. To account for ethnic identity, we have to look at shifting assertions of similarities, affiliations, differences, and separateness rather than the diverse pieces arranged in "mosaics." In lieu of this, two main approaches characterize the literature: the first is *the single group monographic approach,* studying particular groups (Assyrians, Kurds, Jews) in particular locales. While many of these are fine ethnographies and monographs of the classical type, they tend by and large to reify the "group" and not to question either its present configuration, its relations to broader society, or the porosity of its boundaries. In this they replicate the disciplinary sins of village studies and tribal studies, but do so even when studying urban locations or conducting multi-local studies. The second approach is more characteristic of political science and could be called *the indexical approach.* This is the Middle Eastern mosaic materialized in a volume, with each chapter representing one "group"; thus an assorted medley of groups are dished up, the religious, sectarian, linguistic, and cultural, each studied independently from the others.

To go beyond the monograph and the index, we have proposed a number of dimensions that could frame the study of ethnic identity and difference in the region, which if taken together would not only go a long way in capturing both the contingency and the power of ethnic identity and various forms of difference in society but would also link the study of these "groups" to broader theoretical and empirical concerns in the anthropological literature. While we emphasize history, we also insist that ethnic and other identities should not be assumed to be either old or stable. Rather, a keen historical sensibility is needed to capture the ways in which these identities unfold and transform over time and through different contexts. In addition, the politics of state and nation-building (which both involve transnational processes) must be the context through which the production of ethnic categories is understood. And finally, the transnational networks and exchanges within which identity formation is linked through migration and the formation of diasporas must also be taken into account. In the steadily growing literature on migration, we have possibilities to explore transformations and transnationalizations that aspire to legitimacy and recognition by both the state and supranational or international institutions.

Inspirations

In 1908, the leaders of the three religious communities of Thessaloniki—Jewish, Christian, and Muslim—demonstrated their solidarity by marching arm-in-arm during a joyful parade to celebrate the inauguration of the new parliament. In 1909, when the governing party, the party of Union and Progress, sent a parliamentary delegation to Sultan Abdul Hamid to declare the parliament's decision to depose him, the five-man delegation included an Armenian, a Jewish, and an Orthodox Christian parliamentarian. They were enacting their Ottoman public identity. The study of ethnic identity and difference in the Ottoman Empire has long been captured by particular understandings of absolutism, "minorities," and the "millet system." While space does not permit us to explore the problems arising out of these understandings, it is important to stress that anthropological sensibilities are highly influenced by these notions, while regrettably rarely by delving into the historical literature or record. A great many impressionistic notions are also projected backwards from late nineteenth century struggles between the Ottomans and various European powers concerning the representation and "protection" of "minorities." The Ottoman Empire was a large, diverse, and changing entity with different types of local and imperial rule and structuring of groups and group relations. At certain points, communal structures and liberties were safeguarded while individual liberties were restricted, and some religious communities were autonomous in communal civic and religious affairs, which often made self-identity coterminous with communal space. At the same time, in other places and institutions (such as the army, palace elites, and the harem) individual mobility and identity transgressions were allowed and even encouraged and/or manipulated. At the turn of the twentieth century, also, Ottomanism as an identity and ideology was promoted as cutting across religious lines while emphasizing a certain urbanity of manners and discourse, and of style and language.

A century later, the Arab popular uprisings of 2011 inspire us to celebrate the social imagination of human beings transforming their societies. We see potential to reorient and reposition the anthropology of the region on many different registers. We may follow the young men and women who use the vocabulary of democracy to connect and mobilize ordinary Arabs of all walks of life. Squares in Arab cities became epicenters for people to imagine new countries; these special turns are "ethnographic moments in most basic sense of the term" (Naguib 2011, 383). At the same time, the somber reality of sectarian and ethnic violence is also present, showing up the poverty of previous discourses of national identity and their inability to be truly inclusive. The drama being played out opens up possibilities to take up old debates and start new conversations about relationships between men and women, social classes, minorities and majorities, generations, and between citizens and the state.

NOTES

The authors would like to thank Elizabeth Smith for her important contribution to earlier phases of this project, especially in assembling the initial bibliography and reviewing some of the works cited. Nadia Khalaf also provided valuable bibliographical assistance for the final draft of the paper.

1. The authors thank Jon Anderson for raising this crucial insight during the discussions at the conference that produced this volume.

2. See for example, "The Mosaic Theory of the Middle East, and Its Rotten Advocates," a post by Issandr al Amrani on the blog *The Arabist*, 9 September 2009:

http://www.arabist.net/blog/2009/9/3/the-mosaic-theory-of-the-middle-east-and-its
-rotten-advocate.html.

3. The interest seems to be located in Europe more than in the U.S. See, for example, "Minorities and Majorities in the Middle East and North Africa" a research workshop at the Department of Islamic and Middle Eastern Studies, University of Edinburgh, 21–22 April 2006; "Religion, Identity and Minorities in the Middle East: Strategies and Developments" Special Issue of the *Anthropology of the Middle East Journal,* Vol. 4, Issue 2 (autumn) 2009; and the conference on "New Voices, New Media, New Agendas? Pluralism and Particularism in the Middle East and North Africa" Zentrum Moderner Orient, Berlin, 10–11 February 2011.

4. In reviewing the literature, we restrict ourselves to anthropological works in English of the past two decades, except when making an explicit point of departure or connection. The assessment would be somewhat different, though not completely so, if we brought in works from other languages and disciplines, especially from history.

3.

ANTHROPOLOGY'S MIDDLE EASTERN PREHISTORY: AN ARCHAEOLOGY OF KNOWLEDGE

Jon W. Anderson

> Interesting work is most likely to be produced by scholars whose allegiance is to a discipline defined intellectually and not to a "field" like Orientalism defined either canonically, imperially or geographically.
>
> —Edward Said, *Orientalism*

What makes anthropology in the Middle East possible? For a generation, the answer has been complicity with power as anthropologists focused on power (and the powerless) in a paradigm of multidisciplinary area studies that Title VI of the National Defense Education Act of 1958 linked to power-focused disciplines. However, modern anthropology arrived in the Middle East under an older model of area studies with a different agenda and reference group, not on the coattails of power but of archaeology, which provided *inter alia* legitimacy, local contacts and connections, and often actual bases for fieldwork, which is the profession's other bracket. Fieldwork begins before we get into the field; for a generation it has often begun at and through institutes established for archaeological research, as well as under the Title VI paradigm. Such institutional arrangements have themselves evolved along with their reference groups, which mediate relations linking "the field" that Said flags with quotes to the ethnographic sense of a site and activity of work. These arrangements matter for the kinds and conduct of anthropological field research in, and production of knowledge about, the region. Some of these intersections belong to a fuller ethnography of the state of the art.

My own interest in the Middle East was sparked in the late 1960s by reading Fredrik Barth's Swat Pathan studies, when there wasn't much else on this region in comparison to other regions of the world. I encountered his *Political Leadership among Swat Pathan* (Barth 1959) bracketed by Reuben Levy's *Social Structure of Islam* (1957) and altogether different concepts of social structure (nomad ecology) in fresh-from-the-field talks by William Irons and Philip Salzman. Looking around, there was Abner Cohen on Arab border villages (1965), which I didn't read until later, Evans-Pritchard on the Sanusi (1949), Edmund Leach on Kurdistan (1940), an Egyptian village here (Fakhouri 1972), a Turkish village there (Stirling 1965), and Barth's other work on *Nomads of South Persia* (1962) as well as his rescension of Robert Pehrson's *Social Organization of the Marri Baluch* (1966). Otherwise, primary recourse could be had to classics in a more Dickensian mold, such as Lambton on *Landlord and Peasant in Persia* (1953) or Granqvist on Palestinian family life (1931–1935, 1947), which morphed from ancient into ethnographic research.[1] I remember a long slog through Berque's *Les Structures Sociales du Haut Atlas* (1955), and, since I was an incipient Afghanist, the colonial-period memoirs and aides-memoire on tribal social structures of Afghanistan and the North-West Frontier of Pakistan.[2] Other work appeared while I was researching or writing my dissertation that substantially—and, more importantly, methodologically—engaged more social-scientific paradigms: Cole on nomads of eastern Saudi Arabia (1975), Fernea on community and authority in rural Iraq (1970), Bujra on stratification in Yemen (1971), Rosen (1984), and Eickelman (1976) on symbolic action in Morocco, Gilsenan's Weberian treatment of *Saint & Sufi in Modern Egypt* (1973), and, by the later 1970s, Pierre Bourdieu's *Outline of a Theory of Practice* (1977) and Michael Meeker's brilliant reuse of Granqvist (1976) and Musil (Meeker 1976). A generation later, the ethnographic corpus is abundant with ethnographies of the power of words, markets of art, dynamics of class, the reaches of religion, the politics of piety, marketing "culture," imagining history, and, above all, literature that explores women's lives and that follows a decisive transfer of interest from countryside to cities.

To some, the anthropology of the Middle East circa 1970 seems quaint: kinship and marriage, especially parallel-cousin marriage, the veil, tribes, and above all nomads, in whom ethnographers of the region sought points of comparison, much as, say, Latin Americanists fastened on peasantry or Melanesianists on kinship. A lost world of studies of lost worlds, so utterly unlike contemporary experience as to appear a caprice, goes the casual judgment of a discourse that subsequently became more interested in power, but above all in alternative continuities. This judgment can be fundamentally anachronistic and certainly more so than the work of the period, which was decidedly anti-Orientalist. In those nomad studies, Richard Tapper (2008) has pointed out, was a decisive thematic shift from oriental historians' concept of a political cycle of nomad-and-state, to an understanding of nomadism as an economic adaptation and way of life. With the concurrent rise of development studies (and projects), this turn—together with a shift in interest away from parallel cousins to strategies of marriages as a whole, and away from tribal structure to local cultures—points to intra-disciplinary dynamics, namely, the advent of modernist anthropology in the Middle East that brought anthropological questions, driven by a disciplinary agenda of professionalized anthropology, before subsequent turns to problems, notably identity, shared with newly allied disciplines in Middle East studies.

Near the end of *Orientalism,* Edward Said invoked disciplinarity as more productive than "a 'field' like Orientalism defined either canonically, imperially or geographically" (1979, 326) and went on to commend contemporary anthropologists' discipline-driven research in the Middle East. Whatever else can be said about Said's critique, this is a professor's view, that disciplinary method is what guarantees knowledge through an independent systematization. Disciplines are systematized in many ways, from building a corpus of studies to institutional arrangements that convey, organize, and bound traditions of works, both building on other works and as practical alliances. Anthropology's alliances in Middle East studies have shifted along with its reference groups under academic regimes that emerged in the 1960s, developed in the 70s, and matured by the 80s into standards of interdisciplinary coordination that encompassed everything from political science to language and literature, swept up history and social sciences, including anthropology, and swept aside anthropology's older—and native—paradigm for area studies. That would be the Kroeberian paradigm, which set a research agenda for ethnography to fill in the ethnographic map and an analytic agenda of comparison based on comprehensive accounts of cultures.[3] In practice, this dual agenda brought to the fore the problems of kinship and marriage, economic lives, and getting a fuller picture of these than the priorities of colonial ethnography ever provided, as well as finally addressing that gaping lacuna in colonial ethnography, religion.

The turn of the Middle East in anthropology when this concept of a fuller picture was most mature killed its enabling paradigm of culture areas. The new proof-text became Fredrik Barth's essay on "Pathan Identity and Its Maintenance" in *Ethnic Groups and Boundaries* (Barth 1969), one of the best-selling anthropology books of all time. Followed by Geertz's and Bourdieu's turns in North Africa from accounting for structures to here-and-now calculus of action, Barth's comparative account of the social negotiation of cultural identities led anthropology of the Middle East away from the Kroeberian paradigm with its comparativist heuristic and into a different configuration of area studies, one populated with other disciplines less interested in differences and more with their own increasingly post-structuralist accents and visions of people "just like us." At least for anthropology, it wasn't Said, but Barth, who abolished cultural distance by, in his case, identifying how it was a social and interactive process.

That's a very condensed story devoid, to be sure, of much nuance and many influences, but schematically good to think with. It returns to issues that were in the first instance discipline-based enablements of anthropology and points up interdisciplinary influences that realigned ethnography away from problems arising within the discipline *after* modern anthropology arrived in the Middle East. It highlights a turn from horizontal comparisons to more vertical ones that link culture to power and identity, from domestic realms to national ones. Today's anthropology of the Middle East has moved from overt comparison to be encapsulated in national frames and concerns that seem primary to our new allies—political scientists, historians, humanists—under the Title VI regime for area studies, but that hardly registered in the Kroeberian view of area studies, where we often consciously made them invisible at the ethnographic level.

Why is not so invisible. Modern anthropology arrived in the Middle East with modernist anthropology's problems, a discontent with tradition, a preference for a broadly structural focus that morphed easily into one on strategies and continuous negotiation of social order; the shift happened after a period that most of us discovered only afterwards or incidentally had been filled with colonial ethnographers. Spies, not to put too fine a point on it, that we were at pains to emphasize were not "like us," with a different problem set. Most late-period Cold War Americans and post-Imperial Britons, but also French in North Africa doing research encountered and were at pains to counter identities pre-figured for us, vouched by experience and couched in conspiracy thinking that our youth and university origins (and research designs; see Tapper 2009) were ill-suited to dispel. Notorious spies, who provided much of the pre-anthropological reporting on Afghanistan (or Iran, Iraq, the Arabian Peninsula), had also been young and, by the period immediately preceding us, had also been qualified from universities (Anderson 1992). We were barely aware of the national service of all but a few of the previous generation of anthropologists, among them Evans-Pritchard, Leach, the colorful Carleton Coon, and—we now know—Pierre Bourdieu (Goodman and Silverstein 2009).[4] Rapport, that entrée into fieldwork, turned out to be something we first had to establish with officials of newly independent nations, from the Foreign Ministry down through provincial governors and local police as well as our own local counterparts. Fieldwork began with getting a visa, certainly with getting a residence permit, even before we could find the proverbial local community that was the site and frame for modernist ethnography.[5]

There, we got our first lessons in patronage and alliance, although the "marginal men" that Kroeber-Mead apocrypha held out to be anthropologists' conduits to fieldwork often turned out in our cases to have been so made by training in universities like ours, or even in disciplines like our own. I don't think any charm on my part, the naïveté of my research proposal, or its deeply intra-professional conception of extending Barth's game-theoretical account of Pathan social structure to face-to-face interaction and to add another group to the corpus persuaded the official who vetted every anthropology project in Afghanistan at the time. Ravan Farhadi had received a doctorate in linguistics in France and was author of a grammar of the Persian spoken in Kabul as well as deputy Foreign Minister at the time and later Afghanistan's Permanent Representative to the U.N. Disciplinary methods were not strange here; they already figured in the intellectual side of nation-building, and their institutionalization was well underway.

Persuasion took something else. A stream of Westerners was coming through Afghanistan at the time, which had recently opened and was on the hippie trail to India. In this stream were growing numbers coming for research—between 1971 and 1973, I met nearly a dozen anthropologists, including several Afghans, trained at Western universities and with university projects—needing local affiliations and, more importantly, legitimacy as scholars. Administratively, I found myself affiliated with a Fulbright office that administered educational exchange and so "represented" the U.S. National Science Foundation, which provided the grant for my research. Legitimacy is more nebulous: what, after all, was anthropology and why should anyone care? The answer to both questions turned out to be its connection to archaeology, which had been practiced professionally in Afghanistan for two decades and was then represented on a continuing basis by Louis Dupree, who had effectively been settled there in 1959 by the American Universities Field Service, an inter-university consortium for sharing overseas researchers that was established in the 1950s by the Institute of Current World Affairs, itself created after World War I to provide expertise on and reports from foreign countries, and as a research associate of the American Museum of Natural History.[6]

Dupree had first come to Afghanistan with archaeological projects that uncovered a series of sites in southern Afghanistan and received his Ph.D. from Harvard in 1955 for a dissertation on one (Dupree 1958). From working with Afghan archaeologists, Dupree extended his acquaintance throughout the cultural intelligentsia of Afghanistan and his work to include folklore, language, ethnography, and contemporary history in the composite anthropology of the time. That is, his work, then his network, extended outward from a base in archaeology into the study of heritages as encompassed by anthropology's global concept of culture.[7] Dupree's salon was a necessary stop for anthropologists (and others) coming to do research in Afghanistan; it vouched for their academic identity, often introduced them to his circle as well as to each other, and generally lent the cultural cachet and legitimacy rooted in the retrieval and recording of "culture" in the senses that anthropologists began extending to that term in the nineteenth century. By then the reigning orthodoxy in departments had linked archaeology with cultural anthropology for a generation.

Cachet, connections, and legitimacy were thusly provided through Dupree's history of excavating/publishing with and training Afghans. More official institutions have filled this role elsewhere, such as the American Research Center in Egypt (ARCE), the British Institute of Persian Studies (BIPS), the Albright Institute in Jerusalem (and its later offshoot, the American Center of Oriental Research, ACOR, in Amman), as well as the Institut français archéologique du Proche-Orient (IFAPO) and Institut français d'études arabes de Damas (IFEAD), but these were absent or under development in Afghanistan at the time.[8] What they all had in common, and have in common with Dupree's salon in Kabul, are foundations in archaeology (or, in the case of American Research Center in Turkey, Hittology and Byzantine studies), service to long-term projects of cultural retrieval, and extensions beyond the manifold legitimacies of archaeology that conveyed modern cultural and social anthropology and anthropologists into the Middle East. They provided institutional bases, enabling connections, and broader cultural legitimacy for modern anthropology in the Middle East and conveyed its ethnography in the domestic academy, where the University of Michigan's museum serials published, among others, Louise Sweet's (1960) and Barbara Aswad's (1971) studies in Syrian villages, Robert Canfield's study of Hazaras in Afghanistan (1973), and William Irons' Turkoman study (1975).

By modern anthropology, I mean the Kroeberian heuristic that in the 1950s and 60s was absorbed into and became aligned with priorities and methods developed for the social sciences generally. Behind its conception is a tortured history of professionalizing the study of Native Americans that the Boasian tradition tied to geography, on the one hand, and to language, on the other, in order to set American Indian studies apart from framings by Euroamerican history.[9] By the 1960s anthropology was aligned decisively with social sciences in U.S. universities and with modern studies. Anthropologists came to Afghanistan—and, by Tapper's account (2009), to Iran—in the 1960s and 1970s to do research on and among tribes, and particularly nomads, not with the regional historian's focus on state formation and dissolution but with modernist concerns with nomad economies and to record a way of life. Principal among these concerns were ecological models that in American archaeology had reoriented the way cultures were sequenced, from vertical lineages designed in a search for origins to more horizontal models of connection across the field. Similar concepts showed up in some studies from Southwest Asia as well.[10] Intellectually, anthropologists came to the Middle East with modernized anthropology after its imperial-period origins and antiquarian framings had become obsolete and in the high period of its transformation into social science in the new division of the academy. With these decidedly ahistorical bases in high-modernist social science, many anthropologists were emphatically at pains to distance our own from the broad-brush "problem" of tribe–state relations by conducting purely local studies; and professional folklore of the period is full of stories of looking for such communities to study and thereby learning what "community" meant.

Beyond this shared institutional context and intellectual affinity in moving away from culture history frames, anthropologists arrived locally on the coattails of archaeologists and often through the connections of specific archaeologists, who were themselves re-founding their discipline on scientific methodologies—they included Robert Braidwood, whom Barth thanked for entrée into Kurdistan (1953, preface), and Robert M. Adams, who introduced Robert Fernea into southern Iraq in the 1950s (1970, viii). Braidwood's and Adams' archaeology was natural kin to modernist ethnography; the two had been joined for a generation in university departments of Anthropology and in archaeology's own modernization that distanced scientific archaeology from some of its more problematic predecessors in the region.[11] Institutional settings matter, and these include institutional settings beyond universities. While ethnography evolved a single-researcher model during the twentieth century, archaeological research is more typically conducted by teams, over the long term, and includes training local cadres, and so tends to form a local community, to build a base carrying on work that extends over time and from retrieving to caring for heritage. Archaeology becomes enmeshed in local intelligentsia and their projects in cultural heritage.

These sorts of presences have, if anything, become more institutionalized under the Title VI regime of area studies as multidisciplinary combinations of social sciences and humanities that emerged in the 1960s. Even if not founded under this aegis, centers such as ARCE in Egypt or ACOR in Jordan, reassembled and repositioned as American Overseas Research Centers,[12] and European counterparts such as IFAO and IFEAD (subsequently absorbed into IFPO)[13] in Syria, or BIPS in Iran, came to serve as channels for additional area studies beyond their foundations for archaeological research. This institutionalization accompanied the inroads of scientific archaeology into Middle Eastern archaeology, on the one hand, but also the regularization of a model of area studies as multidisciplinary, backed by flows of funds to that model, particularly public funds that overmatched the private philanthropy that had hitherto supported Near East archaeology (see, Goode 2007). For the rest of us, these institutes and centers have provided connections, cultural legitimacy, and often a flop, a phone, and a mail drop.

I do not wish to suggest this is universally the case—that all of us got to the field through archaeologists' institutes, or that all of the institutes are archaeological, or that this is the only path to the field. It was not in French North Africa, where national service brought researchers from Jacques Berque to Pierre Bourdieu; and another major exception was Lebanon (and earlier, Syria), where networks of friends and family were typical avenues to fieldwork, outside channels of official sanction for research (e.g., Aswad 1971, iii; Deeb 2006, 29 ff; and cf. Chatty 1986, 1996). Other routes include previous experience in the Peace Corps or as exchange students, many of whom fell in love with the Middle East, and often with Middle Easterners, and returned for research. Turning the comparison around, one might say that the long-term and multi-personnel character of archaeology, as teamwork plus community, plus its ties to cultural heritage provide a kind of institutional counterpart of the *wasta* enacted through kin, coworkers, and other personal relationships. Whichever way the comparison is drawn, these are reference group phenomena by which the weak ties of friends-of-friends link to stronger ties in denser social nodes. What I do wish to suggest is two things, and both are about access.

Access to the field for modernist anthropology in the Middle East was facilitated by archaeology, which had undergone a similar modernization, established an intellectual community, and proceeded on the ground by lending cachet, connections, and legitimacy that archaeologists had established locally. Even where archaeology's institutions were not direct conduits, its penumbra has spread over the paths anthropologists find into the field. A generation of Egyptianists has at least touched base with ARCE, while Fulbright offices for educational exchange (in Cairo and elsewhere) handle paperwork and sometimes broker introductions. In my case it was mentioning that an archaeologist memorialized at ARCE had been an undergraduate classmate that opened stories, and doors, to my inquiries in Cairo, starting with ARCE itself. My own first visits to Syria to study information technology specialists were through their conferences; I have never stayed there at IFEAD, though archaeologists in other countries have suggested it and offered introductions. By comparison, ACOR, spun off the Albright Institute of Archaeological Research in Jerusalem, has been my base for researching IT in Jordan; and I am not the only anthropologist who has found such connections to open doors there and elsewhere,[14] as well as to provide colleagues who further blur the already blurry boundaries of "fieldwork."[15] What this suggests is a general institutional context, with modern archaeology at its core, that has eased the way for modern anthropology in and of the Middle East.

Additionally, it was specifically modern anthropology—an intellectual-institutional amalgam of intra-professional priorities and concerns, not the high politics of State nor an address of the issues of the many senses of nation-building, from development and political economy to "culture" and its contemporary politics. Nothing if not discipline-focused, it was by Said's measure already post-Orientalist. Politicization, actually, came later, under the Title VI regime for area studies, which gave MENA anthropology another reference group actually focused on the state, on power, and by expansive postmodern notions of culture as anything but tradition. Modernist anthropology, arriving in the liberation period, turned from overarching power issues in the Middle East and, particularly at the level of research, away from national frames to claim a different and more strictly academic legitimacy that leveraged—at an institutional level—another one represented by archaeology. But now, both of those contexts have changed.

Archaeologists are not the primary intellectual associates of Middle Eastern anthropology today because those associations have shifted with the Title VI paradigm for interdisciplinary area studies that associates us with history and political science in one direction and the language-and-arts humanities in another. The Kroeberian paradigm for area studies did not survive Fredrik Barth's turn to processual (or actor-oriented) analysis, as it was called at the time, just at the point that modern anthropology arrived in the region. Since then, we have been tied to a different concept, associated with multi-disciplinary area studies that align us with political scientists and humanists and their similar, sometimes parallel, sometimes overlapping, shifts to post-structural models and agendas. That association plays out not only in conferences or in new area studies centers founded under Title VI. It extends to institutions in the region that have broadened their remit—partly in response to Title VI and to more recent programs in Europe—beyond archaeology to include other disciplines. Here, access crosses association; one of the more salient experiences these days is that even if these centers aren't direct channels into fieldwork, they give access to those who manage access, provide sites where we meet other researchers, and not just archaeologists but also political scientists, historians, humanists, and social scientists who today form part of the taken-for-granted professional life of postmodern anthropology.

The Kroeberian paradigm of area studies that united archaeology and anthropology for modernists in both fields was already in decline as a framework for research when that alliance provided cover for modern anthropology with an agenda both broader than predecessor colonial ethnography and, importantly, separate from it. I've met few political scientists and humanists who were even aware that anthropology had a frame for area studies prior to the multidisciplinary collaboration model of the Title VI regime. But its significance is that modern and modernist anthropology was conveyed into the Middle East neither by its nominal precursors nor by its new friends but on the coattails of its own institutional kin, modern archaeology—borrowing its legitimacies and depending on its connections locally. This not only didn't make anthropology antiquarian, but quite the opposite. What arrived was already postcolonial; but, in accumulating new connections under a different, multidisciplinary paradigm for area studies, MENA anthropology acquired a set of priorities more focused on power and generally poststructuralist, in comparison to high modernism in anthropology and the social sciences generally.

Multidisciplinary area studies shifted intellectual alliances to the disciplines, issues, and perspectives assembled under the Title VI moot, where modernist priorities, e.g. bringing studies of the region under modern disciplines, were reset by postmodernist priorities orbiting around identity and expressivity, diversity, and, increasingly, whether "area" had any significance any more or even any meaning. The postmodern orientation expands "culture" to the point that cultures dissolve in a reach for a common humanity, or at least a common discourse, a yearning that surely has institutional as well as intellectual homes. The Africanist Jane Guyer has flagged as "area accountability" running through "collective [i.e., multidisciplinary] Area Studies" (Guyer 2004a, 514) tendencies in area studies across all regions to converge around related issues of indigenous, minority, class, and gender identity, history, experience, and governmentality. Part of the self-evidence of such focuses must rest on an institutional context,

with its new set of alliances and shifts in those alliances under the Title VI model
of multidisciplinary area studies, area studies associations that sponsor conferences and journals—and centers—which bring judgments in other disciplines
to bear on anthropology, particularly on its core discipline, ethnography. Among
collective searches for "emergent linkages and universalities of globalization," she
lists postcolonial and subaltern studies; the supplanting of "development" with
multiple alterities; operations of law, class, and "cultural and religious complexity" that she sums up as presentist visions of "a kind of 'lateral' diversity" (ibid.,
515). This, she implies, is another conversation altogether.

Writing as an Africanist, Guyer goes on to observe that, by comparison to
other areas, "in the Middle East both the traditions of reasoning and the kinds
of power are locally projected onto the big screen, even the global screen" (2004,
517). She calls these "formalities," likening them to economists' "formal sector,"
which consists of analysts' abstractions of what is shared by analysts and those
about whom they write (Guyer 2004b)—in effect, a shared metaphysical project
of joint objectivations. So, is shift of reference group from comparative to local
formation the end of the story? In his wide-ranging essay on "Contemporary
Problems of Ethnography in the Modern World System," George Marcus (1986)
flagged as a new ethnographic ideal Paul Willis' notion of ethnographer as "midwife" to indigenous critical theory for eliciting just such connections. Less than a
decade later, Webb Keane, whose own work focuses on shared spaces of colonizer
and colonized, criticized this objectivation as a muddled concept of agency made
more clear by shifting from a metaphysics of "potentially explicit objectifica-
tions" (2003, 240) to understanding communication as a material process of
making texts (Guyer's "formalities") out of precursors or "turning text analogues
into texts" that engage actors more precisely as shared objects (2003, 232).

If shifting reference groups were the end of the story, it would be a simple
one, but the multidisciplinary format for area studies has not remained stable.
The trending departures of political scientists to pursue globalization and rational choice theorizing increasingly leave cultural studies' preoccupations with
power, identity, and authenticity behind as the mark of area studies.[16] Such institutional shrinkage of multidisciplinary area studies has left anthropology by default more associated with expressive culture and surrounded by methodologies
of critique and reaches for originality derived from the humanities, over the in-
crementalist strategies by which social sciences build on previous research, which
Geertz dismissed as "another village heard from," in favor of "enlargement of the
universe of human discourse" (1973b, 14). While still very much in the heritage
business through which earlier allies introduced us and now conveyed through

centers and institutes that have themselves evolved, anthropologists at least since Boas have had reservations about "secondary rationalizations." Pierre Bourdieu's own attempt to relaunch social theory nearer to the interactive ground was particularly scathing about how analyzing "accounts of the second degree . . . presupposes the structures it analyses," and went on to make his strongest assertion of suspicion that "the constitutive power that is granted to ordinary language lies not in the language itself but in the group which authorizes it and invests it with authority" (1977, 20–21).

Guyer is more subtle—certainly less polemical—in suggesting an area studies dynamic that recalls folklorists' "double voicing" in discourses that are drawn into common alignment.[17] From a world of talk that is sometimes critical or theoretical, sometimes lived experience, rarely merely referential and always skilled performance, the Lebanese anthropologist Fuad Khuri, who was in a position to know, describes his first fieldwork experience as being let in on the "private subculture" of "a theatre in which particular kinds of comedies and tragedies are continuously enacted" (2007, 10). From the rehearsed to rehearsals, Michael Gilsenan (1996) followed stories of violence in the same region as continuities of the actions they recounted, perhaps only imagined, similar to Meeker's earlier (1979) rescension of Rwala tales (but departing from a comparison to J. M. Synge). Deeb (2006) likewise recounted the "enchantments" of aligning material and spiritual progress with a discourse of religiosity in a Hizbollahi suburb of Beirut. Ethnographically, talking about talk joins these qualities, as formalities, to a peculiar kind of intimacy, lying in specific interactions with another, that have a phenomenological immediacy ever problematic for anthropology. As archaeology fades into the background of both the associations of anthropologists in the Middle East and the access of anthropologists to the Middle East, it has become indigenized institutionally in projects, institutes, training, and in a paradigm underlying all of those, teamwork, that is not only collaborative but continues to build on previous work in a praxis of connecting past to present exemplified in its own practices. Archaeology is the science of cultural heritage with something to show, real results realized in a meta-language beyond mere identity in its own PR. What anthropology does like this archaeology in the Middle East comes arguably to rest on forms of interaction that make covert habitus into overt culture, beyond merely identifying or appropriating the present. Multiple participations seem to introduce an indeterminacy that unsettles area studies. The indeterminacy may be less whether areas exist at all than the metonomy of theory, which is not limited to multidisciplinary area studies. The jest in my graduate student days was that Latin America meant peasant studies, Africa meant lineages, and India castes. Guyer, writing more recently from within and as a protagonist for a multidisciplinary area studies that align anthropologists not just with other social scientists but also with humanists, raises the question whether we perhaps too lightly adopt macro-analytical perspectives to contain plurality, alterity, voicing, fluidity, because some local interlocutors do. One such perspective surely is political economy, another is universal humanism; and the anthropology which left behind the Kroeberian paradigm for multidisciplinary area studies may hastily replace its comprehensive conceptions of culture with one or the other to register a borderless world. Alternative realities, voices, and identities, Khuri reminds, are first of all local. Or they have to be brought into the same frame. This analytical move, formalized by George Marcus (1986) as multi-sited ethnography, would locate cultures as partial views or local knowledge of a larger system, which Marcus had to admit is supplied by the analyst in search of local interlocutors to "midwife." In a more robust humanistic inflection, Michael Herzfeld (2004, 2003) identified global hierarchies of value as "everywhere present, but nowhere clearly definable ... shifting signifiers and indices" that function as "homogeneity-producing semiotic legerdemain . . . [against] the persistence of local differences at the level of everyday practice and interpretation."

NOTES

The epigraph is from Said (1979, 369).

1. "Hilma Granqvist visited the Palestinian village of Artas as part of her research on the women of the Old Testament. Granqvist, then, arrived in Palestine in order to find the Jewish ancestors of Scripture. What she found instead was a Palestinian people with a distinct culture and way of life. She therefore changed the focus of her research to a full investigation of the customs, habits and ways of thinking of the people of that village" (Elbendary 2001, 24).

2. The list is long. Some are discussed in "Politics and Poetics in Ethnographic Texts: A View from the Colonial Ethnography of Afghanistan," (Anderson 1992) and by others writing on the northwest frontier of Pakistan, such as Lindholm (1982) and Ahmed (1980, 1976).

3. Substantive features of the "culture area" concept in anthropology referenced a mix of language and geography in broadly ecological terms developed for Native North America (Kroeber 1939) that fits the Middle East poorly, where ecological/subsistence "types" are discontinuously distributed and discontinuous with language. One attempt

to mend this problem was a brief vogue in the 1960s to conceptualize an "arid zone," primarily to give nomad–settled relations an ecological basis in place of a political one."

4. Not to mention more nefarious American examples, chronicled in David Price's *Anthropological Intelligence: The Deployment and Neglect of American Anthropology in the Second World War* (2008).

5. Richard Antoun put it at the time: "As a discipline, modern social anthropology, in particular Middle Eastern anthropology, cannot be understood apart from its traditional locus of study, the small community, and apart from its traditional type of people studied" (1976, 137). Clifford Geertz, opening the literary critical shift in ethnography from speaking-for to speaking-to, was already caricaturing this as "heaven in a grain of sand or the farthest shores of possibility" (1973, 21), while Antoun was casting peasant villages as "part-societies" that necessitate taking account of what is outside the local in order to achieve understanding, starting with how they interpret connections to state and other formal institutions (1976, 140).

6. *New York Times,* 23 March 1989.

7. Which scope was chronicled in Harvard professor Clyde Kluckhohn's text of the period, *Mirror for Man* (1949) and a survey, jointly authored with A. L. Kroeber, *Culture: A Critical Review of Concepts and Definitions* (1952); for its lapses as social science, see Canfield (1973).

8. The South-Asia Institute of Heidelberg University was the most established and institutional in the early 1970s, providing a home and base for a few German archaeologists and German-Austrian ethnologists plus a channel for educational exchange; others, created by Danes and French for projects, had languished; while yet others were aborted with the 1973 and 1976 revolutions.

9. Its apogee would be Kroeber's synthesis of a half-century of research in *Cultural and Natural Areas of Native North America* (1939).

10. In archaeology, the shift was marked by Robert Braidwood and Gordon Willey's *Courses Toward Urban Life: Archaeological Considerations of some Cultural Alternates* (1962) and *Prehistory and Human Ecology of the Deh Luran Plain: An Early Village Sequence from Khuzistan, Iran,* by Frank Hole, Kent V. Flannery, and James A Neely (1969), which became one of the proof texts of the New (i.e., ecological) Archaeology of the 1960s.

11. See James F. Goode (2007).

12. In the words of Irene Bald Romano (n.d., "Collaborative Programs and Leveraging Funding: The Contribution of American Overseas Research Centers to International Education and Diplomacy," Athens: American School of Classical Studies at Athens):

American Overseas Research Centers (AORCs) are key institutions for fostering U.S. cultural diplomacy abroad. The broad mission of these centers is not possible without sustained funding, pooling of resources, and collaboration among centers, with host country institutions, and with other international organizations. . . . Title VI funding has been essential in this regard, providing much needed operating support to allow centers to maintain their programs, staffing, and facilities, especially libraries.

AORCs, with the help of CAORC and other organizations, have found creative ways to collaborate on exchange fellowships that bring both American and foreign scholars at various stages of their careers from one center to another. Since 1994, the Bureau of Educational and Cultural Affairs of the Department of State has given support to CAORC to provide multi-country research fellowships for American pre-doctoral and postdoctoral scholars to conduct cross-regional research.

13. This history is available as a pdf from the website of L'Institut français du Proche-Orient (http://www.ifporient.org/sites/default/files/ifpo-catalogue-presses-07–2009.pdf, accessed 30 November 2009).

14. Susan Slyomovics (1998) thanks ACOR in Jordan, and Jenny White (1994, 2002) ARIT in Turkey.

15. To widen their clientele, ACOR took in their first non-prehistorian, Laurie Brand, then researching her study of *Jordan's Inter-Arab Relations* (1994) (Pierre Bikai, personal communication). Brand records, "a special thanks on the Jordanian front goes to the center where I resided, the American Center for Oriental Research (ACOR) . . . for their assistance and good humor in making a political scientist feel welcome among a host of archaeologists" (1994, ix–x) and goes on to thank "archaeologist Cherie Lenzen who, as early as my first research trip to Jordan in 1984 challenged me to look at the kingdom in new ways."

16. A development registered, and denounced, by the political scientist Kirin Chaudhry (1994) in a heyday of deconstruction.

17. My source for this concept was Mikhail Bakhtin's *Dialogic Imagination* (see Anderson, 1985); but Deborah Kapchan (1993) gives it more precise specification as utterances situating a speaker in two different "oratories" and that bridge them incrementally instead of supplanting one with another.

4.

THE PRAGMATICS AND POLITICS OF ANTHROPOLOGICAL COLLABORATION ON THE NORTH AFRICAN FRONTIER

Paul A. Silverstein

Collaboration has emerged as a salient metaphor for describing the ethnographic method in general, and the anthropology of the Middle East and North Africa (MENA) in particular. It simultaneously calls forth a colonial history, where anthropology all too often functioned as the handmaiden to imperial rule (Asad 1973; Lucas and Vatin 1975), as well as a postmodern fantasy of post-authorial writing characterized by "studying up" (Nader 1969), dialogical representation (Crapanzano 1980; Dwyer 1982), and cultural critique (Clifford and Marcus 1983; Marcus and Fischer 1986). The latter project, in the name of decolonizing the social sciences (Stavenhagen 1971), called attention to the co-production of knowledge that necessarily characterizes all fieldwork, whether recognized or not (Rabinow 1977). In general, fieldwork collaboration has been insightfully characterized as an unequal exchange, where the anthropologist extracts value (in the form of "local knowledge" [Geertz 1983] subsequently transformed into academic capital) from his "subjects" with little long-term reciprocity in terms of either symbolic or commodity goods. While critics like Paul Rabinow (1977, 28–29)—or even their less critical disciplinary ancestors (e.g., Evans-Pritchard 1940; Malinowski 1989 [1967])—never denied the agency of anthropology's indigenous interlocutors, and if anything bemoaned the material "testing" or even blackmail to which they were subjected by their "informants," they nonetheless regarded the two sets of interests as ultimately incommensurable. The dialogue was one characterized by inherent, if sometimes productive, misunderstanding; the collaboration operated across a seemingly impassible gulf of differential knowledge and experience.

Yet, in the contemporary period, while such real-time encounters are sometimes still marked by an incommensurability of collaborators, they are equally likely to occur across a shared epistemological and discursive space. As the anthropology of the Middle East and North Africa moves beyond the older organizing tropes of tribe, bazaar, and Islam (Abu-Lughod 1989) to investigations of urban space, political movements, transnational formations, and the bureaucracies of "middling modernism" that Rabinow (1989) himself would later describe, older conceits about the mutual exoticism and fundamental inequality of anthropologist and informant that underpinned the postcolonial ethical project of anthropology as cultural critique seem quaint. If MENA anthropology's privileged interlocutors were always articulate specialists in irrigation systems, market networks, tribal genealogies, and Sufi esoterica, anthropologists of the region are today as likely to work with collaborators whose knowledge base, epistemological presuppositions, and educational background closely resemble their own. Anthropologists are thus rarely the oddities they may have once been along the (implicitly non-urban) colonial frontier. Rather, as Yaël Navaro-Yashin (2002, 21), Andrew Shryock (1997), and Jessica Winegar (2006, 22–31) discuss in different contexts of Middle Eastern ethnography, they arrive into a "field" that is generally overdetermined not only by a prior history of "Western" anthropological and historical study with which they will necessarily be in dialogue, but also by a rigorous homegrown attention to history and "culture" practiced by native anthropologists and other local researchers sometimes trained in and credentialed at the very same institutions that produced the visiting anthropologists themselves.

Such emergent conditions of contemporary collaboration are not simply reducible to the various phenomena loosely labeled "globalization" or "cosmopolitanism" that Ulf Hannerz (1990) and others have characterized as enabling a transnational intellectual elite. Indeed, there is nothing really new about such "cultural intimacy" (Herzfeld 1997), (neo)colonial mimesis (Taussig 1993), or the "indigenization of modernity" (Sahlins 1993), phenomena that have now explicitly become anthropology's primary objects of study. But little previous attention has been paid to the implications of such mimetic processes for the changing dynamics of anthropological collaboration in the postcolonial period. Since colonial times, "Berber culture" has become an object of indigenous self-reflection in North Africa and the diaspora that has paralleled the attention paid to it by anthropologists. In recent years, a set of Berber (Amazigh) cultural activists, experts, and entrepreneurs have emerged who have maintained a productive and interested dialogue with European and American state agents and researchers. Reflecting on the politics and pragmatics of working with (and on) such indigenous cultural workers can provide insight into the actually existing (if seldom commented upon) forms of collaboration within the anthropology of the MENA.

Colonial Collaboration

The French colonial conquest of North Africa after 1830 was premised on an intimate knowledge of human and geographical terrains, an operation that, much as in the present-day U.S. occupation of Afghanistan and Iraq, required the integration of anthropological and linguistic investigation into military intelligence. Over the course of the nineteenth and early twentieth centuries, French army ethnologists and linguists worked with local informants to map cultural forms onto conquered territory, effectuating a classification of the indigenous populations encountered along a gradient from primitivity to civilization. If many military scholars considered rural and mountain Berber speakers to be less culturally developed than their urban Arab counterparts, they likewise viewed them as less corrupted by dogmatic Islam and Ottoman despotism, as displaying some rudimentary survivals of earlier Christian and Roman influences, and thus as more open to and welcoming of the "civilizing mission" (*mission civilisatrice*) (Gross and McMurray 1993; Hannoum 2010; Lorcin 1995; Silverstein 2004, 35–75). While the colonial administration in Algeria and Morocco never pursued a consistent "Berber policy" (Ageron 1960; Lafuente 1999), it nonetheless did tend to target Berber-speaking populations for labor recruitment, evangelization, and education.

French colonialism profoundly transformed but did not necessarily destroy Berber social worlds. Colonial policies of extensive land expropriation, administrative centralization, the abolition of slavery, and the "pacification" and forced sedentarization of transhumant populations did preclude many of the prior avenues through which social privilege had been consolidated and challenged. Previously marginal merchant castes were promoted by a monetizing economy, and education enabled new, theoretically open channels for the accumulation of prestige and authority. But, if labor migration created unprecedented levels of spatial and social mobility—particularly for those displaced peasants and emancipated sharecroppers (*Haratin*) who accumulated economic capital while working in colonial farms, mines, and metropolitan industries—colonialism nonetheless tended to reproduce extant class structures, with the sons of Berber landed notables and religious scholars achieving positions in the colonial civil service and military. Indeed, local notables generally viewed the French administration as yet another resource for local contests of power that—as Marshall Sahlins (1988) describes for Hawaiian and "Kwakiutl" cosmologies of capitalism—were always considered more significant, enduring, and encompassing than the latest foreign incursion. Thus, in spite of a postindependence narrative of anti-colonial resistance that structures the contemporary historical consciousness of Amazigh ethno-nationalism, the colonial archive attests to as many instances of collaboration with the invading military force as resistance to it. "Resistance" and "collaboration" were but two strategies along a continuum of interlocution that were often alternately taken up by the same elite actors and their dependents.

From the French perspective, the colonial practice of collaboration with extant hierarchies was, in part, purely pragmatic in terms of minimizing disruption, facilitating local administration and the collection of tax revenue (*tertib*), and procuring armed services for further pacification efforts against *les insoumis* (those who continued to resist the conquest) in a complex game of divide, conquer, and rule. On a smaller scale, it reflected the precarious positions of indigenous affairs officers appointed to administer the settled rural peripheries. The officers needed local mediators to help them work with idioms and practices they did not generally master and about which they had to report regularly, both in the name of military surveillance and with the scientific goal of filling out the cultural map of North Africa (as exemplified by the collection of *fiches de tribu* ["tribal dossiers"]). Moreover, they desired interlocutors with whom they could identify and converse, and with whose families they often developed intimate and caring relations.[1] It was more due to this intimacy than out of any Berberophilic ideologies of indigenous improvement that these officers encouraged and supported the sons of Berber notables to pursue educational and employment opportunities beyond their home villages.

As a result of these efforts, a generation of indigenous intellectual and military elite emerged who were equally at home in rural Berber and French colonial urban settings. These included well-known French-educated Kabyle writers like Jean Amrouche, Si Amar Boulifa, Mouloud Feraoun, and Mouloud Mammeri who worked with colonial ethnologists and linguists in the collection of Berber poetry, folklore, and legal codes, later publishing their own collections and ethnographic studies, as well as fictional narratives of their natal cultural worlds (Goodman 2002; see Amrouche 1988 [1938]; Boulifa (1990 [1904]); Feraoun 1997 [1950]; Mammeri 1980). Tragically, these intellectuals often went unrecognized by the French reading public of the time, and moreover were reviled by anti-colonial nationalist ideologues as collaborationists and sectarian traitors to a patriotic cause increasingly defined by Arabic language and Salafi Islam. They nonetheless deployed their Francophone writing to articulate a critique of colonial inequality and a vision of postimperial humanism, and later were iconized by the emergent Berber cultural movement.[2] Even Abdelmalek Sayad—Pierre Bourdieu's student, informant, collaborator, and co-author of ethnographic and anti-colonial political writings on Kabylia (see Bourdieu and Sayad 1964)—lived in exile and largely dependent on his patron, on the margins of French academia until his premature death in 1998 (Silverstein and Goodman 2009, 29–32). Only recently have his stellar contributions to a critical ethno-sociology of Algerian migration been recognized, translated (see Sayad 2004), and honored, with the library at the French National Immigration Museum dedicated to his memory.

Even more complicated was the collaboration of military officers like Saïd Guennoun, a Kabyle recruit who participated in the conquest of Morocco, fought in France in World War I, and later commanded the region of Itzer in the Middle Atlas from which he spearheaded the final campaigns against the remaining *insoumis* (see El-Qadéry 2006). While stationed in Morocco, he wrote a prize-winning ethnography of the Ait Amalou tribe, entitled *La Montagne Berbère* (Guennoun 1929), in which he seamlessly combined a history of the military conquest of the region with geographical, social, economic, and political description of the local Berber groups. He subsequently published an ethnographic novel, *La Voix des monts* (*The Voice of the Mountains*), which included a reflection on the "Berber mentality" and the condition of indigenous intellectuals "incapable of progress" without the instruction of their European mentors, but who would eventually have to fight for their full rights as citizens of the empire (Guennoun 1934, 302; cited in El-Qadéry 2006, 82). While never disavowing the colonial enterprise nor regretting his role in the conquest in Morocco, Guennoun was ultimately frustrated by the limits to his career as an *indigène* and his inability to publish his later, more critical work in France.

Contemporary Amazigh anthropologists Tassadit Yacine-Titouh (2001) and Mustapha El-Qadéry (2006) have characterized the colonial collaboration of this older generation of Berber intellectuals as *tiherci,* as a "ruse of the repressed" that draws on a longstanding Berber practice in the face of domination, a practice folklorized in the trickster figures of the jackal and hedgehog.

In this interpretation, the colonial roles and discourse inhabited by Amrouche, Feraoun, Mammeri, and Guennoun[3] represent a conscious choice designed to mask a more authentic nationalist or culturalist spirit. While this interpretation bolsters a current Amazigh project of cultural avowal, it risks romanticizing the resistance (Abu-Lughod 1990) of these actors and glossing over the more complex structure of interests involved. It projects a contemporary identity politics back onto a very different context of belonging and aspiration.

Rather, as Homi Bhabha (1994) has explored, colonial collaboration is always a deeply fraught project, indexing an ambivalent subject position that is always betwixt and between without any promise of transition, resolution, or *telos*. If anything, these figures are products of the late-colonial predicament; their ambivalence reflects the hybrid social worlds which they inhabit, regardless of the precise politics they adopted or the retroactive interpretation of their collaboration by Arab or Berber nationalists (as treason and resistance, respectively). Indeed, to a great extent, contemporary identity categories of "Arab" and "Berber" should be understood as the performative outcome of these very collaborations. The ethnographic encounters between army anthropologists and informants contributed progressively to the objectification Berber culture as an instrument of rule and a later site for political struggle.

Anthropology in/of Postcolonial North Africa

The contemporary anthropology of North Africa likewise involves an equally complex, if fundamentally different, collaboration. Current native anthropologists like Yacine and El-Qadéry came of age in a postcolonial world in which Arab nationalist states marginalized Berber culture to the rural periphery and private sphere. Moreover, it was a world of emergent politics around identity and autochthony, where the works of Amrouche, Feraoun, Mammeri, Sayad, and other indigenous intellectuals offered a model of engaged scholarship and an archive of knowledge from which to promulgate an official status for Berber language and culture in Algeria and Morocco. Ethnographic methodologies likewise provide a powerful tool for contemporary Amazigh activism, with auto-anthropology considered an art of resistance. If the Moroccan Berber leader Ou Skounti sacrificed his life to avoid the humiliation of surrender to Guennoun's forces, his son eventually became the *qa'id* (indigenous administrator) of the colonial region (*cercle*) of Assoul, and his grandson is today an anthropologist and Amazigh activist specializing in the political ecology of the very mountains and oasis valleys in which he grew up.

Indeed, for some time now, anthropologists working in rural Morocco—a space for social scientific reflection since at least the late fourteenth century work of Ibn Khaldun—have found themselves rubbing ethnographic shoulders with a variety of development professionals and local cultural experts. The children of the Berber landed gentry of the southeastern oases—where I pursued my own anthropological fieldwork over the last decade—achieved particular educational success in the 1960s and 70s, achieving high positions as military officers, state engineers, and decorated educators. While they pursued their training in northern Moroccan cities or in Europe, many of them ultimately returned to the oases to teach in local schools or direct infrastructure improvement projects. They thus conjoined local knowledge of topography and culture with a measure of distant, critical reflection cultivated while abroad.

Such schoolteachers and development workers founded and manned the plethora of Amazigh cultural associations that have been active in the region since 1991. These contemporary activists built on the efforts of Berber-speaking students based in Rabat and Agadir who, beginning in the late 1960s, compiled an archive of Berber cultural media they feared would soon disappear under the pressures of state Arabization policies and rural development efforts. In parallel with political developments in Kabylia, this salvage anthropology operation was soon coupled with grassroots activism to standardize spoken dialects into a pan-Berber written language, Tamazight, and through such efforts to garner popular awareness and state recognition of a pan-Berber Amazigh identity as the autochthonous culture of North Africa.[4] Conflating distance in space with distance in time in much the same way that evolutionary anthropologists "spatialized Time" (Fabian 1983, 15), activists scoured the remote mountainsides and southern oases to track down "authentic" expressive or material forms and commit them to paper, film, or audiocassette before their practitioners died out. Pursuing areas of traditional anthropological inquiry, they have collected genealogies, transcribed oral narratives, recorded rituals, and preserved material artifacts. Concerned with the survival of their language and culture that they view as endangered, these activists have returned to the colonial ethnological and philological archive to establish a baseline for Berber language and culture before Arabization.[5]

In the southeastern Moroccan town of Goulmima, for instance, three separate activists have each for the last decade worked with different blind poets from the neighboring upland, recording, transcribing, and publishing their oeuvres in a breathless and surely competitive fashion. The activists are poets in their own right—though they differ dramatically in style, persona, politics, and preferred media of transmission—and their poetry (as well as their more basic understanding of their culture and history) has been profoundly marked by their archaeological experience. Like anthropology graduate students returning from the field, they ponder over the best mode of archiving the data they have collected, over how to present it in a pithily explanatory fashion, and over how to make it useful for generations to come. They note subtle differences in micro-regional phonology, lexics, and syntax; log archaic idiomatic expressions; and document the ways a given poem has changed over time in relationship to ecological or political events. They search out the genealogies of terms in order to better grasp their poetic resonances, often turning to colonial dictionaries of the Touareg idiom they see as less sullied by Arabic loan words.[6]

Such a turn to the colonial archive for cultural self-confirmation is not an isolated act. Amazigh activists, whether in Goulmima or elsewhere, generally are familiar with the canonical studies of Berber societies, able to reference particular arguments from Robert Montagne, Jacques Berque, or even Bourdieu, and these scholars' findings have been assimilated into activists' self-understanding. One activist recounted to me what I took to be a folktale from the neighboring Ait Hadidou region, which I later discovered was taken nearly verbatim from an actual fieldwork incident related in Michèle Kasriel's monograph (1989, 70). On a visit to Zagora, a local cultural activist pulled out a tattered photocopy of Captain Georges Spillman's 1936 Protectorate-era study of the Ait Atta of the Dra'a Valley, informing me that if I wanted to understand local Berber culture, it was all there. Texts by Spillmann (1936), Edmond Doutté (1908), Georges Marçais (1946), Edouard Michaux-Bellaire (1923), and other colonial scholars fill the libraries of Berber cultural associations across Morocco, sharing shelf space with newspaper copies, village registers, textbooks used for after-school tutoring, and a variety of material artifacts collected by activists over the years.[7] Not only did the colonial myth of a culturally integral Berber society confirm their own politics of autochthony and self-determination, but the material the French military linguists and ethnologists had collected provided invaluable archival data and an essential reference point for judging how deeply their cultural world had been transformed in the last half century.

Fieldwork in such contexts is thus necessarily a fully collaborative process. Much as Andrew Shryock (1997) discusses with regard to his research on Jordanian genealogical nationalism alongside indigenous historiographers and anthropologists, American and European anthropologists arrive as but the latest students of Berber culture whose ignorance activists and other local cultural experts help to temper, and whose research orientation they critically evaluate and try to direct. Which is of course not to say that the interests of activists and anthropologists have always converged. The activists' engagement with anthropological literature and projects indexes their ideological struggles against Arab nationalism more than their scholastic avocation or critical inquiry. Yet in the collaborations that emerge, the two sets of actors nonetheless share a similar interpretive position as engaged scholars for whom Berber culture is an object of conscious reflection.

The political positioning of the activists nonetheless strongly structures the collaborative environment, effectively inverting the hierarchy of research agency under colonialism. By and large activists of any ideological tendency are suspect members of a given community. They tend to be more educated, with personal networks that stretch well beyond their native locality, sometimes with transnational reach. Activists are generally accused of "playing politics [*siyasa*]," of adopting a needlessly oppositional position vis-à-vis the central state (*makhzen*) that could threaten the livelihood of their households, if not the larger community. They are seen as working for their own personal gain and therefore as ultimately untrustworthy. In order to maintain their standing in the community, activists have to hypercorrect in terms of their public moral deportment.[8] In addition, they regularly reach out to various local constituencies and include their particular interests in the larger demands made to the state in the name of "Amazigh culture"—which to a large extent explains the Amazigh movement's recent turn toward material concerns around rural education, economic development, water claims, and land rights (Le Saout 2009; Pouessel 2010, 125–128; Silverstein 2010). Yet even such community outreach has not allayed local suspicion or ongoing accusations by certain Moroccan nationalists that they are reviving colonial sectarianism, that they constitute a veritable *hizb fransa* (French party).

Moreover, this suspect politics can have a moral or religious dimension. Although Moroccan Amazigh activists and those sympathetic to the Islamist Justice and Development Party (PJD) often cooperate in education and development projects, the two groups generally disdain each other. Islamists generally treat Amazigh activists as impious Muslims, if not *murtaddin* (apostates) for seeking to ethnically divide the Islamic community, for emphasizing what they consider second-order dimensions of identity over their religious faith (Ben-Layashi 2007; Boum 2007). Amazigh activists, for their part, regard PJD activists and sympathizers as "fundamentalists" sowing the seeds of terrorism among Morocco's youth (Silverstein 2007). Such ideological caricatures, of course, mask a far more complex reality of belief and identification among individual activists of both camps, gloss over both groups' shared opposition to the *makhzen,* and ignore the multidimensional relations of kith and kin that affectively unite all residents of small-scale places in webs of solidarity (see Rosen 1979).

And, of course, Amazigh activists across North Africa are by no means a homogeneous group, but are rather intricately subdivided by political tendency, local rivalry, and generational culture. Amazigh activists breathe new life into the *leff* checkerboard alliance structure that Montagne (1973 [1931], 36–41) and others have described as historically organizing certain dimensions of Berber politics. Local associations tend to double either along lines of pre-existing segmentation or through a process of fission following disagreements among former allies or even brothers, much as Kabyle villages segment between upper and lower "halves" (*sfuf*) (Silverstein 2003, 96), while simultaneously confederating with like associations one or two mountain peaks or oasis valleys over. Foreign anthropologists must negotiate this fraught landscape whose politics they end up studying by being incorporated into them.

The anthropologist arrives with desirable, useful economic and academic resources: transnational social networks, knowledge of current analytical approaches, access to overseas archival resources, and a professional title that conveys prestige when allied with a particular activist project. Visiting ethnographers are invited to speak at local associations and to be interviewed in activist newspapers. The anthropologist and her findings thus function as a form of political—and occasionally economic—capital to be struggled over. In this way, rather than anthropology serving as an instrument to assimilate a culturally othered world into a stratified colonial regime, it is the (foreign) anthropologists themselves who are assimilated into a larger postcolonial political game between and among activists—a game in which the anthropologists are novice players at best. Collaboration remains a complex terrain of multiple and overlapping, if not precisely equal, interests.

Diasporic Ethnography

The dynamics of collaboration in diasporic settings of anthropology involve their own related dilemmas. To a great extent, Amazigh activism in North Africa today has built on the efforts of Berberophone Algerian and Moroccan immigrant workers and exiled intellectuals in France who, in the wake of Algerian independence, culturally and politically challenged Arab nationalist hegemony in the former French colonies. Beginning in the mid-1960s, these mostly Kabyle activists formed cultural associations to standardize Tamazight, develop a modern Berber literature, maintain language and cultural competence for generations born abroad, and advocate, from the relative safety of being overseas, for the recognition of Tamazight as an official and national language of Algeria and Morocco (Clarkin 2005; Direche-Slimani 1997; Silverstein 2004). Over the years, these activities have received strong support from European state officials who have seen in Berber culture an alternate path to immigrant "integration" preferred over the Islamic piety perceived to be on the rise among those of North African background growing up in France. Berber cultural associations garnered generous financial backing from national Social Action Funds and local municipalities, and they became central sites for after-school tutoring and citizenship classes for all immigrants. Amazigh activists succeeded in introducing Tamazight as an optional subject on the baccalaureate high school exam, and widespread activist support for the 2004 ban on the *hijab* in public schools elicited a promise from the Minister of Education to incorporate Tamazight classes into certain school districts.   Moreover, European intellectuals have bolstered Amazigh activist efforts. Ethnologists Pierre Bourdieu and Ernest Gellner participated in the creation of a "Berber Study Group" at the University of Paris-Vincennes which became a springboard for the subsequent public diffusion of Berber writing, scholarship, and translations. Later, Bourdieu underwrote Mouloud Mammeri's founding of a Center for Amazigh Research and Studies at the Maison de Science de l'Homme (Museum of Human Science) in Paris, whose academic journal of Berber anthropology and linguistics, *Awal* ("Word"/"Speech"), is now directed by Kabyle anthropologist Tassadit Yacine. The very first article published in *Awal* was the second of two dialogues between Bourdieu and Mammeri (2003 [1985]), titled "On the Good Use of Ethnology." In this transcribed and edited conversation, they discuss the pragmatics and politics of native anthropology. According to both scholars, for ethnology to be "good," it has to be politically useful in the specific sense of promoting the survival of people minoritized by hegemonic state language and cultural policies. This necessarily involves the "recovering" of vanishing traditions, even at the risk of bolstering a mythical representation of cultural identity (Bourdieu and Mammeri 2003 [1985]; Silverstein and Goodman 2009, 37–38). These dialogues attest to the intimate linking of anthropology and transnational Berber politics. If the conversation between "Western" and "indigenous" anthropologists has not always been equal, it has certainly been robust.

Moreover, this prior collaboration set the stage for contemporary anthropological research in diasporic settings.

By the time I began my fieldwork on the Berber cultural movement in Paris in the mid-1990s, the context of activism had transformed significantly. The Algerian civil war had forced thousands of Algerian artists, journalists, and intellectuals to seek refuge in France, as Islamist militias were targeting secular cultural production in their campaign to bring down the military government. Outspoken Berber artists and activists were accused of apostasy and repeatedly threatened, with journalist Tahar Djaout assassinated in 1993, folksinger Lounès Matoub kidnapped in 1994 and later killed in 1998, and feminist Khalida Messaoudi publicly menaced with death. The mortal stakes of the conflict polarized the question of Berber cultural and linguistic rights in both North Africa and the diaspora. Amazigh associations divided themselves between the rival Algerian political tendencies of the Rally for Culture and Democracy (RCD) and the Socialist Forces Front (FFS), political parties that respectively advocated "eradicator" and "dialogue" positions vis-à-vis the Islamist opposition. In spite of emergent efforts to integrate transnational Berber political efforts in the form of a World Amazigh Congress (CMA) whose first meeting was held in the Canary Islands in 1997, the stakes of the civil war largely fractured the diasporic activist community. Collaboration between activists was already fraught; with outside researchers it became even more complicated.

As an American researcher I found myself implicated in Berber politics in often unexpected ways. In the first place, I quickly discovered that the activist landscape was saturated with anthropological knowledge production. Many of the exiled activists who had been trained as doctors and engineers in Algeria were regularizing their immigrant status in France through advanced coursework in Berber linguistics and anthropology offered through Yacine's Center for Amazigh Research and Studies at the École des Hautes Études en Sciences Sociales or through the Center for Berber Studies at the Institut National des Langues et Cultures Orientales, also in Paris and directed by Kabyle linguist and activist Salem Chaker.[9] I found myself often attending the same graduate seminars with the very activists whom I was interviewing. Moreover, the various rival associations regularly sponsored lectures by French and Algerian anthropologists of North Africa, and even the Tamzight language courses offered for the children of Kabyle immigrants used textbooks (e.g., Anonymous 1987 [1957]) that were premised on objectified anthropological representations of Kabyle village life (Goodman 2005, 69–72). As yet another interested anthropologist, I was called upon to contribute texts to newsletters and interviews to community radio programs, and was critically engaged in all venues. When I eventually completed the dissertation and shared it with the several associations with whom I had worked, various members quickly read the work with both political interest and analytical depth. As others have remarked in different contemporary ethnographic settings (see Holmes and Marcus 2005), the epistemological distance between anthropologist and informant on which ethnography was historically premised proved illusionary.

Moreover, my own identity as an American Jew factored into the polarized identity politics of the diaspora and conditioned the collaborative environment. The strong anti-Islamism of many of my activist interlocutors was matched by a growing philo-Semitism that regarded the historical Zionist movement as a model for a future Amazigh struggle. Associations sponsored seminars on the historical relation between Jews and Berbers in North Africa, and diasporic activists made trips to Israel, publishing their accounts in association newsletters. While I had initially refrained from underlining my Jewish background, I eventually discovered it to be a basis of imagined solidarity for many of the activists with whom I was working. One interlocutor, upon learning of my heritage, regaled me with his version of Jewish North African cuisine; another simply declared: "I knew it all along [that you were Jewish]. You see, we're cousins."

My American citizenship was less universally embraced. While later, in post–September 11th Morocco, the more extreme Amazigh activists would declare their allegiance to a U.S.-led global War on Terror (Silverstein 2007), in the 1990s the American position at the forefront of anti-Islamism seemed less clear. Indeed, one of my first interactions with Parisian Amazigh activists was with Malika Matoub, who effectively accused me (as an American citizen) of contributing to the kidnapping of her folksinger brother Lounès, insofar as the United States at that point had granted temporary asylum to several Algerian Islamist leaders. However, in other contexts, my American identity provided a relatively neutral status compared to my French counterparts'. If many activists I later encountered in southeastern Morocco maintained a fair amount of nostalgia for the French Protectorate under which their families had generally benefitted, few diasporic activists harbored fond memories of either the French–Algerian war or the racism and structural discrimination that they and their families had encountered in France. The American anthropological approaches to "culture" I deployed were considered compelling insofar as they derived from a context outside of the colonial discourse of Jacobin universalism that tended to regard "culture" as an antithesis to civilization, humanism, and progress. Quickly I discovered my own analytical categories of transnationalism appropriated and redeployed by the activist-scholars with whom I was working in fascinating, if significantly different, ways.

But the primary pragmatic consideration in conducting ethnographic collaboration in the diaspora concerned the polarized political setting. As I would later discover in Morocco, working with one set of activists made simultaneous research with rival parties extremely difficult, if not impossible. A particular idiom for talking about Berber culture I developed in one diasporic research context would have to be censored and revised for a different one. Indeed, even the ethnonyms "Berber" and "Amazigh" indexed two different political tendencies, with neither providing a possibility of neutrality or agreement. Luckily, the mere fact that Paris-based activists were constantly busy with their studies, multiple jobs, families, and political life meant that fieldwork encounters were necessarily constrained, thus keeping any overlap between my different research engagements to a minimum. When moments did arise when activists from different tendencies found themselves together (such as at informal social gatherings I occasionally organized), a tacit collective effort steered conversations away from particularly contentious political subjects. But, even in the best of circumstances, these collaborative ethnographic environments were continually negotiated and heavily politicized.

Anthropologists and Other Cultural Entrepreneurs

Collaboration thus indexes a fraught landscape of cultural objectification and joint knowledge production. In contexts of colonial rule, postcolonial nation-building, and immigrant incorporation, anthropology has played a significant political role in establishing the diacritics of communities of belonging, in outlining the bases of inclusion and exclusion. It is thus a matter of little wonder that activists and other cultural entrepreneurs, in their own claims to cultural recognition and autonomy, in their own attempts to market the commodity of "culture," have embraced ethnographic methodologies, or that their efforts to define and profit from the contours of culture have elicited deep suspicion from nationalist elites and even their village co-residents. The necessarily collaborative efforts of foreign and native anthropologists inherently multiply the political and economic stakes of scholarship, fostering uncomfortable processes of both collusion and conflict. Such challenges deserve further consideration and critical reflection as we embrace collaboration as an ethic and methodology for future anthropological studies of the MENA.

NOTES

1. Indeed, the fear that these relations might become too intimate and jeopardize the officers' judgment or independence from local competitive interests largely underwrote the policy of transferring officers from one bureau to another after relatively short service.

2. For a discussion of a similar humanist project by late-imperial *négritude* critics like Aimé Césaire and Léopold Senghor, see Wilder (2005).

3. Sayad arguably inhabited a similarly ambivalent space, as Bourdieu's critique of colonialism (written from the perspective of a former military recruit) never matched the violent threats Sayad faced or the trauma he experienced at the conclusion of the war that necessitated his own exile (*ghorba*) in France. His fate was nonetheless less critical than that of the tens of thousands of Algerians who had served as auxiliaries to the French army during the French–Algerian war who were massacred in the immediate wake of independence, and the nearly 100,000 who were "repatriated" to France with minimal provisions for housing or employment. The history of "collaboration" of these "Harkis" is still being written, often by Harki activists themselves who forcefully argue for recognition and reparations from France. See Besnaci-Lancou and Manceron (2008), Cohen (2006), Crapanzano (2011), Hamoumou (1993), Kerchouche (2003), Moumen (2003), and Shepard (2009).

4. For a history of Berber (Amazigh) cultural activism in North Africa, see Aourid (1999), Chaker (1998), Crawford (2005), Crawford and Hoffman (2000), Goodman (2005), Maddy-Weitzman (2001, 2006, 2011), Pouessel (2010), Silverstein (2003, 2010).

5. Jane Goodman (2005) has nicely discussed the linguistic processes by which Kabyle cultural activists draw from colonial compendiums of poetry and legal codes (as especially compiled by military ethnologists Adolphe Hanoteau and Aristide Letourneux [1872–1873]) in order to entextualize a rooted vision of Kabyle culture (Tamazight).

6. Very few of these collected oeuvres have yet been published. But see Ouchna (2007).

7. The collection of colonial ethnographic texts is occasionally accompanied by translation projects. In 2007, an Amsterdam-based Amazigh cultural association brought out a Dutch translation of the anthropologist David Hart's 1976 ethnography of the Aith Waryaghar of the Rif Mountains. On the display of material artifacts in Amazigh associations, see Goodman (2005, 1). For the deeper colonial and post-independence incorporation of museum spaces into educational institutions, see Maher (1974, 80).

8. On hypercorrection as a mode of internalization and public reproduction of moral community by marginal figures in Berber-speaking areas, see Sayad (2004, 50).

9. Needless to say, the study of Berber culture was polarized by the politics of the two centers operating in manifest rivalry.

5.

THE POST–COLD WAR POLITICS OF MIDDLE EAST ANTHROPOLOGY: INSIGHTS FROM A TRANSITIONAL GENERATION CONFRONTING THE WAR ON TERROR

Lara Deeb and Jessica Winegar

How can we assess the state of Middle East anthropology today? One way is to turn the ethnographic lens on Middle East anthropologists themselves, to examine how we think about and do our work in relationship to the broader politics in which our field is embedded—the politics of our discipline, of academia, and of national and international relations. And so, like many ethnographies, this one begins with an anecdote about a group of anthropologists who came of age at the end of the Cold War and launched their professional careers in the context of the emerging War on Terror. Examining this generation reveals a great deal about the relationship between anthropological practice, geographical region, and post–Cold War politics as they play out in U.S. academe.

At the 2001 meeting of the American Anthropological Association (AAA), a group of five anthropology graduate students and postdoctoral scholars who research the Middle East began a conversation about the challenges of writing and teaching about the region after the events of 9/11. This conversation continued over email, and led to a survey of other anthropologists' experiences teaching about the Middle East at that time, and to a meeting held during the AAA conference in 2002. At that meeting, the six young anthropologists in attendance, including the authors, quietly inaugurated what they privately, and with a tongue-in cheek reference to early independence-era Arab governing groups, called the Revolutionary Command Council or RCC. Their first two projects were to plan, for the 2003 AAA meetings, a teaching workshop about the "Middle East, North Africa, and Islam" and to ghostwrite and submit four resolutions for consideration by the AAA membership. These addressed the invasion of Iraq, academic freedom, civil liberties for Arab and Muslim Americans, and human rights in Israel and Palestine. Three RCC members signed their names to the academic freedom and Iraq resolutions, other young anthropologists were recruited to sign the civil liberties resolution, and senior anthropologists who work on Palestine signed the Palestine resolution, in order to protect the graduate students who had written it. The group was very disappointed that only the resolution on academic freedom passed.

Yet clearly, a critical mass was forming. At those 2003 AAA meetings, seven people attended a more formal RCC meeting. These individuals were also at early stages in their careers and eager to expand Middle East anthropology's voice within academe and the public sphere. They discussed a range of issues, including de-ghettoizing the Middle East Section from other parts of the AAA, collecting oral histories about Middle East anthropology in different political contexts, actions around the impending Title VI legislation, and outreach in primary and secondary schools.[1] At the end of that meeting, the RCC publicly emerged as "The Task Force on Middle East Anthropology," and drafted a mission statement that read,

> The Task Force is committed to increasing the public relevance, visibility, and application of anthropological perspectives on Middle Eastern peoples and cultures. It supports ending all acts of aggression and occupation in the Middle East, and all forms of prejudice against Middle Eastern and Muslim peoples. First and foremost, the Task Force works to ensure that conditions within the academy permit the open research and discussion of Middle East–related issues that are the foundation of a public Middle East anthropology. Second, the Task Force encourages anthropological participation in public discourse on Middle East issues by facilitating connections between anthropologists and media professionals, and by engaging in regular written and oral commentary in the public sphere. Third, the Task Force works to promote anthropological perspectives on the Middle East in K–12 and university classrooms, through teacher workshops and other activities. Finally, the Task Force works in concert with other academic organizations to create anthropologically informed conference panels, public statements,

and reports on the various issues precipitated by conflicts involving the Middle East.

The group began to actively recruit new members and organize existing members around particular initiatives through a dedicated listserv. In the following years, the Task Force set up a larger listserv (which currently has 210 members) for anthropologists who wanted to share discipline-related news about events in the region and calls to action around issues affecting Middle East anthropologists. Members also planned additional AAA teaching workshops, resubmitted resolutions, published articles and letters to editors, wrote a proposal for a symposium to bring together media professionals and Middle East scholars, and disseminated alerts to anthropologists and academics more generally about changes pushed through to bring Title VI funding in line with War on Terror prerogatives as well as about attempts to pass the right-wing Academic Bill of Rights on college campuses. In addition, Task Force members researched and wrote what has become a widely and internationally circulated document: "Academic Freedom and Professional Responsibility after 9/11: A Handbook for Scholars and Teachers."[2] The group created a website (www.meanthro.org) to document its activities and to provide free dissemination of the handbook. Today, the Task Force boasts twenty-eight members, although its activity has waned with time as its members have begun tenure-track jobs. The growth and waning of the Task Force is indicative of the structural bind of the academy, whereby graduate students have more flexible schedules to dedicate to activist work but are at a moment of career vulnerability; those in tenure-track positions have much less time but slightly more security; and those with tenure may or may not have maintained the energy and hopefulness that initiatives like this require (and may also have accumulated many other career responsibilities).

Looking back self-reflexively at this history, we see both the extent to which the graduate students and postdoctoral scholars who formed the RCC and Task Force felt alone and uniquely impacted by 9/11, and the extent to which they wanted to think analytically about how they came to perceive themselves as disconnected from earlier and continuing political struggles within academia, especially the longstanding political impact of Palestine politics on scholarship, academic freedom, and job searches and security. Similarly, this history reveals an emerging yet pointed sense that the AAA was not taking a strong or public enough stand against Bush Administration policies that were negatively affecting the people with whom we worked. Yet it also reveals a certain naïveté and set of assumptions about anthropologists' political views and commitments, as well as about AAA politics and organizational structures. Finally, this story highlights an emerging feeling that "something needed to be done," that Middle East anthropology in particular had a responsibility to step up—within the field, within the classroom, and in the public sphere—in a collective way that had not, in fact, happened before in the history of the discipline.

The Trigger of 9/11 and the Coalescence of a Transitional Generation

The events of 9/11/01 sparked the coalescence of an academic generation of Middle East anthropologists with a particular set of ideals, concerns, and perhaps misconceptions about the field and its place within anthropology and academe more generally, as well as within the American public sphere. 9/11 emerges as a "trigger action," a "crystallizing agent" (Mannheim 1952, 310) for this generational formation, just as similar kinds of events did for earlier generations of academics (e.g., World War II, the McCarthy hearings, the Vietnam War).[3] Yet we do not ascribe to 9/11 the absolute world-changing force that it is often given. Other historical, political, and intellectual factors, many of them predating that event, also contributed to this generation's formation. They were the first group of anthropologists to come of professional age in a context defined by the end of the Cold War, the poststructuralist/post-Orientalist turn in academia, the rise of the War on Terror, and the corporatization of the American university.

In his classic 1952 essay "The Sociological Problem of Generations," Karl Mannheim argued that members of generational groups (as defined in social rather than solely biological terms) share "a common location in the social and historical process" and that this "thereby limit[s] them to a specific range of potential experience, predisposing them for a certain characteristic mode of thought and experience, and a characteristic type of historically relevant action." It is this location in relationship to social events and processes—such as the geopolitical and institutional changes noted above—that gives members of a generation "certain definite modes of behavior, feeling, and thought" (1952, 291). Generations are both produced and defined through experience of *and* response to particular social events.[4]

Studying a young generation in a field such as anthropology, Middle East studies, or academia is particularly revealing because as youth reach adulthood (which, in academic terms, can mean undergraduate students entering graduate education and the professoriate), they experience a "fresh contact" with the "accumulated heritage" of the discipline and of politics such that they bring to it "a changed relationship of distance from the object and a novel approach in assimilating, using, and developing the proffered material" (Mannheim 1952, 293). Recent anthropologists have used Mannheim's insight into youth as having a "unique historical positioning" that enables them to "mediat[e] processes of cultural change" (Cole and Durham 2007, 16) such as the disciplinary, institutional, and geopolitical realignments we discuss here. Therefore, insights arising from a study of this generation also have the potential to reveal the broader contours of post–Cold War, post-Orientalist, post–9/11 academic work more generally, given that these scholars are part of and shaped by anthropology networks outside of their regional focus, and by Middle East networks in other disciplines such as history, political science, and religious studies (as Jon Anderson also argues in chapter 3 of this book).

"Generation" here is an analytic category, a set of actors or patterns of thought and behavior that belong to a specific group that shares a particular structural position in relationship to life course and historical time. But it is also a "native" category—one in which actors distinguish themselves both in relationship to social/historical processes and events and to notions of other generations. There is a definite sense among many of today's early/mid-career anthropologists of a generational formation in relationship to institutional and scholarly shifts in anthropology as a discipline as well as Middle East anthropology more specifically, and in relationship to broader academic and geopolitical social and historical processes. These coalesce around experiences of graduate training in anthropology after the critiques of representation and the influence of poststructuralist theory, and experiences of the end of the Cold War. Analytically, these individuals can also be called a generation because they share a certain structural location in relationship to these broader processes, and because they share ways of conceiving of and acting in relationship to them that they frequently conceive of as different from previous generations (whether or not such difference is apparent to others). For example, most members of this generation express a desire to integrate progressive politics into multiple aspects of their professional careers, and in many cases also take action in that regard.

Despite significant diversity among our interlocutors,[5] the majority of anthropologists we interviewed self-described their generation as being formed by a set of theoretical interests and approaches made possible by the critiques of/within anthropology and Middle East studies in the 1970s and 80s, in particular critiques of representation and knowledge production. Many of our interlocutors cited the broad influence of Edward Said's work in shaping the ground on which their generational identity stands, and/or as playing a formative role in their intellectual coming-of-age. Repeated memories of reading *Orientalism* for the first time and statements such as "We are the product of a post-Orientalist academia" capture this sense that certain work, and certain kinds of questions, became possible because of that text and its effects. Interlocutors also discussed a range of theoretical approaches that, in retrospect, they feel characterize their generation in terms of its academic training and the approaches brought to bear on dissertation work and first books. These include Foucauldian approaches and poststructuralism more broadly, postcolonial theory, postmodernism, and feminist theory, as well as interests in history, modernity, gender, and globalization. These sets of interests and approaches suggest the powerful influence of the rise of academic focus on interdisciplinarity and the critique of traditional area studies approaches that dominated the 1990s and early 2000s. A few of our interlocutors also spoke in terms of "strains of training," or how one's approach and interests were shaped by one's graduate institution, which suggests potential sub-generations within this one.

Definitions of a generation often involve contrasts or continuities with other perceived generations. Within this group of anthropologists, there is a clear articulation of contrast with an earlier anthropology, in the sense that there is a notion that much of the earlier work in the anthropology of the Middle East, while valuable, was not reconcilable with the theoretical approaches of new graduate training, and in some cases not relevant to the new kinds of research topics that they as anthropologists were now investigating. Some of these views may have been shaped by readings of Lila Abu-Lughod's (1989) *Annual Review* article "Zones of Theory in the Anthropology of the Arab World," in which she similarly notes key important works that are exceptions to a broader field characterized by limiting interest in tribes, women, Islam, and outlying rural areas. This article was the most widely read piece that took stock of the field that these scholars were entering, and it was no doubt influential.

Our interlocutors' sense of distinction from an earlier anthropology was also paired with a strong sense of intellectual indebtedness to a distinct group of scholars who were trained in the late 1970s and early 1980s, such that many argued that young scholars have more similarity and continuity with this immediately preceding generation. These earlier scholars were often spoken of as "role models" or as people who "paved the way for our generation"—by, for example, working to establish space for what one person called "empirically grounded, critical, politically grounded perspectives," by integrating the Middle East into wider anthropological conversations, and by beginning to open doors for research on Palestine.

In addition to theoretical/political approach as made manifest in certain institutional shifts within anthropology, Middle East studies, and academia more broadly, our interlocutors spoke of the effects of the post–9/11 interest in the Middle East/Islam in academia and its related public spheres as contributing to their generational formation. For this group, there is a sense that they are defined by having begun their careers just before or just after 9/11, and for some, that this experience benefited them directly as a generation with new research opportunities, language funding, jobs, opportunities for public speaking and writing, etc. At least half of our interviewees mentioned the post-9/11 experience as linking scholars together in new ways. As one scholar said, "The sudden interest in the region links us all [in terms of] getting anthropology to speak to those issues." Another cited the "tremendous pressure placed on Middle East academics" to do so. This strong contrasting discourse of welcome opportunities and unpleasant pressures is characteristic of this generation's response to 9/11.

Other life experiences related to politics or the Middle East also contributed to a sense of generation for many of our interlocutors. Such time-markers varied widely, with first political memories ranging from Watergate to the assassination of Sadat. The most significant experiences/events include the Reagan Era, the Iranian Revolution and the hostage crisis, the South African anti-apartheid movement, the first Gulf War, and the Oslo Accords. In different ways, these experiences/events were interpreted as raising consciousness of Middle East politics, a critical stance toward state politics and forms of oppression more generally, and a sense of the Middle East as a new post–Cold War obsession. One anthropologist echoed the sentiments of many when she said, "I do feel part of a generation that . . . saw, during graduate school, the Middle East emerge as the new enemy." This generation coalesces around a specific, politicized view of the world and the negative role of the U.S., Israel, and authoritarian Arab regimes within it. Its members share a heightened critical focus on the state, which translates into theoretical and topical approaches, as well as a sense of linked international political struggle.

It is important to note that some anthropologists are hesitant to define a region-wide generational category primarily because they feel that the exact geographic area of their own research is either unique in some way or disconnected from the concerns of the field more generally. This is the case with Palestine scholars, who frequently articulate a feeling of being within a community of Palestine scholars who are not necessarily Middle East scholars, as well as with those whose work is at the "margins" of the Arab Middle East, such as North Africa and Iran. Some of this hesitancy to declare belonging to a generation of

"Middle East anthropologists" stems from training (e.g., whether or not one had a Middle East anthropologist on the dissertation committee; whether one's training was more focused on region as opposed to theory or the discipline at large), as well as from the broader networks in which each scholar participates (e.g., editorial boards, departments of hire, places of language training, etc.). Task Force members, no matter where they worked, tended to feel a sense of generation very strongly, most likely due to their participation in that network.

In general, anthropologists of this generation articulate a politicized relationship to the field. Approximately sixty percent cited explicit political engagement as a key aspect of their decisions to enter anthropology as a discipline or choose the Middle East as a field, including all of those with family ties to the Middle East and half without. For many of these individuals, a political impetus to study the Middle East was formed during the undergraduate years, whether through coursework, study abroad, or campus activism around key events such as the First Intifada. Travel to the region during key political events, during either undergraduate or graduate school, was also a major factor in shaping the choice to work on the Middle East and the topic. As one scholar said, "[my topic] was unfolding before my eyes," and another: "Palestine was an easy choice." Frustration with increasingly negative media images of Middle Easterners in the 1980s and 90s also played a role, with one interlocutor stating her personal mission to be showing that "there's much more in the Middle East than images of Islamist militants." While it is clear that all heritage anthropologists began their careers in Middle East anthropology with political questions and engagements, for half of the non-heritage anthropologists, the decision to work in the Middle East began with what was variously termed an academic, random, aesthetic, or romanticized interest in an "other" that later became politicized, often during first trips to the region, in conversations with friends and family in the United States, and through the theoretical emphasis of graduate work.

It is impossible to overemphasize the centrality and dominance of Palestine in a majority of the narratives about how people came to Middle East anthropology, and even in the narratives of those who do not work on Palestine. Coming to understand Palestine politics was a critical moment in one's academic generational coming-of-age, whether in terms of those making a political choice to study there or not study there, or in getting people interested in the region, or, in the words of one, the ways it "marked a new sense of the urgency of political realities."

At the same time, interest in the region itself was not necessarily a starting point for its study. For half of the non-heritage anthropologists, developing intellectual questions came first, and then a field site was chosen as the place to best answer those questions. Even this formulation had a generational cast. This trend is shaped not only by the fact that most of these scholars did not have pre-existing connections to the region that thrust upon them political and regional considerations, but also—and perhaps more importantly—by the area studies critique that was coming to dominate anthropology, and academia more broadly, during their graduate training. There is a sense among this generation that they were trained in a post-Orientalist, often poststructuralist, increasingly global-ized anthropology to ask questions about power, or about broad topics such as gender, religion, commodity flows, or modernity, as opposed to learning about traits of one region or group of people. Most members of this generation were in fact drawn to anthropology because they saw that it offered flexibility of focus and/or that it offered some space for critical engagement with politics and power.

Yet despite the sense of being part of an emerging post–area studies aca-demic environment, it is notable that many in this group solidified their com-mitment to study in the Middle East as a result of participation in language programs like that at Middlebury College, many of which were initiated in the earlier days of area studies. These included programs supported by Title VI fund-ing of area studies centers, programs such as the Center for Arabic Study Abroad (casa) funded by the Department of Education, and language programs through Foreign Language and Area Studies (flas) fellowships. Area studies–related forms of support also existed in individual's career trajectories in the form of training, postdoctoral fellowships, or jobs. Thus, while there is a sense of intel-lectual distinction from the area studies model and from prior generations, this generation profited from and indeed owes their focus on and expertise in the Middle East to that model and the earlier generations who developed it.

In conclusion, political engagement with the region, whether it shaped peo-ple's initial choice to go into Middle East anthropology or whether it developed later, is key to the formation of this generation. Even those who do not view themselves as directly politically engaged described a commonality of "experi-ence of people who have worked in regions that are more political hotspots." This sense of generation, like most senses of generation, is forming in retrospect, and probably in some cases in response to our project, but always in relationship to the academic and geopolitical circumstances that shape our work. Some people also said that they feel that they came to Middle East anthropology randomly, some said that they were resisting their parents, and some (particularly those who work in North Africa, Turkey, and Iran) said that they feel somewhat discon-nected from Middle East scholarly foci in general. Yet where there are areas of hesitancy around the idea of a "generation of Middle East anthropologists," one finds that there are ideas of generation connected to approaches to a particular region or country or issue in the Middle East, as well as ideas of generation connected to anthropology more broadly. Furthermore, ideas of generation have definitely formed in relationship to the post-9/11 interest in the Middle East/ Islam, and to Palestine in particular, no matter where one works. Most of our interlocutors feel a sense of both continuity and rupture with previous generations and/or academic or political eras. Importantly, the senses of rupture are shot through with experiences and fears of academic politics.

Encounters with Politics

The perception and fear of persecution of Middle East scholars after 9/11 is a central shared sentiment that contributes to the construction of this group of anthropologists as an academic generation. These anthropologists have experienced the recent politicization of the academy during graduate school, and then in the job market, teaching, public speaking, and publishing. Their perceptions of persecution are shaped by both personal experiences and second-hand knowledge about the experiences of other scholars, including those of preceding generations. Importantly, these perceptions, and the discourse of fear through which they are articulated, are greater in volume than the actual episodes of politicized persecution of academics, and thus may actually produce—rather than just reflect—an environment filled with suspicion. Many of our interlocutors realized this tension, and spoke of their position as one of contradiction. On the one hand, they experience unprecedented opportunity; on the other they experience intense surveillance and an ever-present fear or suspicion of threat. It is their unique structural position as new professors which makes them experience this contradiction most markedly. Notably, while fears and apprehensions about the effects of politics on the field and on careers are generalized to Middle East anthropologists no matter where their research is located and were expressed to differing extents by everyone with whom we spoke, the majority of actual attacks and problems faced, whether on the job market, in tenure cases, or in teaching or research, have involved Palestine and/or Israel in some way.

During graduate school, many anthropologists of this generation faced problems, or at least minor issues, that they understood as related to the intersection of field site with politics. These included difficulties explaining research on politically sensitive issues in the Middle East to Institutional Review Boards that insisted on written informed consent, faculty members who withdrew from dissertation committees for reasons that seemed to have been related to Middle East politics, faculty who expressed significant concern about either student safety or the possibility of even doing research in their field sites due to political situations, and incidents where grant funding was denied, or in one case, withdrawn after being awarded. In many of these cases, either the anthropologist had strong suspicions about the politics underlying a problem, such as the withdrawal of a grant, or had learned of the political undertones of a situation from a classmate or professor. Regardless of whether or not politics did indeed have these sorts of effects, this discourse of suspicion both reflects and produces an environment of fear.

One scholar described this fear as "knowing that people who fall on the wrong side can suffer in their careers." Even the small number of anthropologists who have not had any difficulties on the job market or experiences with right-wing attacks on their scholarship or teaching know of others who have had these experiences. There is a universal sentiment among this group that Middle East anthropology is, in the words of several, "a minefield." Several very well publicized right-wing and Zionist attacks and threats to tenure cases—both within Middle East anthropology and within Middle East scholarship outside the discipline—have contributed to this climate of fear and apprehension.[6] In this regard, Middle East anthropologists feel that they are linked to other regional scholars in a larger battle against nefarious forces in or directed at the academy. Many in this generation have witnessed, at their own institutions, both politics that defend academic freedom and those that demonstrate hesitance or hostility, especially around Palestine. The growth of media and the corporatization of universities[7] have also contributed to this climate of fear—and especially to a sense that trustees and media both have more power today than in the past. One of our interlocutors described this as the "feeling that no one will back you up because they need to keep consumers and funders."

When it came to the effects of politics on the job market, this discourse carried a level of Palestine-specificity. Half our interviewees explained that "the word on the street" during graduate school was that if you worked on Palestine you would never get a job. As one person put it, this "was the common wisdom, it was in the air." This common wisdom was mainly expressed by other students, although in a few cases advisors shared similar sentiments. One anthropologist was explicitly told not to locate her research in Palestine/Israel because she would not get a job if she did, and that she should wait until after tenure to do research in that area. A second anthropologist, who did work on Palestine despite the word on the street, had faculty directly express concerns about her job market chances in relation to her field site, both to her and to her friends. A third, who was never herself discouraged by faculty from working on Palestine, noted that those same faculty "wouldn't touch Palestine with a ten-foot pole."[8]

Palestine also rose as a specter in job interviews for this generation, including for those whose research bore no relationship to either the conflict or the place. A Palestine scholar was asked directly by search committee members more than once whether she encountered problems because of her research. In her words, "It's not what I said, it's the subject I work on . . . people don't want to open themselves up to controversy . . . once the word Palestine is there, people go 'why do we want to make everyone upset.'" Those whose research is in other countries have also often had faculty try to figure out their "Palestine politics" during campus visits, sometimes via point-blank questions; for example, one interviewee was asked on two separate visits to articulate a solution to the conflict. On one of these occasions, the questioner then revealed himself to be pro-Israel and attempted to engage the job candidate in conversation about her views of Israel's politics vis-à-vis the Palestinians. Other than Palestine, the other problems that arose in job interviews were related to gender, or, for scholars with Middle Eastern heritage, to religious or ethnic background. Heritage scholars often have their allegiances questioned or probed through those identity frameworks, and one turned down a job offer because of this experience.

Yet in addition to and despite this discourse of fear and apprehension in relation to the job market, there simultaneously exists a discourse of unprecedented opportunity. For some, this sense of opportunity was linked to the idea that the path had been paved by older generations of Middle East anthropologists, especially those who had struggled to work on Palestine. For others, this sense of opportunity reflected ideas about an increase in the availability of jobs focused on the Middle East and especially Islam after 9/11. For this reason, many anthropologists of this generation see their regional focus as an asset on the job market, not a liability—except, notably, Palestine scholars, many of whom view their focus as an extreme liability on the job market. One of our interlocutors even went so far as to say that *not* working on Palestine was an asset.

Actual job market experiences do not necessarily live up to either the discourse of fear or that of opportunity, for the situation in the past decade has been quite complicated. While everyone we interviewed is employed in academia, nearly half found employment outside the discipline of anthropology, whether in other fields such as religious studies or in area studies departments and programs. For some, this move was deliberate, and involved reframing projects in new ways after 9/11 in order to find employment; for others, their eventual location outside anthropology came as a coincidence or surprise. This trend reflects both the tendencies toward interdisciplinarity among this generation of anthropologists and the ways in which much of the increase in Middle East– or Islam-related jobs took place in fields other than anthropology.

There was a significant increase in *Anthropology News* (AN) job ads for which the Middle East was one of the preferred areas after 9/11, although not as much as the increase in fields such as history, political science, and religious studies. In significant contrast, during most years between 1996 and 2001, there was at most one search dedicated to hiring a Middle East anthropologist, and one or two in anthropology where the Middle East was one of several preferred areas of specialization. These numbers doubled in 2002 and then growth slowed until 2006, though the region continued to be mentioned in more job ads than it had been prior to 9/11. A major jump took place between 2006 and 2008, when there was an average of thirteen possible positions a year, several of which were dedicated specifically to the Middle East. The economic crisis precipitated a small decline in 2009. Overall, then, 9/11 led to a small increase in lines dedicated specifically to the Middle East. Perhaps more critically, the region emerged on the radar of far more departments—or their institutional administrations—as one of the areas in which they were interested in hiring.

Members of this generation feel a great deal of anxiety not only on the job market, but also in the classroom. Once again, stories about other anthropologists or other Middle East faculty who had classroom-related problems combined with personal experiences to produce an environment of significant concern and fear. Concerns about teaching on Palestine are central. Half of our interlocutors discussed issues that arose in their classrooms specifically when teaching about Palestine/Israel. Many—though not all—of those whose research is not located in Palestine expressed extreme reluctance to teach any anthropological work on Palestine, in part due to feeling "on less sure ground" because it is not the focus of their research.

This generation is very worried about classroom censorship and surveillance, either by faculty committees or by "student spies" working for various organizations. Again this fear outweighs the actual number of accounts of censorship and surveillance. Only two of our interlocutors described having their teaching reported on Campus Watch, the most thorough and robust of the conservative and Zionist websites that collect reports on anthropologists and other scholars of the Middle East. Nonetheless, geopolitics and/or concern about potential difficulties in the classroom shaped the content and practice of teaching for several people. Faculty have altered syllabi to include language that forbids the recording of class lectures or discusses maintaining respectful classroom interactions, and they choose texts more carefully than they would for other non-region-specific courses. Some of these shifts in the preparation of teaching materials may have been due to advice contained in the aforementioned Task Force handbook on teaching,[9] but much of this advice itself was relayed to authors of the handbook by teachers who had devised specific strategies to avoid classroom difficulties they were already experiencing.

By far the most commonly expressed sense of how politics have impacted scholarly life is in relation to the newly perceived pressure to speak publicly about the Middle East and Islam, no matter what one's actual topic of research. This was sometimes understood as a responsibility to bring balance or a different perspective to the classroom or public media. One interlocutor termed this sense a "poison chalice," highlighting the contradictory feeling of fear and opportunity that we discussed earlier. While a small number of anthropologists resisted this new imperative, explaining that it assumed a politicization that was not part of their scholarly work, most scholars shared a sense that they now faced an ethical imperative to speak to the public, a product of feeling greater responsibility to do so as well as a confidence that comes at a later stage in one's career. It is less clear whether this is in fact a response to 9/11 and its political aftermath, or simply a reflection of the professional "coming of age" of this generation of anthropologists within institutions.

Along with speaking publicly, whether about one's research or about current political events, came having to learn to deal with hostile audience responses. A few of our interlocutors described the public altercations they had with Zionist audience members whenever they lectured in public events on campus or elsewhere. As one put it, "all of us have the experience of dealing with aggressive audiences, aggressive questioning from audiences—questions that are off topic, like where Palestinians should be relocated—when I'm trying to make a point about Foucault!"

This pattern of experience points to a broader concern among this generation about how their work has been politicized in ways they did not want or intend. Some anthropologists reframed their dissertations or books in response to the emerging political situation, and many described adding extra caveats or taking a more polemical tone than they believe they would have otherwise. Despite these concerns, however, only two of our interviewees had seen politics affect the publication process. One noted that "sometimes you can tell from the reviewer comments that there are political issues involved" and that occasionally reviews are delayed for this reason. A second person reported pressure from an academic press to explain how the topic of her book relates to suicide bombings (it does not), but added that the press dropped its request when the author refused to oblige.

Finally, as this generation of scholars begins their post-dissertation research projects, politics have clearly affected the choices many are making regarding field site and/or topic. Many continue to shy away from Palestine/Israel. The other significant pattern in the shaping of research has been the move of a few scholars whose earlier work was not about religion toward studies of Islam. The increasing focus on Islam within anthropology was noted by many of our interlocutors, some of whom expressed concern that religion was beginning to stand in for the region as a whole.[10] There are also growing concerns around several issues: access to field sites, losing control over the use of one's work, what one person described as "a polarization between those who are working on topics that are of more popular interest and those working on other things," and the new "security" environment around studies of the Middle East and Islam. Many scholars have been contacted by government agencies, Washington-based think tanks, and military subcontractors of various sorts.

As has become clear, Palestine/Israel is a marked topic, a locus of our interlocutors' encounters with politics at all stages and in all aspects of their careers. This is the area in which the fears have a strong correlation with the *potential* for attacks, though there have not been widespread attacks on this generation of anthropologists. On the Campus Watch website, Middle East anthropology or anthropologists were popular topics (with nearly one hundred articles), the vast majority of which concerned Palestine/Israel in some way. For example, Barnard/Columbia anthropologist Nadia Abu El-Haj's tenure case garnered eighty articles and is essentially about the Palestine issue, and several other articles focused on Columbia University's Israel/Palestine controversies more generally. The next item to gain significant media attention on the Campus Watch website was anthropologist Richard Antoun's murder by a Saudi graduate student, about which the site had posted thirty-six articles. The remaining themes or anthropologists have fewer than twenty mentions each on the site.[11] The issue of Palestine/Israel also dominates the smaller Discover the Network and the David Horowitz–sponsored "Students for Academic Freedom" websites—though these have far fewer anthropology-related articles than Campus Watch. These website themes highlight that the majority of attacks are not on Middle East anthropology in general but concern Palestine, including those on non-Palestine scholars who take public anti-Zionist stances.

Despite the fact that the majority of attacks and media attention have to do specifically with Palestine, the more generalized discourse of fear and apprehension itself has had significant effects on Middle East anthropology scholarship, career trajectories, and teaching. These include effects on scholars' self-presentation on the job market; concerns about misrepresentation or misuse of one's work; feeling pressured to speak out in public; effects on the content of scholarly work in terms of both topic and form; and effects in the classroom in terms of syllabus content and teaching practice. Tenure is an obvious area where one might expect to see the impact of the contemporary political climate. In this area, while there have been several highly visible and publicized cases, none have involved anthropologists of this generation, in part because many of them have not yet reached the point of applying for tenure. Thus those effects remain in potential state and continue to provoke apprehension above and beyond the usual tenure anxieties.

Two more, somewhat contradictory, impacts of the political climate on this generation return us to the history of the Task Force on Middle East Anthropology with which we began. First, approximately half of our interlocutors, including all of those who were Task Force founders, spent time and energy as graduate students or postdoctoral scholars ghostwriting documents such as letters to the editor and AAA resolutions, and then asking senior tenured faculty to sign them in their stead. Essentially this was a generation so scared of its own discipline that its members were actively making their labor invisible. Second, many of these anthropologists felt, at least at first, that becoming more active in the AAA was an important way to enhance knowledge of and engagement with Middle East issues in the discipline at large. This sense of responsibility to engage via AAA structures is by no means unique to this generation.[12] Notably, our interlocutors did not feel similarly about the Middle East Studies Association (MESA), and many of them had never attended a MESA meeting. This is related in part to structural and institutional issues: the annual meetings of the two organizations frequently overlap, and job interviews and other "career advancement" activities tend to take place at the disciplinary rather than the area studies meetings. In addition, there is a sense among some anthropologists that MESA is "for historians and political scientists" and that the AAA "is more inspiring" because it is organized around intellectual questions rather than regional issues. Despite this attitude toward our disciplinary organization, this generation's attempt to engage with the AAA on political issues is a story of increasing empowerment and growing disillusionment.

Encounters with the American Anthropological Association

Most members of this generation distinguish clearly between ideas about AAA content as represented by both meeting panels and AN, and AAA political stances. In terms of content, they feel that the region is still not visible enough within anthropology as a whole, though there has been improvement in the last decade. There is also a sense that meeting programs take an uneven approach to the Middle East, with some areas far better represented than others, and the idea that a regional focus may not be the best way to organize meeting content in the first place. Overall, however, this generation views AAA content much more positively than organizational politics.

A quick survey of AN for the last twenty years demonstrates an increase in the visibility of the Middle East as a region within the discipline that correlates in part with geopolitical events. In the 1990s, there were very few articles related to the Middle East in AN. In the four years after 9/11, coverage of the region increased from one article a year to between two and four. Both the initial lack of coverage and its nominal increase post–9/11 are related in part to the ways AN reflects broader media trends. For example, articles about Abu-Ghraib began to appear just after the publication of Seymour Hersh's famous piece on the prison in the *New Yorker*. The shift in coverage is also related to the dependence of AN on the initiative of individual scholars to contribute pieces, and the increased interest in writing about the region for a broader anthropological audience that emerged among anthropologists of this generation and the immediately preceding generation alike.[13] The importance of individual initiative is perhaps best exemplified by the significant increase in articles about the region in 2006 and 2007, the result of a special section or series edited by Susan Slyomovics and Kamran Ali, via the Committee for Human Rights, titled "Anthropologists and the Middle East." That initiative brought the number of articles related to the Middle East to twelve during 2007, with an additional eleven articles published that year concerning anthropology's relationship to the War on Terror, including debates about the ethics of Human Terrain Systems (HTS). In 2007–2009, coverage focused almost entirely on the ethics of HTS, again reflecting broader media, political, and anthropological concerns.

Despite the positive increase in Middle East articles in AN, many of our interlocutors were distinctly unimpressed with the AAA's response to Middle East–related resolutions. As mentioned at the beginning of this chapter, one of the first things the Task Force did was ghostwrite a series of four resolutions that were submitted to the AAA at the 2003 business meeting; that experience and the aftermath significantly shaped the responses of all of our interviewees who were aware of this process (half), and contributed to their disillusionment with the organization and its politics when it came to the Middle East. To understand this disillusionment, it is worth telling the story of the resolutions in greater detail.

A senior anthropologist who submitted a resolution on Palestine to the AAA in 2002 received a rejection letter from the Executive Board explaining that it had been refused because it did not make adequate reference to Israeli victims of suicide bombings and that she could redraft and resubmit.[14] She passed this information on to the Task Force, whose members revised the resolution to include more "balanced" language, including language about Israeli victims. They resubmitted this resolution in 2003, along with three others: one condemning the U.S. invasion of Iraq; one calling on the AAA to take a stance in support of academic freedom in the political climate of the war on terror; and one calling on the AAA to take a stance in support of the civil liberties of Arab, South Asian, and Muslim Americans. All four resolutions came to a vote at the 2003 business meeting and all passed by a large margin. There was no quorum at that meeting, however, which meant that the resolutions became "advisory" to the Executive Board, which was to discuss them and decide whether to pass, reject, or send them to the full AAA for a vote.

The Board passed the resolution on academic freedom in spring 2004 and rejected the other three without submitting them to AAA membership for a full vote. Each letter of rejection was accompanied by an explanation and the new set of guidelines for the submission of resolutions that had been set up by the board after the 2003 AAA meeting. The reason given for the rejection of the Iraq resolution was that the issue was outdated, a reason that in retrospect seems very short-sighted, to put it mildly. The letter read, "While the Board appreciated the spirit of the motion, and while it agrees that Iraq is an issue of critical importance, the Board decided that many of the specific issues raised in this motion are no longer relevant, given the passage of time and current events." The reason given for rejecting the civil liberties resolution was that the issue was outside anthropological expertise. The letter contained the following assessment:

> The Board favored the entire spirit of your Resolution, and they share your concerns about the targeting of specific groups. However, they believe that it is important for us as anthropologists to narrow the focus of this motion to that of anthropological interest and expertise. It was agreed that the AAA

President should redraft this motion to focus on targeted groups and this will be done in consultation with the Middle East Section.

To our knowledge, that follow-up by the AAA President never took place, and the authors were confused as to how supporting civil liberties is beyond the realm of anthropological expertise.

Finally, the reason given for rejecting the Israel/Palestine resolution was that it was not considered well-crafted:

While the Board believes all citizens should be concerned about civil liberties in the aftermath of September 11, the statement itself was not crafted in a way to gain authority. I refer you to the guidelines to understand the criteria the Board will consider when making a public statement. It was determined that your statement in its current form did not meet these criteria.

Oddly, this reasoning—in a letter explicitly responding to the resolution on Palestine/Israel—seems to refer instead to the resolution on civil liberties for Muslim Americans, which suggested either secretarial oversight or Executive Board antipathy to the entire group of linked resolutions.

Gregory Starrett wrote a comprehensive article in AN about these resolutions in 2005, criticizing the Executive Board's refusal to pass them or to submit them to the larger membership for a vote. He concluded that the message these rejections sent to the AAA membership was that anthropologists only cared about Middle Easterners when they were scholars like them, hence the support of the resolution on academic freedom to the exclusion of the others. This assessment perfectly captures one of the sentiments expressed by anthropologists of this generation when discussing the resolutions and their rejection. Their frustration stems in part from the feeling that there is a double standard at work in the AAA. As one of our interviewees put it, "you can yell all you want about the Yanomami or Guatemalans but not about Palestine." The Yanomami case was one where an anthropologist (Napoleon Chagnon) was directly accused of various ethical breaches, fitting more clearly within the Executive Board's standard of a narrowly defined purview of "anthropological relevance." However, it is more difficult to understand how the issues facing other Central American communities are more anthropological than those facing Middle Eastern ones. One scholar echoed the views of many when she said, "Anthropologists like to think of themselves as progressive, but they can't get on the right side of this issue" (here she was referring specifically to Palestine). Many others explained that they believed that the rejections of all three resolutions were due to political reasons and that the process for considering resolutions was "hazy and nontransparent."

The disheartenment that emerged from the resolutions experience is also related to differing ideas about what the AAA *should* do. Some anthropologists of this generation contested the official AAA response about anthropological relevance by arguing for a broader ethical imperative for the discipline. As one person explained, "It *is* related to what we do because anytime we go to war we affect people." At the same time, all of our interlocutors expressed a deep skepticism of the utility of resolutions. The desire to see the resolutions passed by the AAA was not rooted in ideas about action in the real world or the literal utility of such statements. Rather, these anthropologists expressed a desire to see resolutions because they raise awareness of issues within the discipline and because it demonstrates for the sake of the historical record that one's profession has taken an ethical stance. When the resolutions were rejected, the sense emerged that the AAA "is more concerned with protectionism of the discipline," as one interlocutor put it, than they are with the people who live in the region where we work.

Interestingly, the AAA tide seems to have shifted in recent years. At the 2006 meetings, a rare quorum approved two resolutions, one condemning the war in Iraq and a second condemning the "use of anthropological knowledge as an element of physical and psychological torture." These were then both adopted in a vote by the entire membership in spring 2007. The AAA website contains no official statements, resolutions, or letters concerning the Middle East posted prior to 2006, a finding that was tentatively confirmed by the AAA Director for Public Affairs, Damon Dozier.[15] In contrast, since 2006, there have been nine official statements by the AAA related to the Middle East, including several resolutions that were passed in quorum and reports that were commissioned. Four press releases detailed, respectively, the passing of the 2006 resolutions, the report on engagement with U.S. security agencies, the opposition of the AAA to military action against Iran in 2007, and the AAA critique of the Pentagon's Minerva project. The organization has produced five official letters, one expressing concerns about Minerva; one to the State Department in support of an Egyptian anthropologist who was to present at the meetings but whose visa requests had been denied; and two in collaboration with MESA about the arrest of an Iranian anthropologist and about Gaza Fulbright students denied exit for study in the U.S. The fifth letter was written by the Committee for Human Rights to the governments of Israel, the U.S. and the E.U. about the 2009 siege of Gaza. Subsequent to this letter, the Executive Board tightened its protocols for committees issuing letters and statements such that they now have to be vetted by the Board first. The official

AAA position on this matter is that the Executive Board had long been consider-ing tightening these protocols due to concerns about subcommittee statements being understood as representing official statements of the entire AAA. However, while this new procedure was announced in these general terms, to many who work on the Middle East, the coincidence of timing confirms suspicions that there is discomfort among organization leadership when it comes to taking a stand on behalf of Palestinians.

Further research is required in order to fully understand what has changed, along the lines of David Price's thorough treatment of the relationship of an-thropology to war at a very different moment in U.S. history, and taking to heart his caution to historicize these shifts beyond a "presentist concern about anthro-pological contributions to warfare" (2008, xiv). Possible factors contributing to the shift include changes in AAA leadership and staff, and the passing of time such that by 2006 it was quite clear that the Iraq war was indeed not "outdated." However, this discursive shift and apparent disciplinary interest in the Middle East and the War on Terror also has to do with broader shifts in political climate, a greater awareness in general about regional politics, and, most crucially, the direct implication of anthropology in the War on Terror.

Clearly, the Middle East has become a much broader concern within the discipline. The 2006 resolutions were put forward without a single Middle East anthropologist's participation. Similarly, the Network of Concerned Anthropologists, which is behind much of the recent criticism of HTS in particu-lar, does not include among its founding members any anthropologists whose research is in the region. And at the 2009 meetings, a panel on Gaza was, as one scholar put it, "finally organized by non-Gaza folks." She interpreted this as si-multaneously indicating how bad the situation in the Middle East had become and a growing political agreement among anthropologists, an agreement also indicated, she said, by the striking lack of audience argument at that panel. These initiatives by anthropologists whose research focus is not in the Middle East re-veal a broader awareness of and interest in political events and issues that impact the region. The AAA's approach to Middle East politics seems to have changed in the wake of specific events such as the war on Gaza and the Abu Ghraib torture scandal, and at a time of widespread media and political critique of the war in Iraq and a potential, if small, shifting of the tide on Palestine such that Jon Stewart has recently been able to host peace activists on his television show.

Yet this awareness and interest may have less to do with the region and its people and more to do with the changing relationship of the discipline of anthropology to the War on Terror. Broader interest in speaking out against the

Iraq War, torture, and HTS appeared only after the inauguration and wide media coverage of the HTS program, and the renewed appearance of CIA recruitment ads in AAA publications, so that anthropologists and anthropology itself was suddenly (again) directly and publicly implicated in contemporary politics and warfare in a way that could not be ignored. To build on the critique of one of our interlocutors, the importance of HTS in particular to this shift simply reinforces the AAA's narrow definition of disciplinary relevance. In this person's words, "it is good that people finally took a stand, but the concern is still too narrow and about the discipline, rather than about a broader ethics." As a result of this sense of disciplinary limitation, most of the anthropologists with whom we spoke did not view this apparent shift as one that would have lasting or significant effects when it came to Middle East anthropology in particular. Another anthropologist opined, "I'm glad that HTS has been discussed seriously, but in general I have not felt like the AAA would support me if the shit hit the fan [meaning if she became the victim of politicized attacks on her teaching and research]." But, more importantly, the sentiments of several of our interlocutors suggest that those comments by Gregory Starrett, written in response to the 2003 resolution episode, are shared by many:

> One communication the AAA has sent to its members is a perverse one that confuses narrow professional focus . . . for humanity. It says that the people of the Middle East, unlike the people of the Americas, rate official attention only when they are . . . scholars like us; when they fit into a romantic model of exotic primitivism . . . or when, like the restless souls in Saddam's mass graves or the makers of Sumerian cylinder seals, they are already dead. (Starrett 2005, 12)

Despite this lack of official AAA attention allotted to the people of the Middle East, anthropologists whose work is in the region continue to chart new directions in the field, and to navigate its minefields as they do so. The field is both shaped by and responds to the heightened U.S. engagement in the Middle East and the related heightened politicization of the U.S. academy. The state of Middle East anthropology is forever tied to the Palestine issue; one of our colleagues wisely noted that members of our discipline, who are keen to denounce oppression and inequality wherever they find it, and who critique nationalism and nation-states as a matter of course, just cannot seem to do the same when it comes to the actions of the State of Israel. Finally, Middle East anthropology impressively developed earlier subfield interests in colonialism and local politics into broad and deep concerns about Western power in all of its forms, and about the connections between Western power and politics at multiple levels and in all locations—from the field site to the Pentagon, and from the academic institution to the public sphere. It remains to be seen how the recentering of politics at the core of the Middle East anthropological practice will shape the fields of anthropology and Middle East studies at large, but the effects will largely depend on whether the U.S. government and the American public radically change their engagement with the region.

NOTES

We thank Sherine Hafez and Susan Slyomovics for inviting us to present an earlier version of this chapter at the State of the Art of Middle East Anthropology conference, and all of the participants for their engagement and critical questions. We also are deeply grateful to the many anthropologists we interviewed for this project for their generosity and trust. Vanessa Agard-Jones, Damon Dozier, and Daniel Segal provided additional assistance and encouragement. Any errors in analysis are our own.

1. Information about these meetings is kept in their minutes.

2. Members worked with cohort peers from other disciplines in constructing this Handbook in order to make it relevant beyond anthropology.

3. Recent work by David Price further illuminates the impacts of the McCarthy era (2004) and World War II (2008) on the anthropologists and anthropology of those eras.

4. Recent work in anthropology has built on Mannheim's classic insights to develop this contextual understanding of "generations." See especially Borneman (1992), Cole and Durham (2007), Christiansen, Utas, and Vigh (2006), Vigh (2006), and Winegar (2006).

5. We conducted semi-structured ethnographic interviews lasting between one and three hours with eighteen anthropologists who began their graduate training between 1992 and 2001 (between the end of the USSR and 9/11). These were supplemented by: reflections on our own experiences as part of the Task Force; archival data collected from the AAA (including meeting minutes, job advertisements, resolution proposals, and committee reports and letters); articles from right-wing websites that discuss Middle East anthropologists; and articles on Middle East anthropology from various academic trade publications and academic association publications. We selected our interviewees so as to achieve diversity within a set of structural similarities, including training within U.S. institutions at the aforementioned historical juncture. Thus, we selected scholars of various genders, ethnic backgrounds, graduate training programs, topics and countries of focus, types/regional locations of institutions of employment, and political involvement in academic associations.

6. Examples: (1) the tenure cases of Nadia Abu El-Haj—John Gravois, "A New Fact on the Ground," *Chronicle of Higher Education,* 2 November 2007 (http://chronicle.com /article/A-New-Fact-on-the-Ground-/39883); (2) the tenure case of Joseph Massad—Anna Kelner, *Huffington Post,* 1 July 2009 (http://www.huffingtonpost.com/anna-kelner /joseph-massads-tenure-and_b_223659.html); (3) the attacks on Sondra Hale along with other UCLA faculty—Jon Wiener, "The Dirty Thirty," *The Nation,* 26 January 2006 (http:// www.thenation.com/article/uclas-dirty-thirty).

7. Many books have been published in recent years on the shift to neoliberal policies and ideologies and the subsequent effects on teaching, scholarship, and academic freedom. See, for example, Tuchman (2009).

8. It is also worth noting that the importance of Palestine was not quite universal; for three of our interlocutors, the political struggles they faced had to do with minefields or battles other than Palestine/Israel or U.S.-related concerns, and were instead located at the level of national politics within their field sites.

9. The popularity of this handbook is evident in the hundreds of requests received for it, as well as the doubling of the membership of the general Middle East Anthropology listserv immediately following its publication.

10. It is notable that a number of young anthropologists think that contemporary Middle East anthropology is perhaps too focused on Islam, something Abu-Lughod (1989) identified as a major trend in the field over twenty years ago. Discussions with colleagues suggest that the concern is with too much focus on pietist or reformist Islam in particular.

11. These included attacks on Middle East anthropologists, the Task Force's teaching handbook, and the AAA report condemning of the U.S. military's Human Terrain Systems program.

12. See, for example, the 2006–2007 AN series edited by Susan Slyomovics and Kamran Ali.

13. A survey of those articles shows a high percentage of contributions from Task Force members as well as repeat contributions from a number of engaged scholars more senior to this generation.

14. This is not the only resolution concerning Palestine that has met a similar fate. A resolution was submitted in 2004 calling on the AAA to condemn the separation wall being built by Israel. Although it was submitted by distinguished senior anthropologists—Lila Abu-Lughod, Michael Gilsenan, Catherine Lutz, and Brinkley Messick—it was similarly rejected.

15. This may also be related to the organization's record-keeping practices, and a search through the archives for documents prior to 2006 continues.

PART 2.

SUBJECTIVITIES: YOUTH, GENDER, FAMILY, AND TRIBE
IN THE MIDDLE EASTERN AND NORTH AFRICAN
NATION-STATE

6.

ANTHROPOLOGY OF THE FUTURE: ARAB YOUTH AND THE STATE OF THE STATE

Suad Joseph

The Arab Spring began in January 2011 in Tunisia, and moved quickly through Egypt, Yemen, Bahrain, Libya, and Syria, with rousing applause from many corners of the world. It was a ringing indictment of authoritarian governments, corruption, unemployment, inadequate educational institutions, and the lack of political will on the part of Arab national leaders to address the real and urgent problems of their peoples. Throughout the Arab Spring countries, the majority of those engaged in the protests and in critical leadership positions were youth. The Arab Spring and its constituent elements should not have been surprising; yet it caught scholars and political commentators off guard.

This chapter, originally presented as a paper in April 2010 at the University of California, Los Angeles conference from which this volume is drawn—a year before the Arab Spring—calls upon anthropologists to address the pressing problems of Arab youth. Quickly, after January 2011, a surfeit of papers, lectures, online discussions, and panels at professional conferences emerged analyzing the questions presented by the Arab Spring. Most of these drew on commentaries and the expertise of journalists, political scientists, and public intellectuals from different disciplines. Some of these projects, preliminary in their formulation and empirical depth, began to examine the conditions facing Arab youth.

Sociologist Samir Khalaf and English scholar Roseanne Khalaf quickly produced the insightful collection *Arab Youth* (2011). The volume included the works of five political scientists, five anthropologists, three journalists, and one each from the fields of demography, history, urban planning, creative writing, and Middle East studies.

At the Middle East Studies Association (MESA) Annual Meeting in Washington, D.C., in December 2011, twenty panels focused on the Arab Spring, with a number of them reflecting, to some degree, on Arab youth. At that same meeting, Marcia Inhorn and I, in our capacity as members of the MESA Board (I was president at the time), organized a mini-conference, "Anthropology of the Middle East: A New Millennium." As the deadline for submission was after the launch of the Arab Spring in January 2011, the anthropologists we invited to organize panels had an opportunity to respond to the immediate situation by proposing panels on Arab youth or adding papers on youth to their panels. Eighteen panels, of the forty-six submitted for this mini-conference, were accepted by MESA—none of these were on Arab youth (the one specifically on Arab youth was rejected by the MESA Program Committee). The MESA meeting did feature two other panels on Arab youth, however, one organized by the *Encyclopedia of Women and Islamic Cultures,* of which I am General Editor. Anthropologists, reeling from the panorama of issues dizzily imploding before them with the Arab Spring that they largely missed, have much thinking and research to do to understand the on-the-ground experiences of youth in Arab countries. Why have Arab children and youth been so understudied by anthropologists?

Arab children and youth constitute two-thirds of the populations of almost all Arab countries. In an area of the world that produces critical sources of world wealth, the rates of poverty, illiteracy, unemployment and underemployment, and health problems among children and youth is staggering. Since World War II, when most of the states of that region gained independence, the story of state-making and of nation-building has been a story of stunning failure. Nationalist and pan-Arab nationalist movements stalled, never started, or were unsuccessful. Wars and violence have wracked the region. Huge movements of populations fleeing wars, violence, and economic uncertainty have exited their states for other regional states or global destinations. Most of these movements have been of young people.

For over the past half century, perhaps the majority of the children and youth of the Arab world have grown up at high risk, with a cloud (often foreboding violent storms) over their futures. The current adults themselves emerged from years of political instability. While the Arab world has one of the lowest crime rates in the world, it has one of the highest rates of wars and political violence. For in the Arab world, the state has offered no future, no national future. Some citizens cleave to possibilities available to them, often routed through kin and family systems—dually sites of security and/or sources of oppression. Many try to leave their natal countries. Many migrate internally, willingly or unwillingly. Many are unemployed or underemployed. Some are mobilized into militias, nationalist movements, resistance movements, or sectarian/religious movements. Islamist movements, which have swept through the region since the 1980s, are among a variety of attractive alternatives for youth who try to claim a vision for their future.

This paper examines children and youth in Lebanon in the aftermath of the Lebanese Civil War (1975–1990), as an example of research that anthropologists need to do to understand the contemporary dilemmas of the Arab world and the prospects for the future of its youth. I focus on outlining the conditions which created dilemmas for children and youth and consider how anthropologists might address these issues, particularly in light of the Arab Spring—and perhaps its Fall. Whatever work anthropologists do, in addressing children and youth, we are addressing the majority of Arab society.

Arab Children and Youth: Defining the Majority

Arab children are often defined as those 0–14 years of age. Arab youth are variously defined as between the ages of 14–25 or 15–29 or many combinations in between. As these categories are artificial, rather new, and largely the inventions of Western state and international counting agencies, for the purposes of this paper, it is more compelling to address the issues of children and youth together. Largely, I focus on those twenty-nine years old and younger. I rely on data and statistics from agencies which make other age distinctions, however. Therefore the shifting categorizations of children and youth, of necessity, find their way into this analysis. The "categories" themselves are part of the problematic of this project.

The age structure of the Arab region is striking: Children aged 0–14 accounted for over 120 million people, or 34 percent of the Arab population, in 2010 (a decline from 45 percent in 1980) (ESCWA [Economic and Social Commission for Western Asia] 2009, 6). Navtej Dhillon and Tarik Yousef, defining youth as

15–29 years old, observed in 2007 that Arab youth had passed the 100 million mark, making them 30 percent of the Arab population. This is often called the "youth bulge" (ibid., 6). Taken together, these figures indicate that almost two-thirds of the Arab population is twenty-nine years old or younger. By other calculations over half the Arab population is less than twenty-five years old (Piven 2010), and in some countries youth and children account for up to 75 percent of the population.

Arab Youth: Demographics/Profiles

The Arab population increased two-fold in three decades, one of the fastest population growth rates in the world, with figures from 2–2.45 percent (Piven 2010). In 1980, the Arab population was 173 million; in 2009, it was 352.2 million (just a little over the population of the United States). The Arab region accounts for 5.2 percent of the world's population and is projected to constitute 5.6 percent, or 428.4 million, by 2020. Egypt alone is expected to reach almost 100 million by 2020. The population of the Arab world is growing almost twice as fast as that of the rest of the world: 2–2.45 percent per annum as compared to the 1.5 percent average growth rate for the rest of the world. In real numbers, the population of the Arab region has increased by 6.2 million persons annually over the past three decades (ESCWA 2009).

The population in the Arab region is significantly affected by international migration. The U.N. Department of Economic and Social Affairs (cited in ESCWA 2009, 8) projected that 26 million of those living in the Arab region in 2010 would be migrants, of which only 36 percent were female (mostly Asian domestic workers). Hence, 64 percent of the international migrants in the Arab world are male (around 17 million). Over a third of the Gulf Cooperation Council countries' populations are migrants (ibid., 8). These labor figures have a large impact on the domestic market and its capacity to absorb newly economically active Arab youth.

Fertility appears to be declining in the Arab region with the rise of girls' education, workforce participation, and delayed marriage, what is sometimes called "wait-hood" (ibid., 4). The age of marriage in the Arab world has risen by an average of five years in the past three decades (since 1980), and Arab women are now bearing an average of three children as compared to six children in their mothers' generation (Piven 2010). This fertility however, is still higher than in Asia and Latin America and higher than the world average (2.6 children per woman). While age of marriage is going up, Arab women still tend to marry young relative to other regions: 70 percent of Maghribi women and 86 percent of Mashriqi women marry by the age of thirty (Piven 2010). Life expectancy in the Arab region has increased by nine years since 1980, to sixty-eight years for males and seventy-one for women (ESCWA 2009, 5).

Globally, about half of the world's population lives in urban areas (ibid., 3). In the Arab region, 55 percent of the population was urban in 2005. Urban living is expected to grow to 60 percent of the population of the Arab world by 2020 (ibid.), which places the majority of Arab youth in cities.

Literacy in the Arab world is rising but is still low by world standards. The World Bank Development Indicators report that literacy for adult females (fifteen and over) was 65 percent and for males 82 percent. Arab adults (15–64) had a literacy rate of 64 percent, while those Arabs over sixty-five had a literacy rate of 4 percent (ESCWA 2007). By most calculations, about 30 percent of Arabs are illiterate (ALECSO 2008, quoted in Al Fin 2008). Some countries, however, such as Lebanon, Palestine, Jordan, and some Arab Gulf countries, have literacy rates around 90 percent or more. On average, two thirds of the illiterate Arab adults are women. ESCWA reports that in 2002, almost half of the adult Arab women (fifteen and over) were illiterate (ESCWA 2007, 3). This implies that the nearly half of the children and youth of the Arab world are being raised by illiterate mothers.

According to the World Bank Development Indicators, in 2007, the overall rate of literacy for Arab children (0–14) was 32 percent. That report finds the literacy rate for Arab male youth (14–24) to be 93 percent, compared to 86 percent for female youth. According to a 2005 UNESCO report by Hassan R. Hammoud, youth (15–24) in seven Arab countries (Tunisia, Bahrain, Jordan, Lebanon, Libya, Oman, Qatar) had illiteracy rates of less than 5 percent; and four other countries had illiteracy rates of 5–8 percent (Algeria, Kuwait, Saudi Arabia, UAE). Three countries had illiteracy rates of 10–18 percent (Syria, Djibouti, Sudan); and five had illiteracy rates of 24–55 percent (Morocco, Egypt, Yemen, Iraq, Mauritania) (Hammoud 2005, 8). This means that the largest country, Egypt, which accounted for 20 percent of all Arabs, had one of the highest adult (fifteen and over) illiteracy rates—17 percent for males and 41 percent for females (CIA 2010). While literacy is not a sufficient indicator of educational adequacy, by most measures, the schools in Arab countries are not preparing children and youth for the labor market or for adult self-sufficiency.

Unemployment is high in the Arab countries. A March 2010 meeting of Arab ministers, organized by the Arab Labour Organization (ALO) in Manama, Bahrain, promised to reduce unemployment by 7 percent by 2020. The head of the ALO, Ahmed Mohammed Lukman, observed that unemployment is at "its worst levels" and that it "threatens social harmony and national security, as it constitutes a source of extremism, of terrorism and of desperation. It undermines trust between government and the people" (Jones 2010).

Unemployment figures for Arab countries as a whole are figured as anywhere from 14 percent (ESCWA Global Migration Group 2009) to 25 percent (compared to the current 9.5 percent in the U.S., which is considered to be a major crisis). More critically, the United Nations Development Program estimated unemployment among youth between 15–24 years old is as high as 40 percent (Jones 2010)—35 percent for Saudi Arabia, Bahrain, and Oman (ESCWA 2009, 9). In 2004, Arab youth, on average, were unemployed at the rate of 21 percent, over double the unemployment rate of adults. Unemployment among women and young women was even higher, with 24 percent of young Arab women unemployed in 2004 (ESCWA 2007, 4). U.N. ESCWA recently estimated that youth unemployment rate in the Gulf Cooperation Council (GCC) was the highest in the world, at about 22 percent, and represented half of all unemployment in those countries (ESCWA 2009, 9). Economic participation of Arab women was calculated at 29 percent (ESCWA 2007, 4). Regardless of any critique of the way economists count, these figures still represent the lowest rate of economically active women in the world.

Political participation has also been low. Given the predominance of autocratic regimes, political participation—as measured by NGOs, political party activity, and democratic electoral politics—has been low for both men and women in the Arab world until the Arab Spring. Despite some improvements at ministerial levels, women's share of parliament seats in the Arab world was only 8 percent in 2006, the lowest in the world with women in the Maghrib having the highest rate (10 percent) and women in the GCC region having the lowest (2 percent). Iraq had the highest rate—32 percent (ESCWA 2007, 5). While women lost rights in the U.S.–supervised constitution in 2005, Iraq did institute quotas for parliament and cabinet offices of 25 percent women. These are only some of the statistics. Anthropologists can critique and question the numbers generated by economists and demographers. Nevertheless, they collectively paint a picture that compels attention and captures some critical aspects of the social realities confronting children and youth in the Arab world.

Arab Youth: Context/Contests for Future

What is the context in which these "numbers" are lived by Arab children and youth? With few exceptions, there has been a failure of nation/state formation in the Arab world. Pan-Arab nationalism failed in the 1960s and 70s. The Arab states lost every war with Israel (perhaps with the exception of the 2006 war on Lebanon). The internal wars and violent unrest within and between the Arab countries have been crippling and unproductive (Algeria, Somalia, Yemen, Lebanon, Iraq, Sudan). In the fall of 2011, a civil war was raging in Yemen and Syria. The Libyan uprising unseated the Qaddhafi regime, but it remained unclear, at this writing, what direction the Libyans would take. The Egyptian Revolution, youthful and hopeful, appeared to be on the brink of military reconsolidation or Islamist takeover. The repression of the Bahraini revolt was unabated. Tunisia, which triggered the Arab Spring, appeared to be quietly regrouping political power centers. In all the regimes, there appeared to be a regrouping with some degree of victory for Islamist political forces in electoral politics.

One can say there has been a failure of Arab liberalism, with few countries recognized as practicing electoral democracy. Most Arab regimes have been monarchies, military dictatorships, or civilian/tribal/family authoritarian regimes. Political participation for the population at large, and the youth in particular, has been controlled and censored, with little space tolerated for civic debate or discourse. Until the Arab Spring, there was a gulf between young people and their states. They felt no direct connections or loyalty to nationality. Until the Arab Spring, there seemed to be a disconnect between youth and their states.

Citizenship, in terms of active participation, had been minimal. It has been more constrained for women, who, in many countries, achieve citizenship through their fathers and cannot pass it on to their children or husbands. In most Arab countries, religious laws govern family law, with no or few civil law alternatives. Although Egypt and Morocco have made some strides in the past decade, gender equality or equity is far off the horizon in most Arab countries. Even after Saudi Arabia made a concession in 2011 by allowing women the right to vote and run in municipal elections, their ability to exercise these rights was still controlled by men, since they may not travel without permission of their male kin, or drive cars.

The "youth bulge" has inflated the Arab working-age population (25–65). They are expected to constitute 45 percent of the population by 2015 and 48 percent by 2025 (escwa 2009, 7). Demographers and economists call this a one-time opportunity to increase productivity and economic development (ibid., 7). Their concern, however, has been that few efforts have been made focused on youth, who constitute the largest percentage of the unemployed in the working-age population.

To the degree that the oil states provided employment release valves for the region, that opening has diminished. The improvement of education coupled with the decline in job possibilities has created a volatile cocktail, frustrating most youth. Isobel Coleman argues that, "There is a dire mismatch between the skill sets companies are seeking and what most regional high schools and colleges are producing. . . . The result is an explosive combination of millions of young people with high expectations and no hope of fulfilling their dreams." Of the images Arab youth see on American TV and internet, Coleman adds, "We're exporting this hyper version of material success" (quoted in Beehner 2007).

New research argues that the youth bulge is directly related to civil conflicts and has been a destabilizing factor on developing countries (Beehner 2007). Population Action International (PAI) released a study demonstrating a strong correlation between countries with a high rate of civil strife and countries with a rapidly expanding youth population. They argue that the youth bulge has a high risk of destabilizing developing countries. The study found that between 1970 and 1999, over a period of three decades, 80 percent of the countries in which civic conflict occurred had a population with 60 percent of residents under the age of thirty—a profile matching that of most Arab countries. Sixty of the sixty-seven countries with youth bulges had high levels of civic unrest and violence (cited in Beehner 2007). Likewise, many of the countries which have gone through significant revolutions in their history had a youth bulge at the time (France, Japan, Latin America). The PAI report calculates even higher rates for the Middle East (not just Arab world), where 60 percent of the population is under twenty-five years old (ibid.).

While the authors do not argue that youth "cause" civil unrest (affected countries also exhibited such relevant factors as poverty, corruption, religious/ ethnic differences, non-democratic institutions, and the like), the combination of variables summarized above, they argue, can convince policy makers to see youth as a "problem." Especially of concern to these authors are the rapidly expanding youth population, inadequate education systems, rapidly expanding working-age population with high rates of unemployment among youth, prolonged dependency on parents (including delayed marriage), failed nation states which do not operate by rule of law and which give little hope for national futures, restricted arenas for political participation in national life, and lives lived in zones of chronic wars, violence, and civic instability.

These factors are a formula for frustration, discontent, and unrest—and most of all for the young who want to hope for a future. However one looks at the data, the evidence is dauntingly clear that there is a crisis for children and youth in the Arab world. Given that children and youth constitute two-thirds of the population, this means there is a crisis of society in the Arab world. The Arab Spring would appear to be a validation of these predictions.

Lebanese Youth: Demographics/Profiles

Lebanon has manifested many of the patterns of Arab countries, some in very exaggerated levels and others in reverse. With a small population (four million), Lebanon seems "modern" in many of its statistics: 87 percent of its adult population (fifteen and over) is literate. This figure includes 93 percent of the adult males and 82 percent of the adult females (CIA 2010). Expected duration of schooling is fourteen years for males and thirteen for females (CIA 2011). The age structure is not young: 26 percent of the population is 0–14 years old, 67 percent is 15–64, and 7 percent is sixty-five and over, with a median age of twenty-nine years (half of the population is twenty-nine or younger, as compared to 60–75 percent in other Arab countries). The population growth rate is only 1.1 percent (LookLex Encyclopaedia, www.looklex.com), in the Arab world second only to Somalia in terms of slowness of population growth rate. Lebanon has a fertility rate of only 1.9 children per woman, just barely maintaining the population, and is expected to experience an aging population based on its declining fertility (ESCWA 2009, 8). Life expectancy in Lebanon is about seventy-five years (seventy-three for males and seventy-six for females) (CIA 2011). The nation is highly urbanized, with 87 percent of the population living in cities in 2008 (CIA 2008; cf. ESCWA 2009, 3, same figure for 2005). It is the fourth most urbanized Arab country, after Kuwait, Qatar, and Bahrain. This data makes Lebanon look modern. Other aspects of the profile complicate the picture.

If Lebanon does not have as much of a youth bulge as other Arab countries, this is partly because so many of its young people left over the past thirty-five years or more of chronic civic unrest. At certain points, 25 percent of the population left Lebanon. Many returned and left repeatedly as violence cycled through the past four decades. Few Arab countries, Palestine excepted, have had as long a period of violence and political turmoil as Lebanon.

The official unemployment rate was 9 percent in 2009, but was 20 percent in 2008 and 2007 (Index Mundi online, accessed in 2011). On the ground it has seemed much higher. Some predict an unemployment rate of up to 50 percent within the decade (*Daily Star* 2009). Unemployment among Lebanese youth has been at 29 percent. While the minimum work age is fourteen years old (it was eight years old until 1996), child labor has not been uncommon, especially among the rural poor and the Palestinian population. Twenty-eight percent of the population has been considered below the poverty line. Remittances from Lebanese abroad float the economy, having brought in $5.6 billion a year (one-fifth of the economy), and adding $1,400 per capita every year (Nassib Ghobril, head of research Byblos Bank, quoted in Worth 2007).

Lebanon employs between 1.25 million (Agence France Presse 1996) and 2.25 million foreign workers (Xinhua News Agency 1996). This includes 200,000 domestic workers, almost all of whom are women (5 percent of Lebanon's population is domestic workers). Workers from all over the world make up a quarter of the population. Since before it became a state in 1943, Lebanon was called upon to house political and economic refugees: Armenians, Palestinians, Syrians, and Arab political exiles. Armenians were given citizenship when they arrived before World War I and in 1939. Other refugees, on the whole, were not. Lebanon is home to 400,000 Palestinians who have no legal status, cannot legally work or own property, while 300,000 Syrians (15 percent of Syria's workforce) work in Lebanon and remit to their families, but they are technically illegal in Lebanon.

Lebanon is not only divided by the huge number of non-Lebanese residents, but also internally through a system of political representation based on religious sects. Lebanon formally recognizes eighteen religious sects who can have representatives in Parliament. Sixty percent of the population is Muslim (Shi'a, Sunni, Druze, Ismaili, Alawite, Nusayri) and thirty-nine percent Christian (Maronite Catholic, Greek Orthodox, Melkite Catholic, Armenian Orthodox, Syrian Catholic, Armenian Catholic, Syrian Orthodox, Roman Catholic, Chaldean, Assyrian). Each religious sect has their own legally recognized family law dealing with marriage, divorce, child custody, and inheritance. The Lebanese state does not offer civil family law alternatives. Politics in Lebanon has never been driven simply by religious affiliation, however, as the complexities of current alliances and coalitions demonstrate (the Shi'ite Hizbollah aligned with Maronite parties, for example). Nevertheless, religious affiliation has contributed to the havoc of political instability and has been a source for recruiting youth into political activism.

Lebanon became independent in 1943, in many ways a nation carved out to serve France's interest in the region. Before the Civil War (1975–1990), Lebanon already had had several crises shaking the foundations of a state that had yet to establish itself:

- The 1948 founding of Israel, which gave rise to a large Palestinian refugee population residing in Lebanon, the highest in the Arab world.
- The 1958 civil unrest, including the landing of U.S. troops in Lebanon;
- The 1967 Arab–Israeli War, which, even though Lebanon did not participate, led Palestinians to use Lebanon as their main military staging area against Israel.
- The 1969 Cairo agreements, which gave Palestinians in Lebanon the right to military control of their own camps.
- The 1973 War with the Palestinians, who by that time accounted for 300,000 of Lebanon's population of three million.
- The 1975–1990 Civil War, which witnessed Syria sending in 25,000 troops to occupy large parts of Lebanon in 1976. They remained until 2005 when they were accused of the assassination of former Prime Minister Rafik Hariri. Syria had and has extensive intelligence networks in Lebanon; has been accused of controlling the Lebanese government; and, as the United Nations Tribunal on the assassination of Hariri has exposed, appears to have been involved in systematic assassinations of leading Lebanese political figures for many years.
- Israel's repeated military incursions into Lebanon, attacks on its civilians, bombings, assassinations of Palestinian and Lebanese figures; occupation of Southern Lebanon from 1982–2000, including major military incursions in 1993 and 2006.
- The 1983 bombing of the U.S. embassy which resulted in American bombing of Lebanon.

During Lebanon's civil war, the state, which had hardly yet consolidated, fell apart. Over 150,000 people were killed, reducing the refugee population by over 25 percent. It led to the emigration of 25 percent of the population, and devastated civil society and state. Many of the youth and some children in Lebanon were mobilized to fight in the militias. The generation of young adults that now forms the bulk of the socially and politically aware population grew up during the war. Many of them were in militias and fought and killed other Lebanese. Most families lost some members during the war. Many families resisted the militias' efforts to recruit their children. At times, it was as much a war between families and militias over the hearts and minds of the young as it was among different political sects.

It was the youth of Lebanon who fought the civil war. They died in disproportionate numbers from 1973 (when the first skirmishes heralding in the official outbreak of war in 1975) onward, and have continued to fight and die in the episodic incursions within and on Lebanon until the present. In 2005, when former Prime Minister Rafik Harriri was assassinated in Beirut, tens of thousands of anti-Syrian protesters, mostly youth, males and females, took to the streets. In March, a pro-Syrian demonstration in Beirut, organized by Hizbollah, drew between half and 1.5 million people, largely young women and men. A week later, in March, a million demonstrated in a nonsectarian movement. Mainly populated by youth, the demonstrations continued for months, as did the assassinations. Sometimes called the "Cedar Revolution" or the *Intifada al-Istiglal* ("Independence Uprising"), the demonstrations and international pressure led to the withdrawal of 14,000 Syrian troops from Lebanon after an occupation of almost thirty years. Facebook, YouTube, and other social media kept the protesters and the world tied to the compelling events on the streets of Beirut and triggered sympathetic demonstrations by Lebanese in the diaspora. Feeds on social media focused on the young faces of hope, as the overwhelmingly youthful demonstrators dashed themselves into history.

The 2006 Israel invasion of Lebanon dislodged one million people, 25 percent of the population, from their homes. It was the youth, largely of Hizbollah, who fought back, and took credit for what might be the only Arab defeat of Israel—forcing Israel to withdraw its occupation of Lebanon. After the devastation of Israel's war on Lebanon, it was the youth who went door to door to help the families clean up and rebuild in South Lebanon.

Five years later, though, Lebanese youth did not rise up with the Arab Spring of 2011. They watched on TV, Facebook, Twitter, and other social media sites. They were particularly concerned about the impact of the uprising in neighboring Syria. While the Syrian regime has had strong support among Hizbollah's following in South Lebanon and Beirut's southern suburbs, many other parts of Beirut and Lebanon were ambivalent about the possible fall of the Bashar Al Assad regime. Lebanese Christians and secular thinkers in particular saw the possibility of an Islamic government, even Salafi state, in Syria as even a greater evil than the Al Assad regime. Though the Lebanese state has been reconstituted, it has been stalemated between an empowered (Shi'a) Hizbollah party and its Christian allies on the one hand and the other Christian parties with their Sunni and Shi'a allies on the other. An ever-watchful youth looks on, wondering whether to throw their fortunes onto an airplane bound for anywhere else but Lebanon, or to try once again to build.

In June and July of 2011, I spent considerable time in Lebanon discussing events and interviewing Lebanese in lay and leadership positions. With so much of the Arab world topsy-turvy, it was fascinating to see the cafés, theaters, playhouses, and nightclubs of Beirut filled with Lebanese and tourists relatively disconnected from these events. For a people who had been in violent political turmoil for four decades, there appeared to be little appetite for more unrest. Perhaps more to the point, there was little belief that violent protests in Lebanon would bring about positive political change. Most of the youth I interviewed were focused on their families and their work. They wanted little to do with the state and politics. They were frustrated with the economic impossibilities, the dysfunctionality of the state, the lack of vision of most political leaders and political parties. They were also frustrated with world and regional powers whom they saw as using Lebanon as a pawn in larger political games.

Why Have Anthropologists Glossed Over Arab Children and Youth?

These statistics, data, and case studies condense aspects of the stark realities of children and youth in the Arab world. They are compelling evidence for the need for research. Why were anthropologists, up until the Arab Spring, not compelled to focus on children and youth?

While there are, no doubt, many explanations for the relative lack of research by anthropologists focusing on Arab children and youth, one possibility stands out that I offer up for theoretical reflection. As mentioned above and in a number of previous articles (especially Joseph 2008), family is widely recognized as the center of social action in the Arab world; yet, there has been relatively little rigorous research, especially theoretical work, on families and youth in the region—even by Arab feminists. The Arab Families Working Group stands out as an exception trying to address this vacuum.[1]

Given the centrality of families to Arab youth, and the immersion of children and youth in families, I suggest that one reason that anthropologists have not separated children and youth for targeted research is that Arab societies tend not to separate out children and youth socially. Arab societies are not age-graded. Children and youth tend to spend most of their leisure time with their families, undifferentiated from adults and elders. There are few "youth" organizations or clubs which are truly age-segregated. Most of the "youth" groups tend to include adult men and women in their thirties, forties and even older. In Lebanon, my research has consistently found that *shibab* (youth) rarely means those twenty-nine or younger or those 14–24 or 15–25 or any demographic definition of youth used by Western scholars. Rather, youth tends to be used to mean either "unmarried" or "robust," especially for males. In a longitudinal study of children and youth in a village in Lebanon starting in 1994, I have done extensive observation of visiting, leisure activities, study-time, and the like for children and youth. Consistently in this now seventeen-year study, I have found that children and youth rarely spend time together alone. Overwhelmingly they spend time with a wide generational mix, based on family and neighborhood. Spending time with grandparents, who, in this village, are often in the same building or very close by, spending time with uncles and aunts, spending time with older siblings and cousins (as well as parents) is usually the preferred activity. In individual interviews in July of 2011, I asked two women in their early twenties and their two teenage brothers whom they wanted to spend their leisurely time with. All of them replied that they preferred their own siblings and family as leisure-mates and best friends.

While many Arab governments have ministries for "youth," what they mean by youth ranges broadly into the middle end of "adulthood" by Western demographic calculations. The phenomenon of "waithood," delayed marriage, throughout the Arab world, has meant protracted periods of living with parents. Typically, in any case, men and women in the Arab world live with their parents until marriage. This is partly because of the preference of the young to be with their families, and also because they cannot usually afford housing on their own. It is not uncommon for married couples to live with the parents (usually the husband's parents) after marriage for a period of time. In the "village" (in quotes because it is, in many ways, a suburb of the Greater Beirut area) in which I am carrying out the longitudinal study of children and youth, most parents build multistory apartment buildings to house each of their children (males first) after they are married. This housing preference reconsolidates families inter-generationally for some time. Children grow up with their grandparents, uncles and aunts, and cousins as their immediate, and at times, often exclusive social world. If parents cannot afford to build these projects, sometimes brothers either build together or buy together within the same building. While these patterns vary significantly from country to country, and from villages to cities, and by class, what remains common throughout the Arab region is the centrality of family in social structure and the primacy of family in the social world of children and youth. What I suggest is that perhaps anthropologists, immersed in the social worlds in which they research and write, have taken as a given the inseparability of children and youth from their families. Perhaps, as a result, anthropologists have glossed over the burgeoning of children and youth as a demographic that calls out for specific research attention.

Research Agendas on Arab Children and Youth

Other than key works by scholars such as Susan Schaefer Davis (1989) (who submitted a panel on Arab youth for the MESA mini-conference mentioned above), Dawn Chatty (2005, 2010a) and a few others, anthropologists have largely left the field of studying children and youth to sociologists, demographers, economists, and political scientists (see Khalaf and Khalaf 2011 for new research). Some focused research on children and youth has been carried out by psychologists, but that discipline appears to be consolidating a research foothold in the region much later than anthropology.

What are the questions anthropologists might research that would be of relevance to Arab children and youth of the twenty-first century? The question I pursued was: How does a society raise children for active citizenship when the state and civil society have been shattered? Investigating how children are taught their rights, responsibilities, and identities in relationship to family, village, religion, and state by family and neighbors has revealed problems in the production of citizens and "civility" in countries like Lebanon. Given the escalation of violence around the world, it is critical for us to understand how children growing up in zones of political violence and civic and economic unrest learn to be civic adults. My hypotheses were that family was a more central institution than the state as the source of loyalty and stability. I found that there were significant dis/continuities between the rights, responsibilities, and identities learned in the family and practiced in the sphere of public citizenship. This research in Lebanon, the overview of children and youth in the Arab world, and the immediate events of the Arab Spring, triggered a template of questions for anthropological inquiry, outlined below:

1) Anthropologists need to do research on the impact of (a) violence and warfare and (b) the failure of the nation-state paradigm on children, and youth. To understand children and youth in most societies, one needs to understand the state-building project and the consequences of the state-building project

for family systems. In Lebanon, the state-building project has been continually aborted, by wars, violence, or regional disruptions. What does it mean to a child or youth to be Lebanese when multiple regional and global powers continually intervene to direct the affairs of the state; when the state is divided by sectarianism, barely delivers services, and cannot protect its citizens; when almost every family becomes a transnational family with key members living abroad, some never to return? Under these conditions, how do families teach their children to become citizens?

Most of us have grown up in nation-states. The nation-state has conditioned/regulated our education, our health, recreation, our security, our identities, our relationships with our families (and even who gets to be considered family). It is hard to imagine the socialization of children for adulthood outside the nation-state paradigm. Lebanon was a failed nation-state even before the Civil War in 1975. Like so many political entities, it was an artificial nation-state, a map drawn on European tables for strategic interests having little to do with the people who lived in those lands. Since 1975, the Lebanese state has struggled for basic functionality. Even after the Taif Agreements in 1990, it has not been able to protect its own boundaries, regulate its own people, or execute the basic administrative operations of a state. The Israeli occupation until 2000; the Syrian occupation until 2005; constant vulnerability to Israeli military invasions at will, with no global consequence; multiple assassinations of Lebanese leaders, directed by its neighbors—these experiences hardly inspire confidence that the Lebanese state can protect its citizens. Lebanon has been a political football kicked around by local and international superpowers with little regard for the human toll and its economy has been whipped by events that it does not control. This has left children and youth to look to other associational sites for organizing resources, security, and a sense of self.

2) Anthropologists need to research the impact of massive migration, transnationalism, internal displacement, and forced migration on children and youth. In only two months in 2006, Israel's war on Lebanon left 25 percent of the population (one million people) displaced. Since 1975, Lebanese have repeatedly lost their homes. Palestinians have been continually displaced. The new division of the Sudan into two countries triggers possible movements of peoples. The unrest in many Arab countries, Iraq, Syria, and Libya in particular, has displaced millions of Arab children and youth.

3) The failure of the educational systems and the failure of national and global economies to prepare a marketplace for newly economically active youth calls for research.

4) Anthropological studies are lacking on the gendered implications of the failure of the nation-state, the failure of citizenship, the failure of educational systems and the market place.

5) Similarly investigations are needed of the gendered implications for female children and youth of the failure of the rule of law, the gendering of nationality and family law, the advances and retreats of the rights of women.

6) The rise of new forms of sectarianism and ethnic conflict also has critical implications for children and youth, especially females.

7) It is important for anthropologists to consider policy implications of research, including drawing up policy recommendations or carrying out research that has relevance for policy makers. Anthropologists might train themselves to work with policy makers and decision makers. While anthropologists are rightly wary because of the misuse of anthropology in our early history and even in the 1950s–1970s, it should not keep us from trying to use anthropology for social good, especially in relation to children and youth, and particularly for the females among them. It is time for anthropology to think in terms of research that has an impact on policy, including social, economic, cultural, and foreign policies.

8) How can anthropology think about the field of education among Arab youth? What does anthropology have to offer to Arab studies after its half century of studying education (see Linda Herrera 2008)? How can we intervene in the conversations about the failure of the educational system to address the needs of children and youth in the Arab world?

9) We need more systematic studies of Arab families. This is the place where children and youth live. This is the most critical institution for Arab society, and 60 percent of the population spend most of their time within this circle.

10) After more than half a century of economic anthropology, political economy, study of globalization and markets, what does anthropology have to offer Arab societies in terms of understanding the job market and the fit between the job market and the educational system?

Anthropology of the Future: Context/Challenges

The street protests which overthrew the twenty-three-year authoritarian rule of President Zine el Abidine Ben Ali of Tunisia on 14 January 2011 appear to have been ignited by the 17 December 2010 self-immolation of Mohamed Bouazizi, a twenty-six year-old street food vendor in Sidi Bouzid. The story quickly spread virally on social media that Mr. Bouazizi was beaten and humiliated by forty-five year-old Fadia Hamdi, a female police officer, along with her fellow officers. His wares, his livelihood, were confiscated, as they had been numerous times before, because he did not have a vending permit (some reports indicate a permit was not required, but bribery of officers was). Facebook, Twitter, and other social media flashed updates and clips of the deadly events from street to street as thousands of youthful demonstrators, males and females, confronted police in what was dubbed the "Jasmine Revolution" or as one report called it, the "Twitterized Revolution."

In short order, the authoritarian states Egypt, Yemen, Bahrain, Libya, and Syria were challenged by thousands, and in some cases hundreds of thousands, of citizens taking to the streets to protest their lack of voice in their own polities. Overwhelmingly the protesters were youth. Again, Facebook, Twitter, cell phones, the internet social media of all types and stripes were mobilized in a technological revolution that swept through aging and corrupt regimes. Zine el Abidine Ben Ali (Tunisia) and Hosni Mubarak (Egypt) fell and Muammar Qaddhafi (Libya) fled. The battles for Syria, Yemen, and Bahrain rage as of this writing. Leaders around the world applauded the protestors (though some leaders held on to pillars of economic self-interest even in the face of the democratic movements they rhetorically idealized); and even some Arab leaders called upon others of their fellow leaders to step down. It has been a historic moment, a watershed, an unfolding few scholars or pundits predicted.

This historic moment calls our attention to the authoritarian regimes, the lack of civil society, the suppression of public speech and press, and the corruption in many Middle Eastern governments—all of which are well known. However, they also point us toward the faces in the crowds, the possibilities of their futures, and the technologies they master to navigate their circumstances. They point us to the youth of the Arab world, the conditions of their livelihoods, the institutions facilitating/obstructing education, the doors open/closed for jobs, the avenues open/closed for political engagement. In each of these sites, the stories are disturbing.

Yet, most Middle Eastern youth only obtain some education, barely manage to create a livelihood, a family, a path toward a bit of a future. A majority of the youth are disillusioned with their political leaders and governments. They focus on their families and their lives. They have shown the world that they are capable of momentous political and social action through the events in Tunisia, Egypt, Yemen, Bahrain, Libya, and Syria. Their aspirations can be tapped. Their hopes can be ignited. Their humanity can be stirred to action. They are using new technologies to animate their actions regardless of their levels of education. For scholars of the Arab world, these events call for us to read them, understand them, translate them beyond the easy and ready-made categories of analysis.

It is telling that the mother of Mohamed Bouazizi, the Tunisian youth whose self-immolation triggered the fall of a political dictator, contended that his suicide was not for politics or an ideology. It was for dignity. She claimed it was the humiliation that he suffered that he could no longer tolerate. The widespread protests in the Arab world also appear to manifest the cry of a failed human condition, the demand for human integrity, the insistence on openings for futures free of authoritarian regulation—futures which facilitate the possibilities of creative human production. This too, is part of our responsibilities as researchers of the Arab world—to capture the human condition by describing, analyzing, and translating the humanity we have chosen as the focus of our scholarly production.

NOTES

1. http://arabfamilies.org.

7.

THE MEMORY WORK OF ANTHROPOLOGISTS: NOTES TOWARD A GENDERED POLITICS OF MEMORY IN CONFLICT ZONES—SUDAN AND ERITREA

Sondra Hale

To remember is to know that you can forget.

—E. Valentine Daniel, "The Coolie."

Introduction

A salient method of anthropologists in dealing with the military and civil conflicts of the twentieth and twenty-first centuries has been memory work.[1] It has become an indispensable approach to reading the conflicts of the last fifty years or so. Memory work in the ethnography of conflict situations is one way of reading the slippery "truth" of violent encounters and generating theoretical ideas that enhance our thinking about the politics of memory.

The memory work of anthropologists has been in the avant-garde of the field for more than a decade, perhaps propelled into greater visibility and significance with the rise of self-reflexive and narrative anthropology and the contribution of allied fields and methods such as oral history and person-centered ethnography. Although memory-as-ethnography was not at the core of the field of anthropology until recent years (at least not under the rubric of "the politics of memory"), in its recent iterations, especially within postcolonial theories, memory work is very much an epistemological, theoretical, and political force for the future of the field. After all, it is in the heart of ethnography where people may confront each other with the past and refute each other's telling of the past.

Likewise, until recent decades, anthropological studies of war, conflict, and genocide were rarely at the center of the field—certainly not as they are today. The intersecting of conflict and memory work is an innovation that weds a thematic with a methodology or approach. I have been exploring the ways in which people recount their memories of conflicts—as they are living them, recalling them during lulls and "peacetime," and as they are lamenting the phenomenon of continuous conflict. I have noted any number of modes of behavior regarding memory. People and/or governments/parties may not only try to kill their adversaries, but may attempt to annihilate or alter the ideas their adversaries hold about their own past. Individuals, ethnic groups, armies, and governments may try to colonize each other's pasts or, in the case of governments or ruling groups and others, they may try to create a past that never existed. People recognize, at least unconsciously, that what they might experience in the future may very well depend on memories of the past. A great deal is at stake.

Pressing into a conflict with the past tucked under a group's collective memory and reconstructing, post-conflict, the group's present while remembering the past are both processes of the politics of memory salient in viewing the Middle East and North Africa's many conflicts over the last century and into this one.[2]

That these processes, if taken into account at all, are gendered is seldom dealt with as central to various theoretical approaches. It is here where I make my intervention: by using memory work and the gendered study of conflict with reference to Sudan and Eritrea. I recognize that it is not sufficient to demonstrate that people—men and women, different ethnic groups, the state and it citizens—remember conflicts differently. It is how these memories are operationalized that is relevant. This is the politics of memory.

The politics of memory is integrally related to time and space. The various strategies for eliminating/diminishing memory or colonizing that memory involve rupturing time and space and annihilating culture, e.g., forcing name changes on people and places; removing historical landmarks; desecrating cemeteries; withholding education or teaching only the "history" of the vanquisher; forbidding local/vernacular languages; forcing religious conversion; and much more that may be more personal and close to home, e.g., forcing upon a marginalized group a custom of the dominant group, one historically rejected by the marginalized group, such as female circumcision; relocating people away from the homeland and/or forcing them to live among different ethnic groups; and controlling and shaping the lives and bodies of women. Other powerful and violent strategies are land alienation and the extermination of intellectuals and cultural figures. These are some of the strategies of violent conflicts that are designed to coerce forgetting but cannot be forgotten.

The Significance of Sudan and Eritrea

Sudan and Eritrea have a clear significance in studies of gendered conflicts. Sudan is the epitome of the poetic "things fall apart"—two sections of the country ruled strikingly differently during British colonialism and after independence (1956) unable to build a strong enough state (even with military force) to hold the parts together. One of the consequences is that we have witnessed a violent, long-lasting, and intermittent civil war between the north and south (1955–2005) which eventually ended in the south's secession 9 July 2011; a massive conflict in Darfur in the west that continues as of this writing; a continuous series of conflicts in the Nuba Mountains in the west-central area, which was under a tenuous ceasefire from 2002 until 15 June 2011, and then exploded into war; and other regional conflicts of varying intensity. No one discounts the possibility/probability of more conflict between the two Sudans and within each. In all of these conflicts women have figured prominently as symbols, pawns, victims, guerillas, perpetrators, and witnesses. Their testimonies in various forms have been part of our memory work.

Eritrea, too, was a paragon of a different sort—a more positive model for revolutionary struggles. The region fought a thirty-year war for independence from Ethiopia (1963–1993), and the two adversaries engaged again in an even bloodier conflict from 1998–2000. The Eritrea People's Liberation Front (EPLF) became famous in liberation circles not only for its progressive views about how revolutions should be fought and won, but also because women figured so prominently as guerilla fighters (over 30 percent) and were seen as icons of "liberated women." The center did not hold, however, and things fell apart.[3]

As the two Sudans near their own brand of "truth and reconciliation," whether formal (as in a series of hearings and testimonies), individual, conscious or unconscious/subconscious, the past will have to be reckoned with, and as in

South Africa, Bosnia, and Rwanda, women are having their say, bearing witness in ways that often run counter either to the official state story or to the men in the struggle with them or against them.

The Eritrean state, mired in post-conflict intransigence, is still not recognizing the various renditions of the history of the war(s), choosing, instead, to persecute and prosecute those who express versions that depart from the official story. Eritrea, therefore, has come to stand for a severe attempt to impose a collective memory of the war(s) on its people.

The Significance of Palestine/Israel in Memory Work

People who have survived violent strategies tell stories about them. It is the telling and the pointing that reinforce the memory of the events. Oral histories (storytelling) are often transformed into ethnographic data (Slyomovics 1998, xxi). We act on this ethnographic data as if it is real, not as if it is imagined. These stories become a contested history, as we see so vividly in studies of Arabs and Jews in Palestine/Israel and other locations where even the name of the state is contested. Susan Slyomovics, for example, in *The Object of Memory* (1998), explores the visions and memories of the homes of the Arab inhabitants of Ein Houd (Palestinian village displaced/replaced by Jewish Israelis after 1948) and Ein Hod (the Jewish village). In this process historical narratives are formed and nationalist discourses developed. Slyomovics addresses the larger questions of how we memorize/memorialize space and develop a kind of environmental memory and how this, in turn, shapes our sense of identity and belonging.

In the ethnographic film *In Search of Palestine,* narrated by Edward Said (Bruce 1998; Hale 2000a), the viewer is invited to experience a historical event: the return to Palestine after forty-seven years by the most internationally known Palestinian intellectual at the time, the late Edward Said. Memory and space, two concepts crucial to the politics of recent years, intersect in the film. *In Search of Palestine* proves that merely seeing is not sufficient. The film carries the viewer on a journey of remembering, expressing, feeling, and experiencing. The subject matter is tangible and abstract, material and metaphorical.

This film explores the politics of memory. The challenges to conventional epistemology have for some time included the recognition that individual and collective memory are forms of knowledge. Therefore, what is significant may not be what is written and codified by the accepted knowers (official Israeli state history, for example, or official Sudanese or Eritrean state history), but truth can be known in other ways, including the memory of a society or group as a whole. In this film Edward Said, by remembering his childhood in Palestine, is both part of a collective memory and a contributor to it.

Both space and what fills space are significant. Said narrates that so much of what had been there before is still there; however, the entire context is changed. Of course, so much is also gone, contributing to the changed context. What is absent becomes even more significant than what is present. What is not spoken lingers in the air. These are important factors in our analyses of South Sudan or the Nuba Mountains and should guide a great deal of our thinking about Darfur.

Space, as we know, is a fluid, dynamic reflection of culture and politics. The geographies and histories that we have all invented, constructed from our individual and collective memories, may be outside the mold. Nowadays we map ideologies that shape the way we think of Africa or the Middle East.

The film raises viewers' consciousness about the cultural and political importance of personal and place names, labels and place-markers, of people who appear in yearbooks who are no longer there, of a school history that abruptly ends. Viewers grow conscious of the insidious "weapons" of covering up, building over, changing names, and demolishing. Theodor Herzl in *The Jewish State* said in 1896 that "If I wish to substitute a new building for an old one, I must demolish before I construct" (quoted by Slyomovics 1998: 29). We have become aware of house as both material and metaphor and of the power of stones (as in "my house was built of stone," and "I lived a stone's throw from there"). So much of the Nuba Mountains in west-central Sudan was destroyed or moved around to make way for new structures that confused and scattered the local people.

Time can be so specific and yet is easily altered by distortion, conflation, telescoping. It can be shaped by the removal of history. In the film the viewer is compelled to ask if this is the Palestine of yesterday, with the dislocated Palestine Liberation Organization? Or, is what we are experiencing along with Said the Palestine of today under Palestinian authority? Some developments of great political and cultural significance may not be measured within a conventional time-frame. Was Said removed from this time-frame, or was he inserted into it? When one thinks about Palestine it is not possible to ignore the concept of return, but we seldom think of return as a nonlinear process.

One aspect of the conflict for Palestine/Israel is culture—culture in the form of memory and representation of the past. Jews and Arabs remember their past differently—their separate pasts and their common past. Both of these groups stress the past as a political and cultural weapon. Each group has constructed a radically different past, one overlaying the other, a profoundly ramifying story told over and over again for political effect and personal solace.

The act of forgetting is also a significant cultural act. Edward Said himself has written on it. Forgetting can be a crisis of national significance, as is the obscuring of one memory by another. It is imperative that a society not only remember, but keep the history alive. Retrieving the past may be a moral duty, leading to a compulsion to bear vicarious witness. Said returned to Palestine not solely for his own sentiment and nostalgia, or even political effect; he returned to bear witness.

During his visit to Palestine, Said engages in what Slyomovics refers to in *The Object of Memory* as the "repeated gesture" (1998),[4] which specifically involves pointing to a remembered site, pointing at history, as it were. Many times in *In Search of Palestine* the viewer sees Said pointing over and over again at a site. His hand, magnified close to the lens, is in the way of the camera. Obviously, the gesture is more important than the aesthetics of photography; the repeated gesture reminds us, reminds him, and marks the landscape. His individual memory contradicts the official memory and creates a history.

In Search of Palestine is Said's "Memorial Book," a topic so well developed in *The Object of Memory.*[5] He begins the film, in fact, looking at a family photo album and showing us a very old home movie of him and his sister playing on the front steps of their large stone house. The film cuts to Said in contemporary Jerusalem, in front of that same house, and no one can deny he lived there, right there. He stresses the themes we might expect: the land, landscape, place, house, and most importantly the possibility—or impossibility—of return. Throughout the film, land, like house, is both material and metaphor. More than once in the film, Said admits that the Palestine of his childhood cannot be retrieved, that no Palestinian truly hopes to retrieve the lost landscape, at least not as it was. Therefore, even though Said has returned, he is, in a sense, out of place. He is an awkward presence on a landscape that has moved beyond his memories. Before our eyes he lives the story of displacement, of confinement, of keys to a house that is occupied by someone else, and that someone else has locked the door with his or her own version of history. He tells the story of bulldozers doing their dirty work in the name of the state. He spent much of his life trying to produce a discourse to counter the bulldozer.

Said and other Palestinians do not have a passive memory. They engage in active remembrance, attempting to stave off the inevitable, to ensure cultural and political survival. Pointing a finger at history is a form of resistance. These collective memories have produced a poetry in exile, while inside both Israel and Palestine one finds the reality of sixty years of apartheid.

Constructing and Subverting Collective Memory

As early as 1959, ethnographer Ian Cunnison, in *The Luapula Peoples of Northern Rhodesia* (Zambia) argued that most histories in the Luapula Valley were "personal" renditions, except for the "impersonal" and general history of the Kazembe Kingdom. He describes a situation in which two groups have entirely opposite views of the history of the valley and act on those different versions as if their truth is *the* truth, causing years of conflict (Cunnison 1959; see also Gordon 2006). Ethnography, for example, is the imagined description of a people and their history and cultural life, but these are creations by anthropologists, and their descriptions and renderings of the past become imprinted into the memory of the people themselves, or into the memory and epistemology of the intended readership. People remember their "homelands" differently and in the course of conflicts attempt to alter the Other's homeland and the objects of memory, as in removing guideposts, markers, place names, and entire villages. The strategy is to erase one another's land, and if one marks it with one's own objects and memories, the land will be one's own. The process is both abstract (memory) and material (real objects that symbolize a culture). Another strategy is to remove one's adversary's language and replace it with one's own. A further strategy is to create myths of origin, to make claims to who was on the land first (e.g., the Afrikaners in South Africa, who claim to have arrived on the land before the Bantu-speakers); or to try to demonstrate that that land was always farm land or always pastoral land; or to pronounce that river or well as a marker, a boundary, and say it has always been that way. As we know all too well, colonials were experts at creating and inventing boundaries, in essence, marking and demarcating other people's histories and cultures.

Attempts to alter collective memory/history may involve what Eric Hobsbawm and Terrence Ranger (1983) see as the reinvention of tradition. People create their own pasts and they do it by leaving out things, adding things, reconstructing our memories. People reconstruct these pasts differently from each other. Sometimes, as in the Israeli Jewish and Palestinian case, Israelis have altered the history of the area in very material ways, for example by building their own villages on top of forcibly vacated Arab villages, changing the names, making claims to who was on the land first.

Perhaps one of the most famous attempts to alter collective memory has been by The Mothers of the Plaza de Mayo in Argentina, who persisted in putting a face on the disappeared, forcing people to remember, but attempting far more than that. Margaret Burchianti (2004) explored the group as a site through which social memories are transmitted and connected to the realities of Argentina's present:

> The conjuncture or disjuncture between people's direct and individual memories of the past, their memory of the society's collective past, and the "official" history can be used as a prism for seeing how power and resistance work through and reinforce a complex political economy. By giving testimony and re-contextualizing the events of the dictatorship, the Mothers have been able to challenge the historical narratives of the state and construct competing ones. Furthermore, the present-day activism and goals of the Mothers, as individuals and as a collective, are based on political commitments that have arisen in great part out of maternal relationships and maternal memories. (Burchianti 2004, 133)

Consider also the attempts by the state or dominant groups to force people to *forget,* or attempts that the subjects themselves try to forget—from individual "retrieved memory" that was repressed to the suppression of public events, as in post–World War II Germany; the Lebanese civil war of the 1970s and 80s (no one talks about it and nothing is resolved); the Japanese-American internment (which the Japanese-Americans were too ashamed to talk about until the last two decades); the Turks' suppression of free discussions about the Armenian genocide or their strategy of negating or neutralizing the grievances by putting their own victimization side-by-side with the Armenians for the same set of events. Memories of black-on-black slavery in Sudan are suppressed in "official" history, and are either not taught or de-emphasized in the schools.[6]

There are many mechanisms and strategies for evoking both individual and collective remembering. Certainly, memorials are one mechanism. A recent work by Paul Williams (2008) refers to the "global rush to commemorate atrocities," which is the subtitle of the book. If one looks at museum practices throughout the world, we get significant insights into how objects, images and exhibition spaces contribute to the politically charged field of commemoration and remembrance. The last twenty-five years have seen a flourishing of this new cultural phenomenon—the memorial museum. Williams claims his is the first work of its kind to map these new institutions and cultural spaces.

People also engage in memory maps; they map loss; they photograph loss; they engage in autocartography; they tell stories, write histories, give testimonies, recite, and point, among many other methods. With the internet now such a prominent feature in many people's lives, it is difficult to fathom the endless mechanisms that may be upon us in the future. We also do our remembering through *nostalgia*. An example is what Renato Rosaldo points to as "Imperial Nostalgia" (1985). Memories of colonialism are discussed in a number of sources, such as Ann Laura Stoler and Karen Strassler's "Castings for the Colonial: Memory Work in 'New Order' Java" (2000). They point out that there is a very strong fascination recently with "the contrast that memories of colonialism afford between the 'elegance' of domination and the brutality of its effects" (2000, 68).[7] In their words:

> While images of empire resurface in the public domain, colonial studies has materialized over the last decade as a force of cultural critique, political commentary, and not least as a domain of new expert knowledge. One could argue that the entire field has positioned itself as a counterweight to the waves of colonial nostalgia that have emerged in the post–World War II period in personal memoirs, coffee table books, tropical chic couture, and a film industry that encourages . . . audiences to enjoy "the elegance of manners governing relations of dominance and subordination between the races. (2000, 68)[8]

Stoler and Strassler mention Nietzsche's warning against "idle cultivation of the garden of history,"[9] and say that it resonates today and argue that it is not always easy to detect if statements about colonialism are critical or if the speakers/writers are "vicariously luxuriating in it."[10]

The Social Construction of Subjective Experiences

How much is memory about identity? Jonathan Boyarin (1994) theorizes that memory is all about identity. Individuals manipulate, change their minds, reinterpret, lie, engage in self-delusion, distort, repress, and forget their experiences of the everyday world. People construct/invent their lives in such a way that they can live in a more or less noncontradictory way. And when they cannot do it in "fact," they do so in their minds or memories.

However, in terms of gender politics, when women attempt to align their memories to mitigate contradictions, they are often maligned. For example, there has been a great deal of focus in the U.S. on "false memory," and women have more often been the object of these particular kinds of memory debates. The politics of gender has influenced and shaped the contemporary debates over sexual abuse and memory (e.g., Gardner 2000). Why are a woman's memories often questioned when she claims to have been sexually abused as a child?

To follow up on that point, we can see a difference in the level of scrutiny applied to women accusers when they testify in court, especially when it is a sexual crime such as rape. One needs to look at the different language used to refer to women's testimonies. In *shari'a* (Islamic law) it takes two women to equal one man as a witness in court. The rationale I heard in my research in 1988 on the Islamist movement is that "Women are too sympathetic," "emotional," and are, therefore, less reliable witnesses. Their experience is, thus, denied. What prevails is the notion of "hysterical women," who cannot remember the "truth" because their emotions get in the way.

Who is validated as bearing witness to the past is very political. The past is always contested, and there are always *gatekeepers.* The politics of memory is about what the past means to the present. The focus of contestation is not so much about *what* happened in the past. It is about who, or what, is entitled to speak for that past in the present—which is often a conflict over representation—i.e., whose views should be sought. There could be agreement over events, but not over how the truth of these events may be most fully represented. What enters is the role of memory. But both memory and truth are unstable categories (Hodgekin and Radstone 2003).

With regard to gatekeepers and power and memory, anthropologist Mariko Tamanoi's hypothesis is that "The more powerful an individual or a group is, the more effectively such an individual or group member can exercise the politics of memory" (1998, 4–5). Or, with regard to the politics of *forgetting/suppressing,* Tamanoi quotes Rubie Watson (1994) that "[People 'remember'] ... because they share with others sets of images that have been passed down to them through the media of memory—through paintings, architecture, monuments, ritual, storytelling, poetry, music, photos, and film" (2009, 18).[11]

Again, this brings up the issue of identity and representation. As I mentioned above, for scholars such as Jonathan Boyarin memory and identity are nearly the same, a point he makes in "Space, Time, and the Politics of Memory" (1994). To Boyarin there is a "continuing contest to determine how much of what has happened on a nation's territory is contained in its self-image" (ibid., 22). And what is to be hidden? And how much of the nation's self-image is integrally connected?

It is not a jump to move to a discussion of the body when one is discussing self-identity or even the identity of the nation. The link between *memory* and *the body* can be through coded markings. Non-state collectives/groups mark individual bodies in ways that include scarification, circumcision, and so forth; but states often mark to *exclude,* for example by marks of torture that distinguish between torturer and tortured (Boyarin 1994). However, when the torture victim, upon his/her return home, displays his/her marks, it becomes inclusive/collective. It is part of the collective memory. Your scars become mine.

Gendering Memory—Sudan and Eritrea

One of the significant questions I am asking is about the uses and abuses of women's bodies during conflict (Hale 2010). Slyomovics also asks, "Why is there an imaginative link between memories and homeland through the bodies of women?" (1998, xxii).

> Theoretical parallels can be drawn between the feminization of the colonized landscape and a spatial history of Palestine conceived as the indigenous woman penetrated, raped, conquered, mapped, and under surveillance by the colonizer. The Palestinian woman is made to stand for the destroyed villages and the dispossessed land. She represents the "national allegory" of the lost Palestine homeland in much literary and visual imagery as the feminine sphere reproducing, literally, and figuratively, the nation. (1998, 208)[12]

In my fieldwork over many years in Sudan and Eritrea,[13] I have been struck by the various attempts by the state to control memory and the various ways that people have either resisted, altered, redefined, or absorbed those memories and, oftentimes, presented their own. Sometimes the alteration of history and people's memory of their homes has been gradual, oftentimes, sudden. For example, removal of identity has taken many decades in Sudan's Nuba Mountains, a process that has often been referred to as "genocide by attrition" (Hale 2010). Yet, aspects of the process have been very sudden, as in the latest incursion by the government into the Nuba Mountains and the violent rounding up of Nuba.

Since 1989, Islamists in Sudan have attempted to alter areas in very material ways, e.g., through processes of "relocation," by building many mosques that alter the landscape and capture viewers' eyes, guiding them away from other structures and aspects of the environment, such as churches. Furthermore, the "look" of Sudan (especially northern Sudan) has been altered through dress, particularly the dress of women via the imposition of the *hijab*.

The Sudanese state has also attempted to reinvent a kind of Islam that never existed in Sudan, calling it "tradition," or referring to returning to the roots, but actually inventing those roots. This process has gone hand-in-hand with the resuscitation of "Arab" identity and the attempts to build hegemony through that identity. This has involved a series of strategies that have resulted in many of Sudan's conflicts or in prolonging or exacerbating those conflicts (Hale 1996). That women and women's bodies figure prominently in these various attempts to alter memory is one of the themes of this essay.

Furthermore, the color of women and the color of men become factors in these Sudanese conflicts where men conquer partially through women and light skin triumphs over dark skin, even if these differences are barely discernible to the eye of the outsider (or insider). It is the memory of those colors, as they have been invented, that count.

Below I present only brief examples of the different ways groups of people—and I am especially interested in gender dynamics—remember significant events such as war, revolution, or the "heroic life" in times of conflict. These ideas are still in an experimental stage, with much theorizing left to do.

The Gendered Memory of the Eritrean/Ethiopian War
from the 1960s–1990s; *or* Notes on Eritrean Women Fighters

The EPLF put a great deal of emphasis on creating collective memory. I was struck by how many of the stories told to me by both men and women were basically the same. Aspects of everyday life in the bunkers were described with the same or similar vocabulary. However, there were subtle differences, which I outline below (Hale 2000b; 2000c; 2006).

Men and women often told the same battle/casualty stories even if they were in different areas of the war zone and had entered the field at different times. One example of a war story much repeated in my interviews was of a family in which a husband and wife were called to rush into battle at the front. The man went ahead while the woman dealt with their child before joining him and their comrades in the violent confrontation. However, just as she reached where the battle was, he was killed in front of her as she watched; she ran to join him and was killed herself. This was EPLF indoctrination, a constructed collective memory.

However, there were also collective memories women held which were spatialized and temporized differently than men's. Men stressed the pre–"Strategic Retreat" period and the beginning of the movement, not just because they usually entered the movement earlier than women did (with a few exceptions), but because they saw themselves as more significant pioneers, when it was really the women who were pioneers in terms of breaking traditions about the appropriate roles of women. Women talked more about the bunkers (settled life) whereas men talked about the marches, the advances, covering more territory in their recounting than did women.

While most of the Eritreans I interviewed were willing to talk about how violent combat was, in all my interviews only two people mentioned interpersonal violence and conflict, or sexual harassment. No one talked about rape, except to say that it was punishable by death. Few talked about domestic violence.

I was especially interested in the uses of space-time and the performance of political labor. When I asked EPLF ex-fighters—men and women—to tell me their memories of the war, their responses were highly gendered and contrasting. Women described life in the bunkers as if it was family life, demonstrating a collective consciousness; whereas men talked about roads and destinations in a linear, directive, instrumental way. Women talked about being "in the field" (behind enemy lines and the fortified and liberated areas), and communal life; men stressed international relations, especially the relationship to Ethiopia. Women were most struck by the egalitarian division of labor, but men talked more about combat. Women were more willing to tell family stories. The war lasted so long (thirty years) that families were formed and were an integral part of everyday life. In contrast, men were more likely to tell stories about military platoon activities. Women seemed proud of their military training because it was something so different for them and was taken as a privilege. All of the EPLF fighters I talked with boasted about the political education that was given to everyone. I was struck by the fact that many women ex-fighters said they had not thought they would return alive, whereas men talked about their political future after the war, especially civilian politics and civil society. Women did not talk about being wounded, but men did. Men sometimes showed me their wounds; women never did. When I asked about everyday life, women showed me photo albums. Men were more likely to show me their writings and political cartoons, a big pastime in the field.

These different perspectives on the war tended to undermine the EPLF's attempt to build a collective memory, including even the most personal or detailed aspect of life in the field. These contrasts were to have profound ramifications after the war in terms of reparations, benefits, decisions about how to conduct the next war against Ethiopia, which lasted another two bloody years, from 1998–2000. The fact that women were de-emphasized in the second war—not sent in such great numbers to the front, and pulled out of combat when violence occurred (such as the rape of Eritrean women fighters by Ethiopian combatants)—could be argued as a response to EPLF women not fully collaborating in the building of a collective consciousness. Women had their own rendition of the wars.

Notes on Nuba Women and Women of Darfur

It is clearly too early and too difficult to collect memories of conflict from those still engaged in conflict, such as the Darfurians, or subjected to state violence, such as the Nuba after June 2011, or those still trying to hold onto a ceasefire or "peace" in a tinderbox situation (such as the Nuba during the cease-fire or women of South Sudan now). However, as part of my experimental thinking on these issues, I can both speculate and use sketches from dialogues with women and men from these areas.

The particular types of violence that women of these areas have experienced have had a strong impact on the way they remember the conflicts. Because women had/have been raped, held as slaves/concubines, forced to marry outside the group, forcibly moved away from their families to "peace camps" or relocation centers, may be more likely than men to end up in Internally Displaced Persons camps or any refugee camps across borders, etc., they tend to have less attachment to the ethnic group and, therefore, in conversations about what they remember tend to be more broadly focused on extra-national/extra-ethnic issues. Men are more attached to the land/group and hold women responsible to represent the land and the group.

Men and women, therefore, are bound to have very different notions about the personal and group nature and significance of the conflicts. It is my conjecture that women will, however, remember events "closer to home," more personal; whereas men will remember events further from home/camp/village and less personal. These speculations have been borne out by my scattered interviews, with Nuba women in particular. How these will translate in terms of the politics of memory is yet to be researched.

Sudanese Communists and the "Heroic Life"

In an article on the everyday life of the revolution Srila Roy discusses the radical left Naxalbari movement of Bengal (2007). She says that the "heroic life" or the life of the revolutionary is one that supposedly transcends the everyday and the ordinary. The "banal" vulnerabilities of everyday life, however, continue to constitute the unseen, often unspoken background of such a heroic life.

As her examples, Roy uses women's memories of everyday life spent "underground" in the late 1960s. Using interviews with middle-class women activists, she outlines the ways in which revolutionary femininity was imagined and lived in the everyday (we can compare this to the radical chic of Eritrean women fighters with their distinctive Afros, leather jackets, and disdain for femininity). Roy discusses the nature of political labor and also the gendering of revolutionary space. However, unlike the Eritreans, women of the Naxalbari movement found life underground a site of vulnerability and powerlessness. Below I use some of the ideas from the Naxalbari material to analyze Sudanese women communists during the times when the Sudanese Communist Party (SCP) was underground. In the same article Roy also mentions that memories of everyday interpersonal violence remain buried under a collective mythologizing of the "heroic life," which resonates with the SCP case (Hale, forthcoming).

In my research on the SCP and Sudanese women communists, I saw many parallels and contrasts to Roy's Bengali subjects and some parallels to other episodes of "heroic life" (Hale 1993; 1996). Despite having a collective memory of the accomplishments of communism worldwide and in Sudan, women and men of the SCP and its women's affiliate, the Sudanese Women's Union (SWU), much like the case of the Bengali, remember the "heroic life" very differently and have experienced it very differently.

Sudanese men and women communists remember together the comradeship of active Party life—when they were above ground and out in the open. They both remember when women earned the right to vote in 1965; men and a few women ran for Parliament. In interviews over the years I was able to observe, however, that men saw themselves as liberating "their women" during this era; whereas women experienced the era as liberating themselves.

From my interviews, the retelling of SCP history has been fascinating. Men recount their male heroes—the union organizers, their executed SCP secretary general, sometimes multiple stays in prison, often saying these were the best years of their lives. They have related to me that it was inspiring being among men, telling stories, sharing everything, organizing for their return to freedom. Prison space and time were the same.

Women, on the other hand, tell of the sacrifices of raising their families and keeping the family afloat financially when the men got arrested. Some silently resented that their husbands (in their view) did not try to avoid being arrested at moments of heightened political activity. Being arrested was, after all, a badge of honor. I also heard resentments that the Party had so often interfered in their personal lives, especially while the man was in prison; whereas men remember this as the Party taking care of wives of imprisoned martyrs. For many communist women married to communists, the domestic life they had to lead was another form of confinement.[14]

When the scp was banned and driven underground, the men and the Party sometimes thrived. Above ground they were constantly engaged in internal conflicts. Underground there was solidarity, and in prison they still had mobility to do political labor and education. In contrast, while the Party was underground, the women lost the freedom of movement. They were not allowed to attend clandestine late-night meetings in "dubious neighborhoods." The men argued that women's middle-classness would cause them to stand out and would expose everyone else, i.e., the men. Therefore, when the scp was underground, what resulted was yet another form of confinement for women.

Harking back to Roy's point (2007), women kept quiet about sexual harassment and physical abuse, often remembering it as an inevitable sacrifice for the revolution, something to be endured as part of their role. The Party line was that nothing should be recounted about private space, private lives that would discredit the Party. What happened behind closed doors was seen by men as outside the domain of the Party and should not be remembered as part of the "heroic life" of the Party. Furthermore, even when Party cadre or rank and file occasionally acknowledged that domestic violence might sometimes occur, men would say it was "something in the past" that "should be forgotten" so the Party could move on. Temporally, women remembered that sexual violence and physical abuse was on a continuum; in contrast, men saw these as "episodes."

The Sudan People's Liberation Movement/Army (splm/a) and the "Heroic Life"

In a number of his writings and public lectures Jok Madut Jok, a Dinka medical anthropologist, reveals the abuse of both civilian and warrior women of South

Sudan (Jok 1998). He writes of the sexual and health abuses committed by returning SPLA fighters, in particular of their impregnating their wives and partners too frequently, especially under the situation of poor nutrition and stress, and often when they were still lactating from the previous child. Men had expectations of sexual service, nurturing, and psychological sustenance. Women had to see themselves as contributing to the war effort, however that was interpreted. The small number of interviews I have carried out with women of South Sudan (mainly in Kampala) would confirm these notions about how women remember the conflicts. On these pieces of evidence alone we can speculate that women and men of South Sudan will remember these war years differently. With the independence of South Sudan declared so recently (2011), it is too soon for us to have full interpretations from the women, but they will come.

Conclusion

In this chapter I have made reference both to the memory work of anthropologists (and the importance of these methods for anthropological theories) and the memory work of Palestinians, and of Sudanese and Eritrean women who have experienced or are still experiencing violent conflicts and/or life inside a political party or front that sees itself as leading a "heroic life" and attempts to indoctrinate members accordingly. In Eritrea, where the EPLF became the state, and in Sudan, where Islamist forces came to power through a military coup d'état we have seen attempts to build a collective consciousness and to control memory. The SCP relied on its international ideology as a form of collective consciousness. Everything was remembered in "heroic" terms.

Northern Sudanese may not have used some of the more conventional modes of evoking and reinforcing collective memory. It may still be too soon to see memorials to the war built by northerners. Some of my interlocutors argue that we will never see them. Is this because northern Sudanese are trying to forget and encourage/force others to forget more than they try to remember? The war with the south has never been remembered (by most northern Sudanese) as a noble war, only as a necessity that was foisted upon them and deemed essential for nation-building. Newly independent South Sudan has already built a major memorial to the late John Garang, SPLM leader who, ironically, stood for the unity of Sudan. In contrast, Eritreans built a war museum and also have left the detritus from various battles in their last places, transforming military graveyards into museums.

Sudanese and Eritrean women are building memorials with their memories. For women in the conflict zones of various regions of Sudan—especially in the contemporary conflicts in Darfur and the Nuba Mountains—various ethnic groups and people with differing modes of economy remember their pasts differently. Women and men also remember their pasts differently, with Darfurian women singing "praise songs" about the warriors, giving their own versions of the conflicts, while men remember the homeland through women's bodies. In fact, in most instances of gender-based violence memory is linked to women's bodies and the "homeland." In Darfur, the Nuba Mountains, and South Sudan women have been subjected to rape or other forms of sexual violence and incarceration (e.g., domestic slavery). My experiences of talking with men in Khartoum lead me to believe that they want to deny that women have been violated, unless it could directly serve the cause, setting up a different version of the various Sudanese conflicts. In Eritrea, my interviews revealed that sexual violence did occur, perpetrated by both Ethiopians and Eritreans, but the male ex-fighters would not acknowledge this to me, nor to most of the women fighters.

It serves men to cultivate memories where women are standing for the nation or living the "heroic life" side-by-side with the male guerrilla fighters, the communist activists, and the Islamist activists. The "homeland," the struggle, and the past are carved by men on women's bodies, and women often use memory work to resist these processes. The memory work of women engaged in and with conflicts is and will be a crucial element in post-conflict politics. The politics of memory is, indeed, a gendered politics.

One of the goals of this essay was to demonstrate that, to resolve conflicts, we need to recognize that there may be entirely different cognitive views of what has happened, acknowledge those conflicting stories, validate them as authentic to the storyteller and his/her followers, and try to move on. But not move on with amnesia.

NOTES

Some of the material for this essay is forthcoming from Khartoum University Press as "Gendering the Politics of Memory: Women, Identity, and Conflict in Sudan," in *Anthropology in the Sudan: Past, Present and Future*, edited by Munzoul Assal et al., commemorating fifty years of anthropology as a department. Notes from an earlier version of this paper were published in Khartoum in Arabic (Hale 2008). The epigraph is by E. Valentine Daniel, from a draft of his ethno-historical narrative poem, "The Coolie," which is a portion of a larger, epic story of coolies in Sri Lanka. Lecture/Reading at the International Institute, University of California, Los Angeles, 12 February 2008.

1. I am specifically using the term "memory work" to refer to the method of collecting interlocutors' memories through oral histories, dialogues, and interviews.

2. For the purposes of this essay I am categorizing Eritrea as a part of North Africa.

3. Readers will recognize a play on a quote from Karl Marx and Friedrich Engels, *The Communist Manifesto;* Marshall Berman, *All That Is Solid Melts into Air;* and Chinua Achebe, *Things Fall Apart.*

4. Slyomovics makes this point most strongly in chapter 1 when she discusses "Photographing Loss," (1998, 10–14). She says that "what is most important about the pointing finger of the Palestinian peasant within the photographic frame is that the figure need not be physically present and observable in any specific image placed before the reader's eyes" (13). "Thus this image is there when it is not there" (14).

5. See Slyomovics (1998), especially chapter 1, "Memory of Place."

6. Consider other famous attempts at developing *collective memory:* (1) The observance of the Palestinian *nakba* (the 1948 catastrophe, disaster), which was celebrated in 2008 by Israelis as the 60th Anniversary of the formation of their land, their nation; while Palestinians commemorated the disaster as a disaster, Israelis celebrated the event as glorious. Each side is trying to convince the world of the righteousness of their cause by translating the occasion in particular ways; (2) The Armenian–Turkish dispute over what the Armenians refer to as "genocide" while the Turks claim both were victims of pogroms carried out against each other, which has amounted to two entirely different versions of history; (3) The Nazi Holocaust: denied by some, it has been turned into an intellectual and media industry by others; (4) Many others of our more recent calamities—Cambodia, Bosnia, Rwanda, South Sudan, the Nuba Mountains, the Beja (of eastern Sudan), and Darfur—perhaps including the Nubian relocations with the building of the High Dam at Aswan and other projects that are slowly removing Nubian history and culture as Nubians would like to remember it.

7. Stoler and Strassler (2000, 68) are making reference to Rosaldo (1985).

8. Stoler and Strassler (2000) are again citing Rosaldo (1985).

9. Stoler and Strassler (2000, 68), citing Friedrich Nietzsche (1996 [1874]).

10. I can mention a number of films and television series that foreground a white hero against a black South African backdrop, such as *Gandhi, A Passage to India, Sheltering Sky, The English Patient, Jewel in the Crown, Ashes and Dust, Out of Africa,* and a group of films about South Africa, e.g., films about Ruth First, Donald Woods, and others.

11. Tamanoi (2009, 18) is quoting Rubie Watson (1994, 8).

12. Slyomovics (1998, 208) here is using ideas from Fredric Jameson and Partha Chatterjee.

13. My fieldwork in Sudan has spanned decades: 1961–1964; 1966; 1971–1972; 1973–1975; 1981; 1988; and scattered visits from 2004–2012. In the interstices of these years, from 1989–2004, when I was unable to go to Sudan for political reasons, I did research with Sudanese diasporan communities in Asmara, Eritrea; Cairo, Egypt; London, England; Kampala, Uganda; and to some extent in the U.S. Fieldwork in Eritrea was for two summers in 1994 and 1996 and a briefer two-week period in 1999.

14. Of course, some women were also arrested, but their stories are another trope and are outside the scope of this paper.

8.

REJECTING AUTHENTICITY IN THE DESERT LANDSCAPES OF THE MODERN MIDDLE EAST: DEVELOPMENT PROCESSES IN THE JIDDAT IL-HARASIIS, OMAN

Dawn Chatty

Nomads throughout the Middle East have been viewed through a lens of romantic attachment or, latterly, uncomfortable disdain and disparagement. For decades they have been subjected to state-sponsored as well as international settlement efforts in the name of modernity, progress, and more recently environmental protection. Peoples who move have challenged the neocolonial projects of the League of Nations Mandate era as well as the post–World War II independent nation by the sheer fact of their mobility. Movement, as Ernest Gellner pointed out, made these peoples "marginal" to the state, in that they could move out of the orbit of state control (Gellner 1969; also see Scott 2009). Despite efforts by central authorities to control and extend authority over these peoples, a political order outside the state continues to characterize nomads of the Middle East, with their tribal, kin-based social organization.

The Harasiis nomadic pastoral tribe have been, for centuries, the sole human inhabitants of the central desert of Oman. In the 1930s, the reigning sovereign named this desert the Jiddat il-Harasiis in recognition of the tribe's connection with the land. This remote tribe, one of six in the region who continue to speak South Arabian languages predating Arabic, is organized around a subsistence economy based on the raising of camels and goats. Mobility over the vast and largely inhospitable rock and gravel plain of the Jiddat il-Harasiis has been the principle feature of their livelihood, expressed primarily through camel transport and more recently through trucks. The authenticity of their attachment to this region is intimately tied to the traditional distinction in Islamic historiography between *bedu* in the deserts and *hadar* in the towns and cities. Recent decades in the Sultanate of Oman, however, have seen increasing efforts by government, international conservation agencies, and multinational extractive industries to redescribe and classify this land as *terra nullius* (empty of people). Efforts to move the Harasiis out of their encampments, to settle them in government housing, and to turn them into cheap day laborers all point to the rejection of these peoples' claims of belonging to the landscapes of the desert. This paper examines these developmental processes, both national and international, and explores the ways in which the Harasiis have responded by becoming more mobile and adapting their living and herding arrangements as well as by generally becoming unresponsive to state development efforts. A small element of the Harasiis as well as other tribal groups in southeastern Arabia have begun to reject the confines of the state and instead assert their transnational identity across international borders with Saudi Arabia and the United Arab Emirates, where their authenticity as *bedu* is generally recognized.

Authenticity, Landscape, and Identity

The desert-dwelling inhabitants of the Oman, organized in tribes, are recognized as *bedu*, while tribes and extended families in the mountain and coastal settlements of the country are regarded as *hadar*.[1] This *bedu/hadar* distinction has deep roots in Muslim history and historiography (cf. Ibn Khaldûn 1958). In the medieval period Arab writers saw the significant forms of social categories in the dichotomy between the city and the country; or between civilization and its presumed absence. From the perspective of the settled urban historian, the pinnacle of civilization was the city with its government, places of worship, schools, and markets. The city and town dweller was *hadari*. The other extreme, the *badia* (desert), was defined by its lack of *hadar* or civilization and was represented by the social category of *badawi* or *bedu*. The latter were mainly the desert dwellers, the nomadic pastoral camel and sheep herders. The different landscapes of the *bedu* and *hadar* had important cultural and social dimensions in the understanding of human activity.[2] The urban and settled notion of human life versus the rural and nomadic became, over time, a deeply ingrained idealization of social categories; these are, however, no longer clearly defined or distinguished. Furthermore, though the term *hadar/hadari* is hardly referred to any longer, the term *bedu* remains in contemporary use. For the *bedu* such self-identification is a statement of tribal identity and solidarity as well as of attachment to the desert landscape, which is a physical background and social and cultural foreground. This desert is constantly shaped and reshaped by social processes and interactions with the physical environment; it is a physical space and a sociocultural place as well as a form of ambience and a perceptual surround (Hirsch and O'Hanlon 1995). However, when non-*bedu* use the term, particularly contemporary Omani government officials and international civil servants, it is often a statement of contempt, highlighting the presumed backwardness and primitiveness of this social category with no reference to the desert landscape.[3] In general, *bedu* tribes and tribal views of events are relegated to the "moral margins" by settled bureaucrats, government officials, and international experts (Dresch 1989).

Nationalism and identity are two concepts which are at the heart of the processes described above. The Sultanate of Oman had its modern "birth" in 1970 after a "near-bloodless" palace coup brought the Sultan Qaboos to the throne. From that moment the Sultan and his advisors have struggled to create the imagined political community of a unified nation (see Anderson 1983). The first few decades after the birth of this new nation saw campaigns to attract educated and professional Omanis in exile to return to create the modern state (Peterson 1978). This chapter posits that once these outsiders and expatriates had integrated and transformed themselves into "insiders," they set about creating an "imagined" nation which was homogenous and modern. Furthermore, in order to promote the development of its extractive industries, the desert interior was declared *terra nullius*, state land, empty of land claims. Thus the authentic inhabitants in the "background landscapes" such as the deserts (Hirsch and O'Hanlon 1995) became the "outsiders." The tension between the outsider "traditions" and new insider "modernities" appears to be resolved in a representation that encapsulates the political and cultural fiction of a unified nation at the expense of the *bedu* tribes of the interior deserts; *bedu* claims to authenticity are thus increasingly rejected or cast aside as insignificant.

Identity, national or otherwise, is closely tied to language, and the spoken word often becomes an iconic marker of national belonging. The Omani national language, in this case Arabic, is not a neutral tool of communication. It represents the language of the "hegemonic" ethnic group in power, the Ibadi of Oman, rather than the once preferred language, Swahili, of many of the returning expatriate Omanis from Zanzibar and East Africa. The gradual emergence of Arabic as the sole formal language of government in the modern state, replacing Swahili, Baluchi, Urdu, and English is a reflection of the consolidation of power in one ethnic group (Bloch 1971). Many minority groups in exile reinvest in their "native" language to an extent never practiced prior to leaving their homeland or places of origin (see Goody 1986; Chatty 2010a). In other cases, traditional, local languages are part of a specific cultural setting and therefore have difficulty surviving independently from the maintenance of the social ties and networks, the resources and patterns of allocation, and the modes of production on which such settings depend (Crawhill 1999). In Oman both linguistic realities coexist. Some expatriate minorities manage to maintain their traditional languages after return from exile, while other minorities *in situ* struggle to keep their languages alive.

Currently, in addition to the official language of Arabic, Swahili, Urdi, and Farsi, as well as eight local and, perhaps, aboriginal languages are also spoken in the country. They are Bathari, Harsusi, Hobyot, Jibbali, Khojki, Kumzari, Mahri, and Zidgali. Of these, five are unique South Arabian languages spoken in Oman's desert—Bathari, Hobyot, Jibbali, Mahri, and Harsusi.[4] As a cultural heritage, these languages and their oral traditions are not formally appreciated in the country. Unlike Jordan, for example, where the Jordanian Commission for Oral and Intangible Cultural Heritage has presented its *bedu* oral traditions and culture in the regions of Petra and Wadi Rum to UNESCO for formal recognition as part of the world's Intangible Cultural Heritage, Oman officials remain mute about the country's linguistic treasures (UNESCO 2009).

Historical Background

Like so many states of the Middle East, Oman has been inhabited by successive waves of peoples. Settlement in Oman from the desert fringe came from two directions: one along the southern coast of Arabia from Yemen, and the other through the northern gateway of Al-Buraymi. The northern part of Oman is distinctly influenced by the northern migrations via Al-Buraymi and is clearly Arab, Muslim, and tribal. The southern region, Dhofar, also Muslim and tribal, has much closer cultural ties with Yemen and is home to a number of Himyaritic or South Arabian language speakers. These pastoral tribes in the middle of the country are the most remote and marginal peoples in Oman physically; culturally they form distinct heterogeneous groups seemingly at odds with contemporary government efforts to create a unified state. Other migrations into Oman include the Baluch and Persian from southwest Asia, African and Zanzibari from the east coast of Africa, and Hydrabadis from the Indian subcontinent. The latter have settled in the coastal regions and the mountain valleys, mainly of the north of the country (for greater detail of ethnic composition see Peters et al. 2004a, 2004b).

Until 1970, the Sultanate of Oman could justifiably be described as the "Tibet of Arabia" (Eickelman 1989), so complete was its isolation from the rest of the world. This remoteness and sense of separateness of the state was largely created during the long reign of Sultan Said Al Said (1932–1970). It was a time when many urban Omanis fled the country seeking education and livelihood opportunities. During this period the tribes of the desert interior maintained their largely subsistence livelihoods including local trade and barter with coastal settlements. What little transformation took place along the coastal and mountain settlements in the north of the country had little, if any, impact on the desert tribes.

The Al Bu Said Dynasty came to power in 1744 as a result of an election among the Ibadi constituency of the time.[5] This dynasty was able to maintain its hold on power both in the interior of the country as well as abroad (variously in Zanzibar and southwest Asia) for a several generations, with occasional swings in authority and power due to some short-lived rebellions and aborted insurrections.[6] British interests were established in 1798 when Sayed Sultan bin Ahmed agreed in a treaty with a representative of the East India Company to position the country always with Great Britain in "international relations." This marked a formal relationship of indirect influence if not rule by the British. In the mid-nineteenth century a rapid decline in Al Bu Said fortunes ensued and British interests in Oman came to be directed—until Indian independence in 1947—from Delhi rather than from Whitehall.

For the whole of the twentieth century and into the twenty-first, Oman has had four rulers: Faysal (1888–1913), Taymur (1913–1932), Said (1932–1970), and Qaboos (1970 to the present). All four rulers owed their position to British support in one way or another. Although Faysal was not prepared for leadership by the British through any form of specialized education, his peaceful accession to the throne was facilitated by the British, who let it be known that they would not support any competing claims. During Taymur's reign, growing unrest in the interior by the followers of the resurgent Imamate culminated in the British-brokered Treaty of Seeb in 1920. This treaty marked the *de facto* division of Oman into a proto-autonomous interior under the spiritual and religious leadership of an Ibadi Imam and a coastal strip under the secular rule of the Sultan.[7] By the time Said was formally recognized as the ruler of Oman in 1932, the 21-year-old inherited a country riddled with financial difficulties and was hardly able to create any sources of income—outside of levying customs and issuing postage stamps—to repay the mounting debt owed to the British government.

Oil exploration commenced in Oman during the 1930s, and a number of oil companies began making small payments to Sultan Said in order to maintain their rights to exploration. In the central desert of Oman, both the Harasiis and the Jeneba nomadic pastoral tribes were affected by these activities. The Jeneba tribe, closely watching oil exploration in the area, laid claim to the Jiddat-il-Harasiis, maintaining it was their land which they merely permitted the Harasiis to occupy. Sultan Said dismissed the Jeneba claim. Wilkinson suggests that the Sultan's true motive in coming down on the side of the Harasiis was his confidence that the Harasiis had no relationship with the Ibadi Imam and thus potentially were allies in his claim to future oil rights in the central desert interior (Wilkinson 1987).

Oil activity in Oman stopped during World War II at time when Said set out to cooperate completely with the British. British Royal Air Force (RAF) installations were set up throughout the parts of Oman which he controlled and, in return, he received support in modernizing the small armed forces, which, again, the British had established in the country with a contingent imported from Baluchistan in 1921 (Peterson 1978).

In the early 1950s oil activity resumed and pastoral tribes in the north of the country, bordering on areas under the control of the Ibadi Imam, were increasingly drawn into the growing armed conflict between the Sultan on the coast and the Ibadi Imam in the interior.[8] In 1952 the Iman led a rebellion which spilled over into a contestation over ownership of any oil finds by petroleum company exploration teams. In 1959 a combined assault by the Sultan's forces and those of the British on the Jebel Akhdar defeated the Ibadi Imam and his rebels. The success of that campaign heralded a period of genuinely close cooperation with British authorities. Perhaps in recognition of the vital role these forces played in consolidating his authority over the entire country, the Sultan willingly approved significant military expenditure after 1967 when oil revenues began to flow into his coffers. As for other expenditures, Said remained cautious, perpetually searching for a way to gradually develop the country without "modernizing" it.

Ever fearful that "his people" were not ready to move into the twentieth century, Sultan Said prohibited the general importation of cars and severely restricted the enrolment of boys in schools (girls were never enrolled). He took a direct interest in all matters regarding changes to long-held "traditions." He banned sunglasses and flashlights and insisted that the gates of the capital of

Muscat be closed at sunset. Those caught outside had to wait until the next morning to enter the town. He permitted only three schools to operate over the entire country, admitting a total of 100 boys a year, whom he personally chose. Yet Sultan Said himself was cultured and cosmopolitan. Throughout the 1950s and 60s he made annual trips to the United Kingdom, generally in the summer.

In 1964, oil was discovered in the central desert of Oman, and by 1967 it began to be exported. Projected revenues jumped dramatically, but even then Said remained cautious about spending money he did not yet have. Thus, although he commissioned plans for a new port at Muscat and a hospital in Ibri among other projects, he took his time giving the go-ahead to implement these works, waiting first to accumulate the cash reserves to pay for them. Until his overthrow by his son, Qaboos, Said continued to act and behave with the shrewdness and calculation of someone always on the edge of financial ruin.

Omanis had been fleeing the country for decades during Said's reign due to economic hardship, political oppression, and lack of educational opportunities. By the summer of 1970, British forces quietly instigated and supported a coup d'état by Qaboos. After the palace coup, the new Sultan prioritized the modernization and development of his country. Qaboos embraced "progress" wholeheartedly and set about commissioning schools, clinics, hospitals, roads, and other infrastructural development. Unlike that of many of the states of the Gulf, Oman's indigenous population was relatively large and markedly heterogeneous. In the north of the country it included an elite urban merchant class with strong cultural ties and trade links with India and the coast of East Africa. Along the coast, subsistence fishing settlements were common, and in the mountains and intervening valleys, terraced farming communities survived by maintaining ancient systems of water collection and distribution (Wilkinson 1977). The towns of the interior of the country were the centers of local and regional trade as well as of religious learning. These settlements mirrored Oman's long history of successful colonial empire and incorporated East African, Baluchi, Persian, and Indian elements into the dominant culture.

Once he had established his reign, Sultan Qaboos reached out to all Omanis living abroad and encouraged them to return to the country as quickly as possible. This they did in large numbers from Bombay, Mombasa, Liverpool and other Western centers. Along with this returning "citizenry" came skilled European (particularly British) and South Asian expatriate workers to help build a government infrastructure nearly from scratch. The armed forces, the police force, the internal security service, the civil service, and government ministries of health, education, social affairs and labor, agriculture and fisheries, water and electricity, communications and roads, among others, were rapidly set up. The trappings of a modern state were put into place almost overnight. Thousands of miles of roads were tarmacked, and Muscat was connected for the first time by a modern road network to Salalah. The social and economic transformation of the coastal areas and the mountains behind in both the north and the south of the country, funded mainly by petroleum extracted from the central desert, was enormous. The same was not true for the interior desert areas of the country, nor for its nomadic pastoral peoples.

The Harasiis Tribe in Contemporary Oman

The Harasiis, the Wahiba, the Duru, and the Jeneba are the four main nomadic pastoral tribes in the central desert of Oman. The Wahiba tribe of about 7,000 people occupy the southern coast of Oman and the desert interior known as the Wahiba Sands. To the west of the Wahiba Sands live the Duru camel-raising tribe, numbering about 9,000. Spread out along much of Oman's southern coast and adjacent interior are the Jeneba, and their numbers are easily in excess of 12,000. To the south of the Duru and Wahiba are the Harasiis tribe. Moving over what was—until the 1950s—a vast, waterless plain of more than 42,000 square kilometres, the Harasiis are a "refuge" tribe. They are people, largely of Dhofari origin, who have been pushed over recent centuries into this most inhospitable core area of the central desert of Oman. They are the most remote and isolated of already marginal peoples. The region they inhabit separates north Oman from Dhofar. As such, the region has attracted individuals and groups expelled from their own tribes as punishment for major infractions of traditional codes of conduct and honor. The Harasiis tribe speaks a southern Arabian language related to Mahri, an indicator of their lack of contact and relative isolation, certainly in the past few centuries (Johnstone 1977). The tribe's usufruct, or right to access graze and browse found in the Jiddat il-Harasiis, was established in the 1930s when the Sultan and his political advisor, Bertram Thomas, decided to confer the name Jiddat il-Harasiis[9] upon the territory which had fallen to them essentially through the fact of their occupancy and the lack of desire by any other tribe to be there (Thomas 1938).

The Harasiis tribe clearly represent the most excluded element of the Omani peoples. The leadership of the tribe as a whole lies with the Bayt Aksit, whose ancestral forbear is acknowledged to have united the disparate units into one tribe in the middle of the nineteenth century. From about the mid-1930s the Harasiis tribal leader has made annual trips, generally to Salalah, in order to receive cash gifts—along with the other Omani tribal leaders—from the Sultan.

The tribe is small, numbering about 5,000 people. Although their claim to the Jiddat has been, on occasion, contested by other groups, no other tribe has actually attempted to move into this most desolate of landscapes that has few, if any, seasonal grasses, no natural water sources, and is unfit for human habitation during the scorching summer months. It was only with the oil activity of the 1950s that the fortunes of the Harasiis and their grazing lands on the Jiddat were transformed. In 1958 an exploratory party came to a point called Haima in the middle of the Jiddat il-Harasiis and sank a water well there to support its oil activity. Another well was sunk at a point 70 kilometres toward the coast, called al-Ajaiz. These two wells were the first water sources on the Jiddat il-Harasiis, an area approximately the size of Scotland. Al-Ajaiz became something of a magnet attracting pastoral families to its well and its seasonal browse. The Haima well was not used to the same extent as that at Al Ajaiz, because the area surrounding Haima was a salt flat with very little graze or browse for the herds of camels and goats.

The traditional economy of the Harasiis was based on the raising of camels and goats by natural graze for the production of milk rather than meat. At the core of their way of life was migration determined by a combination of seasonal and ecological variables in the location of pasture and water. Survival of both herds and herders made movement from deficit to surplus areas vital. Households were, and are still, generally extended family units, the average family being composed of nine members. Generally three or four adults, of one degree of kinship or another, make up the household. On average a household keeps 100 goats, which are owned by and the responsibility of women and older girls, and twenty-five camels, which are owned by and the responsibility of men. Of these camels, five or six are generally kept near the homestead—these are the heavily pregnant or lactating ones. The remaining camels are left free to graze in the open desert. The whereabouts of these animals are very carefully monitored and an elaborate camel information exchange system operates among all the tribesmen. When they meet, tribesmen first exchange news about the conditions of pastures, then the whereabouts of various loose camels, and finally news items of various family members. Homesteads are generally moved a significant distance three or four times a year.[10]

Basic to the organization of all pastoral people is the existence of sedentary communities in adjacent areas and access to their agricultural products. For the Harasiis tribe, their trading towns have been along the northern desert foothills of the Sharqiyya, particularly Adam and Sinaw, as well as the southern town of Salalah. For the Harasiis, the relationship with the villages reinforced not a cash economy, but a subsistence one. Until the late 1970s, this economic interaction remained stable and unchanging among the Harasiis and extended no further than these border desert villages and towns.

Transforming and Contesting Authenticity

In the early months of 1980, I was offered an opportunity to join a small convoy of vehicles across the desert of Oman. The trip was to start in Salalah, the capital of Dhofar, the southern region of Oman, and to cross the deserts of Oman and end up in Muscat. It was not quite the retracing of the steps of the early twentieth century explorers Bertram Thomas (1930s) and Wilfred Thesiger (1940s), but it still felt a rare opportunity and unique adventure. The purpose of the journey was partially to track several lapsed tuberculosis patients from tribes in the Dhofari interior and, at the same time, to provide immunization vaccines to any children we came across from these communities. Halfway through our journey we came across a small group of nomadic pastoral Harasiis women and children preparing for a wedding. We took the opportunity to stop and to seek their permission to begin the course of immunization against some of the six World Health Organization (WHO) targeted childhood diseases (poliomyelitis, diphtheria, whooping cough, tetanus, measles, and rubella). "Why," we were asked, "did we want to do this?" Our answer was, "The Sultan of Oman wishes to see all Omanis immunized against these diseases." "Why," they continued, "should he want to do this for us?" We were initially at a loss for an answer, having assumed that the sense of belonging to one nation had reached these parts of the country. That did, in fact, develop over time; however, the tie to the desert landscape of the Jiddat, that social construction of belonging to that locale, was not undermined in the process.

The following year, I began a fourteen-year close association with this small nomadic pastoral tribe. My role was to assist the government of Oman in extending social services to this remote community. A Royal Decree had been issued indicating that government services were to be extended into the interior desert "without forcing its migratory people to settle." A policy had been formulated by the Sultan which needed to move through a descending hierarchy of bureaucracy and emerge as a set of discretionary decisions made locally and on the ground.[11] Sultan Qaboos had encouraged the government ministries to push "development" forward into the remote interior of the country to offer its people the same services which the government had extended to the rest of the country during the first ten years of his reign. His perception of the desert landscape as a "created" physical, social, and cultural environment inhabited by nomadic pastoralists was undoubtedly informed by his own mother's origins as a Qara tribeswoman in Dhofar. Yet prior to this, in the 1970s, a British white paper—recognizing the significance of oil discoveries in the region—had encouraged Sultan Qaboos to declare the central deserts a land legally empty of people. These two contradictory positions at the highest level of authority in the country have since resulted in a contestation over identity and landscape.

Over a two-year period, as a "Technical Assistance Expert" with the United Nations Development Programme (UNDP), and with the help of two Peace Corps volunteers, I was allowed by the Minister of Health and the Minister of Education to set up both mobile and sedentary health services as well as a weekly boarding school for boys with day-enrolment for girls (Chatty 2006). Other government services with a relevance to these mobile pastoralists were more difficult to organize. It seemed that the contradictory "hilltop" policy formulations of the Sultan had been manipulated and interpreted by the descending bureaucratic hierarchy to create a landscape in the desert which attempted to reproduce the settled, "civilized" landscapes they were familiar with in the coastal and mountain valley settlements. For example, opening government offices in the remote tribal center of Haima and staffing them with Omani government employees generally meant borrowing all the rules and regulations of a civil service developed around *hadari,* or settled, needs. Thus government welfare benefits became possible for unmarried, widowed, and divorced women, the handicapped and disabled. But to the surprise of the Harasiis community, elderly widowers or bachelors with no family to support them were excluded from government support.[12]

Shelter and housing were particularly problematic, as government officials and ministers were unable or unwilling to conceive of the desert as being previously occupied by temporary camps; they set about creating specific permanent housing settlements. The urban concepts of settled space ruled supreme. The reality of the widespread dispersal of small, impermanent household camps over the 40,000 square kilometres of the Jiddat was inconceivable to government bureaucrats, whatever the Royal Decrees might have suggested. Hence, our 1982, highly successful UNDP program of canvas tent distribution among the Harasiis households met with obstruction and eventually failure when we tried to set it up as a recurrent government program. In an interview with the Minster of Housing in Muscat in 1984 to plead for a continuation of the tent distribution program,

I was told that the Ministry had to be seen to be doing something useful in the interior and tents were not useful or progressive. The Minister added that he needed to show that the Ministry was active and that could only be done with permanent "mortar and cement"; canvas cloth was temporary and undignified. His conclusion was that the government had to build cement housing units for twenty to thirty British-designed two-story townhouses; no matter that such architectural space was more suitable to an English suburb than an Arabian desert.[13] The units were built in 1985 and stood empty for more than a decade. The general lack of cooperation among the Harasiis slowly gave way to limited and begrudging use by some who used the structures to shelter Harasiis goat herds, or hired them out to expatriate laborers imported by local traders and oil company subcontractors. Nonetheless, the government civil servant's outsider view of the desert landscape became more powerful than that of the insider inhabitant.

The distribution of potable water was another area of critical concern to the Harasiis tribe that was not fully understood by a government familiar with their own well-established rules of auctioning time for agricultural watering (see Wilkinson 1977). In the mid-1980s, Harasiis tribal elders petitioned the government to finance a carefully constructed decentralized plan to distribute water to households spread out over the Jiddat il-Harasiis based on a horizontal organization in which all seven of the tribe's lineages were involved. These petitions reached mid-level government bureaucrats who found the demands unfathomable. Much easier, they felt, to extend the system which worked in Oman's towns and villages; to hand over the keys to the water tanker trucks to the tribal leaders recognized by the government and the national oil company, Petroleum Development Oman (PDO). For many years thereafter, water distribution rested in the hands of a few powerful individuals who were cultivating ties with the multinational oil companies and urban leadership rather than with an egalitarian but united syndicate, as the tribal elders had hoped for.

Even the request for agricultural extension—a national program widespread along the coast and in the interior towns of the country and well funded by various international agencies such as USAID and Petroleum Development Oman (known as the PDO), the national oil company—failed to be transferred to the desert interior. In this case, it was the official status of *terra nullius* which compromised Harasiis efforts to access development assistance. Despite numerous requests for assistance from Harasiis tribal elders to government to help them improve breeding stock and experiment in growing salt-resistant fodder, there was no government response. Those in power were ignorant of and disinterested in tribal subsistence and its potential for marketing. Government livestock extension programs in the country were—and continue to be—restricted to the coast and interior towns.[14]

For decades the PDO was perceived locally as the government in the desert. Its exploration activities had resulted in three water wells being left open and maintained for the use of the local Harasiis, a service which was widely appreciated. As the major employer in the region—albeit generally for unskilled and short-term work—it had a grasp of the social makeup and organization of these nomadic pastoralists. Thus, when the international demand for greater social responsibility resulted in the requirement that environmental and social impact assessments be conducted prior to any further oil extraction in the Central Desert of Oman, much could have been expected with regards to the complex nature of the Jiddat "landscape." However, in numerous conversations with local and expatriate petroleum engineers, a technical view of place emerged; the desert in their opinion was a landscape full of promising mineral resources [gas and oil] and devoid of people. These company engineers maintained that people emerged opportunistically from other regions whenever the oil company set up camp.[15] This particular representation of the desert was mirrored in the expert reports commissioned by the oil companies regarding social impact assessments. As late as 2006, Occidental Petroleum carried out a preliminary environmental impact assessment of an important tribal grazing area, Wadi Mukhaizana (Fucik 2006). The "findings" of that report was that the area was devoid of people and thus no social impact assessment was necessary.

Although Mukhaizana may have been physically empty of people at the time of the brief visit of the European consultant, the absence of people and herds at that moment was related more to the lack of rain in that season than a lack of tribal use rights to the Wadi. Only five years earlier the largest oil company in Oman had commissioned a social impact assessment of the same Wadi and found significant numbers of authentic local Harasiis there (Rae and Chatty 2001). Those findings were ignored, and Occidental has since developed a spaghetti junction of oil and gas infrastructure in the Wadi, devastating the grazing area for a large number of Harasiis families. Their rights to this land have been denied and no adequate compensation or restitution has been considered. Overall, the major oil companies in the central desert of Oman take the government view that these concession areas are *terra nullius* (Gilbert 2007). They lay their pipelines across important tribal migration routes, causing disruption if not obstruction for Harasiis herders trying to transport or move their herds from one grazing area to another.[16] A slow and gradual process of dislocation is taking place based on the oil companies' unwillingness to recognize the authenticity of the Harasiis seasonal presence on their traditional grazing lands. This is followed by a process of displacement which is gradually forcing some Harasiis off their lands altogether and into shabby and crowded government low-cost housing at Haima.

Furthermore, conservationists—both national and international—have regarded the central desert of Oman as land empty of people as well. Their immediate and closer contact with the local people is at odds with the fiction of *terra nullius,* and they feel they must ignore the presence and authenticity of its local human inhabitants. Conservationists working in Oman generally do regard the desert as a constructed landscape, but one shaped by plants and animals, not people. Their concern is to restore a balance to this landscape by first returning to it an animal that had been hunted to extinction in the 1970s.

Planned in the late 1970s, the international flagship conservation effort known as the Arabian Oryx Reintroduction Project was set up and put into effect in the Jiddat il-Harasiis in 1980. This process was envisaged from abroad and created in the offices of His Majesty, the Sultan's Advisor for the Environment without any consultation with the local Harasiis tribesmen in the desert. Between 1980 and 1996, 450 Arabian oryx were either returned to "the wild" or were born in the Jiddat il-Harasiis with Harsusi males hired to track them. In 1994, Oman succeeded in getting this conservation project recognized formally as the UNESCO World Heritage Arabian Oryx Sanctuary. But ongoing and constant friction between the Western managers of the conservation project and the local Harasiis tribesmen regarding their "rights" to graze their domestic herds in large parts of their territory—then officially a UNESCO nature reserve—eventually resulted in a distancing from the project by the Harasiis and general lack of cooperation for the conservation project.

Two representations of the desert landscape came to a head: a Western conservation protectionist vision of a pristine landscape of plants and animals, and a local tribal vision of a landscape where there were sets of cultural and historical concepts relating people and domestic animals to desert spaces and places. When between 1996 and 1998 poaching and illegal capture of the oryx by rival tribes resulted in the loss of more than 350 animals, the Harasiis could do little to stop this downward spiral. Other tribes were actively acting out their disaffection. For the Harasiis, their youth had become alienated, and the elders were no longer interested in the transformed landscape in the part of their traditional territory which had been taken from them without their consent. In 2007, the Arabian Oryx Sanctuary became the first World Heritage site ever to be deleted from the UNESCO list of World Heritage Sites. The justification for this unprecedented step was the rapid decline in oryx numbers (from 450 to 65) and the supposed degradation of its grazing area.

Even place names have not been immune to this contemporary move to homogenize the diverse social and cultural landscapes of the modern Omani state. Throughout the country place names that reflect a tribal origin are being changed by civil servants somewhere in a mid-level hierarchy in the public authority responsible for maps and map names. The Wahiba Sands (of the Wahiba tribe) are now officially being labeled as the Eastern Sands. Attempts to drop the name Harasiis from the Jiddat il-Harasiis are also afoot. At a meeting of the Omani Historical Association in 2006, which I attended, it was clearly articulated that there were official government efforts to "neutralize" place names so that they did not reflect tribal affiliation. This pertained particularly to the deserts but did not extend to the interior mountainous valleys of the *hadar* such as the Wadi Beni Kharus or the Wadi Beni Auf. These interior valleys were closely associated with the large and often powerful families serving in government. It seems the neutralization of place names and their separation from peoples traditionally associated with them is only effectively being carried out in deserts where *bedu* live but not in the "civilized places" of the *hadar* interior towns, valleys, and cities. Such moves support the government's action of declaring all land state land and declaring Oman's deserts terra nullius, whereas Oman's coastal plain and mountain valleys are inhabited by *hadar* and there, the rights of traditional occupancy are respected.

Oman's six South Arabian languages were recognized in the early linguistic work of Tom Johnstone in the 1970s. The Diwan of the Royal Palace, on the command of the Sultan, commissioned Miranda Morris in 1980 to write lexicons and dictionaries of each of the six languages. A project of the Palace that lasted nearly thirty years, it was initiated as a "hilltop" policy formulation to recognize the unique contribution that these languages make to Omani and world culture. Despite this program—or perhaps because of the way the "hilltop" policy has not been translated effectively through the bureaucratic hierarchy into local practice—by 2009, five of these six languages—Bathari, Harsusi, Hobyot, Jibbali, and Mahri—were on the UNESCO List of endangered languages (UNESCO 2009). It is one thing to record the linguistic contribution of minority speech, it is another to encourage and promote its use. The Omani education system teaches only Arabic; there is no program to support traditional and local languages, much to the concern of native speakers. Rightly or wrongly, Omani bureaucrats have not acted on the Sultan's interest in the authentic languages of the country; instead they have interpreted the Sultan's wish to see a homogenized Omani national identity requiring all Omanis to speak Arabic. The six South Arabian languages of the country are being systematically disregarded, while world bodies seek to safeguard these unique elements of intangible cultural heritage.

Conclusion

The authenticity of the Harasiis and other nomadic pastoral tribes has been challenged by national governmental and multinational bodies which have their own views on the constructed landscapes of Oman. Recognizing the tensions that exist between the traditional and modern, as well as the *bedu* and the *hadar,* has meant that representations of landscapes are subject to the power of the hegemonic. Space and place are not resolved in a singular representation that encapsulates the political fiction of a unified state. There is no one absolute landscape, but rather a series of related and also contradictory perspectives. Omani policy formulations recognize elements of the authenticity of the Harasiis vision of their desert landscapes. But bureaucratic hierarchy prioritizes and puts into practice landscape perspectives quite contrary: *hadar* landscapes imposed upon *bedu* territories; multinational extractive industry's perspectives of landscapes of no human imprint, but replete with natural resources under the surface; and conservation landscapes of pristine import momentarily unbalanced by humans' disregard for the equilibrium of flora and fauna. These visions explain the lack of interest in the authenticity of Harasiis culture and language, in the lack of government interest in developing or promoting Harasiis livestock-raising economy; and the disinterest by oil companies in Harasiis claims to spaces and places they have inhabited at one time or another for centuries.

The Harasiis are increasingly becoming dislocated by the current prospecting and extractive activity of the oil and gas industry. Their restricted access to areas adjacent to the former Arabian Oryx Sanctuary has also impacted heavily on their sense of mobility and grazing rights. Contemporary government unwillingness to recognize the importance of mobility in their way of life is threatening their freedom of movement as families are increasingly finding themselves tied to government centers in order to access education, health, and welfare for the vulnerable, whether weak, young, or old.

For the first three decades of Oman's modern nation-building history (from 1970 to the present) a truly integrationist approach seemed to hold in which all Omanis from whatever background were called upon to work together to build a new "modern" nation. Now, however, with much of the building in place, an assimilationist outlook and approach seems to reign supreme, which is curiously out of step with global trends. The first few decades after World War II were marked by an assimilationist flavor to nation-state creation as characterized by the International Labour Organization (ILO) Resolution 107 of 1957 regarding the treatment of traditional and local peoples. After successful lobbying by interest groups and member countries from Latin America in particular this Resolution was replaced by an the integrationist ILO Resolution 169 in 1989 to reflect the transformed vision of nation-building held by most of its members. Yet Oman, in its recent failures to recognize the authenticity of its minority tribes in their desert landscapes, seems to have replaced an open-minded, ahead-of-its-time, integrationist vision of the development of the modern state with a backward-looking assimilationist perspective at the expense of the country's unique *bedu* heritage, landscape, and linguistic tradition.

One might ask how those who are rejected from the central construct of national identity and marginalized in the construction of special landscapes maintain their own special forms of collective authenticity (Lindholm 2008, 125). The Harasiis tribe appears to be addressing the challenges to its authenticity and its desert landscapes in several ways. Attachment to place and space is difficult to transform. Disassociation is even harder. Many families are responding by setting up part of the extended group in government housing, while still maintaining their mobile herds of goat and camels with hired shepherds from Baluchistan and the Indian subcontinent. During school breaks and national holidays, these family groups return then to the desert camps where their livestock are being held. Often the older generation of male Harsuusi remain with the herds and the hired help throughout the year. Younger Harsuusi men achieving success in trade and transport businesses and living in permanent accommodation are transforming part of their profits into building up herds of camels and goats with hired help; they visit these livestock camps regularly to "maintain their roots." Others with less means, living in government housing, stubbornly hold on to their cultural identity by keeping a few head of goat or camel in small fenced enclosures adjacent to their cement housing. A few have moved part of the extended family group across borders to the United Arab Emirates, where the national perception of the desert landscape and the place of the *bedu* more closely mirrors their own vision. These transnational families generally maintain their herds in their traditional desert landscapes of Oman. For the Harasiis, identity and authenticity are tied to the desert landscape that includes people, livestock, and wildlife. And although mobility is important, it is not the only defining feature of their self-perception and identity. Although some Western images of an "authentic primitivism" have begun to creep into government discourse—viewing pastoralists who no longer migrate with their animals, like some Harasiis, as somehow no longer authentic—the Harasiis themselves do not make such distinctions (Lindholm 2008, 131).

These moves are not permanent, nor are the settlements static. The Harasiis continue to move back and forth across the borders of Oman. They continue to embrace their marginality in the Gellnerian sense and thus proclaim the continued importance—to them—of a political and social order outside the state. In Abu Dhabi, their sense of "being *bedu*" is reinforced by other tribal groups also moving into these created desert landscapes from Saudi Arabia, Qatar, and Oman. Furthermore, mass education and mass communications (Eickelman 1992) also reinforce their sense of authenticity.[17] The United Arab Emirates national identity is closely tied with both the *bedu* in the interior and the *hadar* merchants in the coastal towns. Here several representations of landscapes encapsulate the imagined state including that of the *hadar* and that of the *bedu*. As with the Kingdom of Jordan (see Layne 1994; Shryock 1995) *bedu* culture and its role in the development of the notion of national identity is important in the UAE. Unfortunately this is not, at present, the case for Oman. There seems to be in Oman no recognition, yet, that assimilating traditional or aboriginal people is not the way to build a strong country (Blackburn 2007). Recognition of the tribes and their authenticity in the desert of Oman would not radically pluralize Oman nor negatively impact on state-building processes. It would instead be a step in the celebration of the unique character and diversity of the Oman nation and its many social and cultural landscapes.

NOTES

1. The term *bedouin* is a French language derivative of the Arabic *badia,* meaning the semi-arid steppe or desert.

2. Landscapes are complex phenomena. In addition to the physical features of geography, there is a widely accepted contemporary understanding that landscapes reflect human activity and are imbued with cultural values. Landscapes combine notions of time and space as well as political and social constructs. They evolve over time, are changed through human activity, and acquire many layers of sometimes contested meanings and versions of reality. Connections with landscapes form part of cultural and political identity; people feel they belong to certain places or regions (Jackson 1984; Aplin 2007). People form meaningful relationships with the locales they occupy and thus transform these

spaces into places. Hirsch and O'Hanlon suggest that landscape in an anthropological sense has two meanings, one as a framing device used "objectively" to bring people into view, the other as a social construct to refer to the meanings people impute to their surroundings (1995, 1).

3. Similar associations are made in other regions where colonial or settler land rights are prioritized over aboriginal ones. Cerwonka considers the way in which Aboriginal land rights in Australia were wiped away by the settler establishment using the legal fiction of *terra nullius* to declare the land empty; this was accompanied by narratives of aboriginal primitiveness and ignorance (2004).

4. A sixth South Arabian language found in Oman, Socotri, is not on the UNESCO list of endangered languages.

5. Ibadi Islam has a long history in Oman. The Ibadi sect of Islam had its origins in Basra at the end of the seventh century when opposition emerged to the transfer of leadership from Ali, the son-in-law of the Prophet Mohammad, to the Umayyad dynasty in Damascus. One of the founders of the sect was the Omani Abd Allah bin Ibad Al Murri al Tamimi. Ibadism today is found in Oman and in pockets in North Africa.

6. Until late in eighteenth century, Oman was ruled by an Ibadi Imam and the state was called an Imamate. However in 1792, in the Compact of Barka, Sultan bin Ahmad was recognized as the secular ruler of Muscat (and the coastal areas), while his brother Said was allowed to keep the office of Imam in the interior of the country (Wilkinson 1972).

7. The combined entity of the "Sultanate of Muscat and Oman" was to emerge out of this treaty and would remain welded together for three uneasy decades. Sultan Said's determination to unify the country under his rule alone resulted in considerable debate at the United Nations. In August 1959, British aggression against the "independent Imamate of Oman" was raised at the Security Council. The "question" of Oman and its contested leadership was included on the UN General Assembly agenda each year until 1971, when the Sultanate of Oman was admitted to the United Nations (Peterson 2007).

8. The long political and military struggle between Sultan Said and the Ibadi Imam over control of the interior of the country in the 1950s is studied in great detail by both Wilkinson (1987) and Peterson (2007).

9. The Jeneba tribe, it seems, protested that this territory belonged to it and the Harasiis were simply being accommodated there because they had no land of their own. The Sultan decided that if the Jeneba wanted to go and live in the region it could be renamed "Jiddat-il-Jeneba," but as long as the Harasiis were the sole occupiers of the Jiddat, it would carry their name (Thomas 1938).

10. In 1980 the Omani government cooperated with the United Nations to implement a two-year anthropological study and needs assessment of the Harasiis tribe. I led this project and as a result was able to promote the opening of a boarding school in 1982

for boys and later a special day school for girls. Increasingly over the past two decades Harasiis families have either camped near to Haima or have taken up residence in "low-cost" housing units on the edge of the center while the schools are in session.

11. Allen Rew has described the constraints regarding policy and practice in development as a pyramid landscape. There is the hilltop where policy is formulated, then the plateau where bureaucratic hierarchy prevails, and at the base a broad expanse of discretionary practice and local coping strategies (Rew, Fischer, et al. 2000).

12. Harasiis concepts of welfare and aid extended to elderly men and women alike. There was recognition that in the extreme environment of the Jiddat il-Harasiis, generation was as important as gender in determining need.

13. Interview with Minister of Housing, Ahmed Al Ghazali, 1984, conducting at the Ministry of Housing, Muscat.

14. The Sultan asked the oil company to set up an experimental farm using artesian water in the desert to show how the "desert could bloom." Rahab Farm was successfully set up near Marmul in the southern province of Oman and proceeded to sell its alfalfa and other grasses locally. But its goat breeding program, which fascinated the local tribes, was closed down without any effort made to introduce these animals into local herds.

15. These views are common globally in the dispute over petroleum exploration in areas of human habitation. In the Amazonian belt, where tribes have sought to remain in isolation, efforts to stop petroleum exploration have resulted in the denial of their existence. Recently the president of Peru, Alan Garcia, was quoted as saying "the figure of the jungle native" is a ruse to prevent oil exploration. Daniel Saba, former head of the state oil company in Peru, added more scornfully, "It is absurd to say there are uncontacted people when no one has seen them. So, who are these uncontacted tribes people are talking about" (Carroll 2009).

16. For a brief period of time in the early 1990s, one oil company did agree to bury any new pipelines at five-kilometer intervals across the desert to facilitate the requirement of the Harasiis and other nomadic pastoral tribes to move themselves and their animals around the desert floor.

17. The use of mobile phones and satellite phones rather than internet, however, suggests that greater affinity with the spoken word rather than the written word remains.

9.

NOTABLE FAMILIES AND CAPITALIST PARASITES IN EGYPT'S FORMER FREE ZONE: LAW, TRADE, AND UNCERTAINTY

Christine Hegel-Cantarella

Al-Sawy stationery store on Gumhurriya Street in Port Said is notable for its tall ceilings and dark wooden shelves stacked neatly with a vast assortment of office supplies.[1] The proprietor is a small man in his seventies dressed neatly in a suit, standing behind the glass display case, who thoughtfully regards each request before retrieving it for the customer and placing it alongside the register. Unlike most of the other stationary shops in town, this one caters to professionals and carries expensive leather desk sets, briefcases, and fine pens. Yet Al-Sawy also stocks the typical array of inexpensive pencil sharpeners, colorful notepads, two-hole punches and other office supplies, as well as a full range of booklets of commercial documents. These include booklets of *shīkāt shīkāt* (non-bank issued checks), *kambiyālāt* (bills of exchange or drafts), and *iyṣālāt amāna* (trust receipts). These single-copy (non-carbon) forms produced by small Egyptian printing companies are used to inscribe and secure various types of delayed transactions.

Among retailers in contemporary Port Said, from appliance shops in the central Arab quarter to variety stores that serve residents of government subsidized housing on the outskirts of the city, trust receipts are the principal technology by which many merchants guarantee retail credit. Likewise, wholesalers routinely employ trust receipts to guarantee the goods that retailers buy on credit. The medium in which transactional pledges are represented is not inconsequential. As Catherine Alexander notes, the efficacy of written agreements may derive from the binding properties of ritual and perceptions of efficacy more than from the potential legal consequences of breaking a bond (2001, 468). As such, my examination of trust receipts as a particular medium of pledge-making and guarantee is premised on the argument that their use in everyday transactions—together with discourses about it—is a barometer by which to examine socioeconomic shifts in Egypt since the 1970s. The deployment and avoidance of trust receipts point to contemporary anxieties surrounding business ethics and the uncertainty of informal and semiformal credit. Locals often point out that only people who cannot trust one another use trust receipts and that their ubiquity is an indication that Port Said is not the community it once was: the power of the "original" and notable families of Port Said has been usurped by the *nouveau riche*. In this way, the medium of pledge-making is a marker of how networked, trusting, and trustworthy are the transacting parties.

Although a commercial document recognized by law, the trust receipt as inscribed and deployed guarantees pledges in a more fluid socio-legal realm. Trust receipts likely came into common use in Egypt during the era of the Mixed Courts in the late nineteenth and early twentieth centuries, yet they are broadly classified among Egyptians as "customary documents" (*muḥarrarāt 'urfī*), in reference both to their paralegal status in the law and to the fact that it is common or typical ('ādī) to use them for transacting.[2] The latter sense of "customary" tacitly points to an array of practical knowledges about trust receipts, among them that they are inexpensive, provide a measure of guarantee for transactions large and small, and make a verbal agreement tangible without the complications of drawing up a contract. Although trust receipts are similar to contractual technologies because they document a private transaction and remain outside the purview of the law unless a legal claim is filed, they are typically inscribed as legal fictions, which has at least two contrary implications. First, the legal fiction creates additional space for verbal agreements through which trust is given, relationships intercede, and mercy may be granted in lieu of litigation. Second, the legal fiction introduces new risks because failure to deliver can result in a criminal misdemeanor rather than simply a civil suit. Despite the fact that the use of trust receipts carves out a potentially larger role for the state in private transactions than was common in the early twentieth century, literal and figurative spaces in documentation practices enable social logics to prevail. This duality is examined in order to consider how discourses about past and present

pledge-making can be more broadly construed as re-valuing continuity and belonging in the context of rapid social and economic transformation.

My focus on the modalities and meanings of secured credit diverges from
recent ethnographic work on law in the region, much of which centers on family
law and the tensions between legal, religious, and patriarchal authority. Yet my
analysis is indebted to studies of marriage contract and *mahr* negotiations that
illustrate how family members both claim and subvert legal rights and contest
legal authority in many registers (Antoun 1980; Mir-Hosseini 1993; Moors 1995,
1999; and Osanloo 2006). This scholarship substantiates the position that legal
reform aimed at expanding women's rights is often undermined by the gendered
landscape in which men and women seek restitution and carve out rights and
obligations. In so doing, it opens up inquiry into facets of identity beyond gender,
including class and status, which constrain and reshape other areas of law in practice, namely the law of obligations. Further, analyses of Muslim marriage contracts
highlight the need to attend to form, content, and inscription practices; doing so
brings into view the intersections between formal legal reform efforts and intimate
politics (Qurashi and Vogel 2008; Zulficar 2008). Likewise, my broader aim in
examining retail crediting in Port Said is to open up for consideration the ways
that the medium of pledge-making might be connected not only to inefficiencies
in legal institutions and judicial authority in an authoritarian political context, but
also to processes of constituting and rearticulating local status.

The development of law and politics in Egypt throughout the late nineteenth and early twentieth centuries has been the subject of debate among anthropologists, historians, and legal scholars (e.g., Asad 2001; Brown 1997; Cuno
1992; Fahmy 1999; Hill 1988). These debates have shaped recent attention to reform movements and rule of law that seek to address the role of lawyers and
judges in reshaping Egypt's political terrain (Moustafa 2003; Shalakany 2006).
This work points a way forward for anthropologists to examine how law constitutes and is constituted by Egyptians beyond the framework of legislation,
adjudication, and reform movements. In his praxiological studies of law in the
Middle East, legal sociologist Baudoin Dupret (2005, 2007) focuses on situated
interactions in courts and other legal institutional spaces in order to interrogate
the ways in which the state legally regulates its citizens. He finds that adjudication
and reporting (i.e., to the police) are processes of meaning-making for both legal
practitioners and litigants, which underlines the fact that the law's substantive
and procedural elements are not autonomous despite the claims of legal positiv-
ists. Rather, the contours, potentialities, and limitations of the law's authority are
wrought through specific engagements. I consider transactional engagements on

the periphery of law; in this space, parties constrain and redirect the law's gaze through the production of legal fictions and use the threat of legal recourse to carve out space for building trust and networks.

The Sons of Port Said and the Capitalist Parasites

In journalistic and historical accounts of contemporary Egypt, Port Said rarely figures into the narrative. Unexpectedly, when government protesters claimed Tahrir Square as the epicenter of resistance to the Mubarak government in the spring of 2011, Port Said was held up as a symbol of resistance.[3] This stands in contrast to the more typical depictions of the city as a site of gross consumerism and new money. Similarly, some Egyptians describe the city as a cosmopolitan port of historical importance, whereas others are inclined to dismiss it as a provincial backwater, populated by uneducated traders from the countryside. These contradictory characterizations encapsulate the changes that have occurred over the past century, which have in turn complicated "business as usual" in the city.

Port Said came into being with the Suez Canal. After obtaining a concession from the ruler, Said Pasha, French engineer Ferdinand de Lesseps designated this strip of coastline hemmed in by the Mediterranean Sea and the sprawling Lake Manzalah as the northern entrance to the canal and broke ground in April of 1859.[4] By the late nineteenth century, the Suez Canal had become an important trade route between east and west and the port and the nascent city provided a wealth of investment opportunities in wholesale import, ship repair and transport, and trade. The major beneficiaries were landed Egyptian families, urban bourgeoisie from Cairo and Alexandria, and European immigrants. This latter group comprised roughly a quarter of the local population at the turn of the twentieth century and controlled a significant portion of the local maritime and mercantile economies.

But Port Said's rise as a cosmopolitan port city began to wane with the nationalization of the Suez Canal and the ensuing Suez Crisis in 1956. This was the point at which foreigners began to depart from Port Said, Alexandria, Suez, and other port cities, as well as from Cairo.[5] Within ten years of nationalization, almost three quarters (68.5 percent) of the city's 282,876 residents had been born in Port Said. This suggests that by mid-century Port Said was an example of reverse cosmopolitanism, with a markedly homogenous Egyptian population.

Egyptian business leaders who hailed from the approximately one-dozen "notable" families absorbed the interests sold and abandoned by Europeans.

Their local influence was further cemented through political ventures and increasing expansion into professions like law and medicine. Among the notables were the Hamzas, whose patriarch, Abdel Malek, was a successful financier and prominent in the new Wafd party. The Lahetas originally made their fortune in coal, and the venerable Aly Bek Laheta represented Port Said in parliament in the 1920s. Mohammad Bek Sarhan and his son, El Sayeed Sarhan, were at the forefront of the import trade in Port Said and built on this foundation for generations to come. These families and others are acknowledged in local historical accounts of Port Said, both oral and written, as the prominent families who "made" Port Said (el-Kady 2004).

Investment Law 43 was introduced in 1974, the first of the Open Door (*infitah*) laws encouraging privatization and opening the country up to foreign investment after almost two decades of state-centered economic policy. One cannot underestimate the degree to which the promulgation of Law 43 and subsequent related laws changed the economic and social climate of Port Said. Included in the original Open Door legislation were the Free Zone laws, including Law 24/1976 and Law 12/1977, which established Port Said in its entirety as a Duty Free Zone.[6] This created a dramatic upswing in import/export, real estate and tourism, and trade, as well as some growth in industry and manufacturing. The Free Zone laws created an environment of opportunity that promoted significant emigration to Port Said from other parts of the country.[7] Construction was booming and some came as laborers, but many were drawn to petty trading in imported domestic goods, popular in part because it was a field that required little experience or capital to enter. As a result of the *infitah* policies, the population in Port Said almost doubled in the last quarter of the century, with most of the population growth occurring in the years immediately following the new laws.[8]

This shift marks the emergence of what locals term the "capitalist parasite" (*al-ṭufailī al-r'asmālīa*, or simply parasite, referencing both the rapid growth of privatization and those who flooded Port Said bent on financial gain.[9] The characterization of post–Free Zone migrants as capitalist parasites expresses at least two ideas. First, it connotes that the new migrants were perceived as taking up residence purely for economic gain rather than out of a sense of loyalty to the city. Second, it suggests a fear that the migrants intended to feed off the flush local economy rather than contribute meaningfully to its continued and long-term growth. The sense of a disrupted social order in the immediate *infitah* years has been noted by many observers, including Egyptian economist Galal Amin. He explains that after World War II and through the Nasser years, social mobility increased and brought about the sudden expansion of the middle class.

This abruptly shifted in the 1970s, he argues, when Egyptians turned away from traditional values toward market culture, a shift most clearly evidenced by the exponential rise in overseas labor migration (Amin 2000). As such, the imputed rise of the capitalist parasite is not specific to Port Said, although characterizations of the *nouveau riche* in Port Said are inflected by claims to status based on longevity in and family ties to a city that has seen dramatic change in the twentieth century.

Less an identifiable subset of the population, the capitalist parasite is more accurately seen as an allegorical figure upon which anxieties about rapid social change are fixed. Moreover, this figure provides a basis against which Port Saidians can reimagine their own status. A well-off retired importer named Aly noted a set of characteristics that other locals also attributed to these newcomers: they lacked education and urban sophistication, abandoned their skilled trades, and got rich quickly. The combination of these factors, he claimed, gave rise to new social ills including overpopulation, informal housing, crime and youth delinquency, and drug use. Further, the figure of the capitalist parasite is mapped onto the city; the *nouveau riche* are associated with a group of high-end apartment buildings near the canal known as *hayy al-budra* (the "powder" [cocaine] district) and other new housing near the sea. In contrast, Aly lives in an old building near the Arab Quarter that he inherited from his father, one of the markers by which he counts himself among the notable families of Port Said: "We're one of the old families, like the Sarhans and the Lahetas." Aly expressed a particularly vehement bitterness about the Free Zone and its impact, but his complaints exemplify the connection many locals draw between the Free Zone, the disruption of the social hierarchy, and new forms of ambiguity in "business as usual."

Discourses about the capitalist parasite represent concern about outsiders converging on the city and the implications of a shifting demography on the status quo. This concern often plays out in the realm of pledge-making related to retail and wholesale credit because of the mutability and risk inherent in delayed transactions. Risk can be offset by prior knowledge of a trading partner and the expectation that both partners desire future or ongoing transactions, but can be heightened when neither of these conditions is in place. Whether forms of contract and guarantee are truly different in the post–Free Zone era is difficult to assess. However, it is possible to identify some shifts in consumption and trade that have undoubtedly reshaped credit and how it is guaranteed.

In the first decade of the Free Zone, the volume of retail and wholesale trade was estimated to run into the millions (EGP) per quarter (al-Sarghany

2005). Commodities moved in and out of the city at such a rapid pace that strict quotas were instituted to curtail the resale of marked-up goods outside of Port Said. Because the city was filled with eager customers and trade was brisk, the credit cycle between wholesalers and retailers was short. According to local lore, petty traders would purchase goods on credit from wholesalers in the morning and pay them back by the evening, having made a profit to reinvest the following morning. Because most traders were making a profit, wholesalers had little concern about extending credit and required nothing more than a reasonable deposit and a promise to repay within a given timeframe.

Yet the brisk market was short-lived and had already begun to shift by the late 1980s and early 1990s due to structural adjustments mandated by the International Monetary Fund (IMF) and the World Bank. Structural adjustment policies gradually reversed most of the duty-free privileges local traders once enjoyed ('Awad 1999; Harik 1998), which meant that the same inexpensive imported goods could be purchased in Cairo just as easily as in Port Said.[10] As of 2009, all duty-free privileges, except those retained in special industrial areas to promote manufacturing and export, were rescinded.

The reversal of the duty-free privileges has made the retail market decidedly local, and this localization plays out in the field of credit as well. Egypt has in the past decades become an emerging market for international banks such as HSBC and Barclays. In 1999, Citibank entered into retail lending in Egypt by offering credit and debit cards, and by 2001 there were nearly 400,000 credit cards in the country. In turn, Egypt-based banks such as ABC bank (*bank al-mu'asasa al-'arabiya al-masriya*), Credit Agricole Egypt (*kredit agricole misr*), and Arab Bank (*al-bank al-'arabī*) have also been advertising the advantages of credit cards and initiating new account holders. One bank employee assured me that credit cards are widely available now in Egypt. Yet the industry has been slow to convince retailers to expand the range of services and goods that can be purchased on credit beyond the major hotels and high-end restaurants in Cairo and in tourist destinations.

Therefore, formal credit markets remain out of reach for average consumers.[11] As scholars have pointed out, rotating credit associations (*jāmi'āt*), a form of informal credit, are common in Egypt (Singerman 1995; Moheideen and Wright 2000). This is true of Port Said, and most of my interlocutors were currently or had been part of a temporary credit association. It is retail credit, however, that is ubiquitous in Port Said. Retail credit entails the extension of credit at the point of purchase from the store to the customer, who typically takes items in exchange for a deposit and an agreement to pay in full via installments. Retail credit may be seen as "semi-formal" in the sense that merchants typically structure crediting into their operation and keep records of some sort.[12] Moreover, retail credit differs from informal credit because it is extended hierarchically such that a more credit-worthy entity lends to a less credit-worthy entity and parallels the extension of bank credit without the oversight and standardized procedures employed with bank loans.[13]

Beyond the fact that few local consumers have a credit card at their disposal, most retailers are loathe to set up service with an international credit company because service charges would reduce their profit per sale and because of the lag between purchase and when the retailer will receive payment from the company, typically thirty to sixty days. Nadim, who manages a high-end children's clothing store in the Mediterranean coast shopping district, pointed out that owners are accustomed to seeing their profits immediately and in cash. Even in instances where customers pay in installments for goods, cash is continually flowing into the store, and hence wholesalers can be repaid promptly and profits can be disbursed to employees and owners.

However, the extension of credit requires a retailer or wholesaler to assume the risk of default that might otherwise be absorbed by a national or multinational corporation in the case of credit cards. Absorbing this risk makes economic sense to the extent that credit is a service that allows retailers to add fees to purchases. As one cynical local noted, "In some stores, they wouldn't even take your cash if you had it. They prefer people who pay on credit because it increases their take!" There are social and long-term economic benefits as well, the analysis of which entails closer attention to the medium of contract and surety used to guarantee retail credit. Hence, we turn to trust receipts and their multiple valences.

Legal Fictions

The Egyptian Trade Law (1999) outlines the provisions for commercial papers, including promissory notes, checks, and trust receipts. A trust receipt is designed to provide surety for a transfer of cash from an agent to a recipient via an intermediary. Such transfers are relatively common in Egypt, where much business is transacted in cash rather than through checks, credit cards, or bank transfers. Failure to deliver means that the intermediary can be accused of breach of trust (*khiyāna amāna*), charged with, and found guilty of a criminal misdemeanor. It is therefore a commercial document that carries the potential of a prison sentence of up to three years for non-delivery, at the judge's discretion. In addition to the misdemeanor case, the plaintiff can also raise a civil case for compensation. Hence, the potential of criminal prosecution upon failure to deliver monies means that the legal consequences for breach of trust are similar to those for "bouncing" a check (knowingly issuing a check in bad faith). One important difference between post-dated checks (PDCs) and trust receipts is that the former pose a risk to the debtor's assets, which can be procured upon presentation of the check unless the funds have been withdrawn. Trust receipts don't transform personal assets or private property into collateral. Rather, they transform the body into collateral; the body is staked as surety through the threat of incarceration.[14]

Further, the practice of signing on the white (*muwaqqi' 'alā buyāḍ*) gives trust receipts particular efficacy. Port Saidians are often expected to, or offer to, sign their names and leave blank the sections in which the amount of the transaction is to be stipulated. While the inclusion of spaces and blanks and the exclusion of important terms and stipulations are commonly found with other types of customary documents like informal and handwritten contracts, the practice of signing on the white with trust receipts has particular juridical implications. A breach of faith charge based on non-delivery of monies stipulated in a trust receipt can result in up to three years imprisonment and fines. The jail sentence is at the discretion of the judge, although lawyers I interviewed pointed out that there was usually a strong correlation between the amount of money involved and the sentence such that a higher sum resulted in a longer prison term.

Trust receipts are much maligned as a medium of pledge. Even those who use them regularly point out that they reveal a lack of trust and turn small debts into major problems precisely because they leverage the threat of a criminal charge. The Civil Law Code, the law of obligations, lays out the framework for valid contracts and provides avenues for legal recourse in cases of breach; as such, it intercedes to adjudicate contractual disputes, determine liability, and award damages through garnishment or seizure of property. In contrast, using the threat of criminal misdemeanor charges to guarantee a pledge appears to make the state more integral to private transactions. Yet, I posit, the potential to leverage state power with trust receipts is frequently mitigated in practice by a host of practical knowledges and moral/ethical concerns about how to deal with customers and clients who fail to pay back their debts.

For instance, Hani, a trader who owns two home goods stores in adjacent working-class neighborhoods in Port Said, provides credit to the majority of his customers. A typical transaction in his store, as in similar stores, operates like this: a customer makes a down payment and can take the goods but is required to sign at least one, typically many, trust receipts. Hani holds the receipts until the debt is paid off. If the debt goes unpaid, Hani will often renegotiate the terms of the installment payments to spread the debt burden out over a longer period of time. But if it continues to go unpaid he can use the honesty receipts to raise a breach of trust case against the customer.

Yet even with an honesty receipt at his disposal, it is expected that a trader will try other means to recoup the debt rather than turning immediately to the courts. Hani related the procedures he tends to follow when someone stops paying installments:

> I call him, after sixty days, two months. After sixty days we begin to act, because he didn't come (to pay his installments). We send him a warning from us. That he has three days to appear or we will raise an action. The warning is in the name of the lawyer, not in the name of the store. From us, but by way of (the lawyer). The lawyer sends the warnings, he has forms in his office that he created for this. After this, if he comes and pays a certain amount, according to his credit, let's say 100LE if he owes 300LE, then fine, we move on, he goes back to paying installments as before, and it's fine, he pays according to his circumstances. If he doesn't pay, we wait until 5 months have passed and we file a formal complaint.

He also explains what he does when he first approaches them about failing to pay:

> First, I ask them why they've stopped paying. Is there some problem, which prevents him from paying the money back. Some people give excuses— I was ill, my wife is ill, he doesn't have work, like that. Some people are making these things up, but I can tell if they're liars or if they're telling the truth. By talking to them like this, I let them know if I believe them, and sympathize with their problems. But other times, I feel like they're lying and I'll tell them so outright. There are people who go from one store to the next, taking things on credit to get the money, burning goods. They'll come here and pay one month, and then they won't pay for three months because they're paying at the other stores they borrowed from. In situations like this, I don't have patience for their excuses because I want my money.

In accordance with the common exhortation that one must always try to resolve problems in a friendly or peaceable way (*bishakl wadi'*), a good trader takes people's circumstances into account when deciding how to proceed when a debt is owed. Later in the conversation, Hani stressed that it was important to be generous, because you will be rewarded for your generosity. Although he didn't explicitly reference religious teachings, he indicated through a gesture of uplifted hands and face that he referred to a spiritual form of reward.[15]

The line between a promise and a written pledge is not absolute. Even where trust receipts are present, they may be functionally absent. A trader named Mahmoud who specializes in selling used cars to taxi drivers pointed out that he uses trust receipts to "ensure his right" if a client stopped payment on a car. At the same time, his right to monies owed is complicated by the fact that much of his business is conducted with family and friends.

> I used to not write trust receipts for friends and the like. We are basically an Eastern society where there is respect and fear among people. So I used to respect people who I know. But in the end, I was the one who lost. In the end, I had no choice but to write trust receipts whether this person is a relative or not. But I can't file a complaint [in court] against a relative. Nevertheless, a trust receipt is considered a kind of threat that makes him worried and makes him want to pay. But if he didn't pay, I really couldn't raise an action.

On the other hand, a trust receipt may be absent from a transaction but "presenced" through its refusal, such as when retailers refuse to allow a customer to sign trust receipts as surety in order to leverage this courtesy for a favor. For instance, Waleed, an English tutor, purchased several pieces of furniture from a trader he had known from his childhood neighborhood. Despite the high value of the goods, the trader repeatedly refused Waleed's offer to sign multiple trust receipts to secure the deal. In reflecting on the transaction, Waleed pointed out that this was an indication both that this man thought of him as family because of their neighborhood connection and that his own reputation for honesty preceded him. Yet, he was unsurprised when some weeks after the initial transaction the retailer began asking him if he was available to tutor his young son in English. Waleed lamented that, although he had made a point of paying his debt installments on time, he would still be expected to provide these lessons for free or at a reduced cost as repayment for having been entrusted to repay without a written pledge.

A trust receipt grants access to law. With it, one has evidence to turn to the police and eventually the courts if an obligation isn't fulfilled. The refusal to exploit its potential can have ethical and moral significance by imbuing a trader with positive qualities (generosity, mercy, and the like). As such, the leverage-value of a trust receipt is constrained by practices that constitute social and familial networks, an example of the familiar tension between short-term and long-term gains in economic decision-making. Waleed found himself doubly indebted to the furniture retailer, illustrating that the absence of a written pledge may also be concretely fruitful. The refusal of surety is a form of currency by which retailers accrue favors and customer loyalty.

Despite concurrence among legal scholars that all contracting is relational to some degree, written and verbal agreements are often viewed as diametrically opposed contractual models.[16] Written agreements are associated with facilitating and anticipating legal recourse, and as such must meet the minimal requirements for validity in addition to outlining stipulations and terms in detail. By contrast, verbal agreements, or promises, may be comparatively imprecise and parties are largely bound by normative expectations, although verbal contracts may in some circumstances be recognized by the court. Legal scholar Jonathan Yovel argues that "promises are not 'skeletal' and legal language is not merely 'about' them . . . because (legal language) shapes and transforms (promises)" (2000, 960). With formal contracts, law's language inevitably interacts with and alters normative mediums such as promises. Trust receipts are a type of minimal contract, documenting a specifically legal obligation with the associated potential for legal recourse. However, trust receipts disrupt the assumed polarity between written and verbal agreements because they house both; they merge these models by virtue of their use as legal fictions. Even when deployed to guarantee an unambiguous delayed transaction, they require the appendage of verbal agreements through which the specific and true terms of the transaction are articulated.

Although there are clear differences between the various types of commercial documents, trust receipts serve a purpose similar to that of post-dated checks (PDCs), which are used in Egypt and in other contexts as a form of guarantee. As Kaufman-Winn notes in relation to the use of PDCs in Taiwan, "[u]sing PDCs to document commercial transactions thus helped maintain the viability of attenuated relationships without forcing the parties to assume the expense and inconvenience of completely converting the transaction from a relational to a legal basis by drawing up a contract that fully expressed the parties' agreement" (1994, 220). Beyond these pragmatic concerns, she also notes that that there is a connection between the use of PDCs and a dominant cultural ideology rooted in Confucianism that prioritizes personal relationships over reliance on state institutions. Port Saidians also use PDCs, although the use of a trust receipt puts even greater emphasis on the relational aspects of the obligation given the higher stakes for default and the more extreme gap between what is owed and what is staked as surety.

Belonging, Obligation, and the Sons of Port Said

Although the uses of trust receipts rely on similar social and business logics to those that framed transactions in the pre–Free Zone era, their discursive association with the post–Free Zone cohort of traders may be integral to revaluing social aspects of contracting. The capitalist parasites were the topic of conversation one evening at the Banks Club (*nādī banūq*), where I often visited with a group of older men, most of whom are current or former bank employees. Mamdouh, an economist who periodically publishes articles on the maritime economy in Egyptian business journals, had this to say:

> Egyptians . . . are willing to sit and talk with one another and find a solution that works for everyone. Each one is not interested in simply taking his right. People have rights and they have duties toward one another in society, and they seek to find a balance between the two. This is true of everyone, it doesn't matter if you are educated or not. With the Free Zone, the capitalist parasites appeared and these traders were not good at working things out in an intelligent and fair and calm way. They thought only of themselves and wanted to get rich right away. Many did, and they lost it just as quickly. It's not just because they are from outside, not the "Sons of Port Said"—there are good and bad people everywhere, and some of these new traders were just not good people, not people who had good sense and a good heart.

According to Kareem, a retired bank administrator, business etiquette among the "Sons of Port Said" emphasized the value of a man's word:

> In the Suez Canal area, people here are used to foreigners. There have always been foreigners here in Port Said, from Italy, Greece, France, Britain, and so forth. And even people of these different groups could sit down and work out a problem peacefully. . . . Traders could call [one another] and make a deal, no papers to sign. A man would call a wholesaler and order things

and say he will pay him back in a week or two, no problem. They were good for their word. Wealthy, pioneering families like Hamza and Laheta, their whole families were involved in trading and they were very experienced in how to do business in a way that looked toward the future, toward building good relations and not just getting rich quick. They dealt with people in a very good way, wisely.

Kareem connects the longevity of "pioneering families" with their business practices that "looked toward the future." He also makes a connection between looking toward the future in business with both "experience" (prior action) and building good relationships (ongoing action), and disconnects it from quick monetary gain. Moreover, he stresses how an element of being a good business-man is building good relationships with others. Although not unique to Egypt, scholars have noted that social networks built across social classes are particularly vital in Egypt and that the bartering of favors is critical for how the majority of Egyptians meet fundamental needs (Ghannam 2002; Singerman 1995). The sons of Port Said were, perhaps above all, deeply networked.

A member of one of these "pioneering" families was a loan officer at a local bank and the landlord for properties near the canal that he had inherited from his family. In discussing how his father conducted business in mid-century Port Said, the loan officer recalled: "You would just call up on the phone and request a certain amount of goods from the wholesaler, and he would send it over. You made a verbal agreement over the phone, and your reputation depended on paying for the goods." He noted that his father had gained local prominence in part because "his word could be trusted." This man also noted that he tries hard to follow in his father's example, to always remain ethical and honest, but finds it challenging. To some extent, the challenges he faces reveal the double edge of being a part of a deeply networked local elite in a new economic era:

It's difficult, my work at the bank sometimes, because I'm so well known in this town. I work in the loan department, and sometimes the local business-men who know me or my family come in wanting a loan. But I've spent time abroad getting training in spreadsheets and background checks and I know that if someone doesn't check out, if they have outstanding debts or if the money they want is more than they will be able to repay, than I can't approve a loan for them, even if our families are connected from years back. There's been more than one prominent businessmen who has smeared my name . . . because I refused to give a loan.

Despite the emergence of a "market culture," in which the desire for cheap goods in vast quantities has increased the pace of exchange and lowered the potential social value of individual transactions, some traders have situated themselves firmly in the market for luxury goods and aim to derive high value from the courtesy of trust. Tamer, who owns a high-end men's clothing store on one of the main boulevards in downtown Port Said, extends credit generously to his regular customers. The suits and shoes he sells are imported from Italy and a dress shirt costs upwards of 600LE, which was roughly equivalent to 100 U.S. dollars in 2006. This is far more than what clothing costs in the Arab district, where a man's shirt can easily be purchased for 60LE. Unlike the overstuffed stores that cater to the middle class, Tamer's store is elegantly decorated, with polished marble floors and custom-crafted wooden cabinets that organize each shirt and suit into a separate compartment for display. He pointed out that for traders like him selling on informal credit to wealthy customers was accepted practice. His brother, who sat beside him, explained how credit works:

> The people who come here, they know Tamer, they have a relationship. So when they choose something they like, they find out the price, and they take the item but don't pay anything just then, or maybe some part of the price. And then over the following months, they'll stop in to say hello and will pay it back gradually. It's impolite to ask for the cash all at once, it's not the way it works here. It's about relationships, it's a way of being nice. And besides, Tamer knows that if he doesn't run his business this way, these men could go elsewhere and buy things, and he would lose business. In the middle-end shops, or the low-end shops, you pay cash. Or if you buy on installment, sure, you write a trust receipt. But not here, not in this kind of store. And sometimes he loses money, it's the way it works.

The extension of trust in this form frames risk as a courtesy to build both reputation and one's client network. Naguib, a trader who owns the shop down the street from Tamer, also selling expensive men's clothing, reiterated that extending unsecured credit and implicit pledge-making are usual at this end of the market:

> Yes, in the [*sura* of the] Cow, it says that you should write things down, no matter how small. But we don't. My customers come and take very expensive goods from me and we don't write it down. It's just not the way it's done. They might take their business elsewhere. If someone dies and they

have debts, on the day of judgment they will be found guilty if they leave debts behind.

In these high-end stores, not only are the terms of repayment—how much per week or month—left unspecified, but also the promise to pay in full is tacit rather than explicit.

An older lawyer, Mr. el-Sibay, pointed out that the notion that Port Said is still a small city where one can implicitly trust business associates lingers. But this trust is often betrayed: informally composed contracts are forged and falsified, debts go unpaid, and people face the possibility of having to go to court to claim their rights.

> Well, people in Port Said are like one big family. For example a person doesn't know me but he might have heard my name somewhere. In Cairo, it's bigger and hard to know people easily. Consequently, because people *almost* know each other [in Port Said], they tend to trust and give money to one another.... But nowadays the pace of life does not allow people to know each other well.

Mamdouh, Kareem, and others, including Mr. el-Sibay, perceive a cultural shift they argue is directly related to the Free Zone that manifested itself in an abruptly depersonalized market. Despite this, transactions are often conducted in ways that increase, rather than reduce, exposure or risk, and this is the case at both the lower and the upper ends of the market. Retail credit is ubiquitous, entails a face-to-face credit transaction, and is often tenuously secured. A trust receipt can reduce the likelihood of default, yet creditors may refuse to pursue a breach of trust case in the courts even when a customer fails to repay monies owed. As illustrated by the examples of Waleed, the English tutor, and Tamer, the owner of a high-end men's clothing store, creditors may refuse to secure transactions entirely. Although the precise reasons for extending unsecured credit vary, the acceptance of risk is a kind of currency that can extend beyond the transaction to rearticulate community networks.

Making Deals and Making Futures

When traders make deals, they don't just make money: they make futures with other traders and with their customers. The forms of contract and guarantee they rely upon are indicative of where in time this future is perceived to be. Jane

Guyer draws connections between structural adjustment policies in Nigeria and the resulting tension between "fantasy futurism" and "enforced presentism," an analysis that is equally useful in thinking about traders and deal-making in Port Said (2004). Although traders might desire to operate in a field of long-term business relationships that enable them to take risks made less risky by virtue of their mutual interdependence, the get-rich-quick climate of Port Said in the 1970s combined with the economic pinch wrought from structural adjustment policies since the 1990s have likely refocused traders' sights on a nearer future. Likewise, in his study of Japanese securities traders, Miyazaki examines anxieties, hopes, and the desire to generate prospective momentum in their work and points out that the experience of "temporal incongruity" is part of knowledge formation (2004). Memory and anticipation make an indelible mark on pledge-making, in that major economic and demographic shifts in Egypt's recent history disrupt the ability to anticipate the distant future and take a more flexible, long-term view of gains and losses in the market; there is increasing certainty that the future is uncertain. The lines drawn in discursive practice between the nouveau riche and old money, trust receipts and verbal contracts, parasites and sons of Port Said, do not map neatly onto the contemporary terrain of deal-making, but rather highlight the struggle to obtain fixity and belonging in an increasingly anonymous market.

This material requires that we reconsider arguments that documents, and in particular financial and legal documents, are "post-social" (Riles 2010, 798). While some documents, such as esoteric financial devices, have effects and uses that are too slippery to map onto social interaction, trust receipts have decided social effects and uses. Legal implications aside, trust receipts are inscribed as part of a negotiated encounter between parties. Moreover, as we can see in the ethnographic data from Port Said, trust receipts are either present or meaningfully absent in everyday delayed transactions. This is particularly so because they obfuscate the nature of a pledge, shifting enforcement to the realm of criminal jurisdiction and expanding the coercive capacity of the state. Their use as legal fictions points to uncertainties in the broader Egyptian legal and political milieu, including inefficiencies in the civil courts that make civil justice uncertain (Hegel-Cantarella 2011).[17]

This material likewise demands that we rethink lingering tropes of Middle Eastern sociality, which might suggest that relational contracting and modes of guarantee should be interpreted as underwritten by "traditional" values of familial, communal, and tribal connectivity. Recollections of "old" and "new" Port Said and the "value of a man's word" do not convey social truths. Rather, when these discourses frame transactional practices they contribute to re-making status and belonging in particular local settings when other indexes of status and belonging have become unstable. Recognizing that pledge-making is enacted within a space of multiple and intersecting temporalities allows us to observe how pledges constitute much more than merely credit and debt.

NOTES

1. Ethnographic data for this essay was collected during sixteen months of field research between 2006 and 2008 in Port Said, Egypt that was funded by the National Science Foundation, the Social Science Research Council, and Fulbright. All names have been changed to protect anonymity except those of well-known local families. I thank the editors of this volume and the anonymous reviewers for their comments on early drafts. This essay was written while I was an assistant research specialist in Anthropology at the University of California, Irvine, and I am grateful for the collegial support and resources that were granted to me by those in the department.

2. Official documents are legally characterized as those produced by a public employee or those "received" by him (notarized). Informal (or customary) documents, on the other hand, are characterized as follows: "If such documents do not assume official capacity, they shall merely have the value of informal documents whenever the parties concerned shall have put down their signature, their stamps or their fingerprints thereupon" (Trade Law 25/1968/Article 10).

3. Some protest songs recalled the bravery of Port Saidians, and El Tanbura, a group of *simsimiyya* musicians from Port Said, regularly took the stage in Tahrir Square; their repertoire includes resistance songs from the Suez War; see Dorian Lynksey, "Ramy Essam, the Voice of the Egyptian Uprising," *The Guardian*, 19 July 2011 (http://www.guardian .co.uk/music/2011/jul/19/ramy-essam-egypt-uprising-interview).

4. Engineers and managers came from England and France to oversee the excavation. Egyptian manual laborers, on the other hand, were conscripted through the corvée system of mandatory temporary labor from among the Egyptian *fellahin* (peasants or farmers). As the canal project neared completion, and the city of Port Said began to take shape, some remained and, along with farmers from nearby Delta villages, were among the original inhabitants to put down roots (el-Kady 1997; Karabell 2004).

5. Suez Canal Company employees were abruptly denied access to their offices by Egyptian soldiers within hours of the declaration of nationalization, and ordered to return to their countries of origin. Jewish families had already begun to emigrate in large

numbers after 1948, and after 1956 Europeans found themselves out of work and at risk of losing property and investments due to new nationalization policies.

6. Law 43/1976 established five free zones: Port Said, Nasr City, Alexandria, Suez, and Ismailiya. Port Said's Free Zone seems to have become the most successful because it encompassed the entire city and not just a designated section.

7. The Free Zone law also gave Port Saidians particular privileges to which other Egyptians were not privy. For instance, they were able to purchase new cars without paying taxes on them, as long as the vehicles remained in Port Said a certain percentage of a given year. Port Said was one of the few places in Egypt where the "black market" did not exist, because trade that occurred outside of the legal regulations in other parts of the country was legal in Port Said. The currency market is one example, as Iliya Harik notes (1998), and the value of the U.S. dollar in 1985 in Port Said ranged between $1.60 and $1.85, as compared with $.70 through the Central Bank of Egypt.

8. The population of Port Said was recently recorded at 529,684 (CAPMAS, 2004). The 1960 census records Port Said's population at 244,000 inhabitants. By 1968, the population was estimated to have grown to 300,000, although this statistic does not reflect *al-hijra*, the migration, between 1967 and 1973. Most residents relocated to other cities between 1967 and 1973 due to concerns about safety because of the war with Israel and because of the closure of the Suez Canal, which severely stunted the local economy. Within the space of approximately forty-five years, the remaining population more than doubled, expanding most rapidly in the latter half of the 1970s.

9. Robert Springborg uses a similar term, "parasitic bourgeoisie," to describe individuals and gangs in the post-*infitah* era who obtained subsidized commodities from the state's retail outlets through bribes, manipulation, or intimidation and diverted them to the black market (1989, 81–85).

10. Structural adjustment policies reduced the special privileges for trade in imported goods in Port Said and some of other Free Zone areas. This meant that it became possible for traders in Cairo, Alexandria, and elsewhere to directly import goods such as European fabric and electronics that previously were only available in Port Said. As al-Fadil shows, shipments entering Egypt through Free Zones like Port Said declined from 101.92 million in 1992 to 53.17 million Egyptian Pounds (EGP) in 1997; that's a decrease of almost half in five years (2002, 102). Thus began a decline in the local economy, exacerbated by the gradual phasing out of almost all Free Zone privileges except those promoting manufacturing beginning in 2002 and culminating in December 2009 (Law 5/2002).

11. Although new banks were established as part of Open Door legislation and the availability of formal credit expanded considerably, lending criteria excluded many poor

and middle-class Egyptians who continued to rely upon informal crediting arrangements (Mayer 1985).

12. I use the term "small" store owners to highlight the fact that in most cases retailers in Port Said own one store rather than retail chains. As such, their operations are of a relatively small scale.

13. There are further parallels between retail credit and bank credit in that retailers may also participate in an implicit credit market known as the "burned goods system"; a high-interest loan is extended by way of a fictional purchase of a high-priced item like a refrigerator. The item doesn't leave the store, and the retailer immediately buys back the item for a reduced price. The customer receives immediate cash for the fictional resale but is still responsible for paying down the debt from the initial purchase.

14. There may be some useful parallels to be drawn with analyses of the criminal incarceration of debtors historically. As Finn points out for eighteenth century England, "By seizing men's bodies for their debts, the civil law substituted persons for things in market exchange, allowing the human body to serve as collateral for goods obtained not through productive labor and the cash nexus but rather through the operation of consumer credit" (2003, 10). This practice was supported by small-claims statutes that gave creditors broad powers and by the legal challenge of seizing debtors' lands and monies. Further, completion of the prison sentence liquidated the debt, such that one could truly absolve the debt with the body (2003, 111).

15. Many traders in Port Said are more explicit about the moral imperative to be patient, merciful, and generous in business practices and link this imperative to specific Muslim teachings. The complex way in which morality and business practices interface in everyday deals in Port Said can be seen as part of a broader phenomenon across the Muslim world, which Charles Tripp describes as the moral economy. He notes that in this context debates about capitalism and its potential to weaken the fabric of society feed into parallel concerns about private law as representative of a kind of individualizing justice and a potential threat to social solidarity and morally-guided modes of adjudication and compensation (2006).

16. For more on this debate, see Bernstein 1992; Macaulay 1963; and MacNeil 1980.

17. The average civil litigation requires between thirty and forty appearances before the trial judges due to poor case management, the referral of cases to the Expertise Office of the Ministry of Justice, and procedural laws that facilitate the introducing of strategic delay. Further, the court's capacity to enforce the payment of damages is limited, and there are well-known strategies for hiding assets to avoid seizure related to a court order (El-Dean 2002; Hegel-Cantarella 2011; Rutherford 2008). Consequently, the criminal courts have often been used to expedite civil justice in Egypt.

PART 3.

ANTHROPOLOGY OF RELIGION AND SECULARISM IN
THE MIDDLE EAST AND NORTH AFRICA

10.

WILL THE RATIONAL RELIGIOUS SUBJECT PLEASE STAND UP? MUSLIM SUBJECTS AND THE ANALYTICS OF RELIGION

Sherine Hafez

The Oriental is irrational, depraved (fallen), childlike, "different"; thus the European is rational, virtuous, mature, "normal." . . . The Oriental lived in a different but thoroughly organized world of its own, a world with its own national, cultural and epistemological boundaries and principles of internal coherence.

—Edward Said, *Orientalism* (1979, 40)

Despite the critical impact of Said's *Orientalism* (1979) on scholarship dealing with Muslim and Middle Eastern cultures and practices, deeply seated assumptions that revolve around conceptions of difference and rationality still persist today. Whereas Said's work has urged scholars to think beyond cultures as "watertight compartments whose adherents were at bottom mainly interested in fending off all the others," (ibid., 348), predominantly Muslim societies and cultures continue to be decontextualized and uprooted from their historical logic. They are framed in terms that Said describes in the above quote, as encapsulated, isolated, and preoccupied with staving off competing ideologies.

Key to this juxtaposition of modern liberalism on the one hand and Islamic movements on the other are deep-seated assumptions that attribute rationality, cognition, and reason to "modern" Western societies while denying it to "traditional" Islamic others. Such unquestioned assumptions underwrite notions of difference, essentialism, and the mutual exclusivity of religion and Western secularism. "If it can be said that the modernist ideology of the post-Enlightenment West effectively separated religion from public life, then what has happened in recent years—since the watershed Islamic revolution in Iran in 1979—is religion's *revenge*," Juergensmeyer writes (2001, 66; emphasis added). Depicting the relationship between Western liberal secularity and religion in this rhetoric evokes a number of assumptions: religion is the oppositional other of liberal secularity; religious movements are regressive because they are not modern; and Islam is anti-secular. Most important, religion is linked to personal feeling, as it carries grudges and seeks "revenge." In short, religion, here—namely Islam, is taken as the backward other of the Enlightenment project which has laid out the foundation of Western modernity and reason.

Thus, conceptions of rationality in hegemonic scholarship merit deeper consideration and especially when examining a postcolonialist Islamic "other" constructed as the antithesis of the modern progressive Western world. Talal Asad points out that rationality is one of the most decisive factors that a number of writers anxious to "explain" Islamic resurgence use to delineate the modern secular subject from Islamic traditionalists who failed to modernize because of, "an irrational reluctance to abandon tradition," (1991, 318). In his book *Formations of the Secular* (2003), Asad argues, by historicizing secularism, that it is no longer viable for anthropologists to view the secular as the natural progression of the religious nor as the epitome of rationality.

Much has been written about rationality in anthropology as in other disciplines, and a number of anthropologists have sought to problematize how conceptions of rationality were instrumental in imperialist politics.

> One of the difficulties is that rationality is a concept which produces basic evaluations but no agreement on how to use the term. The suggestion that rationality is less a universal standard than the incarnation of our particular set of cultural values should be taken seriously. . . . Rationality is part of a world which values achievement of goals, efficiency and control; it thus appears as the subjection of nature (technology) and the subjugation of man (imperialism). The evolution of this value system itself requires ethnographic examination. (Crick 1982, 287)

In what follows I focus on the production of "rationality" in social science and its deployment as a marker of difference in studies of Islamic cultures and societies in the Middle East and North Africa (MENA) region. These frameworks of rationality in foundational studies of religion were the central premise for understandings of Islamic practices and beliefs, with particular significance to issues of cultural relativity, subjectivity, and subject production. In literature on the MENA in particular, religious actors were, as Said illustrated above, described as, "irrational, depraved (fallen), childlike, different." The irrationality, emotionality, even violence of the "religious actor" is implicitly constructed in contrast to the reason and composure of normative secular subjectivity. In the course of my own research of women's Islamic activism in Egypt (spanning six years, 2000–2003 and 2005–2008), I observed a scene of prayer and ritual weeping that provided a context for some of the questions I ask in this essay: How do assumptions of irrationality implicitly attach themselves to Muslim practitioners of the Islamic faith? How do complex and heterogeneous subjectivities become reduced to "religious subjects"? To understand how normative conceptions of rationality develop from wider epistemologies that are often unproblematically employed in studies of Islamic movements and activism, it is necessary to first explore a number of foundational studies in the social sciences. As a unit of analysis, religion is conceptualized by particular histories of colonialism and modernity which demarcate its analytical parameters. Rationality emerges as a significant core assumption around which many of the attempts to "explain" Islamic culture and practice seem to revolve.

Conceptualizing Religion in Early Modern Thought

Asad notes how a conceptual understanding of "religion" that threatens Western statehood continues to be associated with conflict in people's minds (1996). This is because, he notes, "religion" emerges as a central critical element in early Enlightenment thought, with the confrontation between state-building projects and local elite powers framed by the latter through power claims made in religious terms. As historical events in Europe unfolded, the rejection of religious paradigms of knowledge in favor of scientific observation and evidential inference marked the advent not only of the dominance of science but also of the growing significance of the idea of secularism as the antithesis of religious authority. The crystallization of the modern concept of religion was directly linked to the history of the English Civil War (1642–1651) and the French Revolution

(1789–1799), where the struggle between the power of religious dogma and state-building forces took place.

A number of thinkers and philosophers of religion identify fear, incredulity, confusion, and superstition in the modern period as points of departure for understanding religious faith. David Hume (1711–1776), now considered one of the founders of the philosophy of religion from the Enlightenment period, argues that, "The first ideas of religion arose not from a contemplation of the works of nature, but from a concern with regard to the events of life, and from the incessant hopes and fears which actuate the human mind" (1757, 27, in Morris 1987, 141). Hume is known to have emphasized the role of emotions in giving rise to religious belief. He argued that emotions such as fear and the instinctive tendency of humans to "adulate," rather than divine intervention or rational reason, were the compelling motivation behind popular religious belief. For Enlightenment authors, religion began to take shape as an emotional, irrational, and anti-scientific human condition. It was seen to fill the void left empty by the absence of scientific knowledge. Ironically, despite their roots in social and cultural events pertinent to Western history alone, these descriptives still persist in views concerned with the proliferation of Islamic movements around the world today.

Will the Religious Rational Individual Please Stand Up?

Bronislaw Malinowski (1884–1942), a proponent of ethnography as a method of anthropological examination, questions notions of rationality and religious belief so as "to grasp the native's point of view, his relation to life, to realize *his* vision of *his* world" (1922, 25). He sought to affirm primitive man's rational ability for reasoning. He opposed Levi-Bruhl's claim that abstract thinking and systematic thought is not a skill possessed by a "pre-logical mentality." Instead, Malinowski urges us to reflect that "we must surely pause before accepting primitive man's irrationality as a dogma" (1948, 9). Though he claimed that Tylor's ideas of animism attributed too much rationality to primitive man, Malinowski attested to the rational potential of the Trobriand Islanders. He demonstrated their ability to distinguish between what is mystical-magical from what is empirical-pragmatic. The ability to be rational, he maintained, necessitates a distinction between magic and science. Malinowski thus assumed that the criterion for what constitutes rationality is the separation of religion from science.

Malinowski was not short for ethnographic evidence that supported his thesis. He recounted how the Trobrianders were adept at using agricultural tools such as the axe and pointed stick. He described how they possessed knowledge of the seasons and the soil. He commented on the native's rational treatment of death as a dispassionate ending of life, etc. Malinowski finally concluded that in the Trobriand Islands, although magic is linked in some ways to knowledge of gardening, its effects are not interchangeable with the effects of the natives' labor, that is, natives understand and know that their crops are the result of their hard labor but that magic serves to control the uncontrollable variables which might jeopardize them. Malinowski reasons that in differentiating between the roles of the garden magician and the leader of the community, there is a clear separation between the rituals involving magic and secular leadership, yet these are, he admits, occasionally carried out by the same person. To Malinowski, magic serves to reinforce confidence in the face of adversity and is not conflated with logical outcomes, "It is most significant that in the lagoon fishing, where man can rely completely upon his knowledge and skill, magic does not exist, while in the open-sea fishing, full of danger and uncertainty, there is extensive magical ritual to secure safety and good results" (1948, 30–31).

Evident in the examples he cites to demonstrate the rationality of the native Trobriand Islander is Malinowski's assumption that magic should be separate from science. The terms the Trobrianders themselves use are not examined in any great detail in his account. He does not pursue the question as to whether the Trobrianders employed words for religion, magic, or science as they are understood in the West. The portrait of the (ir)rational actor which Malinowski paints is a product not of Trobriand beliefs and social ideals, but of Enlightenment thought and liberal Western principles. Despite his intention to demonstrate the rationality of the native Trobriander, Malinowski only succeeds in reinstating the assumption of the binary construct of faith/reason and religion/secularity. Consequently, the notion of the traditional irrational individual often believed to characterize non-literate societies was not in fact adequately challenged by Malinowski's argument since he did not reject the assumption that *created* the "irrational other" as the religious backward actor versus the rational modern subject. Not surprisingly, similar conceptual frameworks of rationality are employed to examine issues of subjectivity and subject production in Islamic movements. On the one hand, the irrationality, emotionality and even violence of the religious actor is posited against the reason and composure of normative secular subjectivity. How do discursive processes link religious actors to irrationality?

192 Anthropology of Religion and Secularism in the MENA

Re-producing an Idea of Islamic Subjects

Recent literature responding to the growth of Islamic movements in the Middle East has, according to Asad, overwhelmingly attempted to *explain* Islamic revival as a rejection of modernity or a failure to achieve it (1991). The perceived Islamic rejection of Western modernity is somewhat of a myth that many have debunked (Abu-Lughod 1998, Asad 2003, Deeb 2006, Göle 1996, Najmabadi 1991, and others). Yet the structural frameworks that examine Islamic movements persist in assuming the lack of rational cognition among Islamic subjects. As theoretically informed approaches of cultural relativity cast a lens on MENA subjectivity, they posit personhood as collapsible into one-dimensional types or mouthpieces for a bounded and essential culture—a process Paul Rabinow has dubbed a form of "symbolic violence" (Rabinow 1977, 130). In this transformative and reductionist process, rationality as an episteme becomes a justification of Western dominance and progress. While it is rare that concepts of rationality/irrationality are directly addressed or problematized by scholars of the MENA, cultural relativity as a trope for the relativity of standards of rationality becomes an overarching system of intellectual power in the field. The internalization of Western rationality as normative is akin to what Rabinow describes.

> To those who claim that some form of this symbolic violence was not part of their own field experience, I reply simply that I do not believe them. This is not to say that every anthropologist is aware of it, for sensibilities differ. The form and intensity no doubt vary greatly, but they are all variations on a common theme. (Ibid., 130)

A colonialist history, for example, links the cultural pasts (as well as presents) of both Western and MENA cultures and traditions. These hegemonizing processes of appropriation left a strong impact on the nature of cultural exchange. As colonialist European powers ventured into a predominantly Muslim world in the Middle East in the late nineteenth century, they rationalized their superiority as a modern force against an Islamic resistance deemed intellectually unjustifiable because of its association with a religious ideal. Colonialist discourse readily constructed Islamic tradition as a "religion" that was (predictably) anti-modern and irrational (Asad 2003). This transplanting of concepts, particularly that of religion, uprooted from history and firmly lodged at the heart of an altogether alien context, reformulates them into new discursive meanings. The disembedding of local concepts not only intends to erase any historical consideration of their development as part of logical matrixes of social life, but also strips them of credibility as viable discourses and envelops them in a shroud of timelessness and "tradition." As concepts with no history and no context, they are transformed into ahistorical "symbols." Neat and compact, these symbols then act as vehicles of meaning that conjure up on demand the necessary connotations they have been intended to portray.

This is precisely why Asad calls for a consideration of Islamic tradition not as a stage in social development measured against Western historical experiences but on its own terms (1996). The difficulty of doing so, as MacIntyre adds, manifests because Western liberal modernity presents itself as a neutral and universal ahistorical arbitrator relying on an absolutism that is based on an inseparable treatment of ethics and rationality in its philosophy (1988).

These processes of decontextualization characterize, to varying degrees, how Islamic movements are theorized by some social scientists today. Below I select two examples of scholarly treatments of "Islam" to illustrate how insufficient attention to issues of power and normative Western rationality can often parochialize religious traditions into ahistorical and isolated concepts and practices. Although these examples are not anthropological, they crystallize some of the underlying approaches to analysis of the MENA region that have also affected anthropology. I have selected the abundant prolific work of John Esposito to discuss first because of its huge impact on current literature dealing with Islamic studies. Next, I examine Mark Jurgensmeyer's work on religious fundamentalism. The latter's analysis of "religious actors" receives some attention here to illustrate how notions of irrationality, violence, and intense levels of emotions are often normalized in the discussion around religion. Universalistic definitions of religion subscribe to a particular cultural vision and hence obscure the shifting usages and practices that are today part of the modern postcolonialist MENA region. How we recognize religious activism when we see it is informed by the cognition of religious activism as a separate action from other forms of activism.

John Esposito's work has influenced countless studies on the history and culture of the Muslim world. It demonstrates how current attempts at explaining Islam may further reify assumptions that prevail unquestioned in the literature. In his book *The Islamic Threat* (1992), Esposito attempts to dispel certain misconceptions about Islam. He seeks to produce an understanding of Islamic responses through the creation of typologies, following Weber. In an attempt to represent the range of diversity among Islamic states and debunk labels of fundamentalism and conservatism, he further re-inscribes and encapsulates Islamic

states as types: "Saudi Arabia is a conservative monarchy, Libya a populist social-
ist state headed by a military dictator . . . Pakistan under General Muhammad
Zia ul-Haq embodied a conservative Islam, and Saudi Arabia still does; Islam in
Libya is radical and revisionist; clerics dominate in Iran" (1992, 28).

Esposito's point of departure inheres in the claim that Islam runs counter
to modernity and that Islamic movements in the Middle East emerged as a result
of the failure of secular nationalist agendas. In making these claims, Esposito attempts to challenge critics of Islam and Islamic cultures, yet he relies on Western
modern assumptions that otherize religion and categorize it as anti-modern and
opposed to progress. For instance, Esposito's historical survey of Islamic thought
runs as a linear account of events from the eighteenth century to the present. His
intent, which was to dispel misunderstandings regarding Islamic tradition, would
have been better achieved by an effort to delineate its multilayered genealogy.

In his account of Islamic history, Esposito refers to colonialism only super-
ficially. He alludes to the colonialist past by describing its cultural impact and
overlooks the ideological and discursive processes imprinted on the peoples and
cultures of a colonized Middle East. In sum, though extremely prolific, Esposito's
corpus on Islam does not transcend the limitations of modernist views on religion and culture. An example of this is the consistent deployment of a bounded
analytical category of religion that is mired in a Western framework in his work.
There is little or no attempt to complicate this category or its relationship to a
particular ideology of colonialism or a geographic and historic space.

A more thorough consideration of the discursive history of Islamic practices and beliefs could in principle contribute substantially to the kind of debate Esposito seeks. From a modernist perspective, Middle Eastern societies are
viewed in their totality as "traditional" because religion still plays a role in the
public sphere. Hence the idea that these states are failed projects of modernity
(MacIntyre 1988). However, the growing presence of religion in politics can be
witnessed in many countries around the world, where historical and political
processes work to structure diverse conceptualizations of the public sphere.

Despite the complexity of these processes on the current theater of events in
the Middle East, the tendency to select emotional, irrational, and violent aspects
of Islamic movements to illustrate their disruptive potential seems to still persist:

These religious acts of pure violence, although terribly *destructive*, are
sanitized by virtue of the fact that they are religiously symbolic. They are
stripped of their *horror* by being invested with religious meaning. Those
who *commit* such acts justify and therefore exonerate them because they

are part of a religious template that is even larger than myth and history: they are elements of a ritual scenario that makes it possible for people involved in it to experience the drama of *cosmic war.* (Juergensmeyer 2001, 459; emphasis added)

Juergensmeyer's choice of words is particularly significant. The following terms intersperse his account describing the state of mind as well as the political aims of these religious groups: *against modernity* (ibid., 454); "they *hate* secular governments with such a *virulent passion*" (ibid., 455); "they often *loath* their own kind" (ibid., 455); "for that reason they may *hate* not only the politicians in their own countries but also these leaders' political and economic allies in lands far beyond their own national boundaries" (ibid., 455); "the *anger* of the Serbs" (ibid., 456). What is obvious from these accounts and the particular model Juergensmeyer is using to interpret global religious violence is that he has imbued his rhetoric with Western modern liberal vocabulary which paints these movements as emotional, anti-modern, anti-secular, and most importantly *irrational* manifestations of religious zeal that just happen to erupt in these areas of the world due to their historical, traditional past. Absent is an analysis of the wider global contexts and historical background to each of these movements he names. Absent as well is any attempt to question how violence is defined by the state and how nation states have indeed already perfected this *sanitization* of violent symbols in the military.

Most importantly, Juergensmeyer's account projects an unquestioned assumption as to the nature of religious movements versus secular and modern nation states. An implicit binary clearly exists in his analysis that sets each reified entity in intense contradiction to the other. The terms "religious nationalism" or "religionizing politics" do little to resolve the issue itself, the separation of religion as a distinct category from politics, and the liberal assumption that breaching this distinction causes violence, disruption, and war. The fact that religious actors, the participants of these movements, are described in terms which hearken back to the history of European religious wars (with the emerging state's religious opponents constructed as backward fanatics) is too blatantly obvious to ignore. In short, the underlying theoretical framework which Juergensmeyer employs, like that employed by Esposito, attempts to take on the task of interpreting religious movements but fails to do so due to its uncritical appropriation of normative analytical categories.

The subjectivities of individuals involved in religious movements or practices, as in the account by Juergensmeyer, inevitably assume irrational proportions and are constructed as the other of those who are associated with secular practices. This results from the strict binary categorization that views secularism and modernity as the antithesis of religion.

This tendency to view secularism, modernity, rationality, and progress as the polar opposites of religion results in a distortion of Muslim subjectivities and personhood. On the one hand, Islamic activists engaged in political or social militancy are commonly viewed as irrational extremists who act impulsively, are easily provoked, or who are staunchly wedded to ancient scripture and unyielding tradition. On the other hand, those who engage in secular or rational practices are depicted as being somehow less genuine. In this case, their authenticity is questioned and they are represented as simply manipulating religious ideologies that mask their lack of genuine Islamic character. Saba Mahmood's *Politics of Piety* (2005) articulated a strong response to this conundrum and a critique of liberal secular formulations of subjectivity. Her examination of the women's mosque movement in Egypt demonstrates a non-liberal alternative to desire and agency, albeit one shaped by liberal traditions. Recent scholarship, such as Charles Hirschkind's (2006) investigation of the public arena, has aimed at describing a more complex terrain in order to reveal the ways that contemporary Muslims engage in political activism to enact and embody Muslim virtues which also challenge the hegemony of secular liberalism.

The Limits of Relativity: Prayer, Emotion, and Rationality

In what follows, I present a prayer session at a women's Islamic Private Voluntary Organization (p.v.o.) in a Cairo suburb in Egypt as a site of high emotion. The scene provokes a set of questions that revolve around issues of subjectivity, emotions, and rationality. I conclude with a number of questions to initiate a discussion around the epistemology of rationality in Islamic movements and the literature on the MENA. In a scene from *salātu 'id ul-a ādha* (prayer for the Feast of Sacrifice) that I observed at the P.V.O. of Al Hilal, emotions, rationality, and the reactions of the anthropologist in the field cannot simply be explained through a culturally relative lens (Fieldnotes, October 2009).

On the 10th of *thl-hijja*, the last month of the Islamic calendar, a three-day celebration of *'idul adhā*, the Feast of Sacrifice, takes place in Muslim communities. The sacrifice refers to the slaughtering of animals to commemorate Muslims' deepest devotion to their God in remembrance of Ibrāhīm's slaughtering of a ram instead of his son, Ismāīl. "It is not their meat nor their blood that reaches Allah; it is your piety that reaches him," the Qur'anic *sura* or verse (22, 37) asserts.

The flesh and blood of the sacrificial animal (which is mostly distributed to the poor) is not the ultimate goal behind the ritual, explains the verse, rather it is the cultivation of a Muslim's devotion to Allah. The *'id al kabir* (or the Big Feast, as Egyptian Muslims call the Feast of Sacrifice) was going to fall on a Thursday this year. Generally, women do not take part in *salātul'id* as most women are at home with their families the day of the *'id*, probably cooking and preparing the meat from the sacrifice while their husbands go to the mosque to pray. Al Hilal had their own *salāt* a day earlier than is normally scheduled. Because the morning prayer is an important ritual of the celebration, the activist women of Al Hilal with whom I had conducted research for the last few years moved the *salāt* to the day before the *'id* to ensure that the women in the neighborhood could attend. Note how the women's Islamic movements were carving out a space for themselves within the very central traditions of Islamic practice. The events consist of the *salāt* and the following *khutbah*, then the prayer is introduced by a supplication called a *du'a'*.

> *Allaahumma ihdini feeman hadayta wa 'aafini fiman 'aafayta wa tawallani fiman tawallayta wa baarik li fima a'dayta, wa qini sharra ma qadayta, fa innaka taqdi wa la 'aqdi 'alayk, wa innahu laa yadhillu man waalayta wa laa ya'izzu man 'aadayta, tabaarakta Rabbana wa ta'aalayta la munji minka illa ilayk.*

> [O Allaah, guide me (to the right path) among those whom you have guided, pardon me among those whom you have pardoned, take care of me among those whom you have taken care of, and bless me in what you have bestowed, and save me from the evil of what you have decreed. For verily you decree and none can decree but you; and one whom you have cared for is not humiliated, nor is one honored who is your enemy. Blessed are you, O Lord, and exalted. There is no amnesty from you except with you.]

So started the *du'a'* after the *khutba* delivered by Doctora Zeinab, the director of Al Hilal. The *da'iya*, an energetic young medical doctor called Amira, whom I had met earlier, was reciting the *du'a'* from a microphone in her hand. Clear and strong, the microphone carried her words across the prayer hall to the hundreds of women who showed up that day as she recited the supplications. The women in the audience responded either by mouthing the words or interjecting *amin* (amen) in unison as they followed her every word. The prayers kept coming, gaining more intensity as they grew self-deprecating, admitting of weakness in the face of ego, materiality, and the mundane activities of everyday life that dis-tract from devotion to their God. Suddenly it seemed to me that Amira's voice started to waver. First slightly, then more so, she faltered, and it appeared as if she was choking back a wave of emotion that came upon her. The depth of her emotion shook the space of the prayer hall with its force. With tears streaming down her face, however, she continued to describe her love for God and his ever-beautiful qualities, and the worshipper's oblivious disregard for this beauty and bounty. Now Amira was openly weeping. Sobs wracked her slight frame. Still clutching the microphone in her hand, she continued the recital. As she wept, tears rolled down the faces of the women in the audience. Tears of grief, love, regret, yearning, sorrow—it was infectious. Feeling initially uncomfortable with the intensity of emotion in the room, I was surprised to find that my eyes teared up as well. It was impossible not to respond to the deep emotional impact of the performance. Whether or not it was for the same reasons, others too were now weeping or whimpering. Minutes later, Amira's voice called out the last words of prayer and then the *du'a'* ended. At once, the congregation gathered their purses and praying mats, and the bounded volumes of Qur'an they had brought with them, and filed into the front of the hallway. The cheerful burble of conversation rose in the air as the women greeted each other and moved through the crowds to claim the shoes that they had taken off as they entered the mosque earlier. Because there were more than two hundred women in prayer that day, each was given a number at the door to help locate their shoes in the rows upon neat rows on the shelves by the side of the entrance. Here and there, I could hear several women wonder whether they would be able to find their shoes; one joked about walking home barefoot; an older woman wondered out loud to herself why she ever handed her shoes to anyone when she could have simply kept the pair in her purse; and so they went on. It was hard to imagine, as I observed this scene, that only a few moments ago, this sea of faces was wet with tears.

Not a single person mentioned the weeping or the intense emotions they ex-hibited during the *du'a'*. It was as if it had never happened. It was now time to move on to the next part of the day, to celebrate, rejoice, and commemorate the feast.

Rationality and Cultural Relativism

The scene of *salātul-'id* described above illustrates a number of limitations that anthropologists deal with in the field. The ambivalence and then discomfort one feels when presented with heightened drama, the comfort in recognizing our immunity from emotions alien to ourselves, the collapse of the performative roles we assume as we enter the field as "cultural relativists." Without a doubt, as the event I attended unfolded, there was no particular linear or organized pattern to my observations. We submit our fieldnotes to the rigors of legible writing in an aftermath of self-examination. We impose our logical, yes, rational explanations of what transpired in the hope that we will be understood by our readers—if we are lucky enough to have them. My purpose in including this scene in a discussion of rationality and relativity is to illustrate how instinctively anthropologists turn to a set of rational paradigms when describing data collected from fieldwork, despite one's own implication in the scenes one experiences. Perhaps it is because of this very implication—the conundrum of being at once vulnerable in our ethnographic surroundings yet wielding a measure of power over them— that "rationality" develops into a reified skill for the instant translation of what we witness, a crafted tool—if you will—of the anthropologist's ethnographic kit.

A core paradigm in anthropological investigation, rationality (and its cognates the rational, reason, reasonableness) are, according to Barnard and Spencer's *Encyclopedia of Social and Cultural Anthropology,*

> usually ascribed to ideas or thought ("magic is irrational, science is rational"), to action ("cloud-seeding is rational, rain dance is irrational"), or to social arrangements ("feud is [an] irrational feature of social organization, bureaucracy a rational feature"). (1996, 467)

Debates about whether rationality is a universal norm have often centered on the question of whether "natives" follow norms of thinking that are similar to those of anthropologists or whether their thinking patterns are completely outside the norm of Western rationality. This debate has proved highly problematic however, since it assumes Western rationality to be the most progressive and civilized regardless of what natives seem to think. Although most anthropologists do not set out to study rationality in different cultures per se, assumptions about rationality undergird basic anthropological investigative techniques, and particularly the anthropologist's notion of cultural relativism.

Cultural relativity, one of the key concepts in social anthropology, relies upon the "cultural relativity of standards of rationality" (Collin 1997, 47). As social anthropologists going into the field we are prepared to witness and experience norms and practices that can be entirely different from our own. This is because we are trained to appreciate that rationality is deeply connected to human cognition of the world, which invariably differs from one society to another. Hence, principles of relativism enable us to understand social facts and given assumptions as recognizable and justifiable to their context through the rational systems that each society applies (ibid., 53).

However, there are serious limitations to this approach, as many have now pointed out (Lila Abu-Lughod, Johannes Fabian, Michel Foucault, Roger Keesing, Edward Said, and others). Lila Abu-Lughod (1991) notes that cultural relativity as an anthropological staple underscores difference and invariably produces inequality. For how else could cultures be studied except as entities? In which sense can anthropologists grasp the essence of a culture without essentializing it? And how possible is it to explore the tenets of a culture without bringing it back to a Western hegemonic frame of reference? Relative to what? Take for instance, the term "Middle East." Middle East of what? The ultimate example of the impact of a culturally relative vision of the world, the "Middle" refers to the middle of the eastern hemisphere of a world geographically outlined by empire (Hanafi 1998). In the field of the anthropology of the MENA, Stanley Diamond's scathing critique holds particular significance, "Relativism is the bad faith of the conqueror, who has become secure enough to become a tourist" (1974, 110). Although critiques of culture and relativism as discourses of difference-making have gained credence in the anthropology of the Middle East, I question whether cultural relativism can be an effective anthropological methodology in regions so historically and culturally intertwined with the West as the MENA region. How is cultural specificity possible as a starting point to our debates when cultural contexts are globally situated? Consequently, how can we accept rationality as an underlying principle of ethnographic investigation when "rational thinking" seamlessly produces cognitive worldviews across Orient and Occident? Where does the "Middle Eastern" subject begin and where does it end?

Conclusion

Scholars of religion, to varying degrees, debate the extent to which hegemonic definitions of religion dictate interpretations of religious practices and beliefs (Bowen 1998). Religion's common definition as a bounded social category largely determines how studies shape and inform our knowledge of the "subject" involved in religious practices. Data collected from the field does not always adequately address the notion of "religious subjectivities" due to a lack of a critical interrogation of normative conceptual binaries of secularism/religion, reason/faith, rational/irrational, modern/traditional. The subject is viewed in terms which reflect an underlying opposition between a reified emotional religious subject and a scientific secular other.

At the core of these limitations lies the notion of rationality. Conceptually constructed as an ethically neutral notion, Western hegemonic rationality has a hold on anthropological investigation that is difficult to shake. Culturally relative approaches rely on the relativity of rational difference, thus failing to divest the ethnographic process of normative Western rationality. Implicit in the epistemology of rationality is the premise of an essentialist "Orient" that lives in a world of its own—a separate rational existence at best, and an irrational other at worst. This staunchly inflexible viewpoint that persists in seeing cultures as bounded entities fails to recognize the fluidity and seamlessness of interchangeable historical processes. Ignoring this mutuality of history distorts how we understand notions of subjectivity as subjects are shaped through heterogeneous force fields that transcend the simple binary behind the rational/irrational, secular/religious, East/West, us/them constructs.

Early anthropological understanding of the subject engaged in religious activity is derived from the concepts and assumptions that have historically defined religion and religion's place in Western societies. The distinction that demarcates secularism from religion in Western history informs the binary opposition assumed in anthropological literature between religious and secular subjectivities. As historically situated as these categories of thought are, they are nonetheless powerful tools for ordering the world and the people who populate it. The danger has been in the universalizing nature of these sweeping generalizations about religion and its followers. These assumptions' implications for the analysis of subject production, in Western as well as non-Western societies, are immense. The associations of religion with irrationality, emotion, and backwardness that run through many early studies—Tyler, Hume, Weber, Malinowski—continue to impact researchers as they often uncritically employ these normative conceptions in their work.

11.

DEFINING (AND ENFORCING) ISLAM IN SECULAR TURKEY

Kim Shively

The place and role of Islam in the public sphere has long been an issue of intense contention in Turkey. This conflict finds persistent expression in the media, political and public discourse, as well as in private conversations and religious discourse. The debate about religion in Turkey has tended to crystallize around several key points of conflict: the nature of religious education, the presence and role of the *tarikats* or *cemaats* (religious organizations) in public life, and the "headscarf question"—when and where are women permitted to don the Muslim veil, if they so choose. Religious education of all types has progressively come under greater and greater state control, thereby limiting the dissemination of unauthorized religious knowledge. The *cemaats* have been officially outlawed but still continue to be popular and wield considerable social and political influence. And finally, regulations restricting veiled women in public institutions have spurred street demonstrations and political conflicts that have brought down political parties. The Kemalist establishment[1]—especially the military and the judiciary—has been concerned that allowing certain Islamic practices in the public sphere would endanger Turkish-style laicism, and so has been diligent in maintaining at least the semblance of control over religious activities and

204 Anthropology of Religion and Secularism in the MENA

practices. On the other hand, those who oppose government policy agitate for the freedom to practice religion as they see fit.

This debate about the role of Islam in Turkish society arises, in part, from very different understandings of what Islam is. The state's laicist interpretation of Islam maintains that certain unauthorized religious practices should be confined to the private sphere of the practitioner, if not completely eliminated. Yet this characterization of Islam is based on a Western, especially Protestant, concept of religion, where private individual faith is emphasized over social religious practice, such as donning the Islamic headscarf in public or participating in independent (non-state) religious education. Such an interpretation conflicts with other understandings of Islam thriving in Turkey, especially those that maintain that ritual and public practice are essential to genuine Islam. Yet, it is the Turkish state that has the authority and control over legitimate violence to enforce its form of Islam, over and against the wishes of many of its citizens.

The various perspectives in popular discourse regarding the nature of Turkish Islam presented here derive from interviews and participant observation research in various communities in Ankara—as well as one community in Istanbul—and close observation of electronic and print media. The key data are drawn from participant observation research of a women's Qur'an course in Sincan, a famously religious provincial town near Ankara (1997–1999 with subsequent visits in 2004, 2006–2008, 2010). The Sincan Qur'an course was led by Meryem,[2] a charismatic, intelligent, and articulate young woman (she was nineteen when I met her) who had a substantial following among women in the local neighborhood and had in fact worked as a preacher at a local religious radio station before I met her. The course students were generally young, and their educational and economic situations varied: some only had rudimentary formal education, some had graduated from primary school, some from high school, and occasionally a small number of college students took part as well. While the focus of the course was on reciting, memorizing, and understanding the Qur'an, Meryem's sermons and the subsequent discussions almost always turned to political matters. The course often became a platform for analyzing the state's attitude toward religious practice and discussing the ways in which to live a "clean" (*temiz*) form of Islam despite state limitations.

Home-based Qur'an courses like the one in Sincan have become increasingly popular in Turkey as part of the Islamic Revival or Islamic Awakening that has blossomed in Muslim-majority societies around the world since the 1970s. Yet in Turkey these courses are technically illegal because they might serve as arenas in which the wrong ("unauthorized") kind of religion is taught. Even though the laws against these courses are rarely enforced, the Sincan Qur'an course participants were well aware of the state's power to impose its will. A few months before I began my field research, Sincan had been subject to military threats (tanks rolled through the streets) after a display of the wrong kind of religion, in that case, a political-religious rally at the center of town. The coalition government of Turkey was forced out of power a few weeks later by military leaders who felt that this particular coalition and its Islamic agenda had threatened the secularist principles of the country. The course participants were well aware that they too violated these secularist principles. Even though they may fly under the radar of the powerful state, they resent that their interpretations of Islam—views they see as perfectly reasonable—are such an affront to the powers that be.

Religious Identity in Turkey

Turks by and large are a religious people. In all my travels and research in Turkey (since 1992), I rarely heard anyone openly admit that they were atheist. Almost everyone who talked to me about religion readily declared that they were indeed Muslims, because they believed in God and his Prophet Muhammad. This was the case whether my informants were self-declared Kemalists who had never performed ritual prayer (*namaz*), or devoted members of religious organizations (*cemaats*), though the few who did readily admit to being atheists were always vocal supporters of the Kemalist establishment.

Research seems to back up the salience of Muslim identity in Turkey. In a broad survey study conducted on religion and politics in Turkey in 2006, sociologists Ali Çarkoğlu and Binnaz Toprak found that 98.4 percent of their respondents (n=1,492) identified themselves as "Muslim" (2007). This number requires some interpretation since in Turkey, Muslim identity may often be part of national identity, in that the construction of the Turkish nation was often couched in terms of Muslim Turks versus non-Muslim, largely Christian enemies. Muslim identity for some may be in fact more about being Turkish than about being religious. It is nevertheless remarkable that only 1.6 percent of the population declared that they professed faith in no religion.

Furthermore, over ninety percent of the 2006 sample identified themselves as "religious," though what "religious" meant in this context seemed to vary somewhat. Certainly in my own fieldwork, people would label themselves as observant or serious about Islam if they fasted during Ramadan and prayed on holidays. Others argued that real religiosity meant following the five pillars of Islam as best one can, as well as following dietary and clothing regulations, etc. In their study Çarkoğlu and Toprak attempted to gauge respondent's self-perceived religiosity by asking each person to place themselves on a ten-point scale from "secularist" to "Islamist." Almost fifty percent identified themselves on the Islamist end of the scale, while only twenty percent placed themselves at the secularist end. The rest put themselves at point five in the middle. In a separate question on identity, forty-five percent of the respondents—by far the most—described themselves first and foremost as Muslim, rather than as Turkish, Kurdish, or even as a citizen of the Turkish republic, suggesting that religious identity is sometimes more important that national identity (Çarkoğlu and Toprak 2007).

Finally, a "great majority" of the respondents confirmed that having proper faith may be sufficient to be a Muslim, "that if someone believes in God or the prophet he could still be considered a Muslim even if he did not perform the ritual prayer (namaz), did not fast, consumed alcohol or in the case of a woman did not cover" (ibid.). Yet the same survey showed that people who covered or prayed would be for various reasons reluctant to give up these practices. For example, over seventy percent women who wore some sort of Muslim head covering (about seventy percent of the female respondents covered) said that they did so "because Islam commands that women cover" (ibid.). Though many are willing to be generous with others, there still seems to be a strong sense that it is the believer's duty to follow the commands of Islam, however the commands are interpreted.

The strong Muslim identity and the relatively high level of religiosity within the Turkish population exists in the context of a staunchly secularist state. The state has been able to enforce restrictions on what many see as legitimate Muslim practices in the name of protecting Turkey's laicist public sphere, while arguing that people are free to practice "all the Islam they need" in the privacy of their own homes or in state-allocated spaces, such as mosques. Many observant Turks function within these limits without complaint, especially if they live in communities and villages in which they are surrounded by like-minded people who do not enforce the state requirements on religious conduct. But others, such as the women in the Sincan Qur'an course and their families, friends, and neighbors, are indeed affected by the restrictions, and object to them in no uncertain terms. In order to clarify the roots of the tension between the Kemalist establishment and those who critique it on religious grounds, I will investigate the competing ideas about Islam at work in Turkish society, and how those ideas get reproduced in various forms of religious education.

Secularism in Turkey

Before turning to the issue of religion and education, it is necessary to discuss how the secularization of institutions and the public sphere has been a fundamental component of Turkey's modernization project. Many aspects of Turkish society—from education and governance to the public sphere—were officially secularized over a relatively short period of time. The Kemalist secularizing reforms sought not only to remove religious influence from the political arena and place state controls on the public expression of religion, but the reforms also emphasized the reorganization and the "de-Islamization" of patterns of daily life and gender roles and relations. These reforms included the replacement of the Muslim calendar with the Western; the adoption of the Swiss Civil Code and rejection of Muslim law; the abolition of Sufi religious orders; the implementation of secular Western-style education and the abolition of the *medrese* system; the "Alphabet Revolution" (the adoption of the Latin alphabet in place of the Arabic alphabet); and clothing reforms, including the "Hat Law," which banned the fez in favor of the Western hat. Thus, the Kemalist reforms wrought a reorganization of space and time that explicitly sought to disenchant and Westernize the Turkish public sphere. The most striking aspect of the Kemalist reforms is how the dispositions, practices, and lifestyles of ordinary Turkish citizens came under the scrutiny of the state, so much so that the places and appearances of the bodies of Turkish people became the ultimate signifiers of the success or failure of the Kemalist Westernization efforts.

But Turkey is not "secular" in the American sense of the word; it is *laik,* or laicist, in the French sense. To follow the typology of Ahmet Kuru (2006), secularism in the United States is more passive in its exercise in that it maintains neutrality toward various religions, allows for the public visibility of religion, and strives (at least ideally) for a complete separation of church and state. It requires that government make no demands on individuals' religious beliefs or behaviors (within limits, of course) and that religion make no similar demands on government behavior. But laicism (*laiklik*) in Turkey and France—what Kuru classifies as assertive secularism—endeavors to bring religion under the control of the state. The idea is that religion should not be in the hands of a powerful and independent clerical elite that can rival government power, but should be brought under the control of the nonreligious state, where it no longer poses a potential threat to government hegemony (McClay 2000; Davison 2003).

In Turkey, though not in France, the state controls all aspects of public religious practice through the Directorate of Religious Affairs, which formulates all Qur'anic course curriculum, oversees the training of prayer leaders and preachers, and controls the content of Friday sermons (White 2002; Yılmaz 2005). The result has been that the laicist state has not rejected or separated Islam from the state so much as has promoted a particular kind of Islam—one of "belief" and "conscience" rather than political involvement—that better suited the Turkish Republic's goals of rationalization and Westernization. That is, the Kemalist establishment promotes the notion that a secular public sphere is one in which religious symbols and practices—except for those sanctioned by the state itself—are to be delegated to the private sphere and to places of worship where they will not interfere with Turkish "material life and worldly concerns" (Mardin 1982). Thus, the state may proscribe such lifestyle choices as wearing Muslim headscarves and clothing in public spaces, praying in unauthorized places such as in public schools, and participating in unofficial religious education or *cemaat* activity.

Such an interpretation of Islam rests on a set of assumptions that clashed with the religious beliefs of many practicing Muslims in Turkish society, including my informants (see Shively 2008). The first assumption is that there is one essential, apolitical Islam that the state appropriately enunciates and enforces through policy and practice. Other religious practices violate the state principle of laicism and therefore are threats to the secular status quo that supposedly characterizes the Turkish public sphere. The state, especially the military and judiciary, has established itself as a protector of laicism, and thus has the right to limit these practices in the public sphere. It can claim that religious freedom is maintained because it does not necessarily condemn the unauthorized practices altogether. Rather, the state excludes them from the public realm. The practices may be performed in the privacy of the family home or to some extent in designated (and state-controlled) places of worship, so that they do "no harm," that is, present no danger to the political status quo. Kemalists may (and do) argue then that men are free to have an Islamic beard and women are free to cover as they please, but they may not legally take these symbols into public institutions, such as public schools, universities, or government offices. Many public institutions do not allow these bodily practices, with the argument that the religious symbols (the veil or the beard) violate the secular nature of the public, civic sphere. For my informants, all of whom veiled and many of whom aspired to higher education, they either had to discard the veil and violate their interpretation of Islam or go uneducated.

This first assumption depends on other assumptions that are also bound up in the official interpretation of religion's role in society. One notion is that the official, essential Islam is defined primarily by a particular belief or "faith," whereas religious practice—especially certain practices that violate the Republican state's understanding of religion—is subsidiary to belief and therefore may be discarded without harm to the practitioner or to Islam itself. As Ihsan Yılmaz puts it (2005), "In Republican epistemology, religion is imprisoned in the conscience of the individual and in places of worship in society and is not allowed to mix with and interfere in public life." The former president of Turkey, A. Necdet Sezer, articulated this epistemology most explicitly in a symposium on religion. He stated, "Secularism is a way of life which should be adopted by an individual. A 'secular individual' should confine religion in the sacred place of his conscience and not allow his belief to affect this world" (in Kuru 2006).

In a word, there is a "Protestantization" of Islam among many Kemalist Turks and in official attitudes toward religious practice and education. A hallmark of the Protestant reforms of early modern Europe was an emphasis on faith or belief over and against "works" in the form of moral behavior and penance. Martin Luther, the intellectual founder of Protestantism, argued that human sinfulness is so profound that there is basically nothing a person can do to earn his or her salvation. Rather, it is God's gift of grace and the individual's faith that provide the possibility of justification and ultimately salvation. This doctrine of *sola fide* (by faith alone) is the signature belief of Protestantism, though it was adapted in various ways into other forms of Christianity in Europe and elsewhere. Implicitly, though not in terms of any official doctrine issued by the Directorate of Religious Affairs, the emphasis on faith over works has dominated the modern Turkish state's attitude toward Islam. In Turkey, the tacit assumption of official Islam is that religious belief is a matter of the heart, something that one accepts, and belief or faith is the essence of religion. Faith trumps works, belief is more important than deed. As such, some may claim, that it is not necessary to wear a Muslim headscarf, refrain from alcohol, or pray five times a day to be a "true" Muslim. All you have to do is believe. As the Çarkoğlu and Toprak study discussed above makes clear, many Turks agree with this sentiment.

The implicit Protestant bias in official Turkish concepts of religion probably derives from a generalized Protestant bias in Western—including anthropological—understandings of religion and the problems such a bias creates in analyses of Islam, as Talal Asad (1993) has noted. In his 1993 essay, "The Construction of

Religion as an Anthropological Category," Asad critiques Clifford Geertz's famous definition of religion (1973) for its cognitivist slant. That is, Geertz's definition of religion has construed it as being about the moods and motivations of individuals; religion is primarily symbolic and cognitive and it only secondarily concerns actual practice. As such, many religious actions may be optional, excluded without any "real" harm to the essence of religion, namely, individual private belief. In Turkey, as exemplified in the experiences of the Qur'an course participants, pious Muslims are expected to leave certain practices at home when they venture into the public sphere and into certain public institutions. The veil may be shed without harming a woman's true (essential) Muslim identity. Only certain types of religious knowledge and practice may be promulgated in the public sphere, while others must be kept inside the privacy of the home where they supposedly belong.

My informants, and probably most Muslims, would agree that faith is essential to Islam. The declaration of faith—the *shahada*—is the first pillar of Islam, after all, and it is emphasized that one must make the declaration with the proper intention (*niyet*), that is, with sincerity. And certainly, the Qur'an is filled with references to the virtues of "believing men and women" vis-à-vis the *kafirun* (those who do not believe). But my informants did not follow this appreciation of faith with the conclusion that everything else is secondary and therefore disposable. The other four pillars of Islam—prayer, fasting, almsgiving, and pilgrimage—are also incumbent upon all believers who are capable of performing them. The five pillars of Islam are the central duties to God for all believers, and the only reason not to perform them is incapacity, as in the case where poverty prevents the believer from giving alms. Other Muslim law, such as family law (so-called duties to society), has a longer history of debate about what is necessary and what is not, but many Muslims see some of these duties, such as wearing the headscarf or refraining from alcohol, as essential to Islam. Yet, the Kemalist establishment would seem to allow for the discarding of all practices besides faith, or at least make it difficult to maintain some of these practices in the secular public sphere.

I do not intend to judge who is right and who is wrong in regards to the soteriological status of faith versus practice in Islam. Both interpretations—those who take an implicit *sola fide* approach to Islam and those who maintain that practice is also essential—have their theological proponents and detractors. Both the Kemalist establishment and my informants passed judgment over certain types of religious practice, accepting some as proper and others as in some way improper, if not dangerous. But what I wish to emphasize here is that the state's concept of Islam runs afoul of many other interpretations of Islam at work in Turkish society—and the interpretation in the members of the Qur'an course was only one such alternative conception of Islam. Yet the state has the power and authority to enforce its own form of Islam over and against the views and wishes of many of its citizens. In fact, it seems fair to argue that it is the Kemalists themselves who are the real Islamists, since they attempt to impose by law and force a particular interpretation of Islam, while many other religious practitioners, such as the students in the Qur'an course, are closer to true secularists (rather than laicists), since they have articulated a desire to allow for less state control and more freedom of religious practice.

What constitutes the public sphere and what private space is essential to the debate about the role and place of Islamic practices in Turkey. Much recent theory on the nature of the public sphere derives from the work of Jürgen Habermas (1989), who conceived of the bourgeois public sphere as an inclusive discursive realm that serves as a space or structure that intermediates between the state and the private interests of citizens, a space in which private individuals could debate issues of common (public) concern. In the case of religion, for example, the secular public sphere in particular is supposed to provide a neutral or objective arena that allows for people to agree to disagree about religion in a rational dialogue that would yield policies that serve the greatest common good. Furthermore, particular interests and practices that adhere to private space and activity should be set aside from the public debate because they work against the attainment of the desired common good. In this conception, action in the secular public sphere operates on a tenet of what Habermas calls "rational debate" where people with different religious and political viewpoints and motives may subscribe to the same set of political principles. Conflicts that arise over what those political principles may be are resolved through negotiation and compromise, and sometimes by withdrawal.

Such a conception of a neutral public arena in which certain "supra-religious" norms are articulated and negotiated presumes a process of give and take among equals, but most often the parties negotiating over what principles dominate in a secular society are not equals. More commonly, "negotiation amounts to the exchange of unequal concessions in situations where the weaker party has no choice" (Asad 2003, 6). The result of such power relationships is that over time, the realm of "the secular" is delineated along the lines of power, a process that excludes many who have little or no political voice. As such, there really is no such thing as a neutral public sphere.

In the case of Turkey, the Kemalist establishment has determined what types of religious activity are permissible in public spaces and what are not, supposedly in the interests of maintaining a laicist public sphere. But Turkish secularists have gone beyond traditional concepts of secularization of the public sphere "by defining even the living room and the guest room as public spaces and attempting to de-Islamicize every social space but the bedroom" (Tuğal 2006). The state has not only defined the nature of the public sphere in a restrictive way, but has labeled "public" those things that others see as corresponding to the "private" sphere or to the freedom of choice about private concerns, such as clothing and forms of social interaction.

Moreover, the Turkish republican regime casts its restrictions on autonomous religious practice as a matter of national security. A common rhetorical device used against loosening constraints on religious practice is that one need only look at Iran, Saudi Arabia, and Afghanistan under the Taliban to see what happens when Islam gets too involved in or takes over public institutions: religious authoritarianism and repression automatically result. This argument takes many forms. For example, military educational texts—required reading for all students—state that Turkey's very survival as a sovereign nation in the face of foreign threats depends on the its population embracing "Atatürk's principles and revolutions not only at the level of ideas, but also at the level of lifestyle" (Milli Güvenlik Bilgisi in Altınay 2004). By equating lifestyle choices with a Turkish identity conceptualized over and against its enemies, the regime can claim that limits on autonomous Islamic practices serve Turkey's security interests, thereby justifying the use of force to defend its particular version of Islam.

Those devout Muslims, such as my informants, who wish to develop practices and lifestyles they see as being more in accord with the will of God often find themselves with difficult decisions. They may have to continue to break social expectations or even laws (independent religious education, veiling, *cemaats*), hoping that the state will not persecute them (usually it does not). Or they may choose to make painful compromises in which they comply with legal demands in ways that conflict with their religious sensibilities. There were a number of issues that created especially intense resentments. I will use the example of one such issue—the production of religious knowledge—that was especially contentious during my initial fieldwork and remains so today.

Religious Education

A major concern of the laicist state has been to maintain a form of Islam that harmonizes with the principle of laicism and how to prevent the rise of rival and potentially subversive forms of Islamic thought in the Turkish polity. Controlling religious education is, of course, an essential method of "domesticating" religion and guaranteeing that it remains relatively harmless to laicism. Though compulsory education has been secular since the founding of the Republic, "Religious Culture and Ethics" courses have been offered in primary and secondary schools, and have been required for all students since 1982. The importance given to religious education in public schools arose especially as various political and military leaders looked to Islam as a means to try to unify Turkish society after the bitter battles and the communist threat that caused such turmoil in the 1970s and instigated the 1980 military coup (Kaplan 2002).

But the state has also sought to guarantee that "proper" Islam would be imparted to school children, that is, an Islam compatible with nationalism and modernity. Such an education would guarantee that children would not be unduly influenced by "false" family beliefs or other sources. According to the general secretariat of the National Security Council, Atatürk himself is said to have argued that "religion must be taken out from the hands of ignorant people, and the control should be given to the appropriate people"—those who would teach a suitably tame form of Islam (in Kaymakcan 2006). This rationale for state religious education was made explicit in the standard instruction manual, *The Elementary School Program:* "The teacher must draw the pupil's attention to the wrong and harmful traditions that they encounter in their families and persuade them to get rid of these traditions" (in Kaplan 2006). In sum, the state provides venues for the production and circulation of religious knowledge, but only the kind of "tame" Islam that fits the needs of the state. All other unofficial forms of religious education, especially of children, are technically illegal, lest "wild" (unsanctioned) forms of religious knowledge contaminate the Turkish population.

Ironically, the nature of religious education in modern Turkey has unwittingly maintained certain aspects of the *medrese* education characteristic of the Ottoman Empire, with its authoritarian approach to religious knowledge. As under the Empire, religious education in the public schools promulgates only one interpretation of Islam—the state's version of Hanafi Sunni Islam—and does not allow for questioning or for discussion of any other interpretations, such as those held by Turkey's Alevis (Kaymakcan 2006). The curriculum and textbooks used in the courses outline the beliefs and practices of basic Hanafi Sunni Islam (the Five Pillars, the Six Beliefs[3]) and emphasize how good Sunni Muslims should conduct themselves in relationship to family, community, and nation. Nationalist concerns frame the material, so that the textbooks invariably open with the words of the Turkish National Anthem, *İstiklal Marşı* ("Independence March"), as well as a portrait of Atatürk and a copy of his famous "Speech to the Youth." But other issues that were of concern to my informants—proper dietary practices, clothing practices, gender relationships, purification rituals, knowledge of Arabic, Qur'anic recitation and memorization, etc.—are absent from the curriculum.

The courses, as such, teach some of the central elements of proper belief (orthodoxy), but very little about proper practice (orthopraxy) beyond basic moral precepts. In general, official religious instruction (outside the universities) tends to be vague and general, so as not to offend any group or to show bias toward any of the *tarikats* that, though officially outlawed, are still very influential in Turkish society. As Elisabeth Özdalga has noted (1999, 434), this standardization of religious instruction creates a very watered-down and repetitive course content, where what was taught in primary school is simply repeated, with slight elaboration, in secondary school. For secularist students, then, religion class represents only a boring burden of meaningless repetition—a complaint I heard from a large number of students and their parents. And for religiously observant students, the courses are superficial and unsatisfactory (ibid., 436). Critics such as Özdalga have noted that the goal of the state's form of religious education is to create a monoculture in which one essential form of Islam reigns, just as there is to be one culture (Turkish), one language (Turkish), and one future (progressive). Education serves to bring the people into this monoculture, so that "order" and "progress" are given more importance than ideas such as freedom and liberty (ibid.).

Religiously conscious (*şuurlu*) students, then, must look elsewhere for more meaningful religious instruction, though by law (if not by practice) the state controls all forms of religious education. And the state does offer other options: there are religious high schools, *imam-hatip* schools, which offer a mixture of secular curriculum and religious instruction. These schools also offer separate classrooms for girls and boys, and girls are usually permitted to wear the headscarf. For boys and girls from devout families, these schools have been popular alternatives to secular high schools. But over the past two decades, the Islamist movement in Turkey has taken a more prominent role in Turkish politics, leading to government attempts to control religious discourse and education in many arenas (Pak 2004, 332). The *imam-hatip* schools have often been targeted as places in which radical religious youth become politically mobilized by religious-right political parties and other groups. Thus the *imam-hatip* schools have been under strong and continuous pressure to maintain a "moderate" curriculum, which may not include the types of religious knowledge that some students desire. Also, for students who are college-bound, attending these schools mean they receive a severe point deficit on the national college entrance exams, which creates a major barrier to college matriculation. Finally, because the *imam-hatip* schools are secondary schools, they are not an option for students who, like my informants, are beyond high school age or who do not choose to attend high school (education is only compulsory through eighth grade).

Through the *Diyanet İşleri Başkanlığı* (Directory of Religious Affairs), the state also offers official Qur'an courses to teach the book to anyone who wishes to learn. But these courses are tightly controlled and fairly insipid, taught by teachers who are certified by the Directorate of Religious Affairs to give religious instruction according to the needs of the laicist state. None of my devout informants found this a useful option. Several individuals complained that these courses grant a certificate upon completion, but it is almost worthless. One cannot even become a Qur'an course teacher with this certificate. One *cemaat* member I interviewed complained that the state courses tend to teach only very basic information but nothing very interesting—nothing about dietary restrictions or Qur'anic exegesis or even the basics of Arabic beyond recitation of verses (and sometimes not even that).

So there are officially acceptable options for religious education, a point state officials readily make when criticizing those who would set up alternative—illegal—forms of religious instruction. But unless one can go to college or attend the *imam-hatip* schools, one learns only basic aspects of belief and some practice, and not much else that would be meaningful to a devout practitioner. More significantly, all the members of the Qur'an course made it clear that religious study is a life-long pursuit that is important to the maintenance and enhancement of piety. A number of the Qur'an course students had attended and even graduated from the *imam-hatip* schools, but all believed that one does not simply establish once and for all an essential body of religious knowledge that is "good enough" for being a Muslim. Rather, as a good Muslim one pursues religious understanding and persistently attempts to shape one's life according to the will of God. This is an ongoing struggle (*cihad*), as many observant Muslims reminded me. The situations and innovations of the age—and of any age—require constant return to scripture and ongoing guidance from religious adepts. A diploma from an *imam-hatip* high school or a certificate from a Qur'an course is only one step in this continuing journey toward self-perfection. The repetitive and narrow curricula offered in state-sponsored religious education programs are incomplete guides in this journey—at best.

Meryem and her students were interested in a more rigorous morality than the bland discussions provided in the *Diyanet* Qur'an courses or in the

public school classes. The students instead explored an ethical system that emphasized lifestyle choices by which the individual could shape her whole life according to the will of God. They maintained similar concepts of ethics as those
expressed by the women studied by Saba Mahmood in Egypt (2005), in that
they saw disciplined pious activity as a means of creating and enhancing devotion to God, rather than assuming that ethical thought (belief) must precede
and give rise to pious activity, as implicit in most Western, specifically Kantian,
conceptions of ethics. They assume that ethical behavior follows naturally from
ethical thought—again, a cognitive and Protestant bias—whereas the women
in Mahmood's study, as well as the women in the Sincan Qur'an course, interpreted the relationship between thought and behavior in more dynamic ways.
They believed that disciplined pious activities shape a certain desired religious
subjectivity, which in turn inspires consciously ethical behavior. Meryem made
this especially clear in a sermon she gave to her students, where she stated, "It is
necessary to follow the many rules in the Qur'an—following such rules causes
one to think, to think about one's own role in relationship to God, what one
should do."

The Sincan women therefore saw much of their activity as inherently ethical
since the activity not only reflects their piety but also shapes it. Thus, the Qur'an
course members concerned themselves not only with wearing appropriately
modest clothing as a means of pleasing God, but of creating a moral attitude
and social order in which sexual desire is expressed in appropriate ways. Women
must veil, I was told on many occasions, so that men may not be provoked by
women's beauty and women are not tempted to put themselves on display for
men. As one young student put it: "An apple will rot faster if it doesn't have its
skin." She was suggesting that the veil is necessary for a woman to maintain her
purity internally. A woman needs a headscarf as a material reminder that prevents her from stepping outside the social norms of feminine modesty. A woman
on display—without the veil—will be spoiled no matter what. For her, the veil is
essential to the identity of a good woman.

Clothing was not the only moral issue of great concern among the course
members. Rules relating to gender segregation were also a focus of discussion.
Environments in which men and women could properly inhabit their separate
gendered spheres were sought out: gender-segregated education, tea parks, meeting facilities, etc., were all seen as preferable to corresponding non-segregated
spaces. The various resort towns along the western coast of Turkey, with their
displays of bodies and the endless parties and alcohol consumption, were especially condemned, but the women were also concerned to avoid television

programs and films that display unchaste and impious lifestyles. Other issues, such as dietary restrictions, were recurrent sources of conversation as well. Such detailed understandings of ethics and ethical behavior had no place in the state religious education classes and curriculum, where ethics is treated only in generalized and rather simplistic terms, such as being kind to others and serving one's family and nation.

The most common complaint that pious Muslims lodged against state-sponsored religious education is the issue of control—of content, of interpretation, of curriculum, and of course, the control of political discourse. The Turkish state dictates religious content in all public contexts in order to make sure religious messages do not clash with or threaten state conceptions of religion, with its implicit emphasis on belief over practice. But many pious Muslims also criticized the way in which Islam itself has been categorized and marginalized by the Turkish state. They want to teach Islam the way they understand Islam—spiritually, socially, ritually, as well as politically—without interference. The Qur'an course students and many observant Muslims argue that this is a basic right of freedom of conscience and belief (*vicdan ve inanç özgürlüğü*). But "uncontrolled," autonomous religion is precisely what the Turkish establishment finds threatening enough to warrant making laws forbidding religious instruction outside of state supervision. While the laws are often aimed at the *cemaats,* who may use religion courses to organize militant opposition groups, they have the effect of suppressing all types of independent religious instruction. In an effort to keep the public sphere "free" from problematic Islam, the state reached into what the Qur'an course students considered to be their private lives, dictating how they should dress and how they should practice their religion.

Even as the Kemalist state has attempted to suppress those forms of Islam that it has deemed harmful, I do not mean to suggest that the Sincan Qur'an course represents "genuine" Islam and that the state's form is less genuine. I am not reversing the state's evaluation of "true" versus "false" forms of Islam, though the students' own goal in the Qur'an course was to develop an understanding of what for them was genuine or "clean" (*temiz*) Islam. Indeed, the Qur'an course members and some other citizens of Sincan and similar neighborhoods also maintain a critical stance toward those forms of Muslim practice that they see as corrupted or lacking basis in Muslim textual sources. Meryem and her family and students were pointedly critical of the ecstatic practices associated with certain *cemaats,* noting not only their lack of faithfulness to textual traditions but also their lack of rationality. Rationality, in the form of clearheaded study of the Qur'an, the *ahadith,*[4] and other sources of recognized religious authority, was also a watchword of this particular group of pious Muslims, even if it was a form of rationality not recognized by the state outside of the religious bureau-cratic organization. Rather, the Qur'an course students rejected some types of practices because they represent ignorant, corrupted Islam, rather than the clean, "orthodox" Islam that the women of Sincan attempted to cultivate (cf. Hart 2009). Similarly, they criticized the state's restriction on religious education, not because the state's curriculum is irrational or wrong, but because it is limited.

Despite official policy, unauthorized Qur'an courses are not uncommon, especially in conservative neighborhoods in major cities. For the most part, the illegal status of the neighborhood Qur'an courses are not a great cause for con-cern. As with many laws in Turkey, it is difficult for the government to enforce its ban on a relatively widespread (and popular) practice, and so it doesn't try very hard—except when the state feels itself threatened by the religious right, as it did following the "soft coup" of 1997, when an Islamist-leaning welfare government was forced out of power by the military. Since Sincan had been a major site of military action leading up to the coup, the women of the Qur'an course were still quite nervous about their own situation during the principle period of my field-work in 1997–1999, and they took steps to conceal what it was they were doing, such as meeting in different homes every day. In retrospect, their caution was almost certainly unnecessary, since the Turkish state has shown little stomach for tracking down and putting a halt to these informal courses. Yet, there is no doubt that the Kemalist tendency to privilege and enforce by law a certain type of Islam—one that favors the private interior aspects—over and above other interpretations of Islam is bound to create a sense of resentment and oppression among those on the losing side of the exercise of state power.

Conclusion

The period of my initial fieldwork from 1997 to 1999 was an especially tense time in the extended debate over the place and role of religion in Turkish society. I began my fieldwork soon after the soft coup of 1997, and I completed my field-work in 1999, soon after events surrounding national elections that eventually led, in 2001, to the forced closing of another Islamic-leaning party, the Virtue Party. The subsequent establishment of the mildly Islamic Justice and Development Party (AKP: *Adalet ve Kalkınma Parti*) changed the dynamics of the tension over Islam in Turkish public life. The AKP has established what many see as a more moderate, "reformist" religious-oriented movement under the leadership of a controversial former mayor of Istanbul, Recep Tayyip Erdoğan. The AKP has been very mindful of the fact that a religious agenda cannot be pushed very far and so has tread very carefully, focusing on economic and legal policies that appeal to broader constituencies than did the policies of the previous religiously oriented parties (Dağı 2006).

This moderation paid off when the AKP won a clear majority (thirty-four percent) of the vote in the 2002 national elections and solidified that majority in local elections in 2004. Indeed, the religiosity of the Turkish population, as revealed in the Çarkoğlu and Toprak study, expressed itself clearly when the AKP managed to win a stronger majority (forty-six percent) in the 2007 elections. Still the party and its supporters have remained vulnerable to attack from Kemalist components of society, especially the military, who are worried that the party maintains a secret agenda to slowly tear down the Kemalist/secularist reforms to ultimately create an Islamist state. Various events—such as the appointment of AKP former foreign minister Abdullah Gül to the presidency in 2007 and the attempt by the party to lift restrictions on headscarves in universities—have stoked anxieties and provoked such strong responses from Kemalist supporters that AKP has remained an object of great suspicion and distrust by the military and judiciary. The Constitutional Court attempted to forcibly disband the AKP on accusations of anti-secularist activities, and though the accusations were upheld, the vote for party closure fell short and the party was permitted to continue, though it received financial penalties. Even though the power of the military has weakened in the last few years, military generals still regularly issue warnings against what they interpret as violations of the secular order, and given the regularity of military coups in Turkish history (four coups between 1960 and 2000), those threats take on a sharp edge.

What these successive iterations of Islamist, conservative, religiously oriented parties over the past fifteen years have provoked in Turkish public discourse is a heightening concern about the nature of "proper" Islam, that is, a type of Islam that does not threaten the Kemalist establishment. Each party, from Welfare to AKP, has tested the limits of Kemalist toleration for independent, unauthorized religious behaviors and discourses, in the process crystallizing and clarifying the state's concept of true, proper Islam. This form of Islam—what I call "tame Islam" (Shively 2008)—is one defined by belief that is confined to the individual's conscience and does not affect this world. Clearly, the state needs Islam, as the developments after the 1980 coup have revealed, but an Islam that is tightly controlled, confined, and domesticated to fit the requirements of the state.

One could say that the Kemalist state apparatus has done precisely what it has frequently accused the Islamist parties of doing: using religion for political ends and inciting "enmity" among those religious citizens who are not entirely sympathetic to all the tenets of Kemalist doctrine. However, the Kemalist establishment has normalized and naturalized its own interpretation of Turkish Islam, such that any alternative constructions of Islamic practice and belief are seen as not only dangerous but deluded. Alternative religious expressions, such as wearing the veil or belonging to a religious community or conducting independent religious education, are often publicly pathologized in a variety of ways: as holdovers from a dark past (the late Ottoman Empire); as a mark of "primitive," premodern thinking; or more perniciously, as signs of allegiance with malevolent internal or external forces. They are not usually—at least in public—discussed as reasonable alternatives to the Protestantized Islam of the Kemalist state.

For pious Muslims the Turkish state's conception of religion is essentially cognitive, private, and pushed into the shadowy "corners" of society. It is in direct opposition to Muslim history and belief. For them, the Turkish Kemalist establishment has bought into Western imperialist doctrine, thereby jettisoning genuine Islam in the name of modernity. Many devout Muslims who see themselves as the true practitioners reject Kemalist doctrines that violate their understandings of religion, and they break Turkish law in order to fulfill the laws of God. Women wear the headscarf in public institutions or people establish unauthorized Qur'an courses in their neighborhoods. They attempt to bring their understanding of religion out of the hidden corners of society to make space for themselves in the public sphere.

NOTES

Acknowledgements: The research for this article was made possible by grants from the Wenner-Gren Foundation, the Institute of Turkish Studies, and the Sachar Fund of Brandeis University. I would also like to thank Sherine Hafez and Susan Slyomovics for organizing the conference "State of the Art: Anthropology of the Middle East and North Africa" at UCLA in April 2010, at which a draft of this paper was presented.

1. The Kemalist establishment are those who adhere to the principles and revolutions (*ilke ve inkilap*) of Mustafa Kemal Atatürk, which include secularism, nationalism, republicanism, populism, etatism, and reformism. The Kemalist establishment is often identified as including the Constitutional Court, the Council of State, the military generals, and certain politicians, such as members of the Republican People's Party (Atatürk's

original party), as well as all those who support these institutions and actors. Traditionally, the Kemalists have dominated Turkey politically, socially, and militarily throughout the history of the Republic, though their power may be waning somewhat in the twenty-first century (White 2007).

2. All names of research participants are pseudonyms.

3. The six beliefs of Islam are: (1) belief in the one God, (2) belief in the angels, (3) belief in the books (Qur'an), (4) belief in the prophets, (5) belief in the Day of Judgment, and (6) belief in fate and predestination.

4. The *ahadith* (the plural of *hadith*) are a complicated collection of texts, begun as oral history and eventually put into writing. They record the sayings and actions of the Prophet regarding religious and social practices. These "words and deeds of the Prophet" are not thought to be sacred in the same way the Qur'an is considered sacred—commandments from the Qur'an are categorized as requirements, or *farz*, for Muslims. Rather, the deeds and sayings of the Prophet (*sunnah*) are considered to be strongly recommended for believers to follow in order to lead a pious and moral life.

12.

SHARI'A IN THE DIASPORA: DISPLACEMENT, EXCLUSION, AND THE ANTHROPOLOGY OF THE TRAVELING MIDDLE EAST

Susanne Dahlgren

> Any Western politician, judge or religious leader desiring instant fame or a dose of controversy has an easy option. All you need do is say "Shari'a" in public.
>
> —*The Economist* (16 October 2010)

How is the Middle East "present" in today's world? The question began to interest me as I followed the burgeoning anti-Muslim debates in Europe and North America sparked by the 9/11 terror attacks. The Middle East and its people, labeled "Muslims," are increasingly visible on other continents, particularly in Shari'a controversies—debates over how much of "their religion" "we" can accept in "our" societies. What Shari'a, the divine law of Muslims, is, and how it has become the subject of some of today's fiercest public debates, are the questions I address in this chapter. When looking at today's debates, I compare them to similar controversies that took place during the colonial era when European countries extended their empires to the Middle East and North Africa, and in this endeavor, took Muslim law as a means of strengthening the legitimacy of the state. Similarly today, as I argue here, at issue is how the Western hegemonic state is attempting to control the bodies and minds of its subjects. For contemporary anthropologists, today's Shari'a debates represent a barely explored field that can broaden our understanding of how legal practice, in terms both of actual practice in and outside of courtrooms and of the discourse concerning that practice, can be studied ethnographically to show how subjects from different power positions participate in struggles for hegemony, control, and exclusion. Typical to our era, these debates often take place on the internet and satellite TV, where new meanings of Shari'a, devoid of a particular grounding place, are created and contested.

In a 2007 German court case, a judge refused a divorce appeal by a Moroccan woman trying to escape a violent husband, on the basis that wife-beating is sanctioned in the Qur'an. In the court it became evident that the husband had regularly beaten his wife and had threatened to kill her. But because the husband and wife were both from Morocco, the judge saw fit to adjust the case according to her understanding of the litigants' cultural background. Wife-beating is a standard practice in Morocco and the Qur'an sanctions it, the judge was reported to have commented (Medick and Reimann 2007). Newspapers around the globe reported how a Western liberal country had taken the Qur'an as the basis for a court decision.

The case was condemned by German Muslim organizations as well as the press. The head of the Central Council of Muslims in Germany criticized the judgment and proclaimed that wife-beating is not in accordance with the teachings of Islam (Landler 2007). Still, this was not the first time a European court had used cultural background to inform its verdict. Regarding family violence, there have been a number of cases in European courts where the perpetrator's culture of origin was considered to be a mitigating circumstance.[1]

While the above is an extreme case of multiculturalism gone wrong, as scholars of Muslims in Europe and human rights activists alike would assert, it is also illustrative of the platforms upon which today's globalized debates over Shari'a are taking place. At one pole, there are Muslim activists advocating the need for Shari'a, and at another, protectors of "Western values" for whom Shari'a merely stands for injustice. In between lie those migrant individuals whose marital problems remain in limbo in courts not sensitive to legal matters linked in one way or another to Islamic jurisprudence.[2]

In this chapter,[3] I contrast two moments in history when European empires meet with Islamic law: first, when Anglo-Muhammadan law came to light during the British colonial era, and second, the era of today's emerging "Euro-Sharia."

I suggest that similar to the classical colonial period of the eighteenth through twentieth centuries, when the blurred phenomenon understood as Shari'a emerged in Western scholarly discourse and legal practice, a similar phenomenon is unfolding today in Europe and North America. During the colonial era when European states occupied Muslim lands, processes of interpreting, restructuring, and displacing Islamic law were at play. In these processes, Islamic judges and others learned in the science of Islamic jurisprudence were excluded from the process of how the law was interpreted and practiced. Both eras separate the processes of learning and education in Islamic jurisprudence from the practice of law.

In order to make my point, I examine uses of Islamic law in past colonial and present-day neocolonial social realities as particular manifestations of diaspora. As James Clifford has elaborated, diaspora means experiences of displacement and attempts to construct home away from home (Clifford 1994). When discussing particular groups of people and their diasporic encounters, the notions of border, travel, creolization, transculturation, and hybridity are relevant. These notions are also applicable when looking at how legal corpuses, judicial practices, and normative systems move to places where they have no previous history. Severed from their roots, such as systems of learning, they necessarily must adapt to another logic, that of the hegemonic culture.[4]

Colonialism displaced not only people but also their normative systems, and transformed them into something new; in today's diasporic scenes in Europe and North America similar trends have emerged. It is a process where the Middle East and its cultural legacy travel, not only when people migrate but also when legal corpuses cross borders, thus constituting new homes and sensitivities of displacement. What is happening today in the Middle East is deeply connected to both North American and European recent histories in terms of warfare, exploitation, and trade. Still, the Muslim diaspora from the Middle East brings this interconnectivity even closer; in this (unbalanced) interaction, normative and legislative constructs that diasporic people carry with them acquire new meanings. Middle Eastern anthropology has engaged in unfolding the experiences of various countries under Anglo-Muhammadan law (and the equivalent French and Dutch renderings of Muslim justices) that not only transformed the textual basis of Islamic law through translations and textbooks but also set up particular court practices that merged English common law with local custom and Islamic jurisprudence. Today, similar processes unfold in our own neighborhoods. As anthropologists, our task is to make visible the interplay between people, power, and textual legacies where new forms of Muslim justices are created and contested.

Naturally, legal pluralism in judicial practice and law is nothing new in legal history. From the very outset after the death of the Prophet Muhammad, the formation of Islamic law was embedded with other systems of jurisprudence and local customary law (Hallaq 2005). Throughout history, each era and place has created its own formulations of how Shari'a should be understood and ideally practiced by Muslims. Here I want to emphasize how both Anglo-Muhammadan law and Euro-Sharia are acts of governance and how they represent methods of disciplining Muslim subjects. In both cases, a process of constitutive exclusion (Laclau 1995) is taking place: it is about how the law is practiced *for* Muslims, as well as about how much law the hegemonic Western states can allow their Muslim subjects in the first place. In the same way that Anglo-Muhammadan law acted as a tool to transform Muslims into colonial subjects, Euro-Sharia is administered today to contain, if not the outright "Muslim threat," then at least the danger that emerging Islam is opposed to democracy, or, in more abstract terms, to so-called "European values." At the core of these struggles is the hegemonic state's attempt to control the minds and bodies of its Muslim subjects, a hegemony that it wants to appropriate from the Muslim community. In Europe and North America, Muslims have entered the public space with religious and cultural signs of Islam as they shake off the status of invisible migrants. As the Turkish sociologist Nilüfer Göle has asserted, it is largely around the theme of Islamic visibility that public passion and debates are mobilized today (2011, 11).

As there is so far no better name for the emerging entity of Islamic law in Europe and North America (in Britain it is known among the South Asian population as *Angrezi Sharia* [English Shari'a]), I call this phenomenon Euro-Sharia, purposely misspelling the word. Further, I suggest that a Middle East anthropologist's exploration of this field of contemporary Shari'a in the diaspora is important from another perspective as well, namely that of area studies. Just as Anglo-Muhammadan legal practice is about transnational rather than local processes of discursive formations, today's MENA and West Asia are present in Europe and North America in such a way that a traditional area studies approach is useless. In a broader context, Euro-Sharia goes back to the old colonial enterprise of the European states in collecting, organizing, commenting on, excluding and including, as well as combining and blurring the "religion and culture" of Muslim subjects.

Colonial Law as Legal Orientalism

During the British colonial era in Asia, Africa, and the Middle East, a sophisticated legal system known as Anglo-Muhammadan law emerged as the legal
practice of colonial rule. It combined elements of English law, classical Islamic
jurisprudence (*fiqh*), and local customs. Colonially authored textbooks, written
by leading Orientalists, explained the technicalities of this mélange to the colonial administrators. In describing how the colonial encounter between Islamic
law and British administration took place in his book *An Introduction to the
Study of Anglo-Muhammadan Law* (London, 1894), Sir Roland Wilson explains

> British statesmanship determines from time to time how much of Oriental
> precept is to be treated as Law in the English sense, how much left to the
> consciences of those who acknowledge it as religiously binding, how much
> forcibly suppressed as noxious and immoral; and when this has been de-
> termined, European scholarship sifts and classifies the Oriental authorities,
> the mental habits of English and Scottish lawyers influence the methods
> of interpretation, and Procedure Codes of modern European manufacture
> regulate the ascertainment of the facts and the ultimate enforcement of the
> rule. (Wilson 1894, 2)

According to Wael Hallaq, a contemporary expert in the history of Islamic law,
Anglo-Muhammadan law played a particular role in the British endeavor to economically dominate the colonies. This law was financially more rewarding than
brute power, he asserts (2009, 85). Regarding European motivation to administer
and adjudicate this law, Leon R. Yankwich, an American law professor and federal
judge, explains in a law journal article from 1947 that

> in the administration of criminal justice by the caliphs, there developed
> what is known as the justice of the divan—the prerogative of the ruler
> (or caliph) which, following the example of Mohammed, rulers performed
> personally, by administering justice in their offices. It was what might be
> called the Harun-Al-Rashid type of justice, if we name it after the great ca-
> liph of Bagdad, whose judgments have become legend. It was a strictly per-
> sonal kind of justice, administered according to the whims of an Oriental

potentate, and having the whimsicalities of all such justice. As already indicated, this work could be performed by every deputy of the caliph. Like
all autocratic justice, it had something of the spectacular about it; it might
achieve quick results in particular cases, and, like other forms of benevolent
despotism, depended a good deal, if not altogether, upon the benevolence
of the despot or ruler. (Yankwich 1946–1947, 347–348)

According to contemporary British law scholar John Strawson, who focuses on
Islamic law as a colonial enterprise, what the colonial English rule did to Islamic
law should be addressed as legal Orientalism. This is a result of complex ingredi-
ents, such as European power, intellectual credibility, and subtlety, as well as pure
racism. Strawson stresses that this is not merely a question of asserting power,
but also one of a colonial power using its superior location to create an intellectual system which necessarily subjected Islam to European evaluation (1995, 21).
He emphasizes that the development of legal Orientalism has taken a different
path from other cultural fields of Oriental encounter because of the particular
role that law played in colonial rule. It is in the way classical *fiqh* texts have been
chosen for translation, compiled, and introduced that we find the Orientalist
methodology (ibid., 22).

During the course of colonial rule (1839–1967) in the Settlement and later
Crown Colony of Aden on the Arabian Peninsula which I have studied, the
British set up civil courts they called "Shari'a courts." In the absence of legislation, British judges relied in these courts upon a legal scholarship that included
English translations of Arabic and Persian manuals, a variety of legal commen-
taries, and precedent cases recorded in the courts of Aden, British India, and
Britain.[5] The declared policy of the British was not to make fundamental changes
in what they understood as Shari'a. Throughout the colonial period, whatever
legislation was enacted took the form of ordinances that were issued with the
intention of reproducing legislation in Aden parallel to that in India and British
East Africa. James Norman D. Anderson, a British jurist and professor at London
University whose book *Islamic Law in Africa* (1954) was used as a reference in
Adeni courts, explains the intentions of the British: "*Shari'a law appears in South
Arabia largely as the tool of the centralized government.*" (Anderson 1954, 11; italics added). According to him, Shari'a was easier for the administrator to control
than customary law (*'urf*). Besides, administering Shari'a gave colonial rule the
opportunity to pose as a champion of Islam, a manner, according to Anderson,
that was imitated from Saudi Arabia and the Kingdom of Yemen (1954, 12n1).

Divide and Rule

In line with how classical Orientalists such as Joseph Schacht in his *Introduction to Islamic Law* (1964) outlined the scope of Islamic law, in Aden the colonial law was applied in public and administrative law, while other areas of legislation, such as family relations, were relegated to the sphere of "religion and custom," which the British were not eager to touch after facing communal unrest in British India (Amin 1987, 31). Such a policy was drafted in Bombay Regulation 4 section 26 of 1827, which stated that the court, in the absence of specific enactments, should apply the "usage of the country" and the "law of the defendant" (J. N. D. Anderson 1954, 2). Under British policy all civil matters were to be regulated by Islamic law and local custom in the case of Muslims, and by the appropriate legislation in the case of other religious groups, in order to allow various religious communities the means to settle family disputes in their own way. Still, as the courts were headed by British judges, the manner in which this mandate was applied relied on officials' capacity, or lack thereof, to interpret local customs.

Until 1932 Aden was ruled from British India and the government of Bombay, and its legal development and practice followed Bombay and the decisions taken in Bombay High Court. In 1932 the colony was placed under the Governor-General of India in Council until Aden became a Crown Colony in 1937 ruled directly from the Colonial Office in London (J. N. D. Anderson 1954, 33, 37; Naval Intelligence Division 1946, 309).

The British viewed Aden similarly to India, as "ethnically" and religiously divided, and thus introduced the British Indian legal system there. This system was drafted in the Hastings Plan of 1772, where civil and criminal courts were charged with the task of applying indigenous legal norms in matters that implicated religious institutions such as inheritance, marriage, and caste. "Indigenous norms" included "the laws of the Koran with respect to Muhammadans" and "the laws of the Brahmanic Shasters with respect to Hindus" (M. Anderson 1996, 5). Local Islamic scholars were excluded from this legal system from the very outset. The courts appointed British judges and attorneys trained in India. The local *fuqaha* (men learned in Islamic jurisprudence) were left with an unofficial "advisory" status. Only the British-appointed *qadhi* (Islamic judge) was charged with the role of marriage and divorce registrar (*ma'dhun*) (Dahlgren 2010, 95).

The practice of British Shari'a courts in colonial Aden differed extensively from court practice before British arrival. At the time of the conquest, Aden was controlled by the neighboring 'Abdali Sultanate, with the Sultan as its ruler. His local representative was the *qadhi*, to whom all disputes were referred. Executive powers were in the hands of the *dawlah* ("state power"). Whenever the Sultan or any other 'Abdali chief visited, both the *qadhi* and the *dawlah* were superseded. The judge applied Shari'a according to his education and supplemented it with the local custom (Kour 1981, 86–87). Under the governorship of Captain Haines, the first British Political Agent, whose initiative it was to annex Aden to the East India Company, the above legal practice was maintained. As the colonial presence expanded and Anglo-Muhammadan legal practice gained ground throughout the British Empire, it began to deviate from earlier local practice. English became the court language, contributing to the alienation of local people.

Anglo-Muhammadan law as it was practiced in Aden differed from local Islamic legal practice in referring to the Shafi'i school of Islamic jurisprudence (*fiqh*) in an eclectic manner alien to local history of that school in South Arabia. As British anthropologist Abdulla Maktari has shown, the Shafi'i school had different legal manifestations in various parts of the Muslim world, particularized both by the influences of different local traditions, and by the provision of legal views in the spirit of reasoning (*ijtihad*) as practiced by the local *fuqaha* (Islamic learned). In South Arabia, where the Shafi'i school had been introduced at the end of the fourth century *Anno Hijra* (tenth century AD) proponents of the school were confronted by a sophisticated system of customary law ('*urf*), parts of which they adopted (Maktari 1971, 4–5).

The textual basis was not the only difference between local Islamic *fiqh* and the Anglo-Muhammadan system. Others included differences in court practice and in the process of litigation. Even though the declared policy of the British was not to touch "religion and custom," the processes of litigation, expressions of conflict, and strategies of litigants were transformed according to the English system. The process of litigation turned marital conflicts into separate "cases" devoid of larger social aspects, which the British judges were in any case ignorant of. Additionally, the colonial system favored single, exhaustive definitions of the local custom and comparisons with precedent cases. Rules of evidence restricted the content of evidence that was considered legally binding. All this was accompanied by implicit arrogance toward "primitive" local law, and an assumption of the inferior status the local custom allocated to women, an attitude the judges occasionally voiced aloud in court. Without further knowledge of the gender balance in Adeni homes, the judges simply took it as the norm that the law should favor men.

Blind Justice—but Not for Women

As the primary tenets of the British legal system maintained that all persons should be treated equally before the law and that justice should be blind, local hierarchies and status differences were in principle set aside in the litigation process. These provisions did not, however, concern the assumed gender hierarchy. As Robert L. Kidder has suggested in his study on the colonial Indian legal system, the notion of isolated law cases, in which distinct rights and duties were argued, simplified the complexities of local relations and violated customary arbitration systems (Kidder 1978, 159–162).

In British India, Anglo-Muhammadan law was slowly replaced by laws of British origin. Practices that the British deemed barbarian, such as *sati* (widow's suicide) and child marriage, were targeted in campaigns for social reform, and modest efforts were made to improve the position of women. Still, there was resistance, and outcries of religion being "in danger" were occasionally heard (M. Anderson 1996, 7–8; Kapur and Cossman 1996, 45). Such measures were never attempted in Aden, for the British viewed it as a military outpost and were thus less eager to introduce social reform. Anglo-Muhammadan law was finally terminated in 1967 when the British presence in this corner of Arabia came to an end after a popular uprising.

The Anglo-Muhammadan system was created to serve order and to facilitate foreign rule. In its own particular way, Anglo-Muhammadan law transformed local people into subjects of colonial rule without altering the ways their religion and custom were administered (Dahlgren 2010). In a similar manner, today Muslim migrants are subjected by host states to practices that attempt to limit their agency in determining how to practice their religion and what kind of customs to engage in. These Muslim migrants are more and more in the process of creating a global Islam without the mediation of the local *faqih*, one instead disseminated by the global *umma* or community of the internet. Islam has increasingly been traveling; that is, it is no longer rooted in a local culture untouched by the distant outside or virtual influences. Despite the nature of the Muslim presence as transnational, it is nation states that engage in processes of control over their Muslim subjects, the same way they did in the colonial era. As Steven Vertovec observed in the case of Muslims in Britain, at the same time as demands for freedoms and minority rights increase among Muslims, Islamophobic tendencies among non-Muslims amplify (Vertovec 2002, 33). The demand for recognition may include rights to worship and practice rituals, but it can also be seen in the way the Canadian philosopher Charles Taylor has explicated, as redressing serious forms of discrimination that arise from a prior withholding of those rights (Taylor 1992). The platforms for arguing ways of being a Muslim in the diasporic communities are both local and global, but the struggles against those who intend to limit Muslim visibility are national in nature. States are the agents that engage in disciplining Muslim subjects in the postcolonial world as in the colonial. To discuss this point, I will take a closer look at three contemporary cases that illustrate how Shari'a controversies arise.

Global Islam and Muslim Lifestyles

In the world of global Islam, Muslim activists operate on transnational and global platforms such as satellite TV and the internet, disseminating ideas worldwide about what Shari'a is. Merely juristic ideas of Shari'a as Islamic law are accompanied by understandings of Shari'a as an individual choice for a good life. Being a Muslim involves manifesting a Muslim identity with visible markers. The markets for the construction and consumption of new Muslim meanings are translocal and global, often with roots in Middle Eastern ways of claiming identity. The global Muslim wears Islamic fashions that materially originate in the Middle East, the birthplace of Islam. The more closely it resembles costumes worn near the cradle of Islam, the more "authentic" an outfit is claimed to be. Meanwhile, as a parallel process, new Shari'as without *fiqh* are emerging for the consumption of the displaced *umma,* that is, Shari'a without roots in classical jurisprudence but which spring from the needs of Muslim immigrants living as minorities in the West.[6]

These voices parallel global discourses, presented in the name of human rights or feminism, that want to separate Shari'a from practicing Islam. Alongside more literalist understandings of Islamic law such as those disseminated by the Salafists, these post-Islamist views participate in constructing ideas for global audiences of what Shari'a really is (Bayat 1996).

In most Western countries experiencing xenophobia and a fear of change, the different Muslim voices tend to become blurred into one "Muslim threat," and the notion of an introduction of Shari'a provokes the ultimate revulsion. Popularized horrific images tend to take simple or abstracted truths as evidence of how unfitting Shari'a is in the modern world, providing emotional fuel to bans on minarets or headscarves as means to prevent Shari'a from spreading. Newt

Gingrich, a former Speaker of the U.S. House of Representatives, reckons that America needs a federal law to ensure that Shari'a is not recognized by any court in the U.S. (*The Economist*, 16 October 2010). In the speeches of Tea Partiers, Shari'a is paraded as one of the evils that America needs to shed.

In his book *While Europe Slept: How Radical Islam is Destroying the West from Within* (2006) author Bruce Bawer draws an image of Muslims becoming a majority in Europe by the year 2050, echoing the prophesy by Bat Ye'or (the pseudonym of Egyptian-British political commentator Gisele Littman) in her book *Eurabia: The Euro-Arab Axis* (2005).[7] According to Bawer, this is being accomplished through the naïve immigration policies of the politically-correct Left and by the explosive growth of the Muslim population, complemented by the phenomenon of "fetching marriage." As the common trope used on anti-immigration websites on both continents puts it, "the hell-hole of leftist multi-culturalism," far worse in Europe than anything seen in North America, allows Muslim men to bring to Europe illiterate females from backward countries, usu-ally as uneducated teenagers, placing them in arranged marriages where they reproduce widely. These new citizens adapt poorly to local customs but qualify for vast welfare benefits in order to produce more Islamist-oriented males and slave-like females, continuing the vicious cycle. These "Muslims" with their ab-horrent lifestyle also perpetrate female genital mutilation and honor killings, while the naïve multicultural relativist authorities allow the culprits to go free. As proof of the inevitability of the Muslim takeover, statistics are given from vari-ous countries, pointing out how Amsterdam, for instance, already has a Muslim majority (Bawer 2006).

Bawer's book is a graphic example of Islamophobia, presented by an American author but representing a trend that is growing throughout Europe.[8] According to such prophecies, once the old continent is majority Muslim, Shari'a will be enacted. An elaboration of what Shari'a would actually mean is not needed in such accounts. It is simply taken for granted that Shari'a is something evil which does not match European standards of rule of law, democracy, and civil and human rights.

Discussions on limiting Muslim women's dress or disallowing the building of new minarets present a similar worry in a more politically correct way when argued in terms of practical or safety concerns. Still, many countries' parliaments have been the scenes where limits have been drawn on how much Shari'a can be allowed as part of the statutory judicial system. Despite attempts to rational-ize veil bans on the basis of "European values" or claims of protecting women's rights, Göle has suggested that growing anti-Muslim populism in Europe itself poses a threat to the European tradition of an "enlightened public." In this process, the public sphere is in danger of losing its role as the ideal vehicle for the expression of common sense (Göle 2011, 12).

Euro-Sharia as a Battlefield

In today's Europe these debates are daily occurrences. Here I wish to discuss three particular cases as examples of what I mean by Euro-Sharia. The first is the case of out-of-court arbitration, which has increased in Britain; the second concerns legal attempts to understand the concept of *mahr* (marriage payment that a man is obliged to pay to his bride upon signing a marriage contract to render the marriage legitimate) in the framework of European jurisprudence; and the third is about legal studies that refute the idea of legal pluralism in family law practice. These are just some examples of a number of both positive and negative approaches currently being taken in different countries in Europe and North America that speak to the need to form new legal principles to cover such issues.

In October 2008, the British Lord Chancellor and Secretary of State for Justice, Jack Straw, announced in a conference on Islamic finance and trade that Shari'a law was not part of U.K. law. Still, as Irish legal scholar Mairead Enright suggests, since 1982 Shari'a councils have operated on British soil. These councils practice what they call *Angrezi Sharia* (English Shari'a) in practices of private ordering such as arrangement of marriages, negotiations and agreements on marriage contracts, solemnization of marriage, regulation of polygamy, and the *talaq* (a husband's right to divorce by repudiation) (Enright 2009, 5). These are often compared to Jewish *bet din* tribunals, which also are not centralized but engage in resolving civil cases. Some of these Shari'a councils belong under the umbrella of Shari'a Council U.K. (SCU), others are under the umbrella of the Islamic Shari'a Council (ISC), while some remain independent local councils. The Muslim Arbitration Tribunals (MAT) resolve legal problems related to contracts.

Close to ninety-five percent of the cases involve divorce, in particular the *khul'*, meaning divorce on the initiative of the wife with compensation for the husband. Still, family law is not the only area of interest. Britain in 2010 saw a fifteen percent rise in the number of non-Muslims using Shari'a arbitration in commercial cases (Hirsh 2010). Even though Jack Straw has appeared to be unaware of it, in many European countries, in the domain of Islamic finances it seems that the market decides how much Shari'a is allowed and European states remain silent. It is evident that in his comment the British minister presented reality in a flawed way. As the Portuguese sociologist Boaventura de Sousa Santos has suggested, maps of law are not neutral, but are bound up in ideology and the purposes of the powerful (Enright 2009).

The U.K. is an exception in the European legal scene. In other countries, aspects of Islamic law have been allowed in state courts with variable results. In Norway, private international law grants foreign law a place in Norwegian courts. Such law cases need to have a stronger connection to another country than to Norway and often deal with issues of marriage, divorce, or child custody (Fredriksen 2007). Still, in applying foreign law, courts have faced problems in defining the legal terms. A case in point is the Islamic institution of *mahr* (marriage payment). The *mahr* is the wife's property and she must not to spend it on supporting the family. In divorce cases, where a wife claims that her deferred marriage payment must be paid, European courts have first to determine what type of legislation is in question. When Muslims who live in Europe sign a contract, private international law is not applicable. In such cases the comparative legal method has been the solution. In France, *mahr* has been discussed as part of contract law, not family law, comparing it to "the sales price a woman claims for herself when marrying." In other European countries *mahr* has been treated as maintenance (Sweden), as a redistribution of property (Sweden), or as a prenuptial agreement and again constitutive of private contracts (England and France). When mixed in a court with the principle of gender equality, the question of a husband's debt becomes further complicated (Løvdal 2011).

Legal Orientalism as a Human Rights Discourse

European and North American legal scholars have also engaged in the debate on how much Shari'a Western states can allow and how far continents should go in admitting what they consider a religiously based legal pluralism. In an article published in the *Washington and Lee Law Review* in 2007, American law professor Robin Fretwell Wilson issues a strong warning against handing over authority in marital disputes to religious communities since, as he puts it, such communities have a tendency to condone domestic violence. Wilson bases his argument on selected psychological and behavioral studies dealing with Christian denominations in the U.S.A. and Muslim communities in different parts of the world. The latter include Jordanian Muslim men, Israeli Arabs, South Asian Muslims in the U.S., and Western Trachian Muslims in Greece. According to Wilson, *"There are countless anecdotes that domestic abuse is on the rise in Muslim communities or*

prevalent among Conservative Protestants" (R. F. Wilson 2007, 1371). In conclud-
ing, Wilson warns that the costs of greater deference to religious views should be
considered before "*we are willing to rob women and children of the state's protec-
tions*" (ibid., 1363–1364).

The German Islamic legal scholar Mathias Rohe (2004) draws parameters
for the applicability of Islamic law in Europe by means of separating Shari'a as a
legal rule from Shari'a as a guideline for religious practice. In Islamic legal history
it has always been accepted that not all Shari'a rules are binding at every time and
place. According to Rohe, this has resulted in efforts to create a broad forum for
the application of independent reasoning (*ijtihad*), thus allowing flexibility in
situations such as diasporic Muslims in a minority community. Rohe suggests
European Muslims may refrain from applying legal rules of Shari'a by accepting
the Islamic principle that such rules cannot be applied outside Islamic territories
and that Muslims are obliged to either respect the law of the land or leave. This,
according to Rohe, serves as a "fundament for a peaceful co-existence in a diaspora situation." Still, as Rohe accepts, the self-definition of a diaspora would not
be very helpful for actively being part of and contributing to society as a whole.
Besides, about one third of all Muslims live outside majority Muslim countries.
He concludes by suggesting that, "*Shari'a in Europe would mean to define Shari'a
rules for Muslims in accordance with the indispensable values of democracy, human
rights and the rule of law governing European legal orders*" (ibid., 345–348; italics
added).

The Common Platform: Euro-Sharia as Legal Orientalism

The above brief examples point out how policies are drawn up to regulate the
scope of Shari'a in Europe and North America. It is an outsider's look at Muslim
(in)justices as well as an administrator at play in a hegemonic position. The way
Islamic Shari'a is debated in the Western public sphere allows only the conservative, misogynist, "true" Islam as the partner in the dialogue, morally distant
enough to be a perfect enemy. In particular, there is a question of how debates on
Shari'a in non-Muslim contexts tend to tally with the broader trend toward reinforcing Western hegemony and setting the limits of what is culturally permissible
with the help of the Western parameters of "democracy" and "human rights."

Furthermore, debates on Muslim justices and injustices take their grounding from the idea of something "constitutively outside" of European values, to
phrase the process using Laclau's notion. In both colonial law and today's Shari'a

debates, hegemonic articulation is applied to limit the definition and scope of the application of legal notions, in order to have mere Islamic law constitute the outside, meaning that which is outside the legal system based on "European values." Anglo-Muhammadan law and Euro-Sharia are discursive formations that exclude the Muslim scholar, educated in the details of Shari'a, from the very act of interpreting, applying, and practicing Islamic law, thus creating the constitutive outside.

In our times of traveling traditions, the Middle East is globally present not only in the form of the gas we put in our cars or threats of new wars but also in the way the postcolonial state continues to play a hegemonic game with Middle Eastern subjects. The normative systems of these people, and their misrepresentations, should be compared with what anthropological studies have revealed about colonial encounters with Shari'a in the era of classical colonialism (1700–1900). In the same way as colonialism displaced local normative systems and their bases of learning, today's policies to mitigate the "threat of Islam" operate on the logic of displacement. In these debates, Middle Eastern anthropology has a contribution to make.

NOTES

1. In relation to so-called honor killings, the courts in Sweden had earlier applied the logic of mitigating circumstances, see Eldén (1998).

2. See Mehdi and Nielsen 2011.

3. Material for this chapter comes from anthropological studies in Southern Yemen since the late 1980s, and from archival studies in the India Office in London.

4. As the Argentinean social theorist Ernesto Laclau has asserted in talking about the need of a society to claim totalization, *"in a society . . . in which its fullness—the moment of its universality—is unachievable, the relation between the universal and the particular is a hegemonic relation"* (Laclau 1995, 153; italics added).

5. British judges consulted the famous Shafi'i manual *al-Minhaj at Talibin* by Muhyi al-Din al-Nawawi in E. C. Howard's English translation from an earlier French rendering, published in 1914 (al-Hubaishi [1988, 54]; Knox-Mawer [1956, 511]). A local nineteenth century manual published in English and Arabic, *A Treatise on the Muhammedan Law,* by Shaikh Abdul Kadir bin Muhammed al-Mekkawi, reprinted in Syria in 1899 and in Cairo in 1959 and originally published in 1886, was also used in Aden courts.

6. On Shari'a without *fiqh* see Bowen (2003). During the classical period of Islamic history minority *fiqh* was produced (see Abou El Fadl 1994), but today's occurrence of

Shari'a without *fiqh* is a new phenomenon embedding other global political discourses. See Césari (2004), Hellyer (2009), and Rohe (2007).

7. Bat Ye'or was also one of the inspiration sources for the Norwegian right-wing terrorist Anders Breivik who killed seventy-seven people in July 2011.

8. A study conducted by the Center for American Progress Action Fund reveals a small, tightly networked group of right-wing experts who stand behind the spread of Islamophobia in the U.S. Wajahat Ali et al., *Fear, Inc.*, American Center for Progress: 2011; pdf may be downloaded at: http://www.americanprogress.org/issues/2011/08/pdf /islamophobia_intro.pdf (accessed on 31 August 2011).

13.

A PLACE TO BELONG: COLONIAL PASTS, MODERN DISCOURSES, AND CONTRACEPTIVE PRACTICES IN MOROCCO

Cortney L. Hughes

The Middle East and North Africa (MENA) has often been portrayed in popular and scholarly discourses as a homogenous entity comprised of countries linked together through culture, ethnicity, and religion. Places as far west as Morocco and as far east as southwest Asia have been included in or excluded from the region in its various definitions. Charles Lindholm points out that "in terms of square miles, the Middle East is the largest 'culture area' of any of those that generally are included in the anthropological division of the world" (1995, 805). How is the MENA conceptualized as a theoretical construct and a geographical place? How do individuals living in the region see themselves as belonging to a nation-state and to the larger region?

My ethnographic fieldwork in Rabat, Morocco on reproductive healthcare challenges the idea in some popular and scholarly discourses that the MENA is a seamless body of nation-states. For example, my interactions with Salima, a lower-middle class Moroccan woman living in Rabat, and with an Imam at a mosque in the Mid-Atlas Mountains, contest this generalized notion of the Middle East and North Africa.[1] One afternoon Salima and I walked from a health clinic tucked away in a working-class neighborhood in Rabat that is run by a non-governmental organization (NGO) with close ties to the London-based International Planned Parenthood Federation (IPPF). We made our way through a very busy open-air market where people buzzed about buying fruit, vegetables, and other household items. Salima was dressed in a long black coat and donned a matching black hijab on this chilly day in February 2008. She had come to the health clinic to see the gynecologist for a *contrôle,* or follow-up visit, for her intra-uterine device (IUD). On our walk I asked Salima if she had children, but she responded with "*pas encore*" or "not yet." Salima was twenty-six years old at the time of our conversation and had been married for only a short period. I then inquired if she and her husband wanted to have children in the future, to which she responded "*inschallah,*" or "God willing," a phrase I had become accustomed to hearing in Morocco on a regular basis from nearly everyone: practicing Muslims, non-practicing Muslims, Americans, and other foreign residents alike.

During our walk, Salima asked me where I lived and what I thought of the people in Morocco. I told her that I lived in a nearby quarter and that I had met some amazing and interesting individuals while in the country. Salima gave me a warm smile and said, "*Bien sûr,*" meaning "of course"; it was almost as if she anticipated my response. She then said that she loved Morocco even though she had family living abroad. I asked Salima why she liked living in the country so much. She explained in a mixture of French and Moroccan Arabic, "Because it's not France. It's not Europe, but it's not Saudi Arabia. It's *islamique.*" She continued, "It's Islamic, but we can do these things here. It's not *haram.*" Haram means "forbidden" in Arabic, and in her response the word "things" referred to contraception.

Salima's comments about Morocco, Islam, and contraception resonated with views held by Imam Khaloub. During a conversation in his office tacked onto the back of the mosque, I asked him about the relationship between modernity and Islam in Morocco, specifically how he thinks they pertain to women's lives. He answered that, "People in Saudi Arabia don't know Islam." I asked him to elaborate on this point. "*Sh f*" (look), he explained, "women can't drive there. That is not Islam. They don't know Islam or modernity [*al-hdatha*]." Women's social status and what they can and cannot do freely are central to Imam Khaloub's judgment of what is considered to be Islamic and what is considered to be modern.

Toward the end of our conversation, and in the midst of children's voices singing in the mosque, the Imam spoke about his wife's experiences at the doctor's office. This served as an example of how the convergence of Islam and modernity works within Moroccan women's lives. He would permit his wife to see a male doctor in a health clinic or a public hospital if a female doctor was not available that day to see patients. This is allowable because nothing is more important than his wife's health. He believed that in other countries in the MENA where Islam is practiced, this type of interaction between male clinical staff and female patients would not be looked upon favorably. It was a crucial point of departure for him.

Salima and the Imam used contraception and women's bodies to position Morocco within the MENA region and to frame the geopolitical context of Islam. Salima's interpretations of Islam are developed as she engages with modern medical practices of reproduction, and in this case specifically, contraception. At the same time, her religious beliefs impact her decision to delay becoming pregnant through the use of family planning. She reminded me that, "Islam is for a good life," which meant that contraception is not only acceptable, but that it is one of the means by which she can follow religious tenets about fertility and motherhood. Contraception is already pious in nature for Salima. Similarly, the Imam distinctly criticized the Islam practiced in Saudi Arabia because he believes it restricts women's movements and may prohibit them from receiving proper medical attention. He believes that Moroccan Islam allows women to engage with modern medical practices while simultaneously upholding proper Islamic values. What can contraception and women's bodies tell us about how people in Morocco imagine the MENA? How do we begin to conceptualize the region as a theoretical construct in our scholarly endeavors and practical work? How do we engage with or critique popular and scholarly discourses that may suppress the social, political, and religious complexity of the region?

Rhoda Kanaaneh (2002) suggests women's bodies are "fields of contest" through which the nation and community are imagined, written upon, and debated. In addition, in their seminal work on reproduction, Faye Ginsburg and Rayna Rapp masterfully argue that reproduction "in its biological and social senses is inextricably bound up with the production of culture" (1995, 2). Given the centrality of women's bodies and reproduction to nation-building, my fieldwork on reproductive healthcare in Morocco challenges the notion that the MENA is a set of seamless nation-states undeniably linked through language, culture, and religion. This chapter demonstrates how Moroccan women continue to grapple with the country's position as a physical and political interlocutor between Africa, the Middle East, Europe, and North America, in addition to the effects of colonial history and current neoliberal ideas of modernity that are circulating. In this process, individuals are creating an unsettled sense of belonging and identity for themselves. While such conflicts are not particularly new, these contradictions are being repackaged around issues of health and the body. Drawing on interview data, observations, and a visual and textual analysis of posters in health clinics and public school books, I suggest that Moroccan women create a place to belong that distances themselves and Morocco from the "conservative" Middle East and brings them closer to "liberal" Europe while simultaneously moving between these two poles. Salima and the Imam's narratives point to much larger theoretical and empirical issues that concern how scholars construct the MENA and the ways that histories and futures become entangled as individuals form their identities and seek out places to belong in their social and cultural contexts.

Reproductive Health Policies and Population Politics in Morocco

Recently, Yassine Mansouri, the Chief of Intelligence for Morocco, stated that "Morocco is threatened, by two extremes—the conservative Wahhabism spread by Saudi Arabia and the Shiism spread by Iran." He went on to say, "We consider them both aggressive. . . . Radical Islam has the wind in its sail, and it remains a threat" (Erlanger and Mekhennet 2009). This quote by Mansouri places Morocco at a political crossroads as the state tries to distinguish itself from other countries in the region, particularly Saudi Arabia and Iran, through a discussion of Islam. My conversations with Salima and Imam Khaloub, as well as other Moroccan women provide insight into how they, as Moroccan citizens, envision the position of Morocco in the MENA, in addition to how they think of the region as a whole—not, however, as an entire entity, but rather as something that is simultaneously connected yet disparate.

Discussions of the shifts in Morocco's development and political agendas in addition to its national family planning program have shaped how medical providers promote contraception and the ways citizens perceive such methods to delay, space, or limit pregnancies. As in many places, reproduction has long taken on salience in discourses of development and in the state's political scheme in Morocco. Fertility was brought to the forefront of the government's concerns with the publication of a report in 1965 by the Economic Planning Department, nine years after Morocco achieved independence from France (Brown 1968). At the time, annual population growth was 3.2 percent, and the report stated that Morocco would face grave economic consequences in employment and education in the future if the growth rate remained that high. In 1966, Morocco launched its family planning program with the establishment of a national population commission and local commissions. However, the program was not accompanied by policies concerning the liberalization of abortion, the accessibility of contraception, or the improvement of women's rights (Maddy-Weitzman 1992). One of its first big accomplishments was the 1967 abolition of a law initially implemented by Morocco's previous French authorities that forbade the advertising and sale of contraception (Ayad and Roudi-Fahimi 2006; see Sargent and Cordell 2003 for more on France's view of family planning).

The family planning program fostered an environment that is conducive to the acceptance of contraception. In the years following the 1956 independence, the government placed heavy emphasis on economic development with the belief that financial gains would address social issues, including decreasing the Total Fertility Rate (TFR), which was at its highest around the early 1970s at 7.4 children per woman (Courbage 1995). Come the 1980s and 90s, Morocco did not see the improvements it desired in areas of poverty, education, literacy, and healthcare, leaving the country open to international criticism (Cohen and Jaidi 2006). After some debate, officials shifted their focus to social development, which came to be seen as a much more plausible solution to improving citizens' lives. This shift came immediately before and during changes in the monarchy when King Mohammed VI, described as a "symbol of hope for a democratic Morocco" (Maghraoui 2001, 218), succeeded his father, King Hassan II, in 1999.

In 2005, King Mohammed VI launched the National Initiative for Human Development (INDH). The INDH is a program that puts Morocco's "social issues at the forefront of the country's political priorities" (Martín 2006, 1). The INDH aims to increase the number of income-generating activities, to improve infrastructure and social services, and to provide assistance to the most vulnerable groups in society (women, adolescents, and the poor). In an address to the United Nations General Assembly, the King said the aim of the INDH "is to . . . free large segments of the population . . . from the yoke of poverty, illiteracy and unemployment, thus enabling them to lead a decent life we wish to offer all our citizens" (Mohammed VI 2005). It is the duty of the government to foster a new mentality in men and women that encourages "entrepreneurship, participation, and production" (Ben-Meir 2005) and discourages the reliance on the state and others for one's well-being. In short, citizens must be prepared to make responsible decisions about their lives, which includes having smaller, more manageable families. The government provides the necessary tools to do so, but it is the responsibility of individuals to use them properly in order to reach their full potential (Zemni and Bogaert 2009). The INDH came just two years after the 2003 bombings in Casablanca that were linked to members of Salafia Jihadia, a North African terrorist group believed to be connected to al-Qaeda, who lived in shantytowns surrounding the city. The initiative then grew out of the government's concern that poverty harbors Islamic extremism that could result in further violence in Morocco or abroad. According to King Mohammed VI, the INDH attempts to counter the rise of political Islam and Islamic organizations that young men and women are joining by opening up new academic and social opportunities for them and by providing them with a wider range of choices (2005).

Reproduction is central to the INDH and to Morocco's political agenda given that the population is relatively young and a large number of men and women have yet to reach reproductive age. This creates fear of a future population explosion if the youth are not educated properly about sexual and reproductive health. As of 2009, roughly twenty-nine percent of the entire population (32 million) is under the age of fifteen. This is in comparison to only seventeen percent in countries classified as "more developed" by the Population Reference Bureau (PRB), and forty percent in countries placed in the "least developed" category (2009). The population growth rate in Morocco remains rather high at 1.4 percent per year, placing it in the "less developed" category in accordance to PRB standards. This is despite the fact that the TFR (total fertility rate) has decreased dramatically in the past several decades to 2.4 children per woman, just above the replacement level of 2.1 children per woman. These demographic trends have sparked concern in the government about education, job growth, and being able to provide the resources needed to enable men and women to have productive lives.

Studying Contraceptive Practices and Identity Formation in Morocco

My research on women's identity formation took place primarily in three reproductive health clinics in working-class neighborhoods in and near Rabat, Morocco, and in selected female patients' homes and local communities over a sixteen-month period from 2008 to 2009. Two of the health clinics are run by an NGO with ties to the IPPF, while the Ministry of Health runs the third. Informal and formal interviews in addition to observations took place in the health clinics and patients' homes. Further interviews were conducted with key community members, such as Imam Khaloub, officials at the Ministry of Health, and staff at development organizations.

It is important to situate my female participants in terms of class because individual practices of reproduction and how women discuss themselves as Muslims and Moroccan citizens are linked to larger national and international discourses of development and health. Socioeconomic status has an impact on women's health, with poorer women fairing worse than wealthier ones, a trend that is not particularly new to global health (Batnitzky 2008; Boutayeb 2006). My female participants do not live in extreme poverty, but they do not have the financial resources of the wealthy. Consistently, women negotiated their economic and social circumstances in their reproductive choices and practices. For example, Amina said to me as she waited to see the doctor with her sister at an NGO clinic, "We don't have a lot, but we're ok." These constraints not only impacted the ways women placed themselves within the nation-state, the region, and the world, but they subsequently informed my analysis. In contrast to the patients I met, the physicians, as well as the clinical and support staff at the NGO and the Ministry of Health, are from the middle and even upper classes. I take these class interactions as moments to examine the varied ideas of citizenship and the nation that emerge through discussions of reproduction and fertility, and to articulate how discourses of health, modernity, and religion converge or diverge among different groups in Morocco, although this chapter primarily focuses upon working-class urban women who came to the clinics for care.

Using Reproduction and Medical Anthropology to Examine Identity and Self-Positioning

My objective is to undermine our own Western ethnocentrism that often homogenizes the MENA, and especially the individuals living in the region (Said 1979). I work to destabilize the seamlessness of the region by examining how citizens see Morocco and themselves as fitting or not fitting in the MENA through discussions of reproduction. To do so, I begin with a notion of "doubleness" to analyze the ways Moroccan women make sameness and difference coherent in their reproductive practices. Stuart Hall reminds us that identity "is not transparent or unproblematic as we think" (1994, 392). He suggests, "We should think, instead, of identity as a 'production' which is never complete" (ibid.). For instance, in Salima's comments there is "doubleness of similarity and difference" (ibid.) as two seemingly different worlds—France and Saudi Arabia, liberal and conservative, secular and religious—collide in Morocco. It is out of this collision, or perhaps more appropriately, convergence, that Salima forms her individual identity.

The convergence occurs, in part, due to the complex histories that Moroccans live in every day. They have long grappled with how to place themselves and their country on the global political and cultural scene. Stephen William Foster writes,

> Moroccans have long been challenged by their country's proximity to Europe, to the Mediterranean, and to foreign powers to formulate a rhetoric of Moroccan identity and political autonomy. Morocco's recently deceased ruler, King Hassan II, liked to compare Morocco to the palms of the desert; Rooted in African soil, they are watered by Islam, and their branches are rustled by the winds of Europe. (2006, 2)

Faoud Ali El Himma, a former deputy Interior Minister and leader of the Authenticity and Modernity Party, echoed this point when speaking about reform: "Morocco 'has always been a country of transit'" (Erlanger and Mehkennet 2009).

In colonial and postcolonial politics, women's bodies and reproduction have been fundamental to the creation of nationalist agendas and new ways of thinking about the self, the future, and the world (Brahimi 1984; Shakry 2007). However, the inclusion of children into a national collective is far from a purely biological phenomenon. Nira Yuval-Davis states, "the central importance of women's reproductive roles in ethnic and national discourses becomes apparent when one considers that one usually joins the collective by being born into it" (2001, 123). Women's reproductive bodies were crucial to the building of Morocco after the country achieved independence from France in 1956. Additionally, they continue to be essential to the creation of the future nation and how Morocco is positioned in the MENA and the world. Mounira Charrad (2001) maintains that the intersection of gender and power was a key factor in building anticolonial nationalist movements in the Maghrib. She argues, "Women's rights as defined in family law are the crux of the matter" (2001, 5).

A report published in Morocco entitled *50 Ans de Développement Humain & Perspectives, 2025* (*50 Years of Human Development and Perspectives, 2025*) acknowledges that women have been excluded from development in the decades following independence, but it notes the state now recognizes women as crucial actors in modernization: "Thanks to the changes in matrimonial and procreative behaviors of Moroccan women . . . and family planning programs in which a large portion of the female population participated, the country was able to manage the development of its population" (2006, 8). The report claims that if Moroccan women regulate the number of children they have, then there will be more opportunities for education and better jobs in the country for future citizens.

A large body of literature exists in medical anthropology on fertility, child-bearing, and the politics of reproduction (Greenhalgh 2008; Paxson 2004). However, Marcia Inhorn and Carolyn Sargent (2006) point out that there is relatively little scholarship on medical practices in the MENA, with a few exceptions (Ali 2002; Inhorn 1994; Kanaaneh 2002). Much of the medical anthropology literature realizes the diverse historical, political, and social contexts of the MENA. Carla Makhlouf Obermeyer (1995) argues that while many of the countries in the region share Arabic as an official language and are predominantly Muslim, there exists a diversity of health and socioeconomic indicators that impact reproductive health and rights. She argues, "The [population] policies formulated over time by various governments have been divergent in both their explicit and implicit goals, even though they must ultimately be justified with reference to Shari'a (Islamic law)" (1995, 7). A more recent work on reproductive technologies is Morgan Clarke's (2009) monograph on in-vitro fertilization (IVF) in Lebanon. She suggests the relationship between Islam and medical technologies of reproduction is flexible and not monolithic in the region or across the globe. In addition, Donna Bowen argues Muslim jurists and scholars hold two main views on abortion. The first forbids the practice altogether, while the second "follows Qur'anic reasoning that the fetus becomes a human being after 120 days" (2004, 130–131). Therefore, an abortion may be permitted within the first trimester. She notes that there is no central authority over Islamic practice, but rather different interpretations and local standards. I build upon this work by arguing that narratives of reproduction are produced in a space where Western and Arab-Islamic meanings exist congruently and yet sometimes in conflict, thus showing that the identities of former "colonial subjects" in Morocco are not predetermined, but form and continuously change as multiple worlds come together and must be navigated.

Since the events of 9/11, there has been an increase in popular and scholarly attention given to the MENA and to Muslim communities worldwide (Goldstone 2010; Mamdani 2002). A concern of medical anthropologists who study the relationship between Islam and medicine or the MENA has been to problematize the relationship between Islam and medical technologies, including contraception and IVF, in order to demonstrate that Islamic beliefs and practices are used by different groups to justify the use or non-use of these options and to show that a variety of popular understandings of Islam exist (Johnson-Hanks 2006; Keefe 2006; Sargent 2006). Medical anthropology of the MENA has masterfully demonstrated that medical and non-medical reproductive practices are informed by religious and cultural beliefs as well as by larger political and development agendas (Bourqia 1995; Obermeyer 2000). Marcia Inhorn's study of how masculinity and gender relations are articulated in the biomedical world of the Muslim Middle East examines males' interpretations of *fatwas* regarding gamete donation. The practice is typically banned in the Sunni world but is becoming more acceptable in the Shi'ite world after recent *fatwas* from Iran justifying the use of donor gametes as a way to save a marriage (2004). Inhorn finds that since adoption is also prohibited in Islam, some Lebanese men will have donor babies so they can secure their marriages.

My focus is at the level of embodiment, where the "body, self and personhood emerge as inextricably linked" (Sharp 2000, 289) and where cultural forces become lived experiences. Several interconnected dimensions of meaning exist for Moroccan women about childbearing. Spacing and limiting pregnancies through contraception exposes a tension, both productive and problematic, between historical traces and memories, modern discourses of health and development, and visions of the future nation and citizens. Marybeth Macphee uses Pierre Bourdieu's "hysteresis effect" (1977, 1990) in her analysis of "the tension between the formation of new cultural dispositions and the persistence of those formed in the past" (2004, 376) in southern Morocco. She discovers that for women living in this rural region there are contradictions between "historically embodied expectations about health and contemporary experiences of the body" (ibid.). Modern technologies and practices cause them to alter how they think of themselves, their bodies, illnesses, and their roles in the community. While methods of contraception are very intimate practices, they actually do much more than just regulate fertility. Contraceptives package together politics, histories, and discourses of development, the body, health, and religion into lived experiences and allow us as scholars see the ways that individuals think of their selves and construct their identities.

The Use and Non-Use of Contraception

The majority of women I spoke with or observed in the health clinics, unless they were pregnant, trying to conceive, or post-menopausal, were using some form of contraception. There were exceptions due to physiological issues, such as their bodies reacting badly to the hormones introduced by the birth control pill or IUD. Some women's husbands were not willing to use condoms for various reasons, including decreased sensation and considering fertility a woman's domain, which increased the chance of them becoming pregnant whether they wanted to or not. In Morocco, as of 2008, approximately 63 percent of women, regardless of age, ethnicity, marital status, or class, are using some form of contraception. Of these women, about 60 percent are using the birth control pill to limit or space their pregnancies or both (Frerichs-Cigli 2008). The director of one of the NGO's health clinics near Rabat emphasized the pill's popularity to me when I inquired about which method most women choose, using hand gestures (making a #1 sign with her index finger) to make sure I understood this.

In the small public health clinic, Centre de Santé, located just outside of Rabat, all contraceptive methods are free, including male condoms. However, the head nurse said that she would not give contraceptives to unmarried individuals. She responded sternly that these methods were for "married people only." In the NGO's clinics contraceptives can be purchased for subsidized prices. Male condoms are available there, as well as in corner shops, pharmacies, and grocery stories. In the 2003–2004 Demographic Health Survey (DHS), the overwhelming majority of women in Morocco who participated knew of at least one method of contraception, whether it was traditional (post-partum taboos, prolonged breast-feeding, the rhythm method) or modern (birth control pills, IUDs). A total of 99.8 percent of women who responded and were classified as being in the bottom tiers of the socioeconomic scale stated they were aware of at least one method.

Breaking Down Borders and Building Divides through Narratives of Reproduction

On our walk, Salima reminded me that Morocco is not like France in its "liberalness," but the country is not like Saudi Arabia either, even though it is *islamique.* Contraception is a way for her to distance herself and Morocco from one region and to draw herself and the country closer to another. Reproductive technology becomes engrained in her identity as a Moroccan citizen, woman, and Muslim. There is a constant movement between two poles in her mind, France and Saudi Arabia. What does this tell us about how physical borders and cultural contexts are perceived? What do we learn about how two regions, divided in space on the map, are conceived of in the minds of Moroccan citizens? How might the "virtual" Europe (Chakrabarty 2000) and Moroccan imaginary come into play?

In addition to Salima, several other women expressed sentiments that the Middle East and Europe are not mutually exclusive. Hajjer, a mother of two female teenagers who worked at the main office of the NGO that ran two of the health clinics, often pondered out loud why poorer women (*les pauvres*) in Morocco continue to have several children. She told me a story about how she tried to help a woman who begged outside of her office by arranging for her to see a doctor free of charge at one of the NGO clinics in order to receive contraceptives.[2] If the clinic would not see her for free, Hajjer even agreed to pay for the services. She said, "I arranged for her to go to the [clinic] for contraceptives, for free. She never went. I don't understand it. They do not have money. If [name of the director] wouldn't accept her for free, then I would have paid the bill." When Hajjer first met the woman, she had three children. Her husband watched the cars parked on the street for a small fee and made very little money. The woman never went to the clinic and instead became pregnant with her fourth child, which upset Hajjer tremendously. She could not understand why they would have so many children if neither of them were making enough money to support them.

Hajjer reiterated to me that contraceptives are widely available and generally accepted, that neither Islam nor the law forbids reproductive technologies. She stated, "There are two things the Qur'an prohibits, abortion and sexual relations outside of marriage. Nothing else is forbidden in Islam." What is striking is that Hajjer would go on to explain that in this sense, Morocco is very much like Europe or the United States because the majority of people have access to family planning on a regular basis from a wide variety of sources. The only connection she ever made to other countries in the MENA was through the general presence of Islam, but she was careful to make the claim of what are and what are not acceptable reproductive behaviors in Morocco. She recognized that differences exist between Islamic beliefs and practices in the country and in other parts of the globe.

To complicate identity formation and the positioning process even further, Layla, a housewife in Rabat and mother of two sons and three daughters, stated that people living in eastern Morocco do not know any better and that is why they do not use contraception to limit their number of children. Her comment came after I mentioned that an international NGO had recently established health clinics and a large-scale reproductive health program in that region. Layla said, "That is very good. They need that. They have nothing there. Why do you think they have so many children? There is nothing, nothing. It's like Africa."

Layla suggested that the eastern Moroccans were closer to Africans, such as individuals from countries like Ghana and Nigeria who lived in Rabat, some of whom used the region as a passageway to get to Europe. She explained that African women only come to Morocco to become pregnant and have children for its better educational and medical resources. She said, "Women from Africa come here to get pregnant. [CLH: By whom?] Moroccan men or Africans. They have their babies in Morocco so they can go to school. Our schools are better than theirs so they want to have their children here." Layla's perception that African women are "over-reproductive" was seconded by a man I spoke to who worked for the Moroccan government in the financial sector. He suggested that in one of the poorer quarters, "There are so many." He said Africans would live ten or fifteen to a single apartment because each woman has at least three or four children.

Layla implied that she is further from being "African" than the women living in eastern Morocco, even though she has five children, exceeding the two or three recommended by the medical community in the country. For Layla, the Middle East did not play as prominent a role in her Moroccan identity as did sub-Saharan Africa. Moreover, Layla also commented that she is an *immigrée* or immigrant to Morocco because her family was of Arab descent and not Amazigh (or Imazighen).[3] Hajjer explained that she, too, is an African woman, but simply because Morocco is located on the African continent. She stated that there is a very clear distinction between North African women like herself and "*une femme d'Afrique noire*," a black African woman.[4]

Linguistically, Moroccan women "travel" in their minds between the regions among which Morocco is geographically and politically located. John R. Bowen writes,

> In the best tradition of dialectical scholarship, anthropologists and others have been deftly plying the tensions of global and local to understand transnational phenomena. If in one moment scholars explore and celebrate new possibilities for movement and communication . . . in another they consider how new cultural boundaries may be generated by such movements. (2004, 43)

Salima, Hajjer, and Layla create new "cultural boundaries" and understandings that draw on the contemporary moment and use of technologies as well as Morocco's colonial past. I am not using the term "travel" literally as Bowen does in discussing the movement of people, ideas, and things, but rather I am referring to the comparisons that Salima, Hajjer, and Layla make between Morocco and other countries in the MENA as they construct their own identities. Contraception is the mechanism that allows them to reconceptualize borders between Morocco and Europe or Africa and to "fragment" the Middle East and North Africa.

However, "fragment" is used cautiously here so as not to imply that the region was ever a complete entity. Marilyn Strathern argues, "What is imagined as fragmentation may no more be derived from a world of fragments than what is imagined as integration comes from a world already a totality" (2004, 22). Salima, Hajjer, and Layla's stories indicate that the MENA has never been a totality. Their discussions uncover how notions of Morocco and the region are multiple, imagined, and ever-changing, with Europe, Africa, and North America always in their midst. Moreover, there is not a consensus among them as to how Morocco is positioned, or where they and their country fit in the region and larger global scene.

Contraception is a reproductive technology that transfuses and is transfused by culture, history, and politics and becomes intertwined into Moroccan women's identity formation. Andrew Russell and Mary Thompson argue that contraceptive methods are crucial "new technological 'facts' on the global stage" (2000, 4). However, of equal importance is that methods of contraception are also mental "conceptions." They are much more than just a means to limit and space pregnancies. Theorizing contraception both inside and outside of the medical domain exposes the work of this "technological 'fact'" within the processes by which Moroccan women come to think of themselves as women, citizens, and Muslims. Even though Moroccans create their identities within the country's complicated geographic and political positioning, contraception is a tangible means around which women are able to tie together Morocco's vivid past, its geographical context, its rapidly changing present, and its outlook toward the future.

Salima, Hajjer, and Layla each articulated unique ways of identity formation with differing points of reference. On the one hand, Salima identifies with France, since in Morocco, contraception is advocated by the state and generally accepted by the public. At the same time, she identifies with the Middle East because the large majority of the Moroccan population is Muslim. Hajjer expresses a similar opinion. Nonetheless, Salima makes an exception for Saudi Arabia, as did Imam Khaloub, because of how they interpreted Saudi Arabia's norms concerning women's bodies and fertility. On the other hand, Layla compares women in eastern Morocco, herself, and Sub-Saharan African women (both those living in Morocco and those she sees on television and in the news), only to conclude that she is not like "them." The women in eastern Morocco are more like Africans because they may not regulate their fertility. Sub-Saharan Africa is the third reference in addition to the MENA and to Europe that helps women make sense of their and Morocco's position. The identities of my female participants are in a constant state of motion, moving through "sameness" and "difference," trying to piece together multiple social and political facets, albeit in ways that are never fully complete or stable.

Images: Tracing Sources of the Collision/Convergence between "East" and "West"

Often Morocco is deemed an interlocutor between the "East" and "West" due to its unique geographical position, just miles away from Spain to the north and yet on the African continent. Two places where this ambiguity of Morocco seeps into women's everyday lives are public school textbooks on sexual and reproductive health and the posters and pamphlets in the reproductive health clinics.[5] For example, in reproductive health posters and textbooks, several different images of the family appear in close proximity to pictures of or text about contraception. In many of these images, families are placed in contrast to one another. One family, with a mother and father, has two children while the second has six. In one particularly interesting photo in a public school book, the families are trying to squeeze under one umbrella to stay dry from the rain. The family with only a few children is successful, while the other is not and members of the family become wet while standing uncovered.[6]

The clothing of the two families differs to indicate the socioeconomic status of each. In taking a closer look at the image of the two families juxtaposed, the family with six children is dressed in dirty, tattered clothing. The mother of the family wears the hijab and the husband dons a *jall'ba*, or Moroccan robe. In contrast, the family with only two children is neatly dressed. The father has dark hair and is wearing a business suit. The mother is blonde and wears a neatly pressed bright green dress. There are several debates as to the meaning of clothing in Muslim communities and whether or not it represents piety (Deeb 2006; Winter 2008). Leila Ahmed states the inherent Islamic nature of the hijab is not static, but is questionable and must be understood in the larger national and global contexts (1992). In my fieldwork, several individuals made connections between women's dress and Islam. One gentleman has worked in reproductive healthcare in Morocco since the 1960s and has played a key role in building the reproductive health services that are provided today in the country. He explained his opinion that nurses and medical staff who wear the hijab have too narrow a focus in their work when they give precedence to religious meanings and tenets while providing services to women. They show that they are not capable of making sound and objective medical judgments in his opinion. Hajjer asked me one day about a family in Rabat with whom we were mutual acquaintances. She inquired about the daughters of the household and whether or not they left the home frequently. She said, "Her husband is very Muslim. He and his wife have some problems. Is she Muslim? Does she wear the hijab? I think she does." Hajjer assumed that if the mother wears the hijab then she is a practicing Muslim. Images of the family such as this in school textbooks conjure up linkages between Morocco's colonial past, Islam, and the state's current agenda for nation building and modernization. It demonstrates that the family continues to be one of the foundational units for conceptualizing society not only in the present but also for the future.

The walls of the NGO's health clinics are lined with posters about reproductive health and child rearing that send powerful messages as to why citizens should adopt a method of contraception. One image in the waiting room of a Rabat clinic depicts the ideal nuclear family. The underlying message is that the mother created a smaller family using contraception. A woman is sitting on the couch with her husband, a young son, and daughter nearby. Her son is playing on the floor while her daughter is reading a book. The mother wears the hijab while sewing. A thought bubble appears above the woman's head that reads, "The pill for protection from pregnancy, easy to use and effective." At the bottom of the poster is a woman's hand holding a one-month supply of birth control pills. A calendar is next to her hand reminding women that they must start a new cycle of pills each month in order for them to work properly. Fatima, the director of the clinic and a counselor, explained that these posters are important sources of instruction for the female patients who come to the clinic for reproductive healthcare. She said, "Sometimes I'm so busy here that I don't have time to teach. I'm supposed to give lessons when it is slow, but when it's like today I don't have any time. The pictures on the wall help the women learn what I was going to say. They are about nutrition, contraception, breastfeeding."

In keeping with the notion that the hijab represents an Islamic identity for some women in Morocco, we can see how this photo encourages the simultaneous adoption of reproductive technologies, development ideologies, and religious discourses. While the 2006 development report in Morocco makes an explicit link between women's use of contraception and the creation of a "modernized" nation, the NGO that produced this image adopted the same rhetoric within the context of Islam. The National Initiative for Human Development encourages individuals to make responsible choices about their lives, including those related to bodily practices and their families. The state encourages citizens to be "active" in their decision-making and in their own governance (Rose 1999). These images, in combination with the development policy, suggest that new ways of being are produced inside the entanglements of modernity, reproduction, the family, and Islam as the past and the future interact with each other in complex ways. Even though reproduction and development are both forward-looking in nature, there is a replaying of what was and what should be as women's bodies and the nature of future generations are defined.

Complexity of Positions: Implications for Anthropology of the MENA

In his interpretation of Abdelkebir Khatibi's autobiography, *La Mémoire Tatouée,* first published shortly after Moroccan independence in 1971, Mustapha Hamil suggests that Khatibi encourages inner reflection as a means to realize one's own subject position within the rapid changes that take place after colonization (2002). Khatibi proposes that meanings are not external or already existing, but rather are complex, elusive, and in motion. My arguments developed out of my own uncertainty as an anthropologist and writer about how to fit Morocco within existing bodies of literature and broader fields of inquiry. Those of us who conduct research in Morocco are often labeled multiple things (an Africanist, Middle East scholar, Moroccan specialist, and/or an anthropologist of North Africa or the Maghrib) and pulled in various directions, which may result in our own scholarly identity crisis. Morocco is located on the African continent, but many Moroccans, including Hajjer, distinguish themselves from other African men and women. In addition, for several decades, Morocco was under French rule with other European colonizers coming before them. Where does this leave us today? In thinking through this conundrum, I turned to the words of my participants for answers rather than drawing upon my own analytic categories. What I discovered from my participants' narratives, echoing to Khatibi's suggestion, was a blurred vision of Morocco, its geographic position, and its citizens. I have tried to allow these convergences and contradictions to speak for themselves in discussions about identity formation and medical practices.

The enduring ambiguity surrounding the politics and geography of Morocco runs rampant through government planning documents and reports concerning family planning and healthcare as well as through popular culture. Moroccan women's bodies have been and continue to be a foundation for public debates concerning politics, development, medicine, and religion. In June of 2008, the cover of a special edition of the news magazine *L'Express* on Morocco read, "Le Duel Tradition-Modernité" ("The Duel between Tradition and Modernity"). The magazine pictured five women standing in front of the Hassan II Mosque in Casablanca, one of the largest mosques in the world. Three are dressed in either skirts or jeans with sweaters while two wear teal-colored *hijabs* with long skirts and boots. Through making women's bodies and contraception the focal point of my analysis, just as this cover image did, I destabilize the image of the MENA as coherent by elucidating the complex matrices of discourses and meanings that Moroccan women negotiate as they construct their identities as citizens, women, Muslims, and mothers. As reproductive technologies become part of the lived human experience, they are also turned into representations of culture and individuals. Many of my working-class female participants use contraception to metaphorically move between times and places as well as between ideologies associated with a geographic region. They have broken and rebuilt divides within the MENA and reconfigured Morocco's connections within the region and abroad, which adds to the complexity of scholarship on Morocco regarding identity and medical practices, among other domains. They demonstrate the theoretical and practical dangers of considering the region as uniform and faultless without intimate ties to other world regions.

NOTES

I am above all grateful to Susan Slyomovics and Sherine Hafez for the opportunity to present an earlier version of this chapter at the *State of the Art* conference at UCLA in 2010. I would like to thank the conference participants for extremely helpful feedback. Susan Greenhalgh, Lara Deeb, Joanne Randa Nucho, Karen Leonard, Thomas Mertes, two anonymous reviewers from Indiana University Press, and my fellow graduate students in the Spring 2010 dissertation writing seminar at UC Irvine offered insightful comments on previous drafts and encouragement. The American Institute for Maghrib Studies and the American Philosophical Society supported my fieldwork in Morocco.

1. All names have been changed. I have not disclosed the exact locations of the health clinics to protect the privacy of patients and clinical staff.

2. The NGO's clinics would offer free services to those who could not afford to pay, but this was a rare occasion. The staff did not advertise that they would cover the costs because they were afraid individuals would take advantage. However, if a woman could absolutely not afford to pay, they would either let her pay later or offer the services at no charge depending on her particular condition and the services rendered.

3. Berber is a name used for Amazigh.

4. Ilahiane discusses the Haratine, an ethnic group in Morocco who possess relatively "low social status and marginality" (2001, 383). The origins of the Haratine are debated among scholars inside and outside of the country. Some believe they are former sub-Saharan slaves due to their darker skin color. The Haratine tend to be agriculturalists in southern Morocco.

5. Not all schools offered this type of education during the time of my research, but certain schools in the areas and suburbs of Rabat where I conducted fieldwork did have such classes.

6. This kind of image is not unique to the family planning program in Morocco. For instance, it also appears on the cover of Kamran Asdar Ali's (2002) ethnography that explores the Egyptian program.

PART 4.

ANTHROPOLOGY AND NEW MEDIA IN THE VIRTUAL
MIDDLE EAST AND NORTH AFRICA

14.

"OUR MASTER'S CALL": MASS MEDIA AND THE PEOPLE IN MOROCCO'S 1975 GREEN MARCH

Emilio Spadola

On 16 October 1975, at 6:30 in the evening, the king of Morocco, Hassan II, ad-dressed the nation via state television and radio regarding Morocco's claim to sovereignty over the then Spanish-occupied Western Sahara. The address fol-lowed more than a year of extraordinary diplomatic action by Morocco to se-cure recognition of its claim, including sending left-wing emissaries to convince European leftists of Morocco's rights, and public and secret negotiations with Mauritania, Spain, and Algeria. Hassan II's address referred more immediately to that morning's judgment by the U.N. International Court of Justice (ICJ), which acknowledged the historical allegiance of Saharan peoples to the Alawite Sultanate, the ancestors of Hassan II, but nonetheless denied Morocco's historical sovereignty (Vermeren 2002, 69; Dessaints 1976, 460). Sitting in an ornate chair, in an elegant blazer, before a bank of microphones, and speaking to his "dear people" (sha'bi al-aziz), Hassan II, with punctuated vehemence and godfatherly calm, demanded a national act.

It is incumbent upon us to carry out a green march, from the north of Morocco to the south, from the east of Morocco to the west. My dear peo-ple: We must stand as *one man*—orderly and systematically [*bi-l-nitham w-al-intitham*]—to reincorporate the Sahara, and to revive our sacred bond with our brothers in the Sahara [*li naltahiq bi-l-sahara wa li-nasil al-rahim ma' ikhwanina fi-l-sahara*].

Looking straight ahead into the television camera he called upon 350,000 Moroccan men and women from among "the people" to carry out an unarmed mass civilian seizure of the Spanish-occupied territory to establish Moroccan sovereignty.[1]

The speech, which marchers described as "our master's call" (*nida' sidna*) or "the king's call" (*nida' al-malik*), precipitated "The Green March" (*al-masira al-khadra*), a mass mobilization of unprecedented scale in Morocco. Hassan II had delineated specific quotas from the nation's provinces and prefectures, requiring that women account for ten percent of the marchers. The response was enthusiastic; within two days 350,000 Moroccans had registered at local state offices, as an estimated total of 500,000 to two million attempted to do so, necessitating a lottery to choose marchers (Weiner 1979; *Lamalif* 1975, 6).[2]

Hassan II's swift mobilization prompted intensive public negotiations with the U.N. and Madrid, with France and the U.S. secretly pressing a weakened Spain, roiled by General Francisco Franco's lapse into coma, to cede the territory to Morocco (Mundy 2006; Hughes 2001, 239). Meanwhile Hassan II's Ministry of the Interior coordinated the operation, assembling food, water, tents, and communications outposts, and commandeering private trucks and scheduling trains to move marchers from thirty cities across Morocco down to the border towns of Tantan, Tarfaya, and Tah (Weiner 1979, 27–29). To the east around Mahbès, Moroccan and Algerian forces clashed as Morocco attempted to seal the border (Howe 1978, 84; Mundy 2006). One week later, on 6 November, Hassan II addressed the marchers via state radio, ordering the advance of two blocs of marchers into corridors hemmed in by Spanish forces. The marchers advanced only a short distance beyond the Spanish borders, but the king's strategy worked; Madrid disavowed its previous support of Saharawi independence and agreed to partition the Western Sahara between Morocco and Mauritania. Hassan II, still broadcasting from Agadir, commanded the marchers to halt and return to their home cities.

As much as Hassan II's gambit astonished domestic and international political observers, more shocking was the sheer scale of the operation, and especially the intense collective enthusiasm which Hassan II's address stimulated across the nation's geographic, class, and political spectrum (Weiner 1979, 31). Zakya

Daoud, editor of the leftist *Lamalif,* and a target of Hassan II's political repression, wrote approvingly of the "unbelievable mobilization" his call precipitated: "people screaming, shouting, singing, and climbing onto the trucks with their red and green flags flapping in the wind" (Daoud 2007, 272).[3] "A national frenzy seized the entire country," *Lamalif* wrote, as unbelievable and awe-inducing as film or fable: "Technicolor production or images from an ancient tome!" (*Lamalif* 1975, 6). Marchers and other firsthand observers, foreign and Moroccan alike, found similar difficulty comprehending the event (Hughes 2001, 240). A veteran French journalist described the euphoric mass of marchers as "the most astonishing spectacle" he had ever witnessed—akin only to Gamal Abdel Nasser's funeral (Desjardins 1977, 88; cf. Hughes 2001). Politically, however, Nasser's funeral at least made sense, whereas this did not. Given Hassan II's authoritarian repression, the masses' and even the left's enthusiastic response was unfathomable, a kind of mass delusion (Desjardins 1977, 82).[4] Abdellah Laroui, attending the march with Daoud and likewise supportive of it, described a psychic transformation: "a moment of the Moroccan people's consciousness," a "psychological reality," "an epic" (1992, 147, 148). He too struggled to analyze it: "The Green March was not only a political act; it was something else. But what? It's not easy to find adequate qualification. Using a formula familiar to French thinkers since Charles Peguy, we will say that it was also a *mystical* act" (ibid., 148, emphasis in original). Finally, Laroui said, the Green March was a *moussem* (Arabic: *mawsim*), or saint's festival, "comparable to those organized by Sufi orders, which brought together members from all corners of the country" (ibid., 158).

Given its tremendous mobilization of Moroccans, its evident emotional resonance, and its long-term political effects, the Green March demands sociopolitical analysis. Geopolitically, the march helps identify the stakes of Morocco's claims to the Western Sahara, as well as persistent Moroccan–Algerian and Moroccan–Sahrawi antagonisms (Mundy 2006; Zunes and Mundy 2010).[5] Domestically, the Green March redefined the political terrain strongly in favor of the repressive monarchy. Coming in the wake of major political, economic, and ecological instability, persistent leftist and emerging Islamist critiques—and following near-lethal coup attempts against Hassan II in 1971 and 1972—the collective enthusiasm for the march helped legitimize what the throne and some left parties (the *extrème gauche* excluded) had for two years sought to brand "Consensus." Mohammed Tozy, voicing a common sentiment within Morocco, describes the Green March as the democratic advent, heralding participatory politics in Morocco.[6] More directly, however, the march reconsolidated the

monarchy's political dominance, permitting its violent liquidation of opponents through subsequent decades of partial political and economic liberalization (Hammoudi 1997, 20; Weiner 1979; Vermeren 2002, 70–71; Daoud 2007, 266).
Due to this dominance the march now, four decades later, still pervades the
political culture. It is celebrated annually with a national holiday and grand trib-
utes in both government-aligned and party newspapers; marchers I interviewed
recall the march in rich detail, and still carry state-granted identification cards.[7]
Popular Green March anthems have also returned to the national stage, in state-
sponsored festivals like *Mawazine,* and on the satellite channel 2M's popular
Studio 2M program.[8]

Why then has the Green March garnered little anthropological analysis
in either Moroccan studies or the broader area studies? The second silence is
perhaps to be expected; contemporary Middle East and North African studies
often treat Moroccan politics as the unique product of local culture and thus
beyond comparative significance. But Moroccanists' neglect of the Green March
requires a brief review of the literature to better explain. Falling at the intersection between conventional lines of argument, the Green March confirms but
also evades standard analyses. It demands novel theoretical approaches attuned
to the distinctly modern, *mass-mediated* nature of postcolonial Moroccan politics. More specifically, it calls our attention to the ways in which mass-mediated
political cultures of nationalism have extended and transformed older cultural
logics of power, and also collude with contemporary state bureaucratic appa-
ratuses (Anderson 2006; Geschiere 1997; Hammoudi 1997; Morris 2000; Siegel
1998). For Morocco this postcolonial period extends from its apotheosis in the
Green March to the current Arab Spring, in which the monarchy, in contrast to
the Tunisian, Egyptian, and Libyan regimes, has managed not only to repress
opposing voices by violence and imprisonment, but simultaneously to mobilize
popular support for its own reforms.

Theorizing Moroccan Politics: Mass-Mediated Culture

Sociocultural studies of Moroccan politics tend to emphasize either the symbolic,
religious force of the monarchy or its structural power, especially its strategic
and violent management and elimination of domestic rivals. Symbolic studies refer to Morocco's particular Islamic institutions and practices, specifically
the Sufi veneration of saints and the political sovereignty granted *shurafa* (sg.

sharif), descendents of the Prophet Muhammad (Combs-Schilling 1989; Geertz 1968; Hammoudi 1997). In Abdellah Hammoudi's reading—the most developed and most representative symbolic analysis—the Moroccan monarchy relies on 1) a deeply felt but only partly conscious devotional order enveloping elites and ordinary Moroccans alike, in which the king (as *sharif*) combines sacred and political authority; and 2) social-economic dissemination of his "blessing"—as material patronage and divine recognition—to his subjects through the medium of competing religious, genealogical, and socioeconomic elites. In contrast, scholars with a structural view of political culture have emphasized the postcolonial regime's strategic repression of potential domestic rivals or "segments" by divide-and-rule tactics as well as by brutal liquidation of opposing voices, even during periods of putative liberalization and "reconciliation" (Leveau 1985; Munson 1993; Slyomovics 2005; Waterbury 1970).

These approaches profitably overlap, notably in Hammoudi's argument that violence itself constitutes a gift of recognition (1997), and in John Waterbury's view of the monarch's legitimation as resting on both classical patrimonialism and Morocco's particular religious tradition (1978). Indeed, at first glance the Green March brings both of these threads together. Hassan II's call and commands deployed Islamic symbology, evoking a Qur'anic concept of sacred familial (blood) connection (*silat al-rahim,* a connection by womb)[9] to describe the primordial belonging of Saharans with Moroccans, as well as material gifts of charismatic recognition: a poster of the king, copies of the Qur'an, state identification cards, and medals (Combs-Schilling 1989, 325; Entelis 1996, 59; Hammoudi 1997, 20; Rollinde 2003; Waterbury 1978, 416). At the same time the march involved the coercive apparatus of the state, including Hassan II's strategic division of social "segments" and over-representation of marchers from more loyal rural provinces, as well as the blunt force of neighborhood *muqaddams* (officials) coercing at least some marchers into signing up (Weiner 1979).

Yet even together symbolic and strategic power fail to explain the scale and emotional intensity of the event, and more specifically its cultural meaning as a *national* event for marchers and their witnesses, rather than a specifically religious act or expression of local identity. What explains the distinctly national and nationalist character of the event, including its national limits of comprehension?

An answer begins with Benedict Anderson's and others' analysis of the nation as a distinctly modern mass-mediated social form, the practices of which have nearly everywhere supplemented rather than wholly eradicated a prior political and religious culture (Anderson 2006, 1990; Ivy 1995; Siegel 1998; Messick 1993; Morris 2000; Pemberton 1994). Hassan II's televised and radio-broadcast announcement of the march, and its subsequent use throughout the march's execution, constituted a "powerful media campaign for the national cause that enflamed the country" (Vermeren 2002, 70). That such a campaign was possible, as a simultaneous broadcast to different cities and rural regions, i.e., a national address, was relatively novel in 1970s Morocco. In the decade preceding the Green March, and especially the first half of the 1970s, Morocco had witnessed a "veritable blast-off" (Jaïdi 2000, 64) in communicative technologies and production; registered TV sets increased from around 8,000 to around 450,000, spreading at the same time from urban Morocco to newly electrified areas of the countryside. This television infrastructure added to radio capacity already in place (given the low cost and high mobility of transistor sets, radios already numbered in the hundreds of thousands, if not millions).[10] The monarchy monopolized radio and televisual media—political parties relied on print media—particularly through Radio-Television Maroc (RTM), directed by the Ministry of the Interior as a political mouthpiece of the state (Jaïdi 2000, 59). The success of the Green March and the "primary role" of TV and radio in it further bolstered these infrastructures, as the march signaled to RTM officials the benefits of new, more powerful broadcasts (Akhchichine and Naji 1984, 213, 201). Tellingly, the march persisted as a theme in the state's subsequent media planning (ibid., 1984, 304).

Scholars have elsewhere noted Hassan II's successful use of mass media—television and radio in particular—to bolster the sacred legitimacy of his regime among nonelite, ordinary Moroccans, that is, "the masses" (Moudden n.d.). Mohammed Tozy identifies the televised rituals of submission of government officials to Hassan II as a way of helping the sovereign's sacrality to be "accepted [intériorisé] by the majority of the population" (1999, 81). I. William Zartman emphasizes the political force of mass-mediated connection itself under Hassan II: "Of all [political actors], only he does not stand for election. Instead he sits for television, using the media as a visible, incontestable channel to his people, the modernization of the direct link between king and countrymen" (1987, 11). Hammoudi suggests that mass mediation amplifies the power of monarchy's ritual stagings:

> In ritual and ceremony [authoritarian power] takes the concrete form of prostration and hand kissing, which every notable must perform at regular intervals. Such images, enhanced by the court etiquette, enter every

household through the media. The exercise of power, as a form of living energy, appears here in all the splendor of absolute and accepted submission. (Hammoudi 1997, 43)

Hammoudi's argument emphasizes the historical specificity of this mass-mediated experience; indeed, he notes that the very discourse of a "direct relationship between the king and his people" is exclusively modern (ibid., 14). Yet his argument for symbolic power on a mass scale rests largely on the face-to-face mediation of the king's sacred power through exclusive relationships, that is, through his personal closeness and gift-exchange with notables—elites and bureaucrats. *National* consciousness—identification with "the people"—demands for its emergence another kind of mediation apart from the patrimonial or neo-patrimonial.[11] But this exceeds Hammoudi's argument: "Has the ever-increasing power of the media in the twentieth century become a decisive determinant in this highly volatile dissemination?" he asks. "I cannot express an opinion on this power. Indeed, a separate ethnography would be required to treat the subject adequately" (ibid., 107).

This chapter offers a prolegomenon by arguing that the Green March rested on the historically and culturally specific conditions of mass-mediated politics in postcolonial Morocco. From a symbolic perspective, the massive popular mobilization required a familiar political culture, finely depicted by Hammoudi, that was suffused with the workings of divine patronage, blessing, and recognition, as well as with terror and awe. At the same time, it required and clearly put to use the state's authoritarian bureaucratic apparatus to coerce and mobilize the masses. But the success of the march rested on something more, namely, the power of mass-mediated connections, which the march both drew on in terms of infrastructure, and itself stimulated—socially and psychically—for the masses of marchers caught up in the undeniable nationalist euphoria. It resulted, in other words, from mass-mediated political culture: on the one hand, the rapidly spreading mass-mediated communications by which hundreds of thousands saw, heard (and heard about) Hassan II's announcement, and, on the other hand, the recognizable discourse of mass, national belonging, "the people," and their putatively "direct" connection to the king, which the Green March put so strategically to use. These symbolic and technological factors were intertwined. Through technological mediation marchers experienced Hassan II's announcement *as a call*—"Our Master's Call" in marchers' words—that is, as a highly intimate command and a promise of social and material recognition to anyone who identified with his "dear people." Crucially, that call, *felt as a call,* produced for marchers a perhaps otherworldly promise of circumventing or suspending the historically embedded *social* medium of elites and patrons, including the coercive and contemptuous apparatus of local authorities. The *nation* was calling them, not the *state*.

As Benedict Anderson has argued, suspensions of ordinary or prior sociopolitical structures for a mass-mediated national and imaginary structure is akin to the liminal period or the pilgrimage (Anderson 2006, 1994; cf. Turner 1967, 1969). But if the resulting feeling (if not reality) of a "direct link" to the exemplary center of Moroccan political culture generated a mass response, this does not mean that Hassan II's call delivered on its promise of recognition. Nor is it to suggest that the formation of a national mass putatively beyond ordinary hierarchy could last. The story of the Green March is in fact the betrayal of that promise.

Participants in the March, Recipients of the Call

Relatively little has been written by or about participants in the Green March. A small number of short memoirs, published individually and under the auspices of the monarchy, have given voice to a few state-affiliated elite participants. Scholarly treatments of the march generally draw on these but especially on Hassan II's recollections (Hassan II 1976). His orders for the march specified that 350,000 Moroccans volunteer, among them 43,500 government ministers, local leaders—*caids, shaykhs, muqaddams*—doctors, nurses, ambulance drivers, and youth scouts. Middle-and professional-class people—"lawyers and Casablanca businessmen" (Daoud 2007, 274; cf. Laroui 1992) volunteered, as did well-known political figures (Aherdan 1976). Urban and rural underclass Moroccans, however, constituted the tremendous mass of volunteers.

The marchers who chose to participate in this research, twenty-one men and five women, belonged to this latter group. Most had registered for the march in Fez or Sefrou, with one each in Taza, Errachidia, and Rabat. As of July 2008, however, all live in the lower-and lower-middle-class neighborhoods of Fez, including the Medina, and in recently built neighborhoods to its north. (None live in the wealthier Ville Nouvelle or in the middle-class villas growing southward toward Sefrou.) In the words of one, Abdelhafid (b. 1945, Sefrou), other marchers he knows are presently "very poor, living in shantytowns"—or they are dead. The most educated men among my interviewees completed secondary school. These two, Si Sbai (b. 1946, Fez) and Si Alawi (b. 1947, Sefrou)—the respectful "Si" for "Sidi," the rough equivalent of "Sir," signals a degree of status—are perhaps the closest to the middle of the struggling middle class in Fez. They and three other men are formally employed—three as doormen, one at a tourism company, and one as an assistant at a government office (*baladiyya*). Four men are retired (two bereft of pensions owed them); the rest, including all the women, are unemployed or underemployed, a common situation in Fez's weak economy based largely on tourism and artisanal crafts. All the women are illiterate.

These marchers described themselves in 1975 as poor and unemployed or struggling on their single salary to support siblings and parents. Si Sbai was the sole breadwinner for his ill father and ten siblings. Si Alawi was marginally better off, but of his seven family members who marched, three were illiterate. Reflecting on their motivations some thirty-three years after the fact, interviewees were candid about their material need and their anticipation of a reward—a house or a shop (*mahal*)—for reclaiming a wealthy Spanish colonial territory, and especially the city of Laayoune. Si Sbai and Si Alawi both viewed such motivations as "uneducated, unaware," and lacking "conscience" (*damir*). Si Alawi said of his own family's uneducated volunteers, "they expected to go and be given everything." Middle-class Moroccans have made similar comments to me during my fieldwork—that marchers thought the Wadi al-Dhahab, Golden Valley, was in fact gold. The implication of these criticisms is that the uneducated poor were motivated by self-interest rather than by some higher ideal which the march ostensibly demanded.

But we must consider the cultural, historical, and technological circumstances in which simultaneously hundreds of thousands of poor Moroccans—and not just elite "notables"—could anticipate a reward or a gift from the king, "to be given everything" for their service. Underclass marchers emphasized this sentiment of service to the king, referring to material motivations and yet, without contradiction, to having "responded to" or "obeyed" (*talbiyya*) the king's or "our master's call" (*nida' sidna*), as one complies with a command or obliges an invitation. Mohamed H. (b. 1946, Errachidia) said "we were illiterate people who said 'Yes' to Sidna [bows his head]." Mohamed W. (b. 1945, Sefrou) said explicitly "I went there for two reasons: because of the king's call, and also to stay and live there." These and similar comments made clear the logic of the event as something involuntary, even arbitrary, but meaningfully so—a call to duty. "I did my duty [*adit al-wajib*] and returned" (Abdelhafid, b. 1945, Sefrou). The meaning derived not simply from the king's call, but from marchers' sense of being a collective who were addressed by the king and who recognized the call's value. As Si Sbai put it, "When the king calls you—you have to obey him. [It's] the nation's call." That duty to obey derived from the collective to which one, in responding, belongs. The king *and* the nation were calling. The call was both a command and recognition of one's belonging.

Middle-class criticisms that reduce marchers' motivation to idiocy or greed miss the broader significance of the call as a promise and of the anticipated material gain as *gift,* that is, as a recognition of Moroccan underclasses' more profound national belonging. The power of recognition explains why marchers I interviewed had kept their identity cards and medals from the march. Something beyond money was at stake, and my research assistant Sanae and I both felt marchers' longing for it pervading our interviews. Sanae said, "They think we're with the state [*dawla*]." I disagreed, saying I had been clear about the nature of the study. She specified: "It's been thirty years—and they're still *waiting* for the state." Indeed. The point to emphasize again is the mass-mediated and mass political nature of this expectation.

The People

We serve you great nation
Our blood for your glory,
As time passes.

To protect the homeland
To pave the way to your glory,
We serve you, the masses.

We serve you dear Morocco,
Protect you at any cost.

We serve you my Great King,
Your soldiers, with our arms aloft.
    —From Mohamed al-Bidawi's "The Nation's Call" (*nida' al-watan*)

The mass-mediated (televised and radio-broadcast) messages disseminated by the state in the announcement and build-up to the march, including Green

March anthems commissioned by the state, reiterated themes of sacrifice for mass belonging, and of mass belonging as the condition for the king's recognition. Indeed, Hassan II's initial call to the nation specifically invoked a history of mutual recognition between the throne and "the People." If such a mode of address suggests intimacy, his notion of exchange emphasized the immediacy of spiritual fusion:

> My Dear People, you and the throne have exchanged, you have exchanged inspiration [*tabadaltum al-wahi*]. Your taking stands has forever inspired the throne to rise up. And the feelings and judgments [*taqyimat*] of your kings have forever inspired you to action. Thus Dear People, each [of us] traces the path for the other, the path of dignity, victory, and the reassertion of Moroccan pride. And now once again we will exchange inspiration and dreams.

Hassan II's images of the people's exchanges with the Alawite sovereigns are of a spiritual unity; exchanging "inspiration" (*al-wahi*) evokes immaterial or immediate communication, even "suggestion" (*iha' thati*, auto-suggestion) and electronic "transmission" (*wahin* as "radio transmitter"). Such immateriality has of course a political message, a message of perfect communication merging the King with the collective will of the people as a unified body. But while Hassan II described the relationship as timeless and ongoing, he also invoked the specific historical ritual of connection between the People and Alawite monarchs—the Oath of Allegiance, *bai'a*—and its specific historical medium of connection, namely, writing. The oath in Morocco, he explained, was "unique among Muslim nations, [in being] never only oral, but always written," and marked by a "special stamp [*tab' khass*]." The mention of a written stamp (as opposed to "inspiration" or ephemeral orality) highlighted a medium that, as Hassan II then elaborated, brought tribal leaders into contact with princes and kings, hand in hand and face to face. Moreover, he said, the *bai'a* was extended to those "unable to read and write" the document itself by virtue of an intermediary, the state notary. These are historical details, he said, but, "for those interested in further study, I can charge the Minister of Culture with providing a public lecture, and a series of articles on the subject."

The mention of the written seal invites listeners to imagine the established power of writing and hierarchy, of the seal and of social stratification. It evokes the power of the state notary who would mediate commoners' exchange with the monarchy. But it does so in a broadcast medium that supersedes and also circumvents these structures. Historically the seal of the sovereign, the *dahir*, used to grant recognition to tribal or Sufi or corporate leaders, was guarded carefully as a literal mark of distinction (Berque 1955). Its value accrued by its singular rarity and even cult status. Now, however, all members of Hassan II's audience could imagine participating in the elite tradition. Indeed, a few minutes later in the same speech, Hassan II specifically noted that marchers would receive their own mark of recognition:

> My Dear People . . . I have provided the means, and ordered governors in each province to open offices from tomorrow on to register men and women volunteers. I will be among the first to put my name on the record of volunteers. I will proudly avail myself of a Participant's Card [*wariqat nakhib*], and I will be proud to have a Volunteer Card [*bitaqa li-tatawa'*] for the march to recuperate the Sahara. This is the real crown, the real scepter, that will last for my children and my grandchildren: the stamp of nationalism [*sibghat al-wataniyya*]—no, I say, the stamp of God [*sibghat Allah*]! And whose stamp is better than God's?

I have mentioned that my interviewees showed me the identification cards (ID) they still carried decades later. Two other marchers I met in Morocco did the same. In one sense the ID or the medal responded to the call for an interview, that is, it marked one's participation. More to the point, ID *proved* something and in so doing held a power to compel recognition even from a stranger (and foreigner). It is this recognizability that matters, binding one's own face to a general system. It is not absurd then that Hassan II claimed the ID, the stamp of nationalism or of God, was "the real crown, the real scepter." It suggested a replication of the great written stamp, the "special seal" of the Alawite throne—as if each person, having responded to the king, receives his or her own "special seal," and so holds that contract with him. It is a striking, and utterly modern, image of royal recognition granted simultaneously to hundreds of thousands of individuals.

The price of this recognition is abstraction, as the ID (like the census), in the service of the nation, discerns not particular human beings but serial subjects whose recognition derives first from their incorporation into the mass. It is significant then that Hassan II's call to action emphasized numbers, enumerating quotas of marchers from each region (306,500), as well as the government officials, doctors, and functionaries needed to guide and care for them (43,500), the number of trucks needed to transport them (7,813), the tonnage of food (17,000) and water (63,000) and fuel (2,590) needed to nourish them. This focus on scale invited marchers to think in terms of a mass collectivity, indeed to realize that collectivity in a physical act. This mode of enumeration and abstraction was celebrated in the Green March anthem, "The Nation's Call" (*nida' al-watan*), quoted above. Like other anthems broadcast on state television and radio in the wake of Hassan II's call, this one reiterated themes of mass national unity—of the people as a unified mass body of atomized individuals—under the king's command: "350,000 parts of your people [*atraf sh'abik*], oh My Lord / Women and men from all parts of your Kingdom." Middle-class Moroccans have alerted me that Hassan II chose 350,000 marchers because the number equaled Morocco's annual birth rate (cf. Weiner 1979, 26). Each marcher was, in other words, expendable. Yet here the number is celebrated. The repetition of "350,000" in the song evokes the massiveness of the event, and more particularly, the grandeur of the marchers as a *mass body*, a composite of similar and even interchangeable subjects, rather than diffuse and disconnected individuals: 350,000 "parts of your people."

The abstraction of a person into serial quantities would make little sense prior to modern census-taking (Anderson 2006, 168); it correlates not at all with the old sharifian social hierarchy and exchange where spatial proximity was social power, that is, where distance and proximity indexed social rank (Hammoudi 1997, 68–75). In this newly national society, anyone can hear the call anywhere, and this very abstraction is the virtuous condition of national consciousness and belonging which "Our Master's Call" celebrated. To respond to that call meant identifying oneself not with one's social qualities (of name, family origin, age), but with its mass addressee, "the people"—that is to say by becoming a number, "one digit in an aggregable series of replicable" nationals (Anderson 2006, 169). The adoption by participants of a rhetoric of mass-mediated belonging, i.e., the saturation of popular by official rhetoric, suggests that indeed volunteers desired this mode of identity and recognition—that the social and even psychological force of the march was inseparable from this mass-mediated identification.

Laroui's description of the march as a *moussem*, a sacred pilgrimage, is thus apt. For Moroccans who responded to the call did so by transcending ordinary social bonds for a national *communitas*. To be sure, this is hardly unique to Morocco. Indeed, Hassan II's call illustrates one of Benedict Anderson's arguments, drawing on Victor Turner (1967), that national consciousness emerged not only in simultaneous reception of messages, but in shared conditions of liminality or "exodus" from prior social identity (Anderson 1994; 2006, chapter 4). James T. Siegel similarly has linked Indonesian nationalism to liminal conditions of pilgrimage and the broader collapse of social referents, permitting the temporary suspension of social differences and the "passage" to "the People" (2000a, 2000b).[12]

To compare nationalisms is not to suggest, however, that conditions of pilgrimage and liminality are generic. Hassan II's call struck a specific cultural nerve, the anticipation of recognition grounded, as Hammoudi argues, in sharifian ritual. Yet the material (literal) striking of that cultural nerve was forged by mass mediation: by mass communication and the discourse of "the people."

"We heard Our Master's call. We got goosebumps."

The presence of mass media was reinforced as Sanae and I asked interviewees how the announcement of the march "reached you" (*kif waslat lak*). Most heard Hassan II's address on the state radio, listening with others, and some heard and saw it on television (RTM). One interviewee, Abdelhafid, described hearing it from TV and from the local officials (*muqaddams*) at a government office in Sefrou where he worked. Bahia (b. 1956, Fez) a woman who first said she had heard the announcement on television, later clarified that she had heard about it "from others who had seen it on TV." In a way that emphasized the feelings of direct connection, several interviewees described hearing about the march "from Sidna," and only clarified on my follow-up question that they meant "from the TV" or "from the radio."

Hearing the call generated for some a sense of excitement and risk. Abdelhafid explained:

———I first heard His Majesty's call—may God give him victory—I was doorkeeper at the *baladiyya* [local government office]. I felt courageous, I was the fourth or fifth to sign up.
———*How did the call reach you?*
———Out of love for the God, Country, and the King.
———*I mean, how did you hear about the march?*
———From the officials [*muqaddamin*] at the *baladiyya* and from the TV. I went directly to register. As soon as I heard His Majesty's call, I went.

Abdelhafid's response to my first question was telling; his receptivity to the call simply assumed the logistical means of hearing it. But the striking matter of courage spoke to his feelings of an extraordinary event, and an extraordinary command. There is no doubt that some marchers did not volunteer, and

were not enthusiastic about the prospect of the march. Despite the surpass-
ing of Hassan II's quotas in all districts, there was surely coercion by at least
some local officials. Yet my interviewees did not describe their experiences in
this way. Indeed, responding to "our master's call" meant *defying* authority. For
Abdelhafid courage meant the risk of losing his job at the local government office. His family, dependent on his employment, argued against his volunteering.
"They said, 'If you go, you'll lose your job, your salary.' I said, 'Who's going to cut
it—*Sidna*?'" Abdelhafid's brashness is unmistakable, as if responding to the king
gave him immunity from all other authority, including family and his superiors
at the government office. Likewise, numerous women joined the march against
the patriarchal rules of their families (Weiner 1979, 31). Naima (b. 1958, Sefrou)
was sixteen and thus ineligible to march, but defied her mother and brothers and
fooled the local officials. She said nothing at home but dressed in a robe (*jellaba*)
and high heels to register. Her mother was none the wiser, nor did Naima or
her mother know that her brothers had also signed up. Naima and her siblings
would later meet on the march, the national body providing the new medium
of familial connection.

Such acts were not personal rebellion against authority in general, but
rather were rejections of one set of authorities at the command of the king and
the nation. As Naima said, "I saw other people going, so I went too. It made me
happy—glorifying *Sidna!*" To feel the immensity of the collective was for some
thrilling: "When we heard the King's call, *we got goosebumps*," said Mohamed
S. (b. 1949, Fez). The presence of a sense of collective identity is suggested by
marchers' common description of their response to the call in the first person
plural. Kamal (b. 1955, Sefrou) spoke of seeing the speech on television, after
which, he said, "We got up and volunteered with firm determination [*nudna
bi kul hazm*] in the name of His Majesty. We participated with a feeling of happiness and joy! [*bi wahid al-frah wa bi wahid al-surur!*]" In Kamal's hometown
of Sefrou this enthusiasm was not unique. He estimated that some 600 people
lined up at the town office to volunteer. Mohamed H., also in Sefrou, heard and
went, like other people: "We heard about the march from the king. We went to
the government office to register. We went (at once) like other people [*mshina
bhalna bhal an-nas*]." Hussein (b. 1958, Fez) described being out of school and
jobless with his friends: "We were home and heard *nida'* Sidna on the radio. We
all went to register. King Hassan was dear to us, so we went to obey our master's
call [*talbiyyat nida' sidna*]. We volunteered all together, all enthusiastic, all one
heart!" Moreover, Hussein said, laughing, "We didn't even know what the word
march meant! Even if we didn't know what was happening, we were one heart!"

Obedience here does not equate to sheer coercion. Violence alone fails to explain the intimacy with the king which my interviewees felt in receiving his call for volunteers. It explains neither the collective enthusiasm nor the specifically *national* feeling of belonging that marchers (and observers of the march) described. Rather, obedience entailed responding to "our master's call" and more specifically to entering the liminal space of "imagined community" (or imagined *communitas*). This imagined community was mass-mediated, both by virtue of the technologies of the call and the discourse of the people and their "direct link" to the king. More speculatively, this community was liminal to the ordinary mediating structures of life and authority—of home and, for those who had it, employment—and perhaps even of the state officials themselves. Such a national discourse of immediacy is not simply eliding the structures of its own power (Mazzarella 2004), but rather highlighting their suspension—"a genuine experience of linkage *despite* social bonds" (Siegel 2000a, 282 emphasis mine). One seeks recognition not on the basis of who one is—but by virtue of a capacity to sacrifice it for the mass, to join the people.

In the Desert

Nearly three weeks passed between registration of volunteers and the beginnings of the movement. Volunteers were called suddenly by the town crier (*barrah*), some taking money and clothes with them, others not.[13] Marchers were loaded onto trucks and taken to Marrakech, and from there to the border. In Tantan, Tarfaya, and Bettah marchers made encampments, women in tents pitched in the middle of a circle of men's tents. Hassan II's plan included the division of groups by prefecture, and then into sections of twenty-five people under the supervision of one leader chosen by the Ministry of the Interior. (Si Sbai, because he was literate, was such a leader.) Groups were given bulk rations of water, wheat, oil, and sardines to be distributed by group leaders.

The presence of the feared Interior Ministry as well as the separation of marchers by locale reiterates the monarchy's successful tactics (surveillance, divide and rule) for maintaining power. Marchers likewise described police beatings—but as necessary to keep order, and as punishment of those who violated the *communitas*. Indeed these tactics did not hinder collective feeling or the occasional intermingling of regional groups. Rather, marchers described the elation and euphoria of collectivity: "There was a feeling of love (*wahid al-mhabba*) between people. . . . We were brothers and sisters" (Abdelqader, b. 1951, Fez). This unity felt particularly intense in moments of collective voice and vision, in some cases through religious symbols—"Everyone was chanting, '*la ilaha ila Allah! Muhammad rasul Allah!*'"—including, on Hassan II's orders, hoisting the Qur'an as a gesture of nonaggression. In some cases people felt unified through drumming and singing pop music by Jil Jilala ("Laayoune, My Eyes," *laayoune 'ayouni*), whose song in honor of the march had received significant airtime on state radio (Weiner 1979, 32). In other moments, marchers chanted anthems broadcast prior to the march, such as "Masira Khadra":

> The valley, our Master [*Sidna*], is my valley.
> Safely we go and return.
> With us are God, the Prophet and Qur'an!

The content of the chants is critical, suggesting both a cultural/religious unity and a mass-mediated one (through pop music, anthems, etc.). But so too is the sheer power of chanting itself, what Jacques Berque described as "the imponderable elements" of nationalism: "mass enthusiasm, the incantation of Arabic words, the intoxicating effect of shouting, that collective hysteria which sometimes escapes all control, and yet that faith in its leaders, that exciting sense that someone has 'arisen' who will govern these forces and give them point" (Berque 1967, 82–83). The king's call stimulated and channeled these forces; the effect was at once to loosen ordinary social bonds, and, in the same turn, to reaffirm the imagined links of the nation.

Hassan II continued to speak "directly" to the people (i.e., technologically) throughout the next stages of the Green March. On 6 November 1975, broadcasting from Agadir on RTM, he urged people to cross the barbed wire barriers bearing only the red flags of the nation, green Qur'ans, and black and white portraits of the king himself. Without marchers' knowledge, the king had negotiated with Spain to permit the marchers to enter a band of the territory, but one which did not actually reach Laayoune. Marchers arrayed at the border, police placing loudspeakers on their Land Rovers to spread the sound. Marchers recalled the order to first lower the flags and raise the Qur'an and then, on a given command, to raise their flags. At two critical moments at least these speeches were definitive in moving people. Everyone said that the Spanish military jets flyovers terrified them. They repeated the *shahada*. But a group of marchers I interviewed agreed that Sidna's speech calmed them, "We relaxed when the King spoke to us to say, 'You should not be scared. You are well protected.'" Evoking Hassan II's historical recall of the King's written "Special Stamp" and its dissemination, a marcher noted, "Very few people had radios. But those who did invited others to circle around, and translated [from classical Arabic to the vernacular] for the illiterate." The speech, one of the interviewees emphasized, "was live, from Agadir"—another feeling of connection with the monarch.

With the successful crossing into the Western Sahara participants witnessed "miracles" (*mu'jizat*). A full red moon rising in a dust storm reminded two men of King Mohammed V's apparitions in the moon reported by masses of Moroccans during his exile in 1953. For others General Franco's death was divine retribution. These miraculous moments occurred right at the close of the Green March. Within another twenty-four hours, on 8 November, King Hassan had addressed the marchers again from Agadir, via commanders' radios, to declare the Green March an unmitigated success. He called a halt and ordered the expectant marchers back to Tarfaya and their homes, without seeing the city of Laayoune.

Awaiting Recognition

All was not well, however; the euphoria of the march was by no means the end of the story. For some the food and water rations were insufficient. Marchers left encampments for the nearby towns to trade what supplies and money they had for additional food. Stopping short of Laayoune was also a surprise. Naima said that she and her brother and "many people" wished to take the city as their just reward:

> There were many people who wanted to settle there. Wheat, oil, everything is cheap. Living there is cheap. Me too, I wanted to stay there because we were poor and my mother was working as our breadwinner but she couldn't take care of everything. We didn't have food. So my siblings and I, each of us decided to work to help her. We wanted to go there to find something, to live there and work there.

But, she continued, "there we found nothing." Many of my interviewees (twenty-three of the twenty-six) echoed Naima's comment, as well as her tone of defeat. "The king assured us that everything would be provided. But on the march the police were controlling who got what, who got water. There was wheat, oil, sardines, potatoes, but very little water" described Mohamed S. At one point, he said, a man grew enraged by his group leader hoarding water "to *wash* himself with!" The man attacked the leader with a knife, only to be taken away by police.

Naima noted that "Sidna gave us everything! Even cigarettes—though I was too young to smoke." But she added pointedly that police jealously guarded food, water, and supplies for themselves: "They were controlling everything" (*msaytrin ala kul shi*). According to Naima, there was clear favoritism, or as Mohamed S. said, "there was stratification" (*kaynin darajat*). The people of Fez in particular were "spoiled" (*mdallalin*), said Naima. They were given water preferentially, and women from Fez looked down on women from Sefrou. The key point for Mohamed S. and Naima was the unexpected injustice, one highlighted by the contrast with the *communitas* the king's call had promised and in certain moments delivered.

Notably, if the king's address to the people established a direct *national* connection, the breach of that connection was, as Mohamed S. and Naima emphasized, the fault of *state* authorities, including police and government officials in charge of logistics. Abdelqader said, "When the march ended, police took off (*hrab*) in their jeeps. A few trucks [that brought the marchers] started taking people back, but only three or four in a truck. We had to wait for two days before more trucks came." When the trucks finally brought them to Marrakech, marchers boarded trains for their home regions. Abdelqader lived within Fez, but marchers from the surrounding villages were offered no further transportation. The government officials who had been so excited were nowhere: "We returned [to Fez] at one in the morning," Abdelqader said. "No rides—and no one there: *no shaykh, no muqaddam, no caid, no khalifa.*"

In bringing up these serious injustices, marchers expressed anger. But as with Abdelqader's list of government functionaries, these were directed at representatives of the state, those well known for their mistreatment and humiliation of ordinary Moroccans. No one blamed or even mildly criticized Hassan II. This may index the repression of political conversation that pervaded Morocco under Hassan II and continues to a lesser extent in Fez today; perhaps marchers displaced their anger at the king onto state officials. Yet these explanations still lack force. People in Fez tend to fear and avoid the neighborhood *muqaddam*, the petty tyrant of the quarter. This fear had emerged during my earlier fieldwork in Fez and it re-emerged in these interviews, including during my discussion with a group of marchers in a living room in the lower-middle-class neighborhood of 'Ayn Qadous. Although we spoke easily for the first hour, news of our interviews spread and more people came to speak or listen. As the small crowd grew out the door of the room and into the apartment foyer, so too did the risk of the *muqaddam*'s appearance. A rumor of his arrival in fact began to circulate, and within a minute—seconds—my interlocutors dispersed. The state is most assuredly feared.

Abdelqader's listing of state officials—"no shaykh, no muqaddam, no caid, no khalifa"—implicated precisely that mediating chain of command which *nida'* Sidna had seemed at least temporarily to obliterate. If the king's call promised a direct connection it was state functionaries—the social intermediaries—who broke the link, denying marchers the promised recognition and reward, by inserting themselves, even by their absence, between the monarch and his people. "They" also meant "no one." Mohamed H. complained that "We got back, and we got nothing, even though they said 'We'll call you.' We saw nothing from it." He had sacrificed for the nation, yet the state failed to reciprocate: "No one came to me. I didn't go to the government office [*baladiyya*] because no one there asked about us." Mohamed S. had criticized others' expectation of a material reward for heeding the call—"they have no conscience" (*ma 'andhumsh damir*)—yet he complained of the lack of recognition in similar terms: "No one even asked about us" (*hatta shi wahid ma saal fina*).

There were similar stories from nearly everyone I interviewed. Mohamed W. (b. 1945, Sefrou) said that upon his return, "They gave us nothing [*ma 'atawna walu*]. We are needy people and we were promised many times to be supported and helped but they gave us nothing. 'We will stand with you, we will help you, we will do things for you.' But we saw nothing from it." Two months after their return "they" gave marchers a party with tea and donuts! Mohamed mocked the absurdity of it. Risking his life for the nation and receiving . . . tea and donuts? "And the donuts were of very poor quality," he laughed with an edge. "Like rubber. *That's* how they welcomed us."

"For a Green March on Facebook!"

As Sanae observed, the longing for some kind of recognition remains nearly four decades after the fact. So too does the fear. Violence is a facet of Moroccan political culture that no one can ignore. But the Green March cannot be reduced to strategic violence. Indeed the Green March promised to suspend ordinary sociopolitical violence. The enthusiasm it sparked rested on the possibility of direct exchange with, and recognition by, the exemplary center of the nation. And just as violence does not fully explain the Green March or mass politics, neither does the historical model of the monarch as master, his blessed recognition transmitted across a person-to-person hierarchy of known disciples. The Green March, in contrast, rested on mass politics and mass media, in which recognition would accrue to those anonymous individuals comprising the serial parts of the imagined community, "the people." Which is to say it was a distinctly *national* act, its conditions of possibility both technological and discursive: the national infrastructure of the call—the shimmering electronic connection with the monarch—and the discourse of "the people" as that imagined body worthy of the king's recognition.

Could the Green March take place today? The event remains a watershed, its popularity renewed by the revival of its anthems. And marchers were adamant: *they* would do it again. But they insisted that the nationalist feelings Hassan II's call ignited no longer pervade Morocco, especially not among the nation's youth. This assertion has proved both prescient and uncertain in the wake of Morocco's pro-democracy and pro-monarchy competing appeals in the summer of 2011, in which media, including mass media and social media, as well as local functionaries knocking on doors, have played a role in summoning and organizing new collectivities. There are of course tremendous differences in the two eras (of broadcast and social media), but the Green March also provides an important historical backdrop for the so-called "Twitter Revolutions" of Tunisia and Egypt that have at least momentarily bypassed state-controlled media outlets. And yet we should be wary of assuming that media proliferation stands in simple opposition to or wholly challenges broadcast and the monarchy. Along with calls for democratic reform, one finds groups on Facebook calling for the Western Sahara's integration into the nation—"*1.000.000 Signatures Contre l'exclusion du Sahara marocain de la carte*" ("1,000,000 Signatures Against the Exclusion of the Moroccan Sahara from the Map")—and for a reiteration of mass political gathering: "*Sahara Marocain: 350.000 Membres, Pour une Marche Verte sur Facebook!*" ("Moroccan Sahara: 350,000 Facebook Members for a Green March!")[14]

NOTES

1. Extracts of Hassan II's 16 October 1975 address are posted online (http://www .youtube.com/watch?v=VV1yPegH6Jk). I have drawn on these for visual descriptions, with additional passages translated from the complete Arabic text of the speech printed in the official organ of the Moroccan Ministry of Pious Endowments and Islamic Affairs, *Da'wat al-Haqq* 17 (4): 12–18.

2. "In every jurisdiction volunteers for the march far outstripped the King's quotas, and marchers had to be chosen by lottery. For example, in Oujda 11,832 volunteered to meet a quota of 1,500; in Chaouen 4,423 for a quota of 500; in Rabat-Sale 20,018 for a quota of 10,000; and in Agadir 66,580 for a quota of 33,000" (Weiner 1979, 31).

3. On the Moroccan Communist Party's enthusiastic participation in the Green March, see Yata and Paul (1977, 16–18).

4. Desjardins noted that "The [Moroccan] left's response is without doubt one of the most astonishing matters of the Western Sahara affair" (1977, 82).

5. Morocco's unresolved "reclamation" or "annexation" of the Western Sahara certainly included other critical material concerns: the wealth of the largest phosphate reserve in the world, mined there since 1963, the potential offshore oil reserves; Atlantic fishing grounds now in a serious state of depletion; 100,000 Sahrawi refugees in Tindouf, Algeria; Morocco's torture of Sahrawi peoples, and suppression of the Polisario, their rebel national liberation movement; the protracted and immensely expensive stationing of tens if not hundreds of thousands of Moroccan troops along its security walls; and not least, the repression of dissent on the Saharan topic within Moroccan domestic politics. For a geopolitical overview of the conflict see Zunes and Mundy (2010).

6. Mohamed Tozy, speaking at Democracy and the Media, a conference organized by the Center for Cross-Cultural Learning, Rabat, 11 November 2000.

7. The research for this chapter took place four and a half years after I completed long-term fieldwork in Fez and earlier research in Rabat, and while it drew on my contacts in Fez, the circumstances of the research in late July 2008, due to the limited time available to me in the field, differed markedly from my ordinary fieldwork. To find marchers for interviews I began by contacting two marchers I knew through my research and friends in Fez, but relied far more heavily on the extraordinary help and ethnographic skills of my longtime research assistant and family friend in Fez, Sanae Ajana, whom I have asked repeatedly to serve as co-author (she has declined). Based on lists of questions and concerns regarding the march, she carried out and recorded initial interviews (in Moroccan Arabic), which we listened to and discussed by Skype in June and early July 2008 (and which she transcribed into written Moroccan Arabic and emailed me). Based on the personal narratives she collected, and on interviewees' willingness to participate, she arranged for in-person interviews (and one group interview) with eight men (Abdelhafid, Abdelqader, Si Alawi, Hussein, Kamal, Mohamed H., Mohamed S., and Si Sbai) and one woman (Naima) during a whirlwind fieldwork stint 12–31 July 2008 in Fez. I have drawn insights for this chapter from all of Sanae's and my own interviews, as well as from my prior fieldwork-based knowledge of Fez. Quotations draw almost exclusively from my personal interviews. In addition, two interviews with American scholars resident in Morocco in 1975, Jerome Bookin-Weiner (telephone interview, 11 January 2008), and Louis Abdellah Cristillo (in-person interview, New York City, 21 October 2009), have been very helpful in gathering a sense of the foreign response to the Green March. I am also especially grateful to Abdelhay Moudden for emphasizing in numerous personal communications the

centrality of "the people" (*al-sha'b*) in Moroccan political discourse, and for sharing an unpublished manuscript on the monarchy's "non-cognitive" influence through audiovisual media in general and nationalist anthems in particular (Moudden n.d.).

8. Clips of these performances are posted on YouTube—a new site of political culture—and vigorously commented on, for example: (1) Ramy Ayach, "The Call of the Sahara" (*nida' al-sahara*) [*sic*], Mawazine Music Festival, Rabat, 2010 (http://www .youtube.com/watch?v=Vd2IeoXy734, accessed 17 October 2011); (2) Studio 2M, 2M Monde, "The Voice of Hassan Calls" (*sawt al-hassan yunadi*) (http://www.youtube.com /watch?v=hMPYenPF0V4&feature=related, accessed 17 October 2011).

9. See, for example, Al-Qur'an 47: 22–23.

10. See Lacouture and Lacouture (1958) on the ubiquity of the radio in post-Protectorate Morocco.

11. Waterbury similarly suggests that the power of the Green March rested on Hassan II's traditionalism and his influence on "public opinion" rather than on patrimonial structures (1978, 416). He does not explore, however, the structural or infrastructural (media) conditions for such a public to form.

12. For Siegel, such passage occurred as crowds listened to President Sukarno, and precisely by virtue of his address as a "performative act," or call that summoned them away from social origins and into a novel mode of belonging:

> No one is born a member of the people nor is it a sociological category. A farmer, for instance, is not a member of the people because of his profession, his place of birth, or the language he speaks. He becomes a member of the people by a performative act. In the Sukarno era he was one of those the president addressed either in the great stadium of the capital or over the radio. When Sukarno, who styled himself "the extension of the tongue of the people," spoke in their name, those listening, even though hearing certain ideas for the first time, found that these ideas did indeed express what they thought. At that point they were members of "the people." (Siegel 2000b, 36)

13. Notably, the crier followed the original call—the presence of the live human voice rendered a supplement to the technological broadcast.

14. Accessed 21 October 2010.

15.

THE CONSTRUCTION OF VIRTUAL IDENTITIES: ONLINE TRIBALISM IN SAUDI ARABIA AND BEYOND

Sebastian Maisel

For the contemporary anthropologist, the word "tribe" is often a reference to the past, where its forms and settings were studied extensively, frequently in combination with the idea of state formation. However, in the twenty-first century, it seems that the "old" tribe no longer fits and is excluded from the process of building national identities. Especially from the official perspective of countries with large tribal communities, the idea of tribal narratives or influence has been considered an obstacle in the development of a modern society.

A current analysis of tribes and tribalism in Saudi Arabia and neighboring countries, however, reveals that tribes have not vanished from the public sphere. A surge in different forms of self-representation and accounts of tribal practices and concepts is clearly evident. Tribal communities and individuals struggle successfully to find their position in the civil society and hierarchy, especially in countries like Saudi Arabia, Kuwait, and Jordan. Due to the rapid and profound changes in lifestyle, interaction, and communication experienced in the modern era, a new chapter in the relationships between tribal and non-tribal members of society has opened. Concurrent social change has brought along with it generational conflicts and new pressures that tribes have to acknowledge and respond to. The proliferation of new technology and media throughout the entire Middle Eastern region started a new process of public discourse and participation. The tribes have found a way to contribute to this ongoing debate by using some of these powerful communication tools while at the same time challenging traditional ways of interaction between tribal members and the authorities.

This study focuses on the new role of tribalism in contemporary Saudi society, in particular the relationship between tribes and the state or central authorities as well as among inter-and intra-tribal connectors. The large Arabian tribes, such as the Anazah, Shammar, Ajman, Mutayr, and Utayba, and their schemes of interaction in the larger Saudi society have been at the forefront of public attention and discourse. Among the main topics of the tribal agenda are:

- The role of customary law in settling legal disputes.
- The emphasis on selected tribal values in the creation of national narratives, such as honor, hospitality, and poetry.
- Specific marriage strategies along tribal lines.
- Voters' behavior during local elections in Kuwait and Saudi Arabia.
- The claims for further political participation made by several tribal leaders.

What is not discussed in this paper is the old, often romanticized notion of the wandering Bedouin tribes with their constant raids and nomadic lifestyle in the deserts, simply because it has been outdated, at least in the north Arabian context. Furthermore, the question or definition of a tribe is put aside. The groups that are the focus of this study consider themselves tribal groups. Their counterparts, state and religious authorities, regard them as tribes as well.

My argument is that a new form of tribalism has emerged, which is primarily represented by a new generation of protagonists who use modern technology to convey their messages. Tribes are still kinship-based organizations with distinct patterns of behavior and representation; however, based on the study of their statements and actions, it appears that they have started to reinterpret the tribe's role in society with regard to the state as well as internal questions of tribal cohesion. The nature of their comments and publications interpret the role of the tribes as more inclusive and less alienated than in the past.

My research on the new form of tribalism and tribal relations in the Saudi Arabian context started in late 1990s with the application of ethnological, historical, and linguistic methods, such as interviewing tribal members, elders, judges, and state officials, working in the few available archives, observing reconciliation cases, and joining the younger generation in their activities—drinking gazillions of cups of coffee and devouring a small herd of lamb and baby camels in the process. Another immensely useful source for learning about tribal patterns and agendas was the audio holdings of the oral history center in Riyadh. They provided the historical and cultural background for comparison with current interpretations. Combining these resources, it seemed that the anthropological toolbox was pretty thoroughly exploited.

However, my fieldwork among tribal groups during the late 1990s was already affected by the introduction of modern technology, in particular here, the constant use of mobile phones. Countless times, a conversation with my informants, interlocutors, and hosts was interrupted by rings from several phones. Often my hosts picked up the phone to call relatives or acquaintances in order to clarify an issue in our conversation. Surprisingly, very often the relative actually resided outside of Saudi Arabia, for example in Mosul, Iraq, Abu Dhabi, or Homs, Syria. The information technology (IT) revolution has clearly changed ways of communication between tribal members, enabling direct contact between groups who have been separated for generations and centuries. It allowed me as the observer to make preliminary transnational comparisons.

In 2009, I revisited Saudi Arabia following reports of a rising neo-tribalism. The media reported extensively about tribal involvement in local elections, legal rulings by *shari'a* courts over tribal issues, and disputes over the role of women in society. While these are all legitimate and profound topics in the current debate, it seemed prudent to analyze these debates from an existential point of view in order to find new references to still unanswered questions about the general rupture in the relations between tribes and the state in Saudi Arabia. Therefore, I went back to the location where it all started, or perhaps more accurately all ended, where the relations between tribe and state were finally cut. During the battle of Sbillah (29–30 March 1929), tribal forces known as the Ikhwan and formerly loyal to King Abd al-Aziz revolted against the ruler due to their belief that Abd al-Aziz had abandoned the straight path of Islam and sided with the infidels. Although this seemed to be a religious argument, the masses and leaders of the rebels were still entangled in tribal lifestyle and values. In the literature and the official Saudi narrative, the battle of Sbillah is portrayed as the last Bedouin battle and the turning point in tribe/state relations, an interpretation emphasizing the notions of progress, unity, and nation-building (Howarth 1964), 168). Tribes were thereafter no longer considered a threat, but incorporated into the newly created Saudi society. Then, modern technology (i.e., cars, telegraphs, automatic weapons) contributed to their subversion into settled, non-tribal groups. It was not surprising to find that Sbillah was still a matter of intense debate both within tribal circles and with "the others." However, the debate was carried along new platforms of interaction and communication.

Not until recently, certainly since the ascension of Abdallah to the Saudi throne and the advent of the IT revolution, have tribal voices become more audible in the public discourse. I duly followed these new developments with additional trips to the area and further interviews with pertinent informants. However, it was almost impossible to retrieve any reflections on the Battle of Sbillah other than personal accounts of the events from contemporaries. It was quite obvious that this was still a taboo topic that should only be discussed along the official line of historiography. What was striking to me, however, was the fact that the young people in the room started to intervene and voluntarily shared their opinions on the battle and its participants with me. These comments were in sharp contrast to those provided by the elders. This alone was a sign that things had changed. Ten years ago this would never have happened. Respecting elders, especially during discussion of tribal matters, was a core value of the tribal society.[1] But, not only did youth now share their thoughts, they also made countless references to other like-minded people. They explained how they participated in lively discussions about these issues. After asking if I could join these sessions, they said, anytime, just go online.[2] Well, I did, and this opened up a new chapter of ethnological fieldwork.

Saudi Society

Saudi Arabia is a very young country with an old history and culture. The population appears very homogenous, predominantly Arab and Muslim. Official census figures estimate 25 million residents in 2008, of which approximately five million were non-Saudi expatriates. A large majority of Saudi citizens trace their nationality back through bloodlines and not geography. The significance of bloodlines and descent are manifested in the tribal nature of the society. However, tribe in the Saudi context no longer refers to a lifestyle or occupation, but to a social network of kinship, loyalty, and identity. While the tribes no longer claim their own territories, pastures, or grazing grounds within Saudi borders, most Saudis still entertain a mental divide between tribal and non-tribal groups. Some common ways that Saudis identify themselves and others are: "this man is from this lineage"; "my relatives belong to another lineage"; and "this family is not even tribal." People of different tribal background might work and live together, but they still respect the invisible line that separates them from the "other" and regulates or limits any interaction. As mentioned above, the main aspects of interaction that are affected by this behavior are marital relations, legal settlements, and public participation.

Being a member of a tribe, large or small, noble or inferior, does not guarantee wealth, success, or political power; however it provides the necessary backup in times of hardship, conflict, and need. Even urbanized and liberal Saudis remember and cherish their kin network during troubled times.[3]

What does it mean to be tribal or to belong to a tribe? Nowadays it is shown in special patterns of behavior. Primarily, a tribal member looks for support within his/her own kin group. For example, children playing with each other; teenagers doing activities together; young people looking for their spouses; women visiting other members of the extended family; businessmen proposing transactions; the unemployed looking for work at a relative's company; helping to organize social events; settling disputes; or following certain conservative values. The first contact person is usually someone from the tribal group. First, one looks at the paternal relatives, then at the maternal side.

The other common descriptor for Saudi society is that of a very young society. Almost sixty percent of Saudis are under the age of twenty-five. The country has one of the highest birthrates in the world (above four percent) and no policies for family planning or birth control. A rapidly growing society, high level of unemployment, and the perseverance of generational customs and hierarchies are just a few of the daunting problems facing all citizens, tribal or non-tribal. The current move toward a stronger emphasis on tribal pattern and networks indicates a possible approach to resolve those problems.

The Internet in Saudi Arabia

Modern technological developments and progress are key factors for social change primarily because they widen the arena of interaction, bringing different actors within societies and cultures into direct or indirect contact and mutual influence. The internet as an unprecedented communication tool has opened new channels of interaction and information flows. From the perspective of cultural anthropology, the internet can be viewed as a cultural phenomenon by examining its influence on interactions within a defined community as well as between social groups. My focus is strictly regional; in this area the internet is documented as a lightly censored medium of expression and information. It has strongly impacted a largely conservative Saudi Arabian society. Different perceptions of priorities and moral values among distinct cultures require different forms of standards, especially in Saudi Arabia, where, as the heartland of Islam, those standards are kept high. According to a study on internet use in

Saudi Arabia, critics have found plenty to fear from the internet. There are too many extreme political beliefs, too much sex, and too many strange religions (Sait et al. 2007, 22). Thus, substantial efforts have been made to block sites that host objectionable content and services. The Saudi government maintains an active interest in filtering sexually *and* non-sexually explicit web content within the kingdom. They succeeded in making the content effectively inaccessible to most users. Those sites are blocked, as they conflict with the country's religious, cultural, legal, and traditional norms. Citing the Qur'an as a legal basis, the government describes its efforts at filtering as "preserving our Islamic values, filtering the Internet content to prevent the materials that contradict with our beliefs or may influence our culture."[4] Saudi Arabia looks at a range of web content beyond just the sexually explicit, including pages about religion (even Islamic sites), culture (humor, music, movies), and homosexuality. However, it should be noted that blocking criteria are quite broad and not consistent. Despite the censorship, many sites with objectionable content remain popular.

Because the internet was desired by many, Saudi Arabia registered the first net providers for public use in 1999. At universities and other research institutions, internet access was available from 1994, and individuals were allowed to purchase hardware and modems to access the net through foreign providers. However, before the entire population was allowed to go online, specific guidelines and measurements were taken in order to protect religion, nation, and culture from negative aspects of net content and immoral pages, such as pornography, gambling, or anything that threatened the social, political, and religious values of the people. Local internet providers are connected to a single, government-controlled proxy housed in Riyadh at the King Abd al-Aziz City for Science and Technology (KAACST), which controls and blocks inappropriate and undesired web content. For example, access to Yahoo and other sites offering private clubs was temporarily banned by the authorities. Saudi authorities, like those in other Gulf States, try to censor everything that seems offensive to the country's values or security; in addition to the categories mentioned above this means content about opposition groups, Israel, drugs, alcohol, and women's rights. They maintain an updated and sophisticated control system to block those sites; however, ways to circumvent the system exist and are exploited by sophisticated computer users. Additionally, for a higher charge, individual users can have unrestricted web access by calling an ISP outside the Kingdom, for example in Bahrain.

Presently, internet access in Saudi Arabia is widespread, with almost five million users (one fifth of the population). According to a recent survey conducted by King Fahd University of Petroleum and Minerals and the National Information Center,[5] a typical internet user in Saudi Arabia is young (under the age of twenty-five) and educated (with at least a high-school diploma). When asked about their main interest in using the internet, many refer to the connectivity, helping to get or stay in touch with people from the extended family as well as with people who share the same interests. Saudis go online mostly at home and sometimes at work or school. Males spend longer hours online, while females use the internet more frequently. The Saudi online community is growing rapidly and enjoying the immense opportunities for social networking by easily connecting with other individuals and groups without major supervision or restrictions.

The Tribal Discussion Board (*al-muntadiyat*)

Despite the government's attempts to spread a culture of national unity, there are still those who reject what they believe is just another attempt to promote the culture and identity of the dominant Al Saud family and their constituency from the central region of Najd. Recently, a heated discussion over camel beauty contests threatened to split Saudi society into those for and against having the contests. That issue was resolved only after senior scholars commented that such contests are permissible unless they can be shown to do irreparable damage to society (*Saudi Gazette*, 30 April 2009). One might ask how a beautiful camel can split an entire nation. But I will leave this to the imagination of the reader, only reminding them of the fierce competition and tribal ownership of the camels as well as the reputation and prize money associated with winning. The animosities between the camels' owners were largely articulated along tribal lines and stand in sharp contrast to the image of a unified Saudi society.

A greater dilemma for state officials, however, is the claim that internet websites dedicated to different Saudi tribes are weakening the ties among members of Saudi society. The following quotes from the print edition of the *Saudi Gazette* highlight the problem:[6]

> The late King Abdul Aziz found the tribes in conflict and concerned with tribal disputes, and he succeeded in turning them into one connected unity. I'm just afraid that such tribal websites will affect the unity of our society. One of King Abdul Aziz's main concerns was to eradicate racism, which is, of course, a factor of backwardness and is, perhaps, a source of terrorism.

I'm not only talking about these websites, but also about the TV channels, poetry contests like the Poet of the Million and the Poet of the Deep
Meaning, and tribal camel beauty competitions. All of these things destroy
the efforts of the late founder of the nation to make all of the country's
tribes into one civilized society. (*Saudi Gazette*, 30 April 2009)

Over the last decade, with the spread of internet access even among rural
communities, a growing number of indigenous testimonies and perspectives on
the social history of tribes have been published, offering a new form of narrative and interpretation of tribes' relationships with others. Using self-censored
discussion forums and bulletin boards, tribal members conceptualize identities across political and hierarchical boundaries. The classical prominence of
tribal identity in Saudi society has found an outlet of expression on the internet.
Tribal discussion boards now proliferate throughout the entire online kingdom,
where they serve multiple, often competing functions: as repositories for information concerning tribal genealogies; as forums for discussion of pressing
local, national, and international issues; and as venues for socializing among
tribe members.

Tribal Identity in Saudi Arabia

In order to conduct a content analysis, discussion boards of three representative tribes, the Anazah, Shammar, and Mutayr, were selected. All three are high-
ranking ("noble") tribes within the social hierarchy. Also note that all major and
most likely minor tribes have their own websites (often more than one, since
no site can claim to be the official representative of a tribe or lineage). To better
contextualize the discussions that take place in the open forum, some historical
background on the tribes and their place within Saudi society is in order.

Historically, all three tribes were camel-herders with additional land ownership in oases. They fought long feuds against each other over tribal territories and
grazing rights in northern Arabia. The dichotomy between Shammar and Anazah
was often referred to as a struggle between archenemies. On the other hand, tribes
rarely acted in a homogenous fashion. Sometimes, sections of one tribe collabo-
rated with the central authority, while others were opposed to them. Sometimes
they formed alliances on the local level while the leadership was fighting against
each other. The rivalry between the leadership of the Shammar (Al Rashid) and
the Al Saud is well documented, as are the animosities between Faisal al-Duwaysh,

supreme sheikh of the Mutayr, and King Abd al-Aziz. Tribesmen from all three tribes figured prominently within the Ikhwan movement as well as the following rebellion. After the formation of the Kingdom of Saudi Arabia, both Shammar and Mutayr faced some difficulties assimilating to mainstream Saudi society due to their previous hegemonic rivalry with the Al Saud. At first, this prevented them from reaching high-ranking positions; however, those distinctions slowly faded out in favor of a generalization of tribal membership, regardless of the past.

Today, the three tribes and their former grazing lands have been contained and incorporated within the boundaries of the modern Saudi state, whose legitimacy is based on the maintenance of an ethos contradictory to the tribes—that of universalizing Saudi identity. The reduction of tribal spatial cohesion is therefore a necessary consequence of citizenship within the kingdom. As is evident from the discussion boards and the earlier descriptions, this process does not take place without resistance.

As former nomadic tribes, the present-day tribes show off their noble pedigrees, which guarantee them top positions within the rigid hierarchy of Saudi society. Tribal pride is richly represented on the discussion boards. Images of falcons, horses, and coffeepots adorn the borders of the tribes' homepages and appear regularly as user icons reinforcing their traditional commitment to Arabian tribal and cultural life. Some users prefer names that include references to a certain lineage, family, or individual. Often, pictures of a generic tribal member in traditional dress are used.

The discussion boards identified for analysis in this study were selected on the basis of their substantial membership as well as for their capacity to reflect the changing dynamics of Saudi tribal society. In what follows, I attempt to analyze three discussion boards representing the Shammar, Anazah, and Mutayr, who used to be physically located in central and northern Saudi Arabia and beyond. Discussion board members can be located anywhere within the kingdom or even abroad. Some boards record the country of origin, i.e., the country from which the user accessed the board. The absolute majority sign in from Saudi Arabia, followed by users from the United Arab Emirates. Occasionally, a user from Iraq, Syria, or a Western country is registered.

After the selection process, the next step included monitoring the postings on these bulletins for resonant content and selecting for analysis popular threads that generated a substantial number of responses. It quickly became clear that although many topics were posted for discussion, only a few actually generated interest. Thus, it was important not only to look at the number of topics, but at the number of replies.

Discussion Board Samples

Discussion Board 1: www.shmmr.net/vb/

This board is affiliated with the Shammar tribe. One of the oldest sites, it went online on 20 August 2001. It includes almost 30,000 members, of which some 1,300 are considered active users providing feedback and posting new threads. The number of postings had reached 900,000 as of this writing, split over 65,000 different topics or groups.

Main topics included separate hosts for discussions about sports, litera-ture, youth, astronomy, education, Nabaty poetry, mobile phones, family issues, Islamic topics, and history. Hosts were considered for special content analysis if their topic made direct references to tribal issues: the city of Hail (432 topics), poetry (3,513 topics), popular and Nabaty poetry (6,914 topics). The large num-ber of entries in the poetry section covers several issues. First, poetry is a popular vehicle of communication among the tribes: it always has been and remains so. Poets are highly respected members of the tribal community, and much of the group's history has been transmitted orally by means of poetry. Thus, the case of the famous Shammari poet Talal Al Rashid, who was killed in 2003 while hunting in the Algerian desert, gained a lot of attention, especially since the circumstances of his death have still not been clarified. Furthermore, poetry can also be used to stir up confrontations and as a tool in intertribal rivalry. The 1968 publication of the book *Abtal min al-Sahra* (*Heroes from the Desert*), by Ahmad al-Sudairi, caused riots between Anazah and Shammar groups because of some offensive poems.

Discussion Board 2: www.3nzh.com/vb/

The second forum is linked to the Anazah tribe, nominally one of the largest tribes in northern Arabia, with members from Aleppo, Syria to Riyadh, Saudi Arabia. This particular site has some 23,000 registered members, less than the Shammari site. However, note again that none of these sites claim or have the status of the official discussion of the entire tribe. Other large-scale boards coex-ist and, as in the case of the Anazah confederation, they often represent smaller fractions, lineages or sub-tribes. Users participated in about 550,000 threads covering roughly 42,000 topics. Among the selected topics are threads on popular heritage, tribal genealogy, historical documents, old stories, Anazah heritage, and links to other sites related to Arab tribes.

Discussion Board 3: www.mutir.com/vbvv/

The third forum is associated with the Mutayr tribe, which largely settled in the eastern part of Saudi Arabia as well as in Kuwait and the Emirates. Due to their historical affiliation with groups in opposition to the government, the Mutayr tribe has not fully integrated into Saudi society. Faisal Duwaysh, the legendary leader of the tribe and the anti-government opposition campaign of the Ikhwan, is held in high esteem and his family still maintains the leading position within the tribe. Perhaps due to the rather nonconformist nature and history of the tribe, the number of members and active participants on the site is unusual high. Over one million postings and more than 100,000 topics are discussed by about 70,000 registered members. Although a variety of topics are present, special themes focus entirely on the tribal history and the relations with the state as well as tribal news, obituaries and eulogies, history and genealogy of the tribe, general history, and the land and people of the tribe.

In reading through the most common and popular thread, several general topics regarding current tribal questions evidently stand out. They are discussed intensively, producing a large number of replies and participations:

- The dichotomy of descent: tribal versus non-tribal
- The discussion and validation of tribal narratives versus state narratives
- The different forms of temporary marriages (*misyar, mut'a, misfar*)
- The importance of tribal endogamy
- The role of women in society and online
- The extent of tribal involvement in the process of political participation

On all three discussion boards, the issue of intermarriage between tribal and non-tribal (*khadari*) status groups plays an important role in reproducing prevalent hierarchies in the Kingdom. As marriage is considered a contract between two families, superior tribes will as a rule avoid marriages to inferior tribes. In several publicized cases, *shari'a* courts annulled marriages between spouses of different tribal origins upon the request of the families. The issue created a flurry of responses clearly pointing to serious divisions over tribal endogamy that exist in Saudi society.[7] It is significant to note the high frequency and popularity of consanguine marriages in Saudi society (El-Hamzi et al. 1995).

Another topic of strong general interest and debate on the bulletins is the question of political participation. Public participation in the political sphere of Saudi Arabia is limited to several influential circles and elite groups closely associated with the Royal family. Tribal leaders, although nominally in charge of their communities, are merely part of the elite as retainers. However, during election time, tribal elements are encouraged to rise in support of their leaders, who run for office in the Kuwaiti parliament or Saudi municipality council. Since campaigning is very limited, candidates use other forms of interaction with the voters. Discussion boards became very popular during these times due to their accessibility and limited state control. However, non-tribal members also logged in to contest the clientelism and patronage system of the tribal constituency.

Opposition to the political system is largely based outside the kingdom, mainly in London. Over the last few decades, using means of modern communication (tapes and fax machines in the 1970s and 80s, cell phones and the internet more recently), opposition groups regularly connected to large segments of the Saudi population and distributed their materials at election time. In a sudden move two years ago, several tribal leaders joined an opposition group, declaring their resistance to the course of the government and renouncing their allegiance (*Al-Quds al-Arabi*, 28 August 2007). The tribal leaders, Talal Al Rashid (Shammar), Mamduh Sha'lan (Anazah),[8] Musaid al-Dhuwaibi (Harb), and Faisal al-Hithlain (Ajman) announced that they would work together on one platform to distance themselves from sectarianism or tribalism. As one can imagine, the thread was picked up quickly and stirred up fresh debate on the different tribal platforms. The newly emerging attitude of tribal leaders became explicit:

> The Saudi regime does not want anything from the tribe other than its folk-lore and camels to parade them in the camel festivals, and also its poets in order to gain a social dimension and a fragile symbol to add to the folklore of the Arabian Peninsula. However, it seems that the tribal groups have woken up, and are no longer satisfied with renting or selling their heritage at the rostrums of the camel races, or with recording it in the encyclopedias of soul poetry. (Al-Rashid 2007)

As surprising as the move of the four tribal Sheikhs to join forces appeared, it was more surprising to realize that the move was actually rejected by the majority of respondents, citing mistrust and historical evidence. Instead, there was a common notion in the arguments that only one tribal leader could be the real leader of the movement—the one from the poster's own tribe, of course. And here, I finally found the information that I was looking for initially. On the discussion boards, users started to compare the current tribal leadership to former tribal heroes, among them the participants in the battle of Sbillah. Detailed biographical material was cited and countless anecdotes told. It helped me to clarify the image of the battle in the national as well as the tribal narrative.

Using the Internet as a Methodological Tool

The internet and in particular discussion boards became a popular source for soliciting opinions on social issues and taboos. For the contemporary anthropologist, they serve as a tool to conduct interviews and participant observation. By nature, those forums have a bipolar, dueling function. On the one hand, they empower the underprivileged and marginalized, and on the other hand, they update their peripheral status. As a whole, they expand the media environment significantly and challenge the state monopoly on information and identity.[9] The opinions presented in those bulletins allow the researcher to look for second opinions. While official state communications often depict and promote only one narrative, online individuals and groups can produce and deliver opposite viewpoints without fear of immediate consequences. The method has become so popular that even state officials started to use the internet to promote their own discussion boards. The Committee for the Propagation of Virtue and the Prevention of Vice (CPVPV) launched an online forum where users can report and discuss what they perceive as offensive toward the official narrative.[10]

Obviously, working with online texts and documents raises a number of questions; some that this chapter has addressed are the origin of the writer, the targeted audience, the reliability of sources, the issue of networking, or the impact on the community, both virtual and real. However, the advantage of expressing opinions in an anonymous setting, without the fear of revealing your identity, name, age, or tribal status, cannot be underestimated. The government has only limited control over these sites and in the past did not block them like they frequently block personal sites or blogs.[11] The medium of a discussion board allows for the solicitation of a variety of opinions under a common, topical umbrella. And last, but not least, the tribal bulletin board helps to preserve the heritage and tradition of the group.

While anonymity is certainly an advantage for the user,[12] it is not so much for the analyst. Registration is simple and can be completed by anyone whether or not they have a tribal agenda. At times, this has been taken advantage of by opponents of the tribe to engage in confrontational rhetoric and rude accusations. However, the large majority of entries and users follow an unwritten, but well-known code of conduct. In addition, administrators monitor the conversation and block users or threads if necessary. The level of self-censorship and self-criticism was surprisingly high.

Regarding the information and sources obtained from these forums, one should consider their level of authenticity as secondary due to the nature of the informants. The users are predominantly from the younger generation and learned about the historical facts through narratives from their elders. Although many topics show a lack of detailed knowledge, very informative threads are frequently posted, representing substantial source work, i.e., peer communications as well as conversations with elders.

As noted earlier, none of the bulletins are considered the official voice of the tribe. Although they each claim to be the sole representative, no permission or endorsement has been granted. Who could grant such permission anyway? While there are several families who are considered the tribal elite, no single member of those families speaks for the entire tribe. Within the Shammar tribe, the Al Rashid family is highly respected, for example, but the Al Ali family has a similar reputation and so does the Al Jarba family for the Shammar in Iraq. Among the Mutayr, the Duwaysh family has a paramount position, but due to their size, several fractions rival for the supreme leadership. And the Anazah are more like an umbrella organization with several semi-autonomous lineages, fractions, and sub-tribes such as the Rwalla, the Wuld Ali, and the Fedan. Each section maintains several websites and discussion boards based on the involvement of local, young tribal members who organized and administer the sites.[13]

The evolution of internet and discussion board technologies has provided an extremely popular tool for a relatively undisturbed public discourse. They cannot replace the public arena nor will they alone achieve progress and change. Nevertheless, they are part of a growing system that undermines the monopoly of the state on information and public discourse. They provide a refreshing catalyst for the bipolar debate between oral and written (documented) history over questions of descent, identity, cohesion, or intertribal relations. The relative autonomy of internet bulletins provides for rather unexpected outcomes. They are the voice for marginalized groups, ethnic, tribal, or religious, to express and often defend their points, ideas, and narratives.[14] The state monopoly on information supported specific stereotypes, but attitudes toward those groups can now be challenged. Tribal members now spread their side of the story and engage in lively internal debate. The expressions of tribal self-assertiveness and self-confidence observable in these threads are clearly an indication of the resurgent tribalism in the region. Eventually, this could lead to a larger-scale process of assimilating or integrating tribal identities into national Saudi identity.

NOTES

1. On generational conflict in Saudi Arabia see Yamani (2010).

2. For an analysis of how the internet has changed the information dynamics in Kuwait, see Wheeler (2003).

3. Shi'ite families in the Eastern province put less emphasis on common tribal descent, but more on the extended family. Sevener Shiites in Najran, however, emphasize membership in their tribal groups, such as the Bani Yam. For more on Shiite identities and networks in the Gulf region, see Louer (2008).

4. Zittrain and Edelman (2002) describe Saudi filtering and blocking practices in detail.

5. See Sait et al. (2007).

6. Mohammed Al-Kinani, "Saudi Tribal Website Raises the Question of 'Dialogue,'" Saudi Gazette, n.d. (http://www.saudigazette.com.sa/index.cfm?method=home.regcon& contentID=2009043036556, accessed 4 December 2010).

7. The case of Mansur al-Timani and his wife Fatima Azzaz gained media attention, but other cases have been reported in which couples have been ordered to divorce based on the claim that the spouse is from an inappropriate lineage or insufficient tribal background.

8. He later renounced his affiliation with the opposition group. See *al-Watan* newspaper, no. 11361/5807, 6 September 2007, p. 23.

9. On the shifting boundaries in information dynamics via the internet see Kraidy (2006).

10. www.pv.gov.sa.

11. On blogs in Saudi Arabia see Meccawy (2008).

12. See al-Khaddaf (2010) on the use of real names versus pseudonyms online.

13. The Anazah forum, however, gained a level of recognition and legitimacy by posting official statements by the tribal leadership of the Anazah tribe.

14. Samin (2008) describes how religious minorities (here Shiites in Saudi Arabia) use discussion boards to debate countercultural perspectives.

16.

YOUTH, PEACE, AND NEW MEDIA IN THE MIDDLE EAST

Charlotte Karagueuzian and Pamela Chrabieh Badine

The current situation in the Middle East brings to light the increasing role of internet technologies in shaping the dynamics of societies and politics at the local, regional, and international levels. Indeed, new media accelerate the building of bridges among a plurality of identities (national, ethnic, religious, social, economic, and cultural). This chapter explores the results of a study on the Iranian blogosphere, and then expands to comment more briefly on the uses and impacts of other social media. This new constellation of internet technologies constitutes a «shift» away from traditional structures characterized by centralized power toward a more horizontal distribution of power among individuals and communities from a variety of affiliations (Sheriffadeen 1997). It is, therefore, necessary to lay some groundwork in the academic understanding of new media in the Middle East to assess its potential at democracy-building in the region, as blogs run by young Arab and Iranian activists promoting interfaith dialogue, human rights, constructive war memory, and peace create alternative spaces to promote a diversity of social identities and political voices or paths.

Blog is the contraction of «web» and «log» (internet log or online diary). The blog is a type of website which often works as a personal journal and invites public and private interactions. In fact, David Weinberger points out that the blog has traced a new border between the private and the public spheres

302 Anthropology and New Media in the Virtual MENA

and constitutes a new kind of interaction and social action, a new rhetorical opportunity that serves the needs of our times (2002). In other words, the traditional lines become blurred, not only between public and private spheres, but also among producers and consumers, social classes, political visions, and religious beliefs. The blog has three main characteristics: reverse-chronological organization, a frequently updated set of links to sites of interest on the web, and a board for readers to comment below each post. In an article posted 13 June 2002, to the blog *Web DevCenter,* Hourihan finds that the combination of links and accompanying commentary is the distinguishing feature of the blog, creating connections that "bind" bloggers into a community. Blogs are usually classified along several axes: content—news/links versus personal; authorship—individual/personal versus collective (directory, format-based types of blogs); format type, including text, photoblogs, videoblogs, audioblogs, and a mix of subgenres; original filter type—personal blog-style (personal diary writing), or mixed; and fiction versus nonfiction. The blogosphere is a community of blogs, a community network or a scale-free network. There is interconnection among blogs; bloggers read each other's blog, send each other notes, reviews, pictures, videos. They refer to each other in their own writing.

The conceptual approach I here apply to the Arab and Iranian blogosphere is interdisciplinary, at the crossroads of peace studies research, particularly sociology of peace movements, and sociology of religions. It is also inspired by the work of Michael Löwy, who advocates the study of religion as a social fact, a cultural construct linked to a certain social formation without being inconsistent with religious faith (2006). It also lingers on web sciences, where the web is comprehended as an infrastructure of languages, where the interaction between artificial protocols (the micro level of analysis) and human behavior generates the web's behavior (the macro level), which contributes to changes in social structures, political systems, civil organizations, and educational institutions (Hendler et al. 2008). Because blogospheres exist in a reality of constant change, traditional procedures where one starts to test theories and hypotheses on a supposedly stable reality cannot be used. Instead, the qualitative approach allows one to journey into unpredictable subjects of study and helps make them intelligible; it enables the discovery and analysis of emerging phenomena and blurred boundaries as it captures the dynamic nature recorded in different contexts and historical moments. Moreover, blogs present the interpretations of insightful individuals and groups, and reflect the inherent diversity of debates going on among individuals and groups. In this regard, thematic content analysis is an appropriate, efficient tool for studying the wide range of opinions discussed in the blogosphere.

Arab identity is a concept encompassing multiple and complex components: an ethnicity, a people or a nation, a linguistic identity, a heritage, a history, a set of cultural traits, and a common destiny. It defines neither a single nationality nor a single religion. Furthermore, the claim of Arab belonging does not imply the negation of pluralism or the acceptance of nationalist claims. Some deny the existence of an Arab identity, but the same commenters are sometimes the most eager to lump all Arab countries together when it comes to criticizing them. The bloggers targeted in this study all identify themselves as Arabs or claim to have an awareness of the Arab identity, whatever the specifics of that identity may be—among the possibilities are a commitment to a transcendent Arab nationality (pan-Arabism), the expression of a dream of unity, a self-construction transcending ethnic differences, a solicitation for solidarity in the face of foreign intervention, or a concept of identity as instrumental to a unification of the Arab majority in each Arab state along with Arab minorities in the Diaspora (i.e., a supranational affiliation, a fight against invisibility). In the meanwhile, the Arab blogosphere has a variety of affiliations other than Arab, often intersecting with regional and international blogospheres (North American, North African, Mediterranean, European), national ones (Syrian, Lebanese, Iraqi, Jordanian, Egyptian), and ideological/political or religious ones (Christian and Muslim in particular). Arab bloggers write in Arabic, English, French, Hebrew, and other languages.

The Iranian identity is a concept determined by such apparent traits as a common nation-state, people, language, territory, and religion, as well as Persian culture and history. The Iranian identity does not imply the negation of ethnic, religious, or linguistic minorities in Iran, as the targeted bloggers identify themselves as Iranians and the definition of the Iranian identity adopted among them is a standard one. A closer look at Iranians' online discussions shows that the Iranian identity is not static, as it faces a challenging political path, it has to deal with a Diaspora in perpetual development, and it aspires for a more suitable place within the international community. The Iranian blogosphere is relatively hermetic, although it eventually intersects with regional and international blogospheres (North American, European, Central Asian, and others). The inner content of the Iranian blogosphere basically consists of interactive clusters dealing with politics, religion, literature, and the arts. Iranian bloggers are located in Iran, but also in other parts of the world, such as North America and Europe. They primarily write in Persian, English, and French.

Blogs, Interfaith Dialogue, and the Quest for an Arab Identity

Most of the Arab traditional media organizations and newspapers have well-established presences on the web. Forums and discussion boards about a variety of topics attract a lot of users. However, blogs remain a small phenomenon in the Arab world, although one which has grown steadily, especially with young generations. Most popular online hosts and aggregators estimate the number of political and nonpolitical blogs together to number more than 30,000. Whatever the exact number, volume might not be necessary for blogs to exert political, social, and cultural influence. Prominent blogs have an extensive and influential audience; they include: *Amarji (A Heretic's Blog)* by the Syrian activist Ammar Abdulhamid, online since 2005; *Dahr Jamail's Mideast Dispatches* by the freelance journalist Dahr Jamail, online since 2003; *The Angry Arab* by the Lebanese activist and Professor of Political Science Asaad Abu Khalil, online since 2003; *Haitham Sabbah* by the Palestinian activist Haitham Sabbah, online since 1999; and *Misr Digital-Digital Egypt* by the Egyptian journalist Wael Abbas, online since 2005.

A large portion of the readers of Arab blogs are political or social activists, journalists, and other influential elites, as well as foreign scholars and governments trying to gauge Arab public opinion. Newspapers such as *Al Masry Al Youm* in Egypt or *Al Balad* and *L'Orient-le-Jour* in Lebanon routinely cite blogs as sources for their stories, offering another indirect route for political, social, and cultural impact. The prominence of certain bloggers has been incredibly important for the human rights scene, at the same time as properties of the system interfere with the ability of new voices to be heard. This might explain why we find sometimes a migration from the free-scale Arab blogospheres to Facebook. Blogs form a counter-public, incubating, disseminating, and exchanging new visions, practices, and belongings which evolve alongside and reshape the mainstream public, little by little, from below.

> Bloggers have had a discernible impact in a wide range of Arab countries, including their role in the Kefaya movement in Egypt (see Rania Al Malky in this issue), political protests in Bahrain (see Luke Schleusener), the turbulent post-Al Hariri period in Lebanon (see Sune Haugbolle), anti-corruption campaigns in Libya (see Claudia Gazzini) and the 2006 Kuwaiti elections. While political opportunities usually come first—around elections, national scandals, or contentious elite debates, for instance—blogs can be catalysts for previously unlikely political mobilization. (Lynch 2007)

Many in the first wave of Arab bloggers—during the 1990s—have tended to be young, technologically oriented, and politically disengaged. Even nowadays, the majority of internet users and especially bloggers are young people, having at least a minimum of technological skills, but not necessarily an advanced knowledge of new media tools. Furthermore, men constitute the majority of bloggers. According to a study conducted by the Berkman Center for Internet and Society, "Demographic results indicate that Arabic bloggers are predominately young and male. The highest proportion of female bloggers is found in the Egyptian youth sub-cluster, while the Syrian and Muslim Brotherhood clusters have the highest concentration of males" (Etling 2009).

The Arab blogospheres are expanding both in quantity and quality; in order of importance, the Egyptian (the largest blogosphere with distinct sub-and associated clusters, such as Muslim Brotherhood or women bloggers), the Saudi Arabian (second largest but focused more on technology), the Kuwaiti (English and Arabic sub-clusters), the Syrian, the Lebanese, the Iraqi, and the Palestinian. In Lebanon alone, there are more than 300 blogs for young activists who use this simple and affordable platform to build and disseminate information, share testimonies, and promote visions and practices in a relatively free environment ideal for marginalized/independent/dissident individuals and groups. Some spread prejudice and hatred, but others offer tools and ideas of dialogue, understanding, human rights, democracy, coexistence, and peace.

At the first conference of Arab bloggers at Zicco House in Beirut, in August 2008, freedom of expression, interreligious dialogue, human rights, and peace building were major topics of concern and analysis of more than thirty bloggers from Lebanon, Egypt, Morocco, Tunisia, Saudi Arabia, Bahrain, Palestine, Iraq, and Syria. Other gatherings of Arab bloggers were held in 2010 in Beirut at Zicco House, Club 43, and T-Marbouta.

Within the highlights of the conference was a focus on how blogs seem to constitute the best tools to enable young activists to express their opinions, to defend their political, social, and religious or nonreligious beliefs. Old or traditional media are very much a top-down affair steered by elites, political leaders, and religious institutions. However, new media, especially blogs, offer accessibility and freedom of expression due to the looser rules, less conventional forms of dialogue, and more creative knowledge building.

Another main point discussed at the conference was that most Arab bloggers write personal observations (diary-style) but are often critical of social injustices, inequalities, and authoritarian regimes. They all advocate for freedom of thought and expression and basic human rights—more commonly than they criticize Western cultures and values. They offer a variety of idiosyncratic perspectives.

Furthermore, it was noted that the use of Web 2.0 (Youtube, Flickr, Skype, wikis) as integral to most of the blogs helps to raise awareness and to attract attention, both to critiques of the inadequacies of governance systems, and to positive Arab experiences and the immense potential that abounds the Arab world. The use of Web 2.0 makes it easier for like-minded individuals to find each other in spite of their physical separation and their immersion in long workdays and commutes; it also allows bloggers to transfer pictures and sounds, thus facilitating the exchange of personal and collective experiences, particularly between the various identities at the political, national, religious, and cultural levels. According to the Berkman Center, "Bloggers link to web 2.0 sites like YouTube and Wikipedia (English and Arabic versions) more than other sources of information and news available on the Internet. Al-Jazeera is the top mainstream media source, followed by the BBC and Al-Arabiya" (2009).

Blogs were also apprehended as communication tools for marginalized individuals and groups in the Arab world, such as women and minorities. For example, there are many reasons why Egyptian women have embraced blogging, but primary among them is that blogs offer a place to express themselves, often anonymously, in a way that would not be possible in other public forums. Most women on the Egyptian blogosphere try to create sites that reflect their personalities; they tell personal stories, share political and cultural views, post favorite pictures, and talk about their daily frustrations. Good examples are *Gay Woman*, *Kolona Leila*, and *Sheer Mental Garbage*. Some women created their blogs in order to free themselves from social and family conservative traditions and to obtain recognition, as in Saudi Arabia, where women represent more than half of the bloggers. Similarly, in the Palestinian territories and Egypt, where famers and workers' movements are usually brutally and violently oppressed, blogging is a way to have a voice. In 2008, Wael Abbas declared in the blog *Menassat*,

Farmers' land would be destroyed, and they would be pushed off their lands, and no one would hear about it. The state used to deny accusations of torture, and claim people used the claims to clear themselves. But the videos of torture and forced confessions published online have proved to be a giant leap forward. The material published on blogs has pushed the civil society to act on issues of torture, women's rights, workers, farmers, street children, monitoring elections and so on. We face some problems when it comes to political parties. We criticize them, so they consider it bad manners or defamation or competition. What I would like to see is political parties stepping up to their role in the society, like the blogs did when they called for democratic change, plurality and honest elections.

According to an article published in the website *Menassat* ("Bloggers of the Arab World Unite in Beirut") on 27 August 2008, bloggers emphasize that access to the internet is a privilege not available in disadvantaged areas. Ahmad al-Omran said on his blog *Saudi Jeans:* "The effect of blogs is still limited in Saudi Arabia, but I expect it to grow, as internet users and bloggers increase." For Ali Abdel Imam, in his blog *Bahrain Online,*

blogs did not appear [in Bahrain] until 2004–2005; as a result, their effect is still minimal. The total number of Bahraini blogs is 200 to 300 blogs only. Forums are more popular here, especially the political forums. These forums have been extremely effective in two main ways. First, regarding political vibrancy, since Bahrain witnesses political events on a daily basis, this makes political forums highly influential over politics. Second, political forums affect political events documented through news and reports. As for blogs, there are none that are really influential so far in Bahrain. Still, blogging is an unprecedented phenomenon when it comes to expressing oneself, especially for the youth. Blogs are being used politically only to feature news such as the arrests of political activists and other stories neglected by the mainstream media. This seems to be the main concern for [Bahraini] bloggers at the moment.

Muhammad Abdullah said in his blog *I'm Leaving and I'm Not Coming Back,*

It's difficult to determine the effect of blogs in Syria, especially with the lack of accurate statistics. The Syrian blogging experience falls behind the Egyptian experience, but precedes the Saudi and Bahraini experiences in terms of the impact it is having on society. The Internet only arrived in Syria in 2001, and Internet users only made a small dent in the general population. Statistics suggest that the number of Internet users in Syria will reach 2 million by 2009, an unprecedented increase for people who a short while back did not even own computers. The number of bloggers is unknown, but they are definitely harassing the government. If this were not the case, the authorities would not fear them so much, would not block their pages or arrest the bloggers. They've handed down harsh prison sentences to scare other bloggers.

Rachid Jankari declared in his blog *I Share, therefore I Exist,*

> We do not possess accurate data on the effect of the Internet on Moroccan society. Still, I am very optimistic about the effect of blogging on political life in my country. As the Internet began to spread in 1996 and 1997, people did not trust it. But in Malaysia several incidents took place that confirmed the importance of the Internet. Because of my blogging, one minister was sacked, and policemen have been discharged for accepting bribes [after incriminating videos were posted online.] In several instances, cases of human rights violations were exposed.

For Shahnaz Abdellsalam, in her blog *An Egyptian Woman,*

> blogging is very important in Egypt. First, it broke the fear barrier of the Egyptians; second, it installed fear in the hearts of the rulers who started to monitor us. We also encouraged people, particularly the youth, to speak out, express themselves and take to the streets. For me, the blogging movement has been a miracle. When we first started, we did not know the response would be big. The outcome was good, and I have hoped that we will persevere, and remain a catalyst for the people, unless something terrible happens.

Finally, Razan Al-Ghazzawi said in his blog *Razanisms / Razaniat—Anarchist Queer from Syria,*

> This issue presents us with a paradox. I believe bloggers are well-off, with time to blog and contemplate. I do not mean that they are wealthy; I mean they are Different from Those Who Have to work all day. This is why I think it's a bourgeois phenomenon. Blogging started as an experiment in Syria, where people started using the English language as a tool of expression, but I do not believe Français express our reality in the same way as Arabic. Syrian blogging at first did not reflect the Syrian reality. Today, it's different Syrian and Syrian writers are addressing issues. I do not feel [this has made much of a] difference, simply because the Syrian people have not yet

reached the point where they are ready to rise up and express themselves. Blogging is not representative of the people. Even Syrian opposition (blogging) is elitist. From this point of view, I do not consider blogging is effective in this context. We understand from the foregoing that blogs are not generally representative. However, they can and should serve to broaden the social, political and cultural-religious in the Arab world and Middle East.

According to Ammar Abdulhamid in *Amarji Has Heretic's Blog,* internet communication, and blogging in particular, is intended to play an important role in social and political changes currently taking place in the region. The "democratic forces" are forced into using them for intercommunication and organization in communities, what he calls "organic solidarity" (Durkheim 1978). In this sense, human beings become aware of their interdependence through horizontal communication.

Issues of freedom, dialogue, and peace are fundamental for most bloggers, who see the Arab world as a region where democracy is declining, and where freedom of expression is increasingly strained. Even with positive changes that new media has engendered in the Arab world, internet freedom is still far from absolute. At least ten dissidents currently languish in jails across the Middle East due to statements made online. The number of other dissidents who have been scared away from sensitive topics or provocative statements is unknown, and probably much higher. However, savvy internet users can often use proxy services to get around state-imposed filters. Also, bloggers living in the Diaspora disseminate unconstrained content.

Following the Zicco House conference, bloggers identified a common vision: sharing the same dream of change, from societies marked by violence toward peaceful societies. However, the varying definitions of peace put forth were difficult to reconcile: the absence of violence, the end of physical fighting, stability and security, human rights, coexistence, conviviality, interreligious dialogue. During the 2006 summer war between Lebanon and Israel, some Lebanese blogs adopted a confrontational tone; examples include *The Perpetual Refugee, Loubnan Ya Loubnan, My Lebanon, Hiroshima in Lebanon, Lebanonesque, Peace4lebanon, Lebanon Under Attack.* These blogs often have in common the presence of numerous photos of bloodied civilian casualties caused by Israeli raids, coupled with regular columns by people detailing their daily plight. However, while condemning the Israeli offensive, other bloggers have tried to establish some form of dialogue between Lebanese of different faiths, advocating a return to peace, even, some suggest, with neighboring Israel. These blogs, such as *Blogging Beirut,*

Letters Apart, Chroniques Beyrouthines (Beirut Chronicles), and *Pour que le Liban vive (That Lebanon May Live)*, are intended to be nonpartisan and emphasize the duty of mutual aid and support among Lebanese.

For some bloggers, peace in the Arab world depends on peace among religions, at the institutional level as well as among individuals and communities. Indeed, most conflicts in the region are perceived as religious wars, like the Israeli–Palestinian conflict (between Jews and Muslims, Palestinian Christian identity being neglected in this case) or the war in Lebanon (including the period 1975–1990 and its usual characterization as a "civil war" or as an "Islamic–Christian war"). In this sense, religion is seen as exploited to fuel violence. In the case of Lebanon, bloggers argue the example of the militias which have been using religious affiliations and symbols at various times during the war. Lebanese citizens were kidnapped and killed because of their faith as discerned by the name on their identity card. In addition, the massive transfers of Lebanese population were based primarily on religious affiliation. It is therefore necessary, according to these bloggers, to free religion from exploitation. This does not involve the separation of religion and politics, but the recognition of religions as a source of peace. In the blog *The Words of Young Muslims,* we read the following statement:

> The debate must be Inter catalyst in these times of tension and international tensions. Dialogue is the tool of peace and serenity in a multicultural society. Should we still define the content and scope of the term interfaith. We must pay attention to all excess frisky attitudes that could tip it into the betrayal of our values and our clear references of their substance intrinsic to our Muslim and ethical foundation of our faith. The Muslim must be careful that the term "interreligious dialogue" does not dilute or eliminate the essential differences that separate Islam from other religions, such description must be rejected. God says in the Glorious Qur'an: "And argue with them in the best manner" (S16, V125). God said, "Judge between them by what Allah has sent down. Do not follow their passions and take care they do not try to walk away a part of what Allah has revealed." (S5, V49). However, dialogue and cooperation between Islam and other religions is an accepted practice, Allah says: "Say: O People of the Book, come to a common word between us and you that we worshiped Allah without associating anything with Him, and that point we take each other for lords besides Allah" (S3, V 64). The Prophet Muhammad who talked particularly with Christians of Najran gave the example it is possible to hold dialogues with other denominations on issues such as the Oneness of God, the mission of prophets or the origin

of mankind. These dialogues should take place in a healthy atmosphere, without using coercion, and avoid belittling others or harm them. . . . Often interreligious conflicts have their origin in the abuse of religions and their followers through manipulation of a few selfish individuals or groups who seek to take more political power. We all have a stake to fight for justice and equality. Our differences must certainly distinguish ourselves but they must contribute to the musical composition of a cantor common people can enjoy and contribute its originality. Every day there are men and women from both sides who build bridges between the two sides. We can now see local, national and international very encouraging. We are now more than ever condemned to live together and interact to avoid and deny most of the theories on the clash of civilizations put forward by Samuel Huntington.

Bloggers have agreed that blogs allow them as ordinary citizens to engage and re-engage in politics, beyond the limits imposed by governments and traditional media, while creating a shared space for building a transnational Arab identity. It is a kind of decentralization of the constructive discourses on dialogue, peace, citizenship, and identity. Decentralization implies no particular leader, hierarchy, or headquarters, but openness and individual decision-making (collective decision-making in the case of group blogs). Decentralization does not imply the atomization or isolation of individuals, nor does it favor the development of the individual at the expense of the citizen. It implies individualization, or greater autonomy and self-determination for individuals, the possibility of having the choice to adopt certain values rather than others, as well as the possibility of interpreting these values. Power and (therefore) the construction of knowledge are distributed horizontally, regardless of political, religious, social, cultural, geographic, or generational affiliations. According to Thierry Crouzet, the internet is the "fifth power," the power of new technologies of communication to federate citizens (2007). It is a power which counteracts the fourth one, traditional media (and by extension business), which itself counterbalances the three traditional powers: legislative, executive, and judicial. For Crouzet, thanks to the internet, it becomes possible to do politics differently.

The Blogosphere, Social Media, and Political Activism in Iran

Some experts claim that Iran has become the third or fourth largest online community in the world. According to Bruce Etling et al. there are about 60,000 actively maintained Persian-language blogs (2008, 2). To capture the entire Iranian blogosphere also requires the recognition of English-and French-language blogs from the Diaspora, as well as Iranian minority language websites. Persian culture and history, religion, poetry, music, movies, and sports are recurrent topics discussed online. However, political discourse is increasingly predominant in the Iranian blogosphere. Political opinions engage in competition on a wide range of issues, such as government decision-making related to the Iranian economy, the place of religion in politics, the treatment of people deemed dissidents by the regime, women's and human rights, and appropriate styles of romance in society.

Blogging took off in Iran in the last decade, as a result of government repression to silence dissent and of state censorship against traditional media organizations and newspapers. The closure of reformist newspapers and their websites by the conservatives in the Judiciary during the presidency of Khatami (1997–2005) encouraged reform-minded Iranians to pursue political debates online. Khatami's "2nd of Khordad" reform political movement also led to exchanges on the internet between the Diaspora and Iranians from inside the country (Farkhondeh 2001). Since then, the Iranian blogosphere has grown exponentially. With today's high internet penetration rate in Iran, 31.85 percent according to the website of the OpenNet Initiative (see the 2009 "Country Profile: Iran"), blogs have become a significant place where Iranian youth, women, minorities, journalists, and intellectuals write about their political thoughts and experiences. More recently, it has also become fashionable for influential elites in Iran, from political reformists to religious conservatives, to have their own websites, so that they can reach out to their own constituencies. The information they broadcast, given their position in the government as well as their personal insights into the situation, is widely disseminated and commented upon throughout the Iranian blogosphere.

The Advent of Social Media

The use of social networking in Iran reached its peak with the events leading up to and following the controversial 2009 presidential re-election of Ahmadinejad, to the extent that some experts described the political events in Iran as a public relations struggle (Mottaz 2009). The Iranian population and political leaders rallied on the internet to voice their arguments and get support, while the government filtered online dissent and condemned it through traditional state-run media. Youth, who constitute about sixty percent of the Iranian population

(Toomey 2009), were particularly active in the political debate online. With their affinity for new media, young Iranians were eager to exchange online information and thoughts about the Iranian political crisis. The youth are quite often marginalized social actors, particularly in paternalistic societies like Iran, and the blogosphere allows them to have a bigger say in the public debate than they would otherwise have; it allows them to reconcile their desire for individual autonomy and their sense of belonging to a collectivity.

New media offer new opportunities for speech in the public sphere by reducing the costs of becoming a speaker. It becomes difficult for the government to control the entire online information flow, because of the decentralized nature of internet technologies. The regime has taken widespread censorship measures, but this can only be partial and temporary. Information is divulged and diffused online before the State can find and censor it. Bloggers can get around State control by claiming anonymity or by changing a website address. Furthermore, the regime cannot shut down internet access entirely, because that would create a significant social backlash. As a result, individual citizens and groups can make public their political contestations. Today, Facebook, Twitter, and blogs represent the most open public communication platforms for political discourse in Iran. The Iranian youth use them as tools to denounce the regime's corruption, incompetence, and archaism. On the Facebook profile of the youth group Green Opposition of Azad University, a video was posted on 5 November 2009. It shows a speech made by Ahmadinejad's Science Minister, Kamran Daneshjou, when he visited the Iranian Sharif University in September 2009 to convince students that the re-election of Ahmadinejad was legitimate. In this video, we see students accusing the Minister of lying to the population. This video shows youth opposition to the results of the 2009 presidential election and to the current government. Arash Pajouh echoes this opposition in a 13 June 2009 post to his blog *Jahani Degar* containing a list of evidence against the legitimacy of the presidential re-election of Ahmadinejad.

Many young bloggers also post online documentation meant to denounce the practice of violence and repression by the local authorities. For example, another post to the Facebook profile of the Green Opposition of Azad University, on 17 July 2009, showed a scan of the ID of the *bassiji* (state-sponsored militia member) who is known as the assassinator of the young Iranian woman Neda Agha-Soltan during a street demonstration. Numerous pictures depicting the arrest of young opposition protestors are also posted to the blogosphere in order to denounce the regime's repression against Iranian civilians and their rights to express themselves. More meaningfully, the online political discourse of many young Iranians is fed by thoughtful individual comments, advocating a path of peace, democracy, human rights, and liberty. A young Iranian blogger makes the following statement in a comment posted to the blog *Jahani Degar* on 13 November 2009, entitled "Be without limits and democracy":

> Democracy means freedom of choice. Each individual should be free to make his own choices. A dictator is someone who considers his opinion superior and tries to impose his points of views on others. Where are you in these definitions? Try not to be a dictator. Let your sister make her own choices and respect her boyfriend. Try to learn that you too, can make your own choices. . . . Fighting for liberty and democracy in your country starts with you having reached democracy in your private life.

Internet technologies allow the formation of a participatory democracy and strengthen civil society (Benkler 2006). They share some similarities with the Tehran "taxi culture," to the extent that they provide a framework for strangers to exchange underground news and rumors. The difference is that the internet communication platform is available to any member of the polity on a more or less equal basis. Internet users can receive and send content, triggering multidirectional information flows. People have the opportunity to find information, events, and people that interest them. The aggregation of these multiple independent preferences builds powerful social dynamics. The result of this democratic and interactive model of communication is the institutionalization of self-organizing political communities. During the demonstration of 7 December 2009, a young Iranian named Majid Tavakoli tried to escape the police by wearing a *chador* (a traditionally female head covering), but he was arrested. As a sign of support for this young man, many bloggers started to take pictures of themselves with their heads covered and posted them to their Facebook profiles or to their blogs. Arash Pajooh says, in a comment attached to a picture of him with his head covered posted to his blog *Jahani Degar* on 10 December 2009: "We are all Majid Tavakoli. You can find pictures of him diffused anywhere. People diffused these pictures and did not fear that such news sites as Fars, IRNA or Rajanews made fun of them."

Effects on Global Media

New media has been used to mobilize international public opinion, most notably when its content comes to be diffused in the international mainstream media.

On 16 June 2009, the Minister of Culture and Islamic Guidance in Iran issued a decree asking foreign media to get an authorization from the Ministry of the Interior if they wanted to cover demonstrations. From that moment, foreign news organizations were excluded from decisive political events in Iran, and, as they had trouble finding new material, many turned to new media sources. According to CBS News Foreign Editor Ingrid Ciprian-Matthes, "We have a whole mechanism we've set up in New York and London with Farsi-speaking reporters trolling websites and blogs for information. We just have to work extra hard to verify what we're getting" (Baum 2009). According to a discussion panel at the Center for International Media Assistance (CIMA), in the post-election period, *Voice of America's Persian News Network* received almost 300 videos per hour from individuals inside Iran (Mottaz 2009). Social networks are very simple to use, offer a variety of tools (text, audio, video, picture), are low-cost, and do not need the approval of a third party for the information to circulate. Contents of any type and from any location can rapidly spread, from a journal article written by a dissident to a street event captured by an amateur. During the protests, Iranian civilians used cell phones and digital cameras; they uploaded the images directly to the internet to share the events taking place on their streets with an international audience, particularly via YouTube. In an article posted to her blog *Chroniques Orientales*, on 18 September 2009, the French journalist Delphine Minoui describes how Iranians have become increasingly reliable and valued "cyberjournalists." Indeed, as they gained experience, they started to create their own conventions for information shared; for example, some videos posted online start with the first page of a local newspaper, allowing the event filmed to be dated. Information with sensational content taken from the internet and disseminated through the mainstream media can have a huge impact on international public opinion. An illustration of this is the circulation of one compelling amateur video on YouTube, showing a citizen named Neda Agha-Soltan bleeding to death on a street in Tehran during a demonstration. Widely commented on the Iranian blogosphere, it was thereafter picked up by some mainstream Western media such as CNN.com (2009).

Social Media and the Diaspora

Another effect of social networking is that it allows the Iranian Diaspora to participate more easily in the political debate in Iran. Electronic publications are accessible at any time and from almost any place. Individuals and groups outside the country can be informed of domestic events with less propaganda. They can also share news, opinions, and analyses very easily with the population inside the country. When YouTube was blocked in Iran, individuals from the Diaspora emailed videos back to the country to keep their relatives informed. As new media offers a faster diffusion of information, the Diaspora and dissidents in exile can engage in the political debate very reactively, and be more supportive of like-minded individuals inside Iran. Many Iranians from the Diaspora have changed their personal profiles on Facebook to include messages and photographs in support of manifestations of opposition. Some also translate information about the events in Iran from Persian into English, in order to make them more comprehensible at the international level (see the blog *Persian2English*).

Interactivity

The Iranian blogosphere has become a tool for coordinating actions against the status quo in Iran. Iranian opposition candidates have continuously used Facebook to mobilize their supporters. As such, the Facebook profile of the opposition leader Mir-Hossein Moussavi has over 125,000 supporters and attracts numerous posts per hour. Opposition candidates disseminate their knowledge of the situation via their websites. They also coordinate news and prepare demonstrations online in ways that allow them to circumvent government restrictions. Many young Iranians opposing the government post online invitations to participate in coming demonstrations. For example, there were numerous calls for the opposition to rally on 22 *Bahman* (11 February 2010), the date of the thirty-first anniversary of the Islamic Republic, posted on the Facebook profiles of young Iranians. Other online youth sources provide information about the government's action against opposition rallies. Following the demonstration of 7 December 2009, a comment posted to the Facebook profile of the Youth Green Opposition of Azad University relates: "There were SMS sent in the Khouzestan province saying 'One should not participate to certain rallies'"; i.e., the government was trying to dissuade the opposition from protesting.

Online youth interactivity sometimes displays bridge-building among different political clusters. In a comment posted to his blog *Jahani Degar* on 6 December 2009, Arash Pajooh, who advocates gradual constitutional reform in Iran, tells about a letter he has sent to Moussavi, knowing that Moussavi remains faithful to the ideology of the Islamic Republic: "I have sent you a letter to ask you where my place will be and what will be the place of those who think like me. You answered me very nicely and very cleverly that 'I am part of you.'" In another comment posted to his blog on 11 January 2010, Arash Pajooh explains why he supports Moussavi:

> According to the Constitution, any party is allowed to be politically active, provided that it does not use force. The request of the reformers in Iran is the respect of this constitutional law, and this is the request of all the Iranian opposition forces today. If the Green movement has called this request a minimum request, this means that we can ask for more requests thereafter. This is not the time to separate from the reformers in Iran on the ground that our maximum requests are not met in their manifest. We need to support the reformers until the time when we can have free elections and go with our own leaders. If we struggle today with the reformers on our different points of views, we will never have free elections.

Other forms of interactivity among different Iranian youth political groups can also be found in the new media. The Youth Green Opposition of Azad University Facebook page is a catalogue of independent-minded Iranians advocating drastic political change in the direction of a new secular regime. An internet user posted a link to a video on 15 January 2010 publicizing a pro-Mujahidin demonstration in Tehran. The video originated from the TV channel *Châbâké Azadi,* which is connected to the leftist organization People's Mujahidin of Iran. The video was clearly tampered with, as the "demonstration" shows no protestors and is mainly centered on a big poster of a Mujahidin political leader. This is a good example of propaganda involving two different political clusters, both seeking the overthrow of the Islamic Republic.

Social networks are, however, limited tools for Iranian youth political interactivity. New media reflects the polarization of the political debate in Iran, as bloggers outlink preferentially to things that they favor (Etling et al. 2008). These links can be blogs, news sites, YouTube videos, or other sites. But overall, collections of websites connected one to another are definite informational worlds reproducing the Iranian political and ideological struggle. There are websites which clearly support the present government and others which remain faithful to the Islamic regime's ideology but engage in factional fighting. Some campaign for a gradual change of the current constitution to a new one, via peaceful civil resistance methods. There is propaganda for this approach from reformers inside and outside the country. Others, mainly from the Diaspora, press for a constitutional revolution to establish a human rights–based socio-liberal constitution.

They support reformers in Iran only for the clear goal of a new secular regime, but they are not as faithful to reformers. Finally, some websites based outside with specific line of thoughts, such as monarchism, socialism, or Mujahidin, advocate armed conflict in order to implement their own constitution. There is sustained interactivity among websites, but it mostly occurs among those which embrace the same ideological approach.

The political dialogue online is also limited by the fact that new media does not offer full participatory democracy and tends to reflect a biased representation of the Iranian political opinion. Nasrin Alavi published a collection of translated Iranians blogs from the Diaspora (2005), supporting the view that most Iranians are looking for drastic political and social change in Iran. In the meantime, new media technologies are concentrated in the hands of the educated people and, therefore, present only the opinions of the Iranian urban elite. Poorer and rural Iranians, who constitute Ahmadinejad's core support base, are less likely to use the internet. Marginalized from the online political debate, their weight tends to be underestimated by the outside world, while online interaction is very much limited to the Iranian youth opposition and the Diaspora. In an article entitled "Révolution Twitter ou révolution tweetée?" in the French newspaper *L'Express*, Tesquet claimed that many Iranian bloggers are supporting the opposition, but it does not represent the points of view of the entire Iranian population (2009). Furthermore, the authenticity of information diffused on social networks is often question. Online sources are sometimes contradictory, and most of the time partisan. Their content lacks the accuracy and credibility that outside actors are looking for, therefore precluding exchanges of information with international mainstream media. Jeffrey Cole, director of the Centre for the Digital Future at the USC Annenberg School for Communication, acknowledged this in an interview given to the *Los Angeles Times:* "Everybody doesn't go to journalism school or adhere to professional standards, but literally everybody can use a cell phone or a camera or sound equipment" (Baum 2009).

Another limitation of Iranian youth interactivity on political events is the censorship of internet undertaken by the local authorities. Since new media is partially and temporarily censored, citizens' freedom of speech is limited and outside actors are being excluded from the political debate. Websites deemed controversial are being blocked and user bandwidth is being constricted, especially during post-election protests. Facebook was unblocked in January 2009, but the ban was reinstituted during the presidential campaign in May 2009, as well as in the period following the presidential elections in June (Daragahi 2009).

Blogs such as *Mowjcamp* and *Rahesabz*, which are key opposition websites, were inaccessible in Iran in December 2009. During demonstrations, the moral police used to take camera phones away from citizens, or sometimes arrest people taking videos. Bloggers are being tracked and sent to prison. According to the website of Reporters Without Borders, an international media watchdog group, at least 100 journalists and bloggers have been arrested since 12 June 2009, and twenty-seven were still in jail as of 18 December 2009. In September 2010, the journalist Hossein Derakhshan, known as the "blogfather" in Iran, has been sentenced to the heaviest sentence ever ruled by the Iranian authorities against an Iranian blogger, nineteen and half years in jail. Many young Iranians denounce, online, the practice of censorship by the Iranian regime. Arash Pajooh, who had been informed that his blog *Jahani Degar* had been censored by the Iranian authorities, explains in a comment posted on 30 November 2009,

> Freedom of speech means the diffusion of ideas that are logical and constructive for the society. It does not mean the spreading of misleading or ideological ideas, which are ideas harming the people. What is the point of filling people's brains with ideological ideas? One should evaluate each idea on scientific grounds to know if this idea is valuable. The weapon to oppose those who diffuse invalid ideas is writing and criticism. But censorship brings the circulation of incorrect ideas. Dictatorships create an environment conducive to invalid ideas in order to mislead the society.

Some internet users also diffuse news from international sources denouncing censorship in Iran. The Facebook profile of the youth Green movement of Azad University posted a comment regarding this issue on 27 September 2009, stating that the European Parliament was currently discussing the option of sanctioning European companies providing internet spying software to the Iranian government.

Blogs reveal that the sociopolitical dynamics are never structured with neutrality. Instead, they consist of subjective discourses and practices. In this sense, the new media becomes a platform for lobbying. Its potential for promoting a cognitive democracy, a democracy that includes marginalized actors, is based on the fact that there is so much such marginalized actors can learn from each other, and is limited by the lack of rationality displayed by social actors. The challenge is to construct a collective intelligence that is inclusive or that limits the exclusions and makes greater room for dialogue.

Blogs, the 2011 Arab Spring, and Peace Building Efforts

The 2011 Arab Spring testifies to the impact of the growing use of new media in the Middle East, and especially of social media such as blogs, Facebook, Twitter, and Youtube, as a successful tool for political activism, able to alter public opinions. It demonstrates how the blogosphere, in particular, creates the opportunity to renegotiate the relationship between rulers and ruled. Digital activism has an important potential to promote civic engagement and to provide virtual spaces for assembly, identity-building, publicity, and forming counter-public movements against established institutions; to undermine authoritarian control; and to be recognized, as pointed out by Salmon, Fernandez, and Post, as a potential tool for "public will mobilization" (2010).

During the Egyptian revolution of 2011, new media avenues enabled effective forms of citizen journalism, provided forums for citizens to document the protests and to spread the word about their initiatives, as well as to disseminate their testimonies to the outside world, as, for instance, among activists in Egypt and Tunisia, as well as among protesters and Arabs in the Diaspora, thus creating a virtual global public sphere. The current demonstrations in Syria are being recorded by bloggers and online activists in order to shed light on the struggle of the opposition against the political regime, and to ensure that authentic voices are heard, especially those of young men and women, the 20–30 year-old age group, who are unsatisfied with the traditional media's version of events. However, one should acknowledge the role of offline, street activism, such as knocking on peoples' doors and rehearsing for major events through mini-protests. This form of activism, which preceded the Egyptian revolution, paved the way for it.

Still, as Sahar Khamis and Katherine Vaughn noted in their study of the Egyptian online revolution (2011),

the National Coalition for Change used a well organized and intertwined communication network that included Facebook, Twitter, and YouTube to get the word out and sent text messages, such as 'Tell your friends' and 'Look what is happening in Tunisia. This is how people change their country'. Facebook's largest impact was in the mobilization of protesters. In fact, it could be said that the Egyptian revolution witnessed the first incident of the "politicization of Facebook" on a grand scale to orchestrate major reform and drastic change. . . . The social network best suited for the task of organizing the protesters was Facebook, where information could be spread to thousands of people in an instant and then shared between friends. . . . This highlights the value of social media in terms of creating networks that enable peer-to-peer communication between users. . . . By combining these multiple functions of different types of online media together in one effective communication network during the January 2011 revolution, it is easy to understand how Egyptian political activists won their battle against the regime, both online and, most importantly, offline.

Cyberactivists in the Egyptian online community have continued to defend free speech advances and civic engagement since the resignation of President Hosni Mubarak, especially for women, as, for example, in the struggles of the activist Bothaina Kamel and the blogger Dalia Ziada. In Bahrain, new media, in particular the growing community of Bahraini bloggers, will, in the long run, promote the growth of civil society, which is the bedrock of democracy. Crowdmaps like *Behind the Wall* or *Syria Tracker* are being used in Syria, Yemen, and Bahrain, aggregating user-generated videos, images, and reports, which are then verified and geoplotted on online maps. However, the impact of these maps remains to be seen. Crowdmaps, Facebook, Twitter, blogs, YouTube, and so many other social media platforms, for all their interest, cannot be seen as the trigger of the Arab revolutions. They are, rather, effective catalysts and vehicles of communication and empowerment. They are powerful tools used to bear witness or testimonies of the crimes being perpetrated by repressive regimes. Still, some Arab civil societies cannot mobilize massive demonstrations using only online resources, especially in areas with low internet access or where online tools only reach small elites, not to mention given the use of censorship by conservative Arab regimes. A combination of radio and mobile phones is often used to create a vibrant political sphere.

Bloggers demonstrate the urgency of implementing a form of participatory democracy, where one seeks capable actors, regardless of their affiliations, as constructors of knowledge on dialogue and peace, based on shared experiences, specific individual awareness, and the recognition of the contingency of their own position and peculiarities. The ideal is not to fall into hyperdemocracy (which rests on an assumption that sovereignty and democratic rights are no longer located in the people as a whole community, but have descended to autonomous individuals), nor to exacerbate the narcissism of small differences, nor to have only a digital democracy, but to draw from the potential of virtual networks for generating an active civic society, as happened both during the 2009 controversial presidential election in Iran and the 2011 Arab Spring, especially in Egypt, and as is still happening in Syria. Rather than consuming a snapshot of an opinion out of its context, like the passive end-users of traditional media, internet users can easily access the details of the ideas discussed online from a variety of sources, as well as participate in their evaluation. This attribute of new media can contribute to a more comprehensive dialogue among social groups and, therefore, constitute a helpful tool in building peace in countries in transition.

REFERENCES

Abou El Fadl, Khaled. 1994. "Islamic Law and Muslim Minorities: The Juristic Discourse on Muslim Minorities from the Second/Eighth to the Eleventh/Seventeenth Centuries." *Islamic Law and Society* 1 (2): 141–187.

Abu El Haj, Nadia. 1998. "Translating Truths: Nationalism, the Practice of Archaeology, and the Remaking of Past and Present in Contemporary Jerusalem." *American Ethnologist* 25 (1): 166–188.

———. 2001. *Facts on the Ground: Archaeological Practice and Territorial Self-Fashioning in Israeli Society.* Chicago: University of Chicago Press.

Abu-Lughod, Lila. 1989. "Zones of Theory in the Anthropology of the Arab World." *Annual Review of Anthropology* 18: 267–306.

———. 1990. "The Romance of Resistance: Tracing Transformations of Power through Bedouin Women." *American Ethnologist* 17 (1): 41–55.

———. 1991. "Writing Against Culture." In *Recapturing Anthropology,* ed. R. Fox, 137–154. Santa Fe, N.M.: School of American Research Press.

———. 1998. "The Marriage of Feminism and Islamism in Egypt: Selective Repudiation as a Dynamic of Postcolonial Cultural Politics." In *Remaking Women: Feminism and Modernity in the Middle East,* ed. L. Abu-Lughod, 243–269. Princeton: Princeton University Press.

———. 2001. "Orientalism and Middle East Feminist Studies." *Feminist Studies* 27 (1): 101–113.

———. 2005. *Dramas of Nationhood: The Politics of Television in Egypt.* Chicago: University of Chicago Press.

Abusharaf, Rogaia M. 2009. *Transforming Displaced Women in Sudan: Politics and the Body in a Squatter Settlement.* Chicago: University of Chicago Press.

Agence France Presse. 1996. "Foreign Workers in Lebanon Total 1.25 Million: Arab League." 9 July.

Ageron, Charles-Robert. 1960. "La France a-t-elle un politique kabyle?" *Revue historique* 223: 311–352.

Aherdan, Mahjoubi. 1976. *La masse . . . ira: ou, Le journal d'un marcheur.* Casablanca: Éditions G. Gauthey.

Ahmed, Akbar S. 1976. *Millennium and Charisma among Pathans.* London: Routledge & Kegan Paul.

———. 1980. *Pakhtun Economy and Society: Traditional Structure and Economic Development in a Tribal Society.* London: Routledge & Kegan Paul.

Ahmed, Leila. 1992. *Women and Gender in Islam: Historical Roots of a Modern Debate.* New Haven: Yale University Press.

Akhchichine, Ahmed and Jamal Eddine Naji. 1984. "*Le contact avec les médias au Maroc.*" Ph.D. dissertation. Rabat, Morocco: Université Mohammed V.

Al-Ali, Nadje. 2000. *Secularism, Gender & the State in the Middle East: The Egyptian Women's Movement.* Cambridge: Cambridge University Press.

Al-Ali, Nadje, and Khalid Koser, eds. 2002. *New Approaches to Migration? Transnational Communities and the Transformation of Home.* London: Routledge.

Alavi, Nasrin. 2004. *We Are Iran.* London: Portobello Books.

Alexander, Catherine. 2001. "Legal and Binding: Time, Change, and Long-Term Transactions." *The Journal of the Royal Anthropological Institute* 7 (3): 467–485.

Al-Fadil, Fathi Abu. 2002. "Exit from Stagnation and Unemployment and the Development of the Future in Port Said." *Development in Port Said.* Center for Research and Future Studies, Suez Canal University, Port Said.

Al Fin. 2008. "Arab World Still Lagging in Education, Literacy." *Al Fin* (blog). 4 February. http://alfin2100.blogspot.com/2008/02/arab-world-still-lagging-in-education.html.

Al-Hubaishi, H. A. 1988. *Legal System and Basic Law in Yemen.* Worcester, U.K.: Billing and Sons.

Ali, Haydar Ibrahim and Milad Hanna. 2002. *'Azmat al-'Aqalliyyat fi al-Watan al-'Arabi* (The Crisis of Minorities in the Arab World). Damascus: Dar al-Fikr.

Ali, Kamran Asdar. 2002. *Planning the Family in Egypt: New Bodies, New Selves.* Austin: University of Texas Press.

Al-Khaddaf, Iman. 2010. "68 Percent of Saudi Girls Drop Last Name on Facebook." *Asharq Alawsat.* 19 February.

Allison, Christine. 2001. *The Yezidi Oral Tradition in Iraqi Kurdistan.* London: Curzon Press.

———. Forthcoming. *Popular Memory in Kurdistan.*

Al-Mekkawi, Shaikh Abdul Kadir bin Muhammed. 1959 [1886]. *A Treatise on the Muhammedan Law, Entitled "The Overflowing River of the Science of Inheritance and Patrimony" Together with an Exposition of "The Rights of Women, and the Law of Matrimony."* Cairo: Moustapha El Baby El Halaby & Sons.

Al-Rasheed, Madawi. 1998. *Iraqi Assyrian Christians in London: The Construction of Ethnicity.* Lewiston, N.Y.: Edwin Mellen Press.

Al-Rashid, Madawi. 2007. "Complicated Relationship: The Tribe and the State in Saudi Arabia." *al-Quds al-Arabi.* 27 August.

Al-Sarghany, Khaled. 2005. *Port Said Governorate.* Cairo: Al-Ahram Center for Political and Strategic Studies.

Altınay, Ayşe Gül. 2004. *The Myth of the Military-Nation: Militarism, Gender, and Education in Turkey.* New York: Palgrave Macmillan.

Amin, Galal. 2000. *Whatever Happened to the Egyptians? Changes in Egyptian Society from 1950 to the Present.* Cairo: American University in Cairo Press.

Amin, S. H. 1987. *Law and Justice in Contemporary Yemen: People's Democratic Republic of Yemen and Yemen Arab Republic.* Glasgow: Royston Publishers.

Amrouche, Jean. 1988 [1938]. *Chants berbères de Kabylie.* Paris: Harmattan.

Anderson, Benedict. 1983. *Imagined Communities: Reflections on the Origin and Spread of Nationalism.* London: Verso.

———. 1994. "Exodus." *Critical Inquiry* 20 (2): 314–327.

———. 2006. *Imagined Communities: Reflections on the Origin and Spread of Nationalism,* rev. and exp. ed. London: Verso.

Anderson, James Norman Dalrymple. 1954. *Islamic Law in Africa.* Colonial Research Publication no. 16. London: Her Majesty's Stationery Office.

Anderson, Jon W. 1978. "Introduction and Overview." In *Ethnic Processes and Intergroup Relations in Contemporary Afghanistan,* ed. Jon W. Anderson and R. F. Strand, 1–8. New York: Afghanistan Council.

———. 1985. "Sentimental Ambivalence and the Exegesis of 'Self' in Afghanistan." *Anthropological Quarterly* 58: 203–211.

———. 1992. "Politics and Poetics in Ethnographic Texts: A View from the Colonial Ethnography of Afghanistan." In *Writing the Social Text,* ed. Richard H. Brown, 91–116. New York: Aldine de Gruyter.

Anderson, Michael R. 1996. *Islamic Law and the Colonial Encounter in British India.* Women Living under Muslim Laws (wluml) Occasional Paper No 7.

Anonymous. 1987. *Tizi-Wwuccen méthode de langue berbère (taqbaylit).* Aix-en-Provence, France: Edisud.

Anscombe, Fred. 2005. "An a-National Society: Eastern Arabia in the Ottoman Period." In *Transnational Connections and the Arab Gulf,* ed. Madawi Al-Rasheed, 21–38. London: Routledge.

Antoun, Richard. 1976. "Anthropology." In *The Study of the Middle East: Research and Scholarship in the Humanities and Social Sciences,* ed. Leonard Binder, 137–213. New York: John Wiley.

———. 1980. "The Islamic Court, the Islamic Judge, and the Accommodation of Traditions: A Jordanian Case Study." *International Journal of Middle East Studies* 12: 455–467.

Aourid, Hassan. 1999. "Le substrat culturel des mouvements de contestation au Maroc. Analyse des discours islamiste et amazighe." Doctoral Thesis, Department of Juridical, Economic, and Social Sciences. Université Mohamed V (Agdal-Rabat).

Aplin, Greame. 2007. "World Heritage Cultural Landscapes." *International Journal of Heritage Studies* 13 (6): 427–446.

———. 1993. *Genealogies of Religion: Discipline and Reasons of Power in Christianity and Islam.* Baltimore: Johns Hopkins University Press.

Armbrust, Walter. 1996. *Mass Culture and Modernism in Egypt.* Cambridge: Cambridge University Press.

Asad, Talal. 1973. *Anthropology and the Colonial Encounter.* London: Ithaca Press.

———. 1986. *The Idea of an Anthropology of Islam.* Washington, D.C.: Center for Contemporary Arab Studies, Georgetown University.

———. 1991. "Afterword." In *Colonial Situations; Essays on the Contextualization of Ethnographic Knowledge,* ed. George Stocking, 314–324. Madison: University of Wisconsin Press.

———. 1993. *Genealogies of Religion: Discipline and Reasons of Power in Christianity and Islam.* Baltimore: Johns Hopkins University Press.

———. 1996. "Modern Power and the Reconfiguration of Religious Traditions." *SEHR* 5 (1), 27 February.

———. 2001. *Thinking About Secularism and Law in Egypt.* Leiden: International Institute for the Study of Islam in the Modern World (ISIM).

———. 2003. *Formations of the Secular: Christianity, Islam, Modernity.* Stanford: Stanford University Press.

Assaad, Ragui and Farzaneh Roudi-Fahimi. 2007. "Youth in the Middle East and North Africa: Demographic Opportunity or Challenge?" Washington, D.C.: Population Reference Bureau. http://www.prb.org/pdf07/youthinmena.pdf (accessed 25 June 12).

Aswad, Barbara. 1971. *Property Control and Social Strategies: Settlers on a Middle*

Eastern Plain. Ann Arbor: University of Michigan Museum of Anthropology, Anthropological Papers.

'Awad, El-Sayyid Hanafy. 1999. "The Influence of the Free Zone on the Social Structure of Port Said" (in Arabic). In *A Symposium on Economic and Social Changes in the Context of the Port Said Free Zone,* ed. Samir Mu'awad, 66–77. Port Said, Egypt: The Frederich Ebert Institute/Association for Port Said Investment.

Ayad, Mohamed and Farzaneh Roudi-Fahimi. 2006. "Fertility Decline and Reproductive Health in Morocco: New DHS Figures, Population Reference Bureau." Available from http://www.prb.org/articles (accessed 10 January 2010).

Badran, Margot. 1988. "The Institutionalization of Middle East Women's Studies in the United States." *Middle East Studies Association Bulletin* 22: 9–18.

Bahloul, Joëlle. 1996. *The Architecture of Memory: A Jewish-Muslim Household in Colonial Algeria, 1937–1962.* Cambridge: Cambridge University Press.

Barnard, Alan and Jonathan Spencer. 1996. *Encyclopedia of Social and Cultural Anthropology.* London: Routledge.

Baron, Beth. 1996. "A Field Matures: Recent Literature on Women in the Middle East." *Middle Eastern Studies* 32 (3) (January): 172–196.

———. 2005. *Egypt as a Woman: Nationalism, Gender, and Politics.* Berkeley: University of California Press.

Baron, Beth, Israel Gershoni, and Sara Pursley, eds. 2011. "Relocating Arab Nationalism." *International Journal of Middle East Studies,* Special Issue 43 (2) (May): 197–325.

Barth, Fredrik. 1953. *Principles of Social Organization in Southern Kurdistan.* Oslo: Universitetsforlaget.

———. 1959. *Political Leadership among Swat Pathans.* London: Athlone Press.

———. 1964. *Nomads of South Persia: The Basseri tribe of the Khamseh Confederacy.* Oslo: Universitetsforlaget.

———, ed. 1969. *Ethnic Groups and Boundaries: The Social Organization of Cultural Difference.* Oslo: Universitetsforlaget.

Batinitzky, Adina. 2008. "Obesity and Household Roles: Gender and Social Class in Morocco." *Sociology of Health and Illness* 30 (3): 445–462.

Battenburg, John. 1999. "The Gradual Death of the Berber Language in Tunisia." *International Journal of the Sociology of Language* 137: 147–161.

Baum, Geraldine. 2009. "From New Media, a New Portrait of Iran Emerges." *Los Angeles Times.* 24 June.

Bawer, Bruce. 2006. *While Europe Slept: How Radical Islam is Destroying the West from Within*. New York: Broadway Books.

Bayat, Asef. 1996. "The Coming of a Post-Islamist Society." *Critique: Critical Middle East Studies* no. 9 (Fall 1996): 43–52.

Beal, E. Anne. 1999. "Financing National Pride: The 1995 MENA Economic Summit in Amman." *PoLAR: Political and Legal Anthropology Review* 22 (2): 27–40.

Beck, Lois. 1980. "Herd Owners and Hired Shepherds: The Qashqa'i of Iran." *Ethnology* 19 (3): 327–351.

———. 1986. *The Qashqa'i of Iran*. New Haven: Yale University Press.

———. 1991. *Nomad: A Year in the Life of a Qashqa'i Tribesman in Iran*. Berkeley: University of California Press.

———. 1992. "Qashqa'i Nomads and the Islamic Republic." *Middle East Report* (177): 36–41.

Beck, Lois and Nikki Keddie. 1978. *Women in the Muslim World*. Cambridge, Mass.: Harvard University Press.

Beehner, Lionel. 2007. "The Effects of the 'Youth Bulge' on Civil Conflicts." Council on Foreign Relations. 27 April. http://www.cfr.org/society-and -culture/effects-youth-bulge-civil-conflicts/p13093 (accessed 1 July 2012).

Benkler, Yochai. 2006. *The Wealth of Networks: How Social Production Transforms Markets and Freedom*. New Haven: Yale University Press.

Ben-Layashi, Samir. 2007. "Secularism in the Moroccan Amazigh Discourse." *Journal of North African Studies* 12 (2): 153–172.

Ben-Meir, Jason. 2005. "Royal Activities: King Seeks to Foster New Citizenship Mentality." *Morocco Times*. 14 October.

Berger, Morroe. 1967. "Middle Eastern and North African Studies: Development and Needs." *Middle East Studies Association Bulletin* 1 (2): 1–18.

Bernstein, Lisa. 1992 "Opting out of the Legal System: Extralegal Contractual Relations in the Diamond Industry." *The Journal of Legal Studies* 21 (1): 115–157.

Berque, Jacques. 1955. *Structures sociales du Haut-Atlas*. Paris: Presses universitaires de France.

Besnaci-Lancou, Fatima and Gilles Manceron. 2008. *Les Harkis dans la colonization et ses suites*. Ivry-sur-Seine, France: Editions de l'Atelier.

Beswick, Stephanie. 2004. *Sudan's Blood Memory: The Legacy of War, Ethnicity, and Slavery in Early South Sudan*. Rochester, N.Y.: University of Rochester Press.

Bhabha, Homi. 1994. "Of Mimicry and Man: The Ambivalence of Colonial Discourse." In *The Location of Culture*, ed. Homi Bhabha, 121–132. New

York: Routledge.

Binder, Leonard. 1976. "Area Studies: A Critical Reassessment." In *The Study of the Middle East: Research and Scholarship in the Humanities and the Social Sciences,* ed. Leonard Binder, 1–28. New York: John Wiley and Sons.

Blackburn, Carole. 2007. "Producing Legitimacy: Reconciliation and the Negotiation of Aboriginal Rights in Canada." *Journal of the Royal Anthropological Institute* 13: 621–638.

Bloch, Maurice. 1971. "'Why Do Malagasy Cows Speak French?'" *!Kung, the Magazine of the London School of Economics Anthropological Society*: 28–30.

Boddy, Janice. 1989. *Wombs and Alien Spirits: Women, Men, and the Zar Cult in Northern Sudan.* Madison: University of Wisconsin Press.

Bonine, Michael. 1986. "MESA and Middle East Studies: An International Perspective from North America." *Middle East Studies Association Bulletin* 20 (2): 155–168.

Bookin-Weiner, Jerry. 2009. Email correspondence. 6 November.

Borneman, John. 1992. *Belonging in the Two Berlins: Kin, State, Nation.* Cambridge: Cambridge University Press.

Boulifa, Si Amar. 1990 [1905]. *Recueil de poésies kabyles.* Paris: Awal.

Boum, Aomar. 2007. "A Berber Heresy in the Arabo-Islamic Borderlands." Paper presented at the Western Jewish Studies Association annual meeting, Portland, Ore., 18 March.

Bourdieu, Pierre. 1977. *Outline of a Theory of Practice,* trans. Richard Nice. Cambridge: Cambridge University Press.

———. 1990. *The Logic of Practice,* trans. Richard Nice. Stanford: Stanford University Press.

Bourdieu, Pierre, and Mouloud Mammeri. 2003 [1985]. "Du bon usage de l'ethnologie." *Actes de la recherche en sciences sociales* 150: 9–18.

Bourdieu, Pierre, and Abdelmalek Sayad. 1964. *Le déracinement.* Paris: Editions de Minuit.

Bourqia, Rahma. 1995. "Women, Uncertainty, and Reproduction in Morocco." In *Family, Gender, and Population in the Middle East: Policies in Context,* ed. Carla Makhlouf Obermeyer, 136–146. Cairo: The American University of Cairo Press.

Boutayeb, Abdesslam. 2006. "Social Inequalities and Health in Morocco." *International Journal for Equity in Health* 5 (1). Doi: 10.1186/1475-9276-5-1 (accessed July 26, 2010).

Bowen, John. 1998. *Religion in Culture and Society.* Boston: Allyn & Bacon.

———. 2003. *Shari'a without Fiqh; the Anthropology of Law without Law? Reflec-*

tions from France. Paper presented at the ISIM Workshop on the Anthropology of Islamic Law. Leiden, Netherlands, 14–16 March 2003.

———. 2004. "Does French Islam Have Borders? Dilemmas of Domestication in a Global Religious Field." *American Anthropologist* 106 (1): 43–55.

Boyarin, Jonathan. 1994. "Space, Time, and the Politics of Memory." In *Remapping Memory: The Politics of TimeSpace,* ed. Jonathan Boyarin, 1–37. Minneapolis: University of Minnesota Press.

Brahimi, Denise. 1984. *Femmes arabes et soeurs musulmanes.* Paris: Tierce.

Braidwood, Robert J. and Gordon R. Willey. 1962. *Courses toward Urban Life: Archaeological Considerations of Some Cultural Alternates.* Chicago: Aldine Publishing Co.

Brand, Laurie. 1994. *Jordan's Inter-Arab Relations.* New York: Columbia University Press.

Brown, George F. 1968. "Moroccan Family Planning Program--Progress and Problems." *Demography* 5 (2): 627–631.

Brown, Nathan. 1997. *The Rule of Law in the Arab World.* Cambridge: Cambridge University Press.

Bruce, Charles, dir. 1998. *In Search of Palestine.* Sixty-minute documentary. BBC.

Brumberg, Dan, Steve Heydemann, Sheldon Himelfarb, and Asieh Mir. 2009. "Iran's Disputed Elections." http://www.usip.org/publications/iran-s-disputed-election (accessed 1 July 2012).

Bryson, Thomas A. 1979. *An American Consular Officer in the Middle East in the Jacksonian Era: A Biography of William Brown Hodgson, 1801–1871.* Atlanta: Resurgens.

Bucholtz, Mary. 2002. "Youth and Cultural Practice." *Annual Review of Anthropology* 31: 525–552.

Bujra, Abdalla S. 1971. *The Politics of Stratification: A Study of Political Change in a South Arabian Town.* Oxford: Clarendon Press.

Burchianti, Margaret. 2004. "Building Bridges of Memory: The Mothers of the Plaza de Mayo and the Cultural Politics of Maternal Memories." *History and Anthropology* 15 (2): 133–150.

Burton, John W. 1987. *A Nilotic World: The Atuot-speaking Peoples of the Southern Sudan.* New York: Greenwood Press.

Bruinessen, Martin V. 2000. *Kurdish Ethno-nationalism Versus Nation-building States: Collected Articles.* Istanbul: Isis Press.

Calotychos, Vangelis. 1998. *Cyprus and its People: Nation, Identity, and Experience in an Unimaginable Community, 1955–1997.* Boulder, Colo.: Westview Press.

Canfield, Robert L. 1972. Review of *Afghanistan* by Louis Dupree. *Ethnohistory* 20 (4): 424–429.

———. 1973. *Faction and Conversion in a Plural Society: Religious Alignments in the Hindu Kush.* Ann Arbor: University of Michigan Museum of Anthropology, Anthropological Papers 50.

Çarkoğlu, Ali and Binnaz Toprak. 2007. *Religion, Society, and Politics in a Changing Turkey.* Istanbul: TESEV Publications.

Carroll, Rory. 2009. "Rumble in the Jungle." *The Guardian Weekend.* 3 July.

Chaker, Salem. 1998. *Berbères aujourd'hui,* 2nd ed. Paris: Harmattan.

Chakrabarty, Dipesh. 2000. *Provincializing Europe: Postcolonial Thought and Historical Difference.* Princeton: Princeton University Press.

Charrad, Mounira. 2001. *States and Women's Rights: The Making of Post-Colonial Tunisia, Algeria, and Morocco.* Berkeley: University of California Press.

Central Intelligence Agency. 2010, 2011. *The World Factbook.*

Cerwonka, Allaine. 2004. *Native to the Nation: Disciplining Landscapes and Bodies in Australia.* Minneapolis: University of Minnesota Press.

Césari, Jocelyne. 2004. *When Islam and Democracy Meet: Muslims in Europe and the United States.* New York: Palgrave Macmillan.

Chatty, Dawn. 1986. *From Camel to Truck: Bedouin in the Modern World.* New York: Vantage.

———. 1996. *Mobile Pastoralists.* New York: Columbia University Press.

———, ed. 2010a. *Deterritorialized Youth: Sahrawi and Afghan Refugees at the Margins of the Middle East.* Oxford, U.K.: Berghahn Books.

———. 2010b. *Displacement and Dispossession in the Modern Middle East.* Cambridge: Cambridge University Press.

Chatty, Dawn, and Annika Rabo, eds. 1997. *Organizing Women: Formal and Informal Women's Groups in the Middle East.* Oxford: Berg.

Chatty, Dawn, and Gillian Hundt, eds. 2005 *Children of Palestine: Experiencing Forced Migration in the Middle East.* Oxford, U.K.: Berghahn Books.

Chaudhry, Kiren A. 1994. "The Middle East and the Political Economy of Development." *Items* 48 (2): 41–49.

Christiansen, Catrine, Mats Utas, and Henrik E. Vigh. 2006. "Introduction: Navigating Youth, Generating Adulthood." In *Navigating Youth, Generating Adulthood: Social Becoming in an African Context,* ed. Catrine Christiansen, Mats Utas, and Henrik E. Vigh, 9–30. Stockholm: Uppsala.

Clarke, Morgan. 2009. *Islam and New Kinship: Reproductive Technology and the Shariah in Lebanon.* London: Berghahn Books.

Clarkin, Alison. 2005. "Claiming Place and Legibility in the Republic. The Making of Berber Citizens in France." Ph.D. Dissertation. Anthropology, New School for Social Research.

Clifford, James. 1984. "Interrupting the Whole." *Conjunctions* 6 (Spring): 282–295.

———. 1988. *The Predicament of Culture: Twentieth-century Ethnography, Literature, and Art.* Cambridge, Mass.: Harvard University Press.

———. 1994. "Diasporas." *Cultural Anthropology* 9 (3): 302–338.

Clifford, James, and George Marcus, eds. 1986. *Writing Culture: The Poetics and Politics of Ethnography.* Santa Fe, N.M.: SAR Press.

Cohen, Abner. 1965. *Arab Border-Villages in Israel.* Manchester, U.K.: Manchester University Press.

Cohen, Erik. 1977. "Recent Anthropological Studies of Middle Eastern Communities and Ethnic Groups." *Annual Review of Anthropology* 6: 315–347.

Cohen, Shana and Larabi Jaidi. 2006. *Morocco: Globalization and Its Consequences.* New York: Routledge Press.

Cohen, William B. 2006. "The Harkis: History and Memory." In *Algeria and France, 1800–2000: Identity, Memory, Nostalgia,* ed. Patricia M. E. Lorcin, 117–134. Syracuse, N.Y.: Syracuse University Press.

Cole, Donald P. 1975. *Nomads of the Nomads: The Al Murrah Bedouin of the Empty Quarter.* Chicago: Aldine Publishing Co.

Cole, Jennifer. 2007. "Fresh Contact in Tamatave, Madagascar: Sex, Money, and Intergenerational Transformation." In *Generations and Globalization: Youth, Age, and Family in the New World Economy,* ed. Jennifer Cole and Deborah Durham, 74–101. Bloomington: Indiana University Press.

Cole, Jennifer, and Deborah Durham. 2007. "Introduction: Age, Regeneration, and the Intimate Politics of Globalization." In *Generations and Globalization,* ed. Jennifer Cole and Deborah Durham, 1–28. Bloomington: Indiana University Press.

Collin, Finn. 1997. *Social Reality.* London: Routledge.

Combs-Schilling, M. Elaine. 1989. *Sacred Performances: Islam, Sexuality, and Sacrifice.* New York: Columbia University Press.

Coon, Carleton S. 1951. *Caravan: The Story of the Middle East.* New York: Henry Holt. (Arabic translation, translator unknown: 1959. *Al-Qafilah: Qissat al-Sharq al-Awsat.* Beirut: Dar al-Thaqafah.)

———. 1965. *The Living Races of Man.* New York: Alfred A. Knopf.

———. 1980. *A North Africa Story: The Anthropologist as OSS Agent, 1941–1943.* Ipswich, Mass.: Gambit.

Courbage, Youssef. 1995. "Fertility Transition in the Mashriq and the Maghrib: Education, Emigration, and the Diffusion of Ideas." In *Family, Gender, and Population in the Middle East: Policies in Context,* ed. Carla Makhlouf Obermeyer, 80–104. Cairo: The American University of Cairo Press.

Crapanzano, Vincent. 1980. *Tuhami: Portrait of a Moroccan.* Chicago: University of Chicago Press.

———. 2011. *The Harkis: The Wound that Never Heals.* Chicago: University of Chicago Press.

Crawford, David. 2005. "Royal Interest in Local Culture: The Politics and Potential of Morocco's Imazighen." In *Nationalism and Minority Identities in Islamic Societies,* ed. Maya Shatzmiller, 164–194. Montreal: McGill-Queens University Press.

Crawford, David, and Katherine E. Hoffman. 2000. "Essentially Amazigh: Urban Berbers and the Global Village." In *The Arab-African and Islamic World: Interdisciplinary Studies,* ed. Kevin Lacey, 117–131. New York: Peter Lang.

Crawhill, Nigel. 1999. "Going to a Better Life: Perspectives on the Future of Language Education for San and Khoe South Africans." *International Journal of Education Development* 19 (4–5): 323–335.

Crick, Malcolm R. 1982. "Anthropology of Knowledge." *Annual Review of Anthropology* 11: 288–298.

Crouzet, Thierry. 2007. *Le cinquième pouvoir. Comment Internet bouleverse le politique.* Paris: Bourin Editeur.

Cuno, Kenneth M. 1992. *The Pasha's Peasants: Land, Society, and Economy in Lower Egypt, 1740–1858.* Cambridge: Cambridge University Press.

Cunnison, Ian. 1959. *The Luapula Peoples of Northern Rhodesia: Custom and History in Tribal Politics.* New York: The Humanities Press.

Dağı, İhsan D. 2006. "The Justice and Development Party: Identity, Politics, and Human Rights Discourse in the Search for Security and Legitimacy." In *The Emergence of a New Turkey: Democracy and the AK Parti,* ed. M. H. Yavuz, 88–106. Salt Lake City: University of Utah Press.

Dahlgren, Susanne. 2010. *Contesting Realities: The Public Sphere and Morality in Southern Yemen.* Syracuse, N.Y.: Syracuse University Press.

Daily Star. 2009. "Major Reforms Needed to Reduce Lebanon's Unemployment." 9 July.

Daoud, Zakya. 2007. *Les années Lamalif: 1958–1988, Trente ans de journalisme au Maroc.* Casablanca: Tarik / Mohammedia, Morocco: Senso unico editions (1st ed.).

Daragahi, Borzou. 2009. "Iran: Authorities Block Facebook amid Heated Election Campaign." *Los Angeles Times.* 24 May

Davis, Rochelle. 2010. *Palestinian Village Histories: Geographies of the Displaced.*

Stanford: Stanford University Press.

Davis, Susan Schaefer, Douglas A. Davis, and John W. M. Whiting. 1989. *Adolescence in a Moroccan Town: Making Social Sense.* New Brunswick, N.J.: Rutgers University Press.

Davison, Andrew. 2003. "Turkey, a 'Secular' State? The Challenge of Description." *South Atlantic Quarterly* 102 (2/3): 333–350.

Deeb, Lara. 2006. *An Enchanted Modern: Gender and Public Piety in Shi'i Lebanon.* Princeton: Princeton University Press.

Delaney, Carol L. 1991. *The Seed and the Soil: Gender and Cosmology in Turkish Village Society.* Berkeley: University of California Press.

Desjardins, Thierry. 1977. *Les rebelles d'aujourd'hui.* Paris: Presses de la Cité.

Dessaints, J. 1976. "Chroniques politiques du Maroc." *Annuaire d'Afrique du Nord* 14: 457–476.

Dhillon, Navtej and Tarik Yousef. 2007. "Inclusion: Meeting the 100 Million Youth Challenge." Middle East Youth Initiative, The Brookings Institution, and the Dubai School of Government.

Diamond, Stanley. 1974. *In Search of the Primitive: A Critique of Civilization.* New York: Transaction Books.

Direche-Slimani, Karima. 1997. *Histoire de l'émigration kabyle en France au XXe siècle.* Paris: Harmattan.

Dominguez Virginia. 1989. *People as Subject, People as Object: Selfhood and Peoplehood in Contemporary Israel.* Madison: University of Wisconsin Press.

Doornbos, Paul. 1988. "On becoming Sudanese." In *Sudan: State, Capital and Transformation,* ed. Tony Bennet and Abbas A. Karim, 91–121. London: Croom Helm.

Doutté, Edmond. 1908. *Magie et religion en Afrique du Nord.* Algiers: A. Jourdan.

Dresch, Paul. 1989. *Tribes, Government, and History in Yemen.* Oxford: Oxford University Press.

———. 2000. "Wilderness of Mirrors: Truth and Vulnerability in Middle Eastern Fieldwork." In *Anthropologists in a Wider World: Essays on Field Research,* ed. P. Dresch, W. James, and D. Parkin, 109–128. New York: Berghahn Books.

Dupree, Louis. 1958. *Shamsir Ghar: Historic Cave Site in Kandahar Province, Afghanistan.* New York: Anthropological Papers of the American Museum of Natural History 46.

Dupret, Baudoin. 2007. "The Rule of a Morally Constrained Law: Morality, Islam, Law, and the Judge in Present-Day Egypt." In *Rule of Law: History, Theory and Criticism,* ed. Danilo Zolo and Pieto Costa, 543–564. Dordrecht,

Netherlands: Springer Verlag.

Dupret, Baudoin, and Jean-Noel Ferrie. 2005. "Constructing the Public/Private Distinction in Muslim Majority Societies: A Praxological Approach." In *Religion, Social Practice, and Contested Hegemonies: Reconstructing the Public Sphere in Muslim Majority Societies*, Armando Salvatore and Mark LeVine, 135–154. New York: Palgrave Macmillan.

Durkheim, Emile. 1978. *La division sociale du travail.* Paris: Presses Universitaires de France.

Dwyer, Kevin. 1982. *Moroccan Dialogues: Anthropology in Question.* Baltimore: Johns Hopkins University Press.

Economic and Social Commission for Western Asia (ESCWA). 2007. The Developments in the Situation of Arab Women. Health, Education, Employment, Political Representation, CEDAW. E/ESCWA/ECW2007/Brochure 1. 22 February 2007.

———. 2009. "The Demographic Profile of the Arab Countries." E/ESCWA/SDD/2009/Technical Paper 9. 26 November 2009.

Economic and Social Commission for Western Asia (ESCWA): Global Migration Group. 2009. "Fact-Sheet on the Economic Crisis and International Migration in the Arab Region."

Eickelman, Dale F. 1976. *Moroccan Islam: Tradition and Society in a Pilgrimage Center.* Austin: University of Texas Press.

———. 1989. *The Middle East: An Anthropological Approach.* Englewood Cliffs, N.J.: Prentice Hall.

———. 1992. "Mass Higher Education and the Religious Imagination in Contemporary Arab Societies." *American Ethnologist* 19: 643–655.

———. 2001. *The Middle East and Central Asia: An Anthropological Approach.* Upper Saddle River, N.J.: Prentice Hall.

El-Amrani, Issandr. 2009. "The Mosaic Theory of the Middle East, and its Rotten Advocates." *The Arabist* (blog). 3 September.

Elbendary, Amina. 2001. "Other Palestines." *Al-Ahram Weekly Online.* 24–30 May 2001.

El-Dean, Bahaa Ali. 2002. *Privatisation and the Creation of a Market-Based Legal System: The Case of Egypt.* Leiden, Netherlands: Brill.

Eldén, Åsa. 1998. "'The Killing Seemed to Be Necessary.' Arab Cultural Affiliation as an Extenuating Circumstance in a Swedish Verdict." *Nordic Journal of Women's Studies* 6 (2): 89–96.

El Guindi, Fadwa. 1999. *Veil: Modesty, Privacy, and Resistance.* Oxford: Berg.

———. 2008. *By Noon Prayer: The Rhythm of Islam.* Oxford: Berg.

El-Hamzi, Mohsen et al. 1995. "Consanguinity among the Saudi Arabian Population." *Journal of Medical Genetics* 32 (8): 623–626.

El-Kady, Dia' El-Dean Hassan. 1997. *Port Said Historical Encyclopedia*, vol. 1. Port Said, Egypt: el-Mustaqbal.

El-Qadéry, Mustapha. 2006. "Saïd Guennoun ou *tiherci* d'un intellectuel 'indigène.'" *Awal* 30: 71–87.

El-Zein, Abdul Hamid. 1977. "Beyond Ideology and Theology: The Search for the Anthropology of Islam." *Annual Review of Anthropology*, 6: 227–254.

Enright, Mairead. 2009. "Mapping Sharia in English Divorce Law." Paper presented at the workshop "Transnational and Cross-cultural Understandings of Legal Culture and Legal Pluralism in the West: The Example of *Mahr*," held at the University of Copenhagen, 21–23 October 2009.

Entelis, John. 1989. *Culture and Counterculture in Morocco*. Boulder, Colo.: Westview Press.

Erlanger, Steven and Souad Mekhennet. 2009. "Islamic Radicalism Slows Moroccan Reforms." *New York Times*. 26 August.

Esposito, John. 1992. *The Islamic Threat: Myth Or Reality?* New York: Oxford University Press.

Etling, Bruce, J. Kelly, J. Faris, and R. Palfrey. 2009. "Mapping the Arabic Blogosphere: Politics, Culture, and Dissent." *Berkman Center Research Publication No. 2009–06.* Cambridge Mass.: Berkman Center for Internet and Society at Harvard University.

———. 2008. "Mapping Iran's Online Public: Politics and Culture in the Persian Blogosphere." *Berkman Center Research Publication No. 2008–01.* Cambridge, Mass.: Berkman Center for Internet and Society at Harvard University.

Evans-Pritchard, E. E. 1940. *The Nuer*. Oxford: Oxford University Press.

Fabian, Johannes. 1983. *Time and the Other: How Anthropology Makes Its Object*. New York: Columbia University Press.

Fábos, Anita. 2002. "Ambiguous Borders, Ambivalent Subjects: Being Sudanese in Twentieth-Century Egypt." In *Auto/Biography and the Construction of Identity and Community in the Middle East*, ed. Mary Ann Fay, 177–190. New York: Palgrave.

———. 2007. "Between Citizenship and Belonging: Transnational Ethnic Strategies of Arab Muslim Sudanese in the Diaspora." *Kvinder, Kön & Forskning / Women, Gender & Research*, Special Issue on Gender and Transnationalism (3).

———. 2008. *"Brothers" Or Others? Propriety and Gender for Muslim Arab Su-*

danese in Egypt. New York: Berghahn Books.

Fahim, Hussein. 1983. *Egyptian Nubians: Resettlement and Years of Coping.* Salt Lake City: University of Utah Press.

Fahmy, Khaled. 1999. "The Police and the People in Nineteenth-Century Egypt." *Die Welt des Islams* 39 (3): 340–377.

Fakhouri, Kani. 1972. *Kafr el-Flow: An Egyptian Village in Transition.* New York: Holt, Rinehart & Winston.

Farkhondeh, Sepideh. 2001. *Médias, pouvoir, et société civile en Iran.* Paris: L'Harmattan.

Farsakh, Awny. *Al-'Aqalliyat fi al-Tarikh al-'Arabi: Mundhu al-jahilliya wa ila al-yawm* (Minorities in Arab History from pre-Islamic Times till Today). London: Riad El-Rayyes Books.

Feraoun, Mohand. 1997 [1950]. *Le fils du pauvre.* Paris: Seuil.

Fernea, Elizabeth Warnock and Basima Qattan Bezirgan, eds. 1977. *Middle Eastern Muslim Women Speak.* Austin: University of Texas Press.

Fernea, Robert A. 1970. *Shaykh and Effendi: Changing Patterns of Authority among the El Shabana of Southern Iraq.* Cambridge: Harvard University Press.

Fernea, Robert A., and George Gerster. 1973. *Nubians in Egypt: A Peaceful People.* Austin: University of Texas Press.

Fernea, Robert A., and James Malarkey. 1975. "Anthropology of the Middle East and North Africa: A Critical Assessment." *Annual Review of Anthropology* 4: 183–206.

Finn, Margot C. 2003. *The Character of Credit: Personal Debt in English Culture, 1740–1914.* Cambridge: Cambridge University Press.

Fischer, Michael M. J. 1980. *Iran: From Religious Dispute to Revolution.* Cambridge: Harvard University Press.

Fluehr-Lobban, Carolyn and Kharyssa Rhodes. 2004. *Race and Identity in the Nile Valley: Ancient and Modern Perspectives.* Trenton, N.J.: Red Sea Press.

Fredriksen, Katja Jansen. 2007. "Shari'a in Norwegian Courtrooms?" *ISIM Review* 20, (Autumn): 44–45.

Foster, Stephen William. 2006. *Cosmopolitan Desire: Transcultural Dialogues and Antiterrorism in Morocco.* Lanham, Md.: AltaMira Press.

Frerichs-Cigli, Melanie. 2008. "On fait le point sur les nouvelles contraceptions." *Citadine*, 1 October: 83–84.

Fuccaro, Nelida. 1999. *The Other Kurds: Yazidis in Colonial Iraq.* London: I. B. Tauris.

Fucik, Kenneth. 2006. *Environmental Impact Assessment in Wadi Mukhaizana.* Muscat, Oman: Occidental Press.

Gaffney, Patrick D. 1994. *The Prophet's Pulpit: Islamic Preaching in Contemporary Egypt.* Berkeley: University of California Press.

Gambetti, Zeynep. 2009. "Conflict, 'Communi-cation' and the Role of Collective Action in the Formation of Public Spheres." In *Publics, Politics, and Participation: Locating the Public Sphere in the Middle East and North Africa,* ed. Seteney Shami, 91–115. New York: SSRC Books.

Gardner, Emily. 2000. "Gender Politics and the Focus on Women in the Memory Debates." *Journal of Child Sexual Abuse* 9 (1): 99–106.

Geiser, Peter. 1973. "The Myth of the Dam." *American Anthropologist* 75: 184–194.

———. 1986. *The Egyptian Nubian: A Study in Social Symbiosis.* Cairo: The American University in Cairo Press.

Geertz, Clifford. 1968. *Islam Observed: Religious Development in Morocco and Indonesia.* Chicago: University of Chicago Press.

———. 1973. "Religion as a Cultural System." In *The Interpretation of Cultures,* 87–125. New York: Basic Books.

———. 1975. *The Interpretation of Cultures.* London: Hutchinson.

———. 1983. *Local Knowledge: Further Essays in Interpretive Anthropology.* New York: Basic Books.

Gellner, Ernest. 1969. *Saints of the Atlas.* Chicago: University of Chicago Press.

Geschiere, Peter. 1997. *The Modernity of Witchcraft: Politics and the Occult in Postcolonial Africa.* Trans. Peter Geschiere and Janet Roitman. Charlottesville: University Press of Virginia.

Ghannam, Farha. 1998. "Keeping Him Connected: Labor Migration and the Production of Locality in Cairo." *City and Society* 10 (1): 65–82.

———. 2002. *Remaking the Modern: Space, Relocation, and the Politics of Identity in a Global Cairo.* Berkeley: University of California Press.

Gilbert, Jérémie. 2007. "Nomadic Territories: A Human Rights Approach to Nomadic Peoples' Land Rights." *Human Rights Law Review* 7 (4): 681–716.

Gilsenan, Michael. 1973. *Saint and Sufi in Modern Egypt.* Oxford: Oxford University Press.

———. 1982. *Recognizing Islam: An Anthropologist's Introduction.* London: Croom Helm.

———. 1996. *Lords of the Lebanese Marches: Violence and Narrative in an Arab Society.* Berkeley: University of California Press.

Ginsburg, Faye D. and Rayna Rapp. 1995. "Introduction: Conceiving the New World Order." In *Conceiving the New World Order: The Global Politics of Reproduction,* ed. Faye D. Ginsburg and Rayna Rapp, 1–17. Berkeley:

University of California Press.

Goldberg, Harvey. 1972. *Cave-dwellers and Citrus-growers: A Jewish Community in Libya and Israel.* Cambridge: Cambridge University Press.

—. 1976. "Anthropology in Israel." *Current Anthropology* 17 (1) (March): 119–121.

—, ed. 1977. "Ethnicity in Israeli Society." Special Issue of *Ethnic Groups* 1 (3): 163–262.

—. 1985. "Historical and Cultural Dimensions of Ethnic Phenomena in Israel." In *Studies in Israeli Ethnicity: After the Ingathering,* ed. Alex Weingrod, 179–200. New York: Gordon and Breach.

Goldstone, Jack. 2010. "The New Population Bomb: The Four Megatrends That Will Change the World." *Foreign Affairs,* January/February.

Göle, Nilüfer. 1996. *The Forbidden Modern: Civilization and Veiling.* Ann Arbor: University of Michigan Press.

Goodman, Jane. 2002. "Writing Empire, Underwriting Nation: Discursive Histories of Kabyle Berber Oral Texts." *American Ethnologist* 29 (1): 86–122.

—. 2003. "The Proverbial Bourdieu: Habitus and the Politics of Representation in the Ethnography of Kabylia." *American Anthropologist* 105 (4): 782–793.

—. 2005. *Berber Culture on the World Stage: From Village to Video.* Bloomington: Indiana University Press.

Goodman, Jane, and Paul A. Silverstein, eds. 2009. *Bourdieu in Algeria: Colonial Politics, Ethnographic Practices, Theoretical Developments.* Lincoln: University of Nebraska Press.

Goody, Jack. 1986. *The Logic of Writing and the Organization of Society.* New York: Cambridge University Press.

Gordon, David M. 2006. "History on the Luapula Retold: Landscape, Memory, and Identity in the Kazembe Kingdom." *Journal of African History* 47 (1): 21–42.

Granqvist, Hilma. 1931–35. *Marriage Conditions in a Palestinian Village.* Helsinki: Finska vetenskaps-societeten, Commentationes humanarum litterarum III.

—. 1997 [1947]. *Birth and Childhood among Arabs: Studies in a Muhammadan Village in Palestine.* Helsinki: Soderstrom.

Greenberg, Jason. "Representing the State: Class, Race, and Nationhood in an Israeli Museum." *Visual Anthropology Review* 13 (1): 14–27.

Greenhalgh, Susan. 2008. *Just One Child: Science and Policy in Deng's China.* Berkeley: University of California Press.

Grendzier, Irene. 1997. "Following the Flag." *Middle East Report* 205 (Oct.–Dec.): 2–9.

Gross, Joan, and David McMurray. 1993. "Berber Origins and the Politics of Ethnicity in Berber North Africa. *PoLAR: Political and Legal Anthropology Review* 16 (2): 39–57.

Guennoun, Saïd. 1929. *La montagne Berbère: les Aït Oumalou et les pays Zaïan.* Paris: Comité de l'Afrique française.

———. 1934. *La Voix des monts. Moeurs des gueres berbères.* Rabat, Morocco: Omnia.

Gulick, John. 1969. "The Anthropology of the Middle East." *Middle East Studies Association Bulletin* 3: 1–14.

Guyer, Jane I. 2004a. "Anthropology in Area Studies." *Annual Review of Anthropology* 33: 499–523.

———. 2004b. *Marginal Gains: Monetary Transactions in Atlantic Africa.* Chicago: University of Chicago Press.

———. 2007. "Prophecy and the Near Future: Thoughts on Macroeconomic, Evangelical, and Punctuated Time." *American Ethnologist* 34 (3): 409–421.

Haaland, Gunnar. 2006. "The Darfur Conflict in Evolving Politico-economic and Socio-cultural Contexts: The 'Games', the 'Players' and the 'Stakes.'" *International Journal of Diversity in Organisations, Communities and Nations* 5 (2): 105–116.

Habermas, Jürgen. 1989. *The Structural Transformation of the Public Sphere: An Inquiry into a Category of Bourgeois Society.* Cambridge, Mass.: MIT Press.

Hajjar, Lisa, and Steve Niva. 1997. "(Re)Made in the USA: Middle East Studies in the Global Era." *Middle East Report* 205 (Oct.–Dec.): 2–9.

Hale, Sondra. 1993. "Transforming Culture or Fostering Second-Hand Consciousness?" In *Women in Arab Society: Old Boundaries, New Frontiers*, ed. Judith Tucker, 149–174. Bloomington: Indiana University Press.

———. 1996. *Gender Politics in Sudan: Islamism, Socialism, and the State.* Boulder, Colo.: Westview Press.

———. 2000a. "Culture and the Politics of Memory." *Aljadid: A Review & Record of Arab Culture and Arts* 6 (3): 9.

———. 2000b. "The Soldier and the State: Post-Liberation Women: The Case of Eritrea." In *Frontline Feminisms: Women, War, and Resistance*, ed. Marguerite Waller and Jennifer Rycenga, 349–370. New York: Garland [republished by Routledge, 2001].

———. 2000c. "'Liberated, But Not Free': Women in Post-War Eritrea." In *Aftermath: Women in Post-War Reconstruction*, ed. Sheila Meintjes, Anu

Pillay, and Meredith Turshen, 122–141. New York: Zed Press.

———. 2006. "The State of the Women's Movement in Eritrea." *Journal of Northeast African Studies* 8 (3): 155–178 [New Series, copyright 2005].

———. 2008. *Siyasat Al-Zakira fi Al-Nizaat Al-Sudania: Alnisaa wa Al-Hawia wa Al-Watan* (The Politics of Memory in Sudanese Conflicts: Gender, Identity, and "Homeland"). Translated into Arabic by Magdi El-Na'im and published as *Ajeras Al-Hurriyya* (*Freedom Bells*, Periodical; Khartoum, Sudan), Four-Part Series. No. 74 (June 30): 5. No. 75 (1 July): 5. No. 76 (2 July): 5. No. 77 (3 July): 5.

———. 2010. "Rape as Marker and Eraser of Difference: Darfur and the Nuba Mountains." In *Gender, War, and Militarism*, ed. Laura Sjoberg and Sandra Kia, 122–141. New York: Praeger, An Imprint of ABC-CLIO.

———. Forthcoming. "Gendering the Politics of Memory: Women, Identity, and Conflict in Sudan." In *Anthropology in the Sudan: Past, Present and Future*, ed. Munzoul Assal. Khartoum, Sudan: Khartoum University Press.

Hall, Stuart. 1994. "Culture, Identity, and Diaspora." In *Colonial Discourse and Post-Colonial Theory: A Reader*, ed. Patrick Williams and Laura Chrisman, 392–403. New York: Columbia University Press.

Hallaq, Wael B. 2005. *The Origins and Evolution of Islamic Law*. Cambridge: Cambridge University Press.

———. 2009. *An Introduction to Islamic Law*. Cambridge: Cambridge University Press.

Hamil, Mustapha. 2002. "Interrogating Identity: Abdelkebir Khatibi and the Postcolonial Prerogative." *Alif: Journal of Comparative Poetics* 22 (2002): 72–86.

Hammoud, Hassan R. 2005. "Illiteracy in the Arab World." Education for All Global Monitoring Report 2006. UNESCO.

Hammoudi, Abdellah. 1997. *Master and Disciple: The Cultural Foundations of Moroccan Authoritarianism*. Chicago: University of Chicago Press.

Hamoumou, Mohand. 1993. *Et ils sont devenus harkis*. Paris: Fayard.

Hanafi, Hassan. 1998. "The Middle East, in Whose World?" In *The Middle East in a Globalized World: Papers from the Fourth Nordic Conference on Middle Eastern Studies*, ed. Björn Olav Utvik and Knut S. Vikör, 1–9. Oslo: Nordic Society for Middle Eastern Studies.

Handelman, Don, and Shlomo Deshen. 1975. *Social Anthropology of Israel: A Bibliographical Essay with Primary Reference to Loci of Social Stress*. Tel Aviv: Department of Social Anthropology.

Hannerz, Ulf. 1990. "Cosmopolitans at Locals in World Culture." *Theory, Culture, and Society* 7 (2): 237–251.

Hannoum, Abdelmajid. 2010. *Violent Modernity: France in Algeria.* Cambridge: Harvard Center for Middle Eastern Studies.

Hanoteau, Adolphe and Aristide Letourneux. 1872–73. *La Kabylie et les coutumes kabyles,* 3 vols. Paris: Imprimerie Nationale.

Harik, Iliya. 1998. *Economic Policy Reform in Egypt.* Cairo: American University in Cairo Press.

Hart, David. 1976. *The Aith Waryaghar of the Moroccan Rif: An Ethnography and History.* Tucson: University of Arizona Press.

Hart, Kimberly. 2009. "The Orthodoxization of Ritual Practice in Western Anatolia." *American Ethnologist* 36 (4): 735–749.

Hassan II. 1976. *Le défi.* Paris: Albin Michel.

Hassanpour, Amir. 1996. "The Creation of Kurdish Media Culture." In *Kurdish Culture and Identity,* ed. Philip Kreyenbroek and Christine Allison, 48–84. London: Zed Books and SOAS Center of Near and Middle Eastern Studies.

Hegel-Cantarella, Christine. 2011."Waiting to Win: Family Disputes, Court Reform, and the Ethnography of Delay." In *Family Law in Islam: Divorce, Marriage, and Women in the Muslim World,* ed. Maaike Voorhoeve, 111–146. London: I. B. Tauris.

Hellyer, H. A. 2009. *Muslims of Europe: The "Other" Europeans.* Edinburgh: Edinburgh University Press.

Hendler, James, Nigel Shadbolt, Wendy Hall, Tim Berners-Lee, and Danier Weitzner. 2008. "Web Science: An Interdisciplinary Approach to Understanding the Web." *Communications of the ACM* 51, no. 7

Herrera, Linda. 2008."Education and Empire: Democratic Reform in the Arab World." *International Journal of Education Reform* 17:4 (Fall): 355–374.

Herzfeld, Michael. 1997. *Cultural Intimacy.* London: Routledge.

———. 2004. *The Body Impolitic: Artisans and Artifice in the Global Hierarchy of Value.* Chicago: University of Chicago Press.

Hill, Enid. 1988. "Al-Sanhuri and Islamic Law: The Place and Significance of Islamic Law in the Life and Work of 'Abd Al-Razzaq Ahmad Al-Sanhuri, Egyptian Jurist and Scholar, 1895–1971 (Part I)." *Arab Law Quarterly* 3 (2): 182–218.

Hines, Ralph. 2001. "An Overview of Title VI." In *Changing Perspectives on International Education,* ed. Patrick O'Meara, Howard D. Mehlinger, and Roxana Ma Newman, 6–11. Bloomington: Indiana University Press.

Hirsch, Eric, and Michael O'Hanlon, eds. 1995. *The Anthropology of Landscape: Perspectives on Place and Space*. Oxford: Clarendon Press.

Hirschkind, Charles. 2001. "Civic Virtue and Religious Reason: An Islamic Counterpublic." *Cultural Anthropology* 16: 3–34.

———. 2006. *The Ethical Soundscape: Cassette Sermons and Islamic Counterpublics*. New York: Columbia University Press.

Hirsh, Afua. 2010. "Fears over non-Muslim's Use of Islamic Law to Resolve Dispute." *The Guardian*. 14 March 2010.

Ho, Engseng. 2004. "Empire through Diasporic Eyes: A View from the Other Boat." *Comparative Studies in Society and History* 46 (02): 210–246.

———. 2006. *The Graves of Tarim: Genealogy and Mobility across the Indian Ocean*. Berkeley: University of California Press.

Hobsbawm, Eric and Terrence Ranger, eds. 1983. *The Invention of Tradition*. Cambridge: Cambridge University Press.

Hodgekin, Katharine and Susannah Radstone. 2003. *Contested Pasts: The Politics of Memory*. New York: Routledge.

Hodgson, William Brown. 1844. *Notes on Northern Africa, the Sahara and Soudan: In Relation to the Ethnography, Languages, History, Political and Social Condition of the Nations of those Countries*. New York: Wiley and Putnam.

Hoffman, Katherine, and David Crawford. 2000. "Essentially Amazigh: Urban Berbers and the Global Village." In *The Arab-Islamic World: Multidisciplinary Approaches*, ed. Kevin Lacey, 117–131. New York: Peter Lang.

Hole, Frank, Kent V. Flannery, and James A. Neely. 1969. *Prehistory and Human Ecology of the Deh Luran Plain: An Early Village Sequence from Khuzistan, Iran*. Ann Arbor: University of Michigan Museum of Anthropology Memoirs.

Holmes, Douglas R., and George E. Marcus. 2005. "Cultures of Expertise and the Management of Globalization: Toward the Re-Functioning of Ethnography." In *Global Assemblages: Technology, Politics, and Ethics as Anthropological Problems*, ed. Aihwa Ong and Stephen J. Collier, 235–252. Oxford: Blackwell.

Hoodfar, Homa. 1997. *Between Marriage and the Market: Intimate Politics and Survival in Cairo*. Berkeley: University of California Press.

———. 2000. "Iranian Women at the Intersection of Citizenship and the Family Code: the Perils of Islamic Criteria." In *Women and Citizenship in the Middle East*, ed. Suad Joseph, 281–313. Syracuse, N.Y.: Syracuse University Press.

———. 2001. "Reproductive Health Counseling in the Islamic Republic Of Iran: The Role of Women Mullahs." In *Cultural Perspectives on Reproductive Health*, ed. C. Makhlouf Obermeyer, 153–174. New York: Oxford University Press.

Hopkins, Nicholas S., ed. 2003. *Upper Egypt: Life Along the Nile.* Aarhus, Denmark: Aarhus University Press.

Howarth, David. 1964. *The Desert King: A Life of Ibn Saud.* Beirut: Continental Publications.

Howe, John. 1978. "Western Sahara: A War Zone." *Review of African Political Economy* (11): 84–92.

Hughes, Stephen O. 2001. *Morocco under King Hassan*, 1st. ed. Reading, U.K.: Ithaca.

Ibn Khaldûn. 1958. *The Muqaddimah: An Introduction to History.* Princeton: Princeton University Press.

Ilahiane, Hsain. 2001. "The Social Mobility of the Haratine and the Re-Working of Bourdieu's Habitus on the Saharan Frontier, Morocco." *American Anthropologist* 103 (2): 380–394.

Inhorn, Marcia. 1994. *Quest for Conception: Gender, Infertility, and Egyptian Medical Traditions.* Philadelphia: University of Pennsylvania Press.

———. 1996. *Infertility and Patriarchy: The Cultural Politics of Gender and Family Life in Egypt.* Philadelphia: University of Pennsylvania Press.

———. 2004. "Middle Eastern Masculinities in the Age of New Reproductive Technologies: Male Infertility and Stigma in Egypt and Lebanon." *Medical Anthropology Quarterly* 18 (2): 162–182.

———. 2006. "'He Won't Be My Son': Middle Eastern Muslim Men's Discourses on Adoption and Gamete Donation." *Medical Anthropology Quarterly* 20 (1): 94–120.

Inhorn, Marcia, and Carolyn Sargent. 2006. "Introduction to Medical Anthropology in the Muslim World." *Medical Anthropology Quarterly* 20 (1): 1–11.

International Journal of Middle East Studies, Special Issue: Relocating Arab Nationalism. Vol. 43, No. 2, May 2011.

Irons, William. 1975. *The Yomut Turkmen: A Study of Social Organization among a Central Asian Turkic-Speaking Population.* Ann Arbor: University of Michigan Museum of Anthropology, Anthropological Papers 58.

Ismael, Tareq, and Jacqueline S. Ismael. 1990. "Middle East Studies in the United States." In *Middle East Studies: International Perspectives on the State of the Art*, ed. T. Ismael, 3–17. New York: Praeger.

Ivy, Marilyn. 1995. *Discourses of the Vanishing: Modernity, Phantasm, Japan.* Chicago: University of Chicago Press.

Jackson, John. 1984. *Discovering the Vernacular Landscape.* New Haven: Yale University Press.

———. 2001. "'In Ways Unacademical': The Reception of Carleton S. Coon's *The Origin of the Races.*" *Journal of the History of Biology* 34:2 (Summer): 247–285.

Jaïdi, Moulay Driss. 2000. *Diffusion et audience des médias audiovisuels: cinéma, radio, télévision, vidéo et publicité au Maroc.* Rabat, Morocco: Al Majal.

Jean-Klein, Iris. 2000. "Mothercraft, Statecraft, and Subjectivity in the Palestinian Intifada." *American Ethnologist* 27 (1): 100–127.

Jennings, Anne. 1995. *The Nubians of West Aswan: Village Women in the Midst of Change.* Boulder, Colo.: Lynne Reinner.

———. 2009. *Nubian Women of West Aswan: Negotiating Tradition and Change,* 2nd ed. Boulder, Colo.: Lynne Reinner.

Johnson-Hanks, Jennifer. 2006. "On the Politics and Practice of Muslim Fertility: Comparative Evidence from West Africa." *Medical Anthropology Quarterly* 20 (1) 12–30.

Johnstone, Thomas M. 1977. *Harsusi Lexicon.* Oxford: Oxford University Press.

Jok, Jok Madut. 1998. *Militarization, Gender, and Reproductive Health in South Sudan.* Lewiston, N.Y.: The Edwin Mellen Press.

Jones, Daniel Christopher. 2010. "Arab States to Cut Unemployment by 7% by 2020." GDS Publishing. 12 March.

Joseph, Suad. 1983. "Working-class Women's Networks in a Sectarian State: A Political Paradox." *American Ethnologist* 10 (1): 1–22.

———. 1994. "Brother/Sister Relationships: Connectivity, Love, and Power in the Reproduction of Patriarchy in Lebanon." *American Ethnologist* 21 (1): 50–73.

———. 2000. *Gender and Citizenship in the Middle East.* Syracuse, N.Y.: Syracuse University Press.

———. 2008. "Familism and Critical Arab Family Studies." In *Family Ties and Ideational Change in the Middle East,* ed. Kathryn Young and Hoda Rashad, 25–39. New York: Routledge.

Joseph, Suad, and Susan Slyomovics. 2001. *Women and Power in the Middle East.* Philadelphia: University of Pennsylvania Press.

Juergensmeyer, Mark. 2001. "The Global Rise of Religious Nationalism." In *Religions/Globalizations: Theories and Cases,* ed. Dwight Hopkins, 66–83. Durham, N.C.: Duke University Press.

Kanaaneh, Rhoda. 2002. *Birthing the Nation: Strategies of Palestinian Women in Israel*. Berkeley: University of California Press.

———. 2008. *Surrounded: Palestinian Soldiers in the Israeli Military*. Stanford: Stanford University Press.

Kanaaneh, Rhoda, and I. Nusair, eds. 2010. *Displaced at Home: Ethnicity and Gender Among Palestinians in Israel*. Albany: State University of New York Press.

Kandiyoti, Deniz. 1996. *Gendering the Middle East: Emerging Perspectives*. London: I. B. Tauris.

Kapchan, Deborah A. 1993. "Hybridization and the Marketplace: Emerging Paradigms in Folkloristics." *Western Folklore* 52 (2–4): 303–362.

———. 1996. *Gender on the Market: Moroccan Women and the Revoicing of Tradition*. Philadelphia: University of Pennsylvania Press.

Kaplan, Sam. 2002. "*Din-u Devlet* All Over Again? The Politics of Military Secularism and Religious Militarism in Turkey Following the 1980 Coup." *International Journal of Middle East Studies* 34 (1): 113–127.

———. 2006. *The Pedagogical State: Education and the Politics of National Culture in Post-1980 Turkey*. Stanford: Stanford University Press.

Kapur, Ratha and Brenda Cossman. 1996. *Subversive Sites: Feminist Engagements with Law in India*. New Delhi: Thousand Oaks.

Karabell, Zachary. 2004. *Parting the Desert: The Creation of the Suez Canal*. New York: Vintage Books.

Kasriel, Michèle. 1989. *Libres femmes du Haut-Atlas? Dynamique d'une microsociété au Maroc*. Paris: Harmattan.

Kaufman Winn, Jane. 1994. "Relational Practices and the Marginalization of Law: Informal Financial Practices of Small Businesses in Taiwan." *Law & Society Review* 28 (2): 193–232.

Kaymakcan, Recep. 2006. "Religious Education Culture in Modern Turkey." In *International Handbook of the Religious, Moral and Spiritual Dimensions in Education*, ed. M. D. Souza, G. Durka, K. Engebretson, R. Jackson, and A. McGrady, 449–460. Dordrecht, Netherlands: Springer.

Keane, Webb. 2003. "Self-interpretation, Agency, and the Objects of Anthropology: Reflections on a Genealogy." *Comparative Studies in Society and History* 45 (2): 222–248.

Keefe, Susi Krehbiel. 2006. "'Women Do What They Want': Islam and Permanent Contraception in Northern Tanzania." *Social Science & Medicine* 63 (2006): 418–429.

Kennedy, John G., ed. 1978. *Nubian Ceremonial Life: Studies in Islamic Syncretism and Cultural Change.* Berkeley: University of California Press / Cairo: American University in Cairo Press.

Kerchouche, Dalila. 2003. *Destins de harkis: Aux racines d'un exil.* Paris: Autrement.

Khalaf, Samir, and Roseanne Khalaf, eds. 2011. *Arab Youth.* London: Saqi Press.

Khamis, Sahar, and Katherine Vaughn. 2011. "Cyberactivism in the Egyptian Revolution: How Civic Engagement and Citizen Journalism Tilted the Balance." *Arab Media and Society,* no. 13 (Summer).

Khosravi, Shahram. 2009. "Displaced Masculinity: Gender and Ethnicity among Iranian Men in Sweden." *Iranian Studies* 42 (4): 591–609.

Khuri, Fuad. 2007. *An Invitation to Laughter: Lebanese Anthropologist in the Arab World.* Chicago: University of Chicago Press.

Kidder, Robert L. 1978. "Western Law in India: External Law and Local Response." In *Social System and Legal Process,* ed. Harry M. Johnson, 159–162. San Francisco: Jossey-Bass.

Kirişci, Kemal. 1998. "Minority/Majority Discourse: The Case of the Kurds in Turkey." In *Making Majorities: Constituting the Nation in Japan, Korea, China, Malaysia, Fiji, Turkey, and the United States,* ed. Dru Gladney, 226–245. Stanford: Stanford University Press.

Kluckhohn, Clyde. 1949. *Mirror for Man.* New York: McGraw-Hill.

Knox-Mawer, Ronald. 1956. "Islamic Domestic Law in Aden." *International and Comparative Law Quarterly* 5 (Oct.): 511–518.

Kour, Zaki Hanna. 1981. *The History of Aden 1839–72.* London: Frank Cass.

Kraidy, Marwan. 2006. "Hypermedia and Governance in Saudi Arabia." *First Monday.* Special issue no. 7 (September).

Kroeber, A. L. 1939. *Cultural and Natural Areas of Native North America.* Berkeley: University of California Press.

Kroeber, A. L. and Clyde Kluckhohn, eds. 1952. *Culture: A Critical Review of Concepts and Definitions.* New York: Vintage.

Kuru, Ahmet T. 2006. "Reinterpretation of Secularism in Turkey: The Case of the Justice and Development Party." In *The Emergence of a New Turkey: Democracy and the AK Parti,* M. H. Yavuz, 136–159. Salt Lake City: University of Utah Press.

Laclau, Ernesto. 1995. "Subject of Politics, Politics of the Subject." *Differences: A Journal of Feminist Cultural Studies* 7(1): 146–164.

Lacouture, Jean, and Simonne Lacouture. 1958. *Le Maroc à l'épreuve.* Paris: Éditions du Seuil.

Lafuente, Gilles. 1999. *La politique berbère de la France et le nationalisme marocain.* Paris: Harmattan.

Lamalif. 1975. "Tenir et maintenir." Nov.–Dec.: 4–10.

Lambton, Ann K. S. 1953. *Landlord and Peasant in Persia.* London: I. B. Tauris.

Landler, Mark. 2007. "Furor in Germany over Court Case Decision on Muslims." *New York Times.* 23 March.

Laoust, Emile. 1930. *Mots et choses berbères.* Paris: A. Challemel.

Laroui, Abdallah. 1992. *Esquisses historiques.* Casablanca: Centre culturel arabe.

Lavie, Smadar, and Ted Swedenburg. 1996. *Displacement, Diaspora, and Geographies of Identity.* Durham, N.C.: Duke University Press.

Layne, Linda. 1994. *Home and Homeland: the Dialogics of Tribal and National Identities in Jordan.* Princeton: Princeton University Press.

Le Saout, Didier. 2009. "La radicalisation de la revendication amazighe. Le sud-est comme imaginaire militant." *L'Année du Maghreb* 5: 75–93.

Leach, Edmund. 1940. *Social Organization of the Rowanduz Kurds.* London: LSE Monographs.

Lebanon Ministry of Social Affairs & United Nations Development Programme. 2004 and 2007. "The National Survey of Households Living Conditions 2004 and 2007: Selected Characteristics of the Youth Population in Lebanon." Beirut.

Leinhardt, Peter. 2001. *Shaikhdoms of Eastern Arabia.* Basingstoke, U.K.: Palgrave.

Leveau, Rémy. 1985. *Le fellah marocain, défenseur du trône,* 2nd ed. Paris: Presse de la Fondation national des sciences politiques.

Levy, Andre. 1997. "Controlling Space, Essentializing Identities: Jews in Contemporary Casablanca." *City and Society* 9 (1): 175–199.

———. 1999. "Playing for Control of Distance: Card Games between Jews and Muslims on a Casablancan Beach." *American Ethnologist* 26 (3): 632–653.

———. 2001. "Center and Diaspora: Jews in Late-Twentieth-Century Morocco." *City and Society* 13: 245–270.

———. 2003. "Notes on Jewish-Muslim Relationships: Revisiting the Vanishing Moroccan Jewish Community." *Cultural Anthropology* 18 (3): 365–397.

Levy, Reuben. 1957. *The Social Structure of Islam.* Cambridge: Cambridge University Press.

Limbert, Mandana. 2005. "Personal Memories, Revolutionary States and Indian Ocean Migrations." *MIT Electronic Journal of Middle East Studies* 5 (Fall).

———. 2010. *In the Time of Oil: Piety, Memory, and Social Life in an Omani Town.* Stanford: Stanford University Press.

Lindholm, Charles. 1982. *Generosity and Jealousy: The Swat Pathan of Northern*

Pakistan. New York: Columbia University Press.

———. 1995. "The New Middle Eastern Ethnography." *The Journal of the Royal Anthropological Institute* 1 (4): 805–820.

———. 2008. *Culture and Authenticity.* Oxford: Blackwell Publishing.

Lockman, Zachary. 2004. *Contending Visions of the Middle East: The History and Politics of Orientalism.* Cambridge: Cambridge University Press.

Longva, Anh Nga. 1997. *Walls Built on Sand: Migration, Exclusion, and Society in Kuwait.* Boulder, Colo.: Westview Press.

Lorcin. Patricia. 1995. *Imperial Visions: Stereotyping, Prejudice, and Race in Colonial Algeria.* London: I. B. Tauris.

Louer, Laurence. 2008. *Transnational Shia Politics: Religious and Political Networks in the Gulf.* New York: Columbia University Press.

Lövdal, Lene. 2011. "*Mahr* and Gender Equality in Private International Law: The Adjudication of *Mahr* in England, France, Norway and Sweden." In *Embedding Mahr (Islamic Dower) in the European Legal Systen,* ed. Rubya Mehdi and Jörgen S. Nielsen, 77–112. Aarhus, Denmark: DJØF Publishing.

Löwy, Michael. 2006. *François Houtart, sociologie de la religion.* Bogota, Colombia: Ruth Casa Editorial.

Lucas, Philippe, and Jean-Claude Vatin. 1975. *L'Algérie des anthropologues.* Paris: François Maspéro.

Lynch, Marc. 2007. "Blogging the New Arab Public," *Arab Media and Society* Issue 1 (Spring 2007). http://www.arabmediasociety.com/topics/index.php?t_article=32#_ftn3 (accessed December 10, 2009).

Macaulay, Stewart. 1963. "Non-Contractual Relations in Business: A Preliminary Study." *American Sociological Review* 28 (1): 55–67.

MacIntyre, Alasdair. 1988. *Whose Justice? Which Rationality?* Notre Dame, Ind.: University of Notre Dame Press.

Macneil, Ian R. 1980. *The New Social Contract: An Inquiry into Modern Contractual Relations.* New Haven: Yale University Press.

Macphee, Marybeth. 2004. "The Weight of the Past in the Experience of Health: Time, Embodiment, and Cultural Change in Morocco." *Ethos* 32 (3): 374–396.

Maddy-Weitzman, Bruce. 1992. "Population Growth and Family Planning in Morocco." *African and Asian Studies* 26 (1992): 63–79.

———. 2001. "Contested Identities: Berbers, 'Berberism,' and the State in North Africa." *Journal of North African Studies* 6 (3): 23–47.

———. 2006. "Ethno-politics and Globalisation in North Africa: The Berber Culture Movement." *Journal of North African Studies* 11 (1): 71–83.

————. 2011. *The Berber Identity Movement and the Challenge to North African States.* Austin: University of Texas Press.

Maghraoui, Abdeslam. 2001. "Political Authority in Crisis: Mohammed VI's Morocco." *Middle East Report* 218: 12–17.

Maher, Vanessa. 1974. *Women and Property in Morocco.* Cambridge: Cambridge University Press.

Mahmood, Saba. 2001. "Feminist Theory, Embodiment, and the Docile Agent: Some Reflections on the Egyptian Islamic Revival." *Cultural Anthropology* 16 (2): 202–236.

————. 2005. *Politics of Piety: The Islamic Revival and the Feminist Subject.* Princeton: Princeton University Press.

Maktari, Abdulla M. A. 1971. *Water Rights and Irrigation Practices in Lahj: A Study of the Application of Customary and Shariah Law in South-West Arabia.* Cambridge: Cambridge University Press.

Malinowski, Bronislaw. 1922. *Argonauts of the Western Pacific.* New York: E. P. Dutton Co.

————. 1948. *Magic, Science, and Religion, and Other Essays.* Boston: Beacon Press.

————. 1989 [1967]. *A Diary in the Strictest Sense of the Term.* Stanford: Stanford University Press.

Mamdani, Mahmood. 2002. "Good Muslim, Bad Muslim: A Political Perspective on Culture and Terrorism." *American Anthropologist* 104 (3): 766–775.

Mammeri, Mouloud. 1980. *Contes berbères de Kabylie.* Paris: Bordas.

Manger, Leif. 1999. "On Becoming Muslims: The Constructions of Identities among the Lafofa of Sudan." In *Muslim Diversity: Local Islam in Global Context,* ed. Leif Manger, 224–256. Surrey, U.K.: Curzon Press.

————. 2010. *The Hadrami Diaspora: Community-building on the Indian Ocean Rim.* Oxford: Berghahn Books.

Mannheim, Karl. 1952. "The Problem of Generations." In *Essays on the Sociology of Knowledge,* ed. Paul Kecskemeti, 276–320. New York: Oxford University Press.

Marçais, Georges. 1946. *La Berbérie musulmane et l'Orient au moyen âge.* Paris: Aubier.

Marcus, George E. 1986. "Contemporary Problems of Ethnography in the Modern World System." In *Writing Culture: The Poetics and Politics of Ethnography,* ed. James Clifford and George E. Marcus, 165–193. Santa Fe: School of American Research.

Marcus, George E., and Michael M. J. Fischer. 1986. *Anthropology as Cultural Critique.* Chicago: University of Chicago Press.

Mardin, Şerif. 1982. "Turkey: Islam and Westernization." In *Religions and Societies: Asia and the Middle East,* ed. C. Caldarola, 170–198. New York: Mouton Publishers.

Martín, Iván. 2006. "Morocco: The Bases for a New Development Model? The National Initiative for Human Development (INDH)." Madrid: Real Instituto Elcano.

Marx, Emanuel. 1975. "Anthropological Studies in a Centralized State: The Bernstein Research Project in Israel." *Journal of Jewish Sociology* 22 (2): 131–150.

Mayer, Ann Elizabeth. 1985. "Islamic Banking and Credit Policies in the Sadat Era: The Social Origins of Islamic Banking in Egypt." *Arab Law Quarterly* 1 (1): 32–50.

Mazzarella, William. 2004. "Culture, Globalization, Mediation." *Annual Review of Anthropology* 33 (1): 345–367.

McClay, Wilfred M. 2000. "Two Concepts of Secularism." *Wilson Quarterly* 24 (3): 54–71.

Meccawy, Maram. 2008. "Bloggers and the Emergence of a New Tribalism in Saudi Arabia: An Insider's Experience." http://meccawy.com/site/wp-content/uploads/2008/06/media_conf_paper_v3.pdf (accessed 1 July 2012).

Medick, Viet and Anna Reimann. 2007. "A German Judge Cites Koran in Court Case." *Der Spiegel.* 21 March.

Meeker, Michael E. 1976. *Literature and Violence in North Arabia.* Cambridge: Cambridge University Press.

———. 1976. "Meaning and Society in the Near East," 2 parts. *International Journal of Middle East Studies* 7 (2): 243–270; 7 (3) 383–422.

———. 2002. *A Nation of Empire: The Ottoman Legacy of Turkish Modernity.* Berkeley: University of California Press.

Mehdi, Rubya, and Jörgen S. Nielsen, eds. 2011. *Embedding Mahr (Islamic Dower) in the European Legal Systen.* Aarhus, Denmark: DJØF Publishing.

Meiselas, Susan. 1997. *Kurdistan: In the Shadow of History.* New York: Random House.

Meneley, Anne. 1996. *Tournaments of Value: Sociability and Hierarchy in a Yemeni Town.* Toronto: University of Toronto Press.

"The MESA Debate: The Scholars, the Media, and the Middle East." 1987. *Journal of Palestine Studies* 16 (2) (Winter): 85–103.

Messick, Brinkley. 1993. *The Calligraphic State: Textual Domination and History in a Muslim Society.* Berkeley: University of California Press.

Michaux-Bellaire, Edouard. 1923. *Les confréries religieuses au Maroc.* Rabat, Morocco: Imprimerie Officielle.

Minow, Martha, Michael Ryan, and Austin Sarat. 1992. *Narrative, Violence, and the Law: The Essays of Robert Cover.* Ann Arbor: University of Michigan Press.

Mir-Hosseini, Ziba. 1993. *Marriage on Trial: A Study of Islamic Family Law: Iran and Morocco Compared.* London: I. B. Taurus.

———. 1999. *Islam and Gender: The Religious Debate in Contemporary Iran.* Princeton: Princeton University Press.

Mitchell, Timothy. 2004. "The Middle East in the Past and Future of Social Science." In *The Politics of Knowledge: Area Studies and the Disciplines,* ed. D. L. Szanton, 71–119. Berkeley: University of California Press.

Miyazaki, Hirokazu. 2004. "The Temporalities of the Market." *American Anthropologist* 105 (2): 255–265.

Mohammed VI. 2005. "Address to the High-Level Meeting of the General Assembly Commemorating the 60th Anniversary of the Creation of the United Nations Organization." Address given to the United Nations, New York, N.Y., September 14–16.

Mohieldin, Mahmoud S., and Peter W. Wright. 2000. "Formal and Informal Credit Markets in Egypt." *Economic Development and Cultural Change* 48 (3) (April): 657–670.

Mojab, Shahrzad, and Rachel Gorman. 2007. "Dispersed Nationalism: War, Diaspora, and Kurdish Women's Organizing." *Journal of Middle East Women's Studies* 3 (1): 58–85.

Montagne, Robert. 1973 [1931]. *The Berbers: Their Social and Political Organisation,* trans. David Seddon. London: Frank Cass.

Moors, Annelies. 1995. *Women, Property, and Islam: Palestinian Experiences, 1920–1990.* Cambridge: Cambridge University Press.

———. 1999. "Debating Islamic Family Law: Legal Texts and Social Practices." In *Social History of Women and Gender in the Modern Middle East,* ed. Margaret L. Meriwether and Judith E. Tucker, 144–177. Boulder, Colo.: Westview Press.

Moors, Annelies, Ray Jureidini, Ferhunde Ozbay, and Rima Sabban. 2009. "Migrant Domestic Workers: A New Public Presence in the Middle East?" In *Publics, Politics, and Participation: Locating the Public Sphere in the Middle East and North Africa,* ed. S. Shami, 151–175. New York: Social Science Research Council.

Morris, Brian. 1987. *Anthropological Studies of Religion.* Cambridge: Cambridge University Press.

Morris, Rosalind C. 2000. *In the Place of Origins: Modernity and its Mediums in Northern Thailand.* Durham, N.C.: Duke University Press.

Morsy, Soheir. 1993. *Gender, Sickness, and Healing in Rural Egypt: Ethnography in Historical Context.* Boulder, Colo.: Westview Press.

Mottaz, Laura. 2009. "The Role of New Media in the 2009 Elections." Report presented at the Center for International Media Assistance, National Endowment for Democracy, Washington, United States, 7 July.

Moudden, Abdelhay. n.d. "Procession of the Immortals: The Nation and the King." Unpublished paper.

Moumen, Abderahmen. 2003. *Entre histoire et mémoire. Les rapatriés d'Algérie.* Nice, France: Editions Gandini.

Moustafa, Tamir. 2003. "Law Versus the State: The Judicialization of Politics in Egypt." *Law and Social Inquiry* 28 (4): 883–930.

———. 2007. *The Struggle for Constitutional Power: Law, Politics, and Economic Development in Egypt.* Cambridge: Cambridge University Press.

Mundy, Jacob. 2006. "How the US and Morocco Seized the Spanish Sahara." *Le monde diplomatique.* 12 January.

Munson, Henry. 1993. *Religion and Power in Morocco.* New Haven, Conn.: Yale University Press.

Nader, Laura. 1969. "Up the Anthropologist: Perspectives Gained from Studying Up." In *Reinventing Anthropology,* ed. Dell Hymes, 284–311. New York: Pantheon.

Naficy, Hamid. 1993. "From Broadcasting to Narrowcasting: Middle Eastern Diaspora in Los Angeles." *Middle East Report* (180): 31–34.

———. 1995. "Recurring Themes in the Middle Eastern Cinema of Diaspora." In *Cinema of Displacement: Middle Eastern Identities in Transition,* ed. H. Naficy, E. Shohat, and Jonathan Friedlander, 3–63. Los Angeles: Center for Near Eastern Studies International Studies and Overseas Programs at UCLA.

Naguib, Nefissa. 2008. "Storytelling: Armenian Family Albums in the Diaspora." *Visual Anthropology* 21 (3): 231–244.

———. 2009. *Water, Women, and Memory: Recasting Lives in Palestine.* Leiden, Netherlands: Brill.

———. 2011. "Basic Ethnography at the Barricades." *International Journal of Middle East Studies* 43: 383–390.

Nagy, Sharon. 1998. "'This Time I Think I'll Try a Filipina': Global and Local

Influences on Relations between Foreign Household Workers and their Employers in Doha, Qatar." *City & Society* 10 (1): 83–103.

Najmabadi, Afsaneh. 1991. "Hazards of Modernity and Morality: Women, State, and Ideology in Contemporary Iran." In *Women, Islam, and the State*, ed. Deniz Kandiyoti, 48–76. Philadelphia: Temple University Press.

Naval Intelligence Division (United Kingdom). 1946. *Western Arabia and the Red Sea*. Geographical handbook series (produced and printed for official purposes during World War II, 1939–45). Oxford, U.K: n.p.

Navaro-Yashin, Yael. 2002. *Faces of the State: Secularism and Public Life in Turkey*. Princeton: Princeton University Press.

Nelson, Cynthia, ed. 1973. *The Desert and the Sown*. Berkeley: Institute of International Studies.

———. 1974. "Public and Private Politics: Women in the Middle Eastern World." *American Ethnologist* 1 (3): 551–563.

Nietzsche, Friedrich. 1996 [1874]. *The Uses and Advantages of History: Untimely Meditations*. Cambridge: Cambridge University Press.

Obermeyer, Carla Makhlouf. 1995. "Reproductive Rights in the West and in the Middle East: A Cross-Cultural Perspective." In *Family, Gender, and Population in the Middle East: Policies in Context*, ed. Carla Makhlouf Obermeyer, 1–15. Cairo: The American University of Cairo Press.

———. 2000. "Pluralism and Pragmatism: Knowledge and Practice of Birth in Morocco." *Medical Anthropology Quarterly* 14 (2): 180–201.

Osanloo, Arzoo. 2006. "Islamico-Civil 'Rights Talk': Women, Subjectivity, and Law in Iranian Family Court." *American Ethnologist* 33 (2): 191–209.

O'Shea, Maria. 2004. *Trapped between the Map and Reality: Geography and Perceptions of Kurdistan*. New York: Routledge.

Ouchna, Zaid. 2007. *Asfafa n Twengimt* (The Awakening of Consciousness). Rabat, Morocco: Institut Royal de la Culture Amazigh.

Ovesen, Jan. 1983. "The Construction of Ethnic Identities: The Nuristani and Pashai of Eastern Afghanistan." In *Identity: Personal and Socio-Cultural*, ed. Anita Jacobsen-Widding, 321–333. Uppsala, Sweden: Acta Universitatis Upsaliensis.

Oxford English Dictionary Online. 2011. "State of the Art." Accessed 24 October.

Özdalga, Elisabeth. 1999. "Education in the Name of 'Order and Progress': Reflections on the Recent Eight Year Obligatory School Reform in Turkey." *Muslim World* 89 (3–4): 414–438

Özyürek, Esra. 2006. *Nostalgia for the Modern: Privatization of State Ideology in Turkey*. Durham, N.C.: Duke University Press.

Pak, Soon-Yong. 2004. "Articulating the Boundary between Secularism and Islamism: The Imam-Hatip Schools of Turkey." *Anthropology and Education Quarterly* 35 (3): 324–344.

Parla, Ayşe. 2003. "Marking Time along the Bulgarian-Turkish Border." *Ethnography* 4 (4): 561–575.

Paxson, Heather. 2004. *Making Modern Mothers: Ethics and Family Planning in Urban Greece.* Berkeley: University of California Press.

Pehrson, Robert N. 1966. *Social Organization of the Marri Baluch.* Chicago: Aldine Publishing Co.

Pemberton, John. 1994. *On the Subject of "Java."* Ithaca, N.Y.: Cornell University Press.

Peteet, Julie. 1991. *Gender in Crisis: Women and the Palestinian Resistance Movement.* New York: Columbia University Press.

———. 1994. "Male Gender and Rituals of Resistance in the Palestinian 'Intifada': A Cultural Politics of Violence." *American Ethnologist* 21 (1): 31–49.

———. 1996. "From Refugees to Minority: Palestinians in Post-war Lebanon." *Middle East Report* (200): 27–30.

———. 2005. *Landscape of Hope and Despair: Palestinian Refugee Camps.* Philadelphia: University of Pennsylvania Press.

———. 2007. "Unsettling the Categories of Displacement." *Middle East Report* 37 (244):2.

Peters, Emrys L. 1990. *The Bedouin of Cyrenaica: Studies in Personal and Corporate Power.* Cambridge, U.K.: Cambridge University Press.

Peterson, John. 1978. *Oman in the Twentieth Century.* New York: Croom Helm.

———. 2004a. "Oman's Diverse Society: Northern Oman." *Middle East Journal* 58 (1): 32–51.

———. 2004b. "Oman's Diverse Society: Southern Oman." *Middle East Journal* 58 (2): 255–269.

———. 2007. *Oman's Insurgencies: the Sultanate's Struggle for Supremacy.* London: Saqi Books.

Piven, Ben. 2010. "Arab World Experiences Rapid Population Explosion." *World Focus.* 23 March.

Poeschke, Roman. 1996. *Nubians in Egypt and Sudan: Constraints and Coping Strategies.* Saarbrücken, Germany: Verlag für Entwicklungs-politik Saarbrücken.

Pouessel, Stéphanie. 2010. *Les identités amazighes au Maroc.* Paris: Non Lieu.

Powell, Eve M. Troutt. 2003. *A Different Shade of Colonialism: Egypt, Great Britain, and the Mastery of the Sudan.* Berkeley: University of California Press.

Pranger, Robert J. 1991. "Nations and Communities." In *The Middle East in Global Perspective,* Judith Kipper & Harold H. Saunders, eds. Boulder, Colo.: Westview and the American Enterprise Institute.

Price, David. 2004. *Threatening Anthropology: McCarthyism and the FBI's Surveillance of Activist Anthropologists.* Durham, N.C.: Duke University Press.

———. 2008. *Anthropological Intelligence: The Deployment and Neglect of American Anthropology in the Second World War.* Durham, N.C.: Duke University Press.

———. 2009. "'Better Killing': Anthropology Goes to War in Afghanistan." *Counterpunch* (Oct. 16–19). Available in the archives of www.counterpunch.org (accessed 1 August 2009).

Quraishi, Asifa, and Frank E. Vogel. 2008. *The Islamic Marriage Contract: Case Studies in Islamic Family Law.* Cambridge, Mass.: Islamic Legal Studies Program / Harvard Law School.

Rabinow, Paul. 1975. *Symbolic Domination: Cultural Form and Historical Change in Morocco.* Chicago: University of Chicago Press.

———. 1977. *Reflections on Fieldwork in Morocco.* Berkeley: University of California Press.

———. 1989. *French Modern: Norms and Forms of the Social Environment.* Berkeley: University of California Press.

———. 2007. "Steps Toward an Anthropological Laboratory." Available on the website Anthropological Research on the Contemporary: http://anthropos-lab.net/working_papers (accessed 25 June 2012).

Rabinowitz, Dan. 1997. *Overlooking Nazareth: The Ethnography of Exclusion in Galilee.* Cambridge: Cambridge University Press.

———. 2001. "The Palestinian Citizens of Israel, the Concept of Trapped Minority and the Discourse of Transnationalism in Anthropology." *Ethnic and Racial Studies* 2 (1): 64–85.

Rabo, Annika. 1999. "Faith and Identity in Northeast Syria." In *Muslim Diversity: Local Islam in Global Context,* ed. Leif Manger, 173–199. Surrey, U.K.: Curzon Press.

———. 2005. *A Shop of One's Own: Independence and Reputation Among Traders in Aleppo.* London: I. B. Tauris.

Rae, Jonathan and Dawn Chatty. 2001. *Participatory Project Appraisal for the Mukhaizana Field Development: A Social Impact Study.* Muscat, Oman: Petroleum Development Oman LLC.

Rassam, Amal. 1977. "Al-Taba'iyya: Power, Patronage and Marginal Groups in Northern Iraq." In *Patrons and Clients in Mediterranean Societies,* ed.

Ernest Gellner and John Waterbury, 157–166. London: Duckworth.

Rew, Alan, Eleanor Fischer, et al. 2000. *Addressing Policy Constraints and Improving Outcomes in Development-Induced Displacement and Resettlement Projects.* Oxford: Refugee Studies Centre, University of Oxford.

Riles, Annelise. 2010. "Collateral Expertise: Legal Knowledge in the Global Financial Markets." *Current Anthropology* 51 (6): 795–818.

Rohe, Mathias. 2004. "Application of Shari'a Rules in Europe: Scope and Limits." *Die Welt des Islams, New Series* 44 (3): 323–350.

Rollinde, Margueritte. 2003. "La marche verte: un nationalisme royal aux couleurs de l'Islam." *Le mouvement social* 2003/1 (202): 133–151.

Romano, Irene Bald. n.d. "Collaborative Programs and Leveraging Funding: The Contribution of American Overseas Research Centers to International Education and Diplomacy." Athens: American School of Classical Studies at Athens.

Rosaldo, Renato. 1985. *Culture and Truth.* Palo Alto, Calif.: Stanford University Press.

Rose, Nikolas. 1999. *Powers of Freedom: Reframing Political Thought.* Cambridge: Cambridge University Press.

Rosen, Lawrence. 1979. "Social Identity and Points of Attachment: Approaches to Social Organization." In *Meaning and Order in Moroccan Society,* ed. C. Geertz, H. Geertz, and L. Rosen, 19–122. London: Cambridge University Press.

———. 1984. *Bargaining for Reality: The Construction of Social Relations in a Muslim Community.* Chicago: University of Chicago Press.

———. 2002. *The Culture of Islam: Changing Aspects of Contemporary Muslim Life.* Chicago: University of Chicago Press.

Roy, Srila. 2007. "The Everyday Life of the Revolution." *South Asia Research* 27 (2): 187–204.

Russell, Andrew and Mary Thompson. 2000. "Introduction: Contraception across Cultures." In *Contraception across Cultures: Technologies, Choices, Constraints,* ed. Andrew Thompson, Mary Russell, and Elisa Sobo, 3–26. London: Berg Publishers.

Rutherford, Bruce K. 2008. *Egypt after Mubarak: Liberalism, Islam, and Democracy in the Arab World.* Princeton: Princeton University Press.

Sadiqi, Fatima. 1996. "The Place of Berber in Morocco." *International Journal of the Sociology of Language* 123: 7–21.

Sahlins, Marshall. 1988. "Cosmologies of Capitalism: The Trans-Pacific Sector of the World System." *Proceedings of the British Academy* 74: 1–51.

———. 1993. "Goodbye to *Tristes Tropes:* Ethnography in the Context of Modern World History." *Journal of Modern History* 65(1): 1–25.

Said, Edward. 1979. *Orientalism.* New York: Pantheon Books.

———. 1994. "Afterword." *Orientalism.* New York: Vintage, 329–352.

Sait, Sadiq et al. 2007. "Impact of Internet Usage in Saudi Arabia: A Social Perspective." *International Journal of Information Technology and Web Engineering* 2 (2): 1–107.

Saktanber, Ayse. 2002. *Living Islam: Women, Religion, and the Politicization of Culture in Turkey.* New York: I. B. Tauris.

Salem-Murdock, Muneera. 1989. *Arabs and Nubians in New Halfa.* Salt Lake City: University of Utah Press.

Salih, Ruba. 2003. *Gender in Transnationalism: Home, Longing, and Belonging Among Moroccan Migrant Women.* London: Routledge.

Salmon, C. T., L. Fernandez, and L. A. Post. 2010. "Mobilizing Public Will across Borders: Roles and Functions of Communication Processes and Technologies." *Journal of Borderlands Studies* 25 (3–4): 159–170.

Samhan, Helen Hatab. 1999. "Not Quite White: Race Classification and the Arab-American Experience." In *Arabs in America: Building a New Future,* ed. Michael Suleiman, 209–226. Philadelphia: Temple University Press.

Samin, Nadav. 2008. "Dynamics of Internet Use: Saudi Youth, Religious Minorities, and Tribal Communities." *Middle East Journal of Culture and Communication* 1: 197–215.

Sargent, Carolyn. 2006. "Reproductive Strategies and Islamic Discourse: Malian Migrants Negotiate Everyday Life in Paris, France." *Medical Anthropology Quarterly* 20 (1): 31–49.

Sargent, Carolyn, and Dennis Cordell. 2003. "Polygamy, Disrupted Reproduction, and the State: Malian Migrants in Paris, France." *Social Science & Medicine* 56: 1961–1972.

Sawalha, Aseel. 2010. *Reconstructing Beirut: Memory and Space in a Postwar Arab City.* Austin: University of Texas Press.

Sayad, Abdelmalek. 2000. "El Ghorba: From Original Sin to Collective Lie." *Ethnography* 1 (2): 147–171.

———. 2004. *The Suffering of the Immigrant.* London: Polity.

Schacht, Joseph. 1964. *Introduction to Islamic Law.* Oxford: Clarendon Press.

Scott, James. 2009. *The Art of Not Being Governed: An Anarchist History of Upland Southeast Asia.* New Haven: Yale University Press.

Shafik, Viola. 2007a. *Arab Cinema: History and Cultural Identity.* Cairo: American University in Cairo Press.

———. 2007b. *Popular Egyptian Cinema: Gender, Class, and Nation.* Cairo: American University Press.

Shakry, Omnia. 2007. *The Great Social Laboratory: Subjects of Knowledge in Colonial and Postcolonial Egypt.* Stanford: Stanford University Press.

Shalakany, Amr. 2006. "'I Heard It All Before': Egyptian Tales of Law and Development." *Third World Quarterly* 27 (5): 833–853.

Shami, Seteney. 1993. "Feminine Identity and Ethnic Identity: The Circassians in Jordan." In *Who's Afraid of Femininity? Questions of Identity,* ed. M. Michielsens and M. Brugmann 147–155. Amsterdam: Editions Rodopi B.V.

———. 1996. "Gender, Domestic Space, and Urban Upgrading: A Case Study from Amman." *Gender and Development* 4 (1): 17–23.

———. 2000. "Prehistories of Globalization: Circassian Identity in Motion." *Public Culture* 12 (1): 177–204.

———. 2009. "*Aqalliyya*/Minority in Modern Egyptian Discourse." In *Words in Motion: Towards a Global Lexicon,* ed. Carol Gluck and Anna Tsing, 151–173. Durham, N.C.: Duke University Press.

Sharoni, Simona. 1997. "Women and Gender in Middle East Studies: Trends, Prospects, and Challenges." *Middle East Report* (Oct.–Dec.): 27–29.

Sharp, Lesley. 2000. "The Commodification of the Body and its Parts." *Annual Review of Anthropology* 29: 287–328.

Shepard, Todd. 2009. "Excluding *Harkis* from Repatriate Status, Excluding Muslim Algerians from French Identity." In *Transnational Spaces and Identities in the Francophone World,* ed. Hafid Gafaïti, Patricia M. E. Lorcin, and David G. Troyansky, 94–114. Lincoln: University of Nebraska Press.

Sheriffadeen, Tengku A. 1997. "Beyond Information Literary: A Malaysian Experiment." Paper presented at the Asia-Pacific Economic Cooperation Conference, Tokyo, Japan, 4 November.

Shively, Kim. 2008. "Taming Islam: Studying Religion in Secular Turkey." *Anthropological Quarterly* 81(3): 683–712.

Shokeid, Moshe, and Shlomo A. Deshen. 1982. *Distant Relations: Ethnicity and Politics among Arabs and North African Jews in Israel.* New York: Praeger.

Shryock, Andrew. 1995. "Popular Genealogical Nationalism: History Writing and Identity among the Balqa Tribes of Jordan." *Comparative Studies in Society and History* 37 (2): 325–357.

———. 1997. *Nationalism and the Genealogical Imagination: Oral History and Textual Authority in Tribal Jordan.* Berkeley: University of California Press.

Siegel, James T. 1998. *A New Criminal Type in Jakarta: Counter-Revolution Today.* Durham, N.C.: Duke University Press.

———. 2000a [1969]. *The Rope of God.* Ann Arbor: University of Michigan Press.

———. 2000b. "Kiblat and the Mediatic Jew." *Indonesia* 69: 9–40.

Silverstein, Paul. 1996. "Realizing Myth: Berbers in France and Algeria." *Middle East Report* (200): 11–15.

———. 2003. "Martyrs and Patriots: Ethnic, National, and Transnational Dimensions of Kabyle Politics." *Journal of North African Studies* 8: 87–111.

———. 2004. *Algeria in France: Transpolitics, Race, and Nation.* Bloomington: Indiana University Press.

———. 2007. "Islam, *Laïcité,* and Amazigh Activism in France and North Africa." In *North African Mosaic: A Cultural Reappraisal of Ethnic and Religious Minorities,* ed. Nabil Boudraa and Joseph Krause, 104–118. Newcastle, U.K.: Cambridge Scholars Press.

Silverstein, Paul, and Jane Goodman. 2009. "Introduction: Bourdieu in Algeria." In *Bourdieu in Algeria: Colonial Politics, Ethnographic Practices, Theoretical Developments,* ed. Jane Goodman and Paul Silverstein, 1–64. Lincoln: University of Nebraska Press.

———. 2010. "The Local Dimensions of Transnational Berberism: Racial Politics, Land Rights, and Cultural Activism in Southeastern Morocco." In *Berbers and Others: Shifting Parameters of Ethnicity in the Contemporary Maghrib,* ed. Katherine Hoffman and Susan Gilson Miller, 83–102. Bloomington: Indiana University Press.

Slyomovics, Susan. 1998. *The Object of Memory: Arab and Jew Narrate the Palestinian Village.* Philadelphia: University of Pennsylvania Press.

———. 2005. *The Performance of Human Rights in Morocco.* Philadelphia: University of Pennsylvania Press.

———. 2012. "Happiness, Human Rights, and the Arab Spring." *American Anthropologist* 114 (1): 14–15

Singerman, Diane. 1995. *Avenues of Participation: Family, Politics, and Networks in Urban Quarters in Cairo.* Princeton: Princeton University Press.

Smith, Elizabeth. 2006. "Place, Class and Race in the *Barabra* Café: Nubian Urban Spaces and Media Identities." In *Cairo Cosmopolitan: Politics, Culture, and Urban Space in the New Middle East,* ed. Diane Singerman and Paul Amar, 399–414. Cairo: American University in Cairo Press.

Spillman, Georges. 1936. *Les Ait Atta du Sahara et la pacification du Haut Dra.* Rabat, Morocco: Félix Moncho.

Springborg, Robert. 1989. *Mubarak's Egypt: Fragmentation of the Political Order.* Boulder, Colo.: Westview Press.

Starrett, Gregory. 1995. "The Political Economy of Religious Commodities in Cairo." *American Anthropologist* 97 (1): 51–68.

———. 1998. *Putting Islam to Work: Education, Politics, and Religious Transformation in Egypt.* Berkeley: University of California Press.

———. 2005. "The Spirit of Your Resolution, or, Political Culture and the AAA." *Anthropology News* (February): 11–12.

Stavenhagen, Rudolfo. 1971. "Decolonizing Applied Social Sciences." *Human Organization* 30: 333–358.

Stein, Rebecca. 1998. "National Itineraries, Itinerant Nations: Israeli Tourism and Palestinian Cultural Production." *Social Text* 16: 91–124.

Stirling, Paul. 1965. *Turkish Village.* New York: John Wiley & Sons.

Stokes, Martin. 1998. "Imagining 'the South': Hybridity, Heterotopias, and Arabesk on the Turkish–Syrian Border." In *Border Identities: Nation and State at International Frontiers,* ed. Thomas Wilson and Hastings Donnan, 263–288. Cambridge: Cambridge University Press.

Stoler, Laura and Karen Strassler. 2000. "Castings for the Colonial: Memory Work in 'New Order' Java." *Comparative Studies in Society and History* 42 (1): 4–48.

Strathern, Marilyn. 2005. *Partial Connections.* Walnut Creek, Calif.: Altamira Press.

Strawson, John. 1995. "Islamic Law and English Texts." *Law and Critique* 6 (1) 21–38.

Swedenburg, Ted. 1995. *Memories of Revolt: 1936–39 Rebellion and the Palestinian National Past.* Minneapolis: University of Minnesota Press.

Swedenburg, Ted, and R. L. Stein, eds. 2005. *Palestine, Israel, and the Politics of Popular Culture.* Durham, N.C.: Duke University Press.

Sweet, Louise. 1960. *Tell Toqaan: A Syrian Village.* Ann Arbor: University of Michigan Museum of Anthropology, Anthropological Papers 14.

———. 1969. "A Survey of Recent Middle East Ethnology." *Middle East Journal* 23 (2) (Spring): 221–232.

———. 1970. *Peoples and Cultures of the Middle East: An Anthropological Reader.* Garden City, N.Y.: Published for the American Museum of Natural History by the Natural History Press.

———, ed. 1971. *The Central Middle East; A Handbook of Anthropology and Published Research on the Nile Valley, the Arab Levant, Southern Mesopotamia, the Arabian Peninsula, and Israel.* New Haven, Conn.: Human

Relations Area Files.

Tamanoi, Mariko. 1998. *Under the Shadow of Nationalism: Politics and Poetics of Rural Japanese Women.* Honolulu: University of Hawaii Press.

———. 2009. *Memory Maps: The State and Manchuria in Postwar Japan.* Honolulu: University of Hawaii Press.

Tapper, Nancy, and Richard Tapper. 1986. "Eat this, it'll do you a power of good": Food and Commensality among Durrani Pashtuns." *American Ethnologist* 13 (1): 62–79.

———. 1988. "Concepts of Personal, Moral, and Social Disorder among Durrani Pashtuns in Northern Afghanistan." In *The Tragedy of Afghanistan: The Social, Cultural, and Political Impact of the Soviet Invasion,* ed. Bo Huldt and Erland Jansson, 38–54. London: Croom Helm.

Tapper, Richard. 1989. "Ethnic Identities and Social Categories in Iran and Afghanistan." In *History and Ethnicity,* ed. Elizabeth Tonkin, Maryon McDonald, and Malcolm Chapman, 232–246. London: Routledge.

———. 2009. "Personal Reflections on Anthropology of and in Iran." In *Conceptualizing Iranian Anthropology: Past & Present Perspectives,* ed. Shahnaz Nadjmabadi, 225–241. Oxford: Berghahn.

———. 2008. "Who are the Kuchi? Nomad Identities in Afghanistan," *Journal of the Royal Anthropological Institute (n.s.)* 14: 97–116.

Taussig, Michael. 1993. *Mimesis and Alterity.* New York: Routledge.

Taylor, Charles. 1992. *Multiculturalism and "The Politics of Recognition."* Princeton: Princeton University Press.

Tesquet, Olivier. 2009. «En Iran, révolution Twitter ou révolution Twittée?» *L'Express.* 15 June.

Thomas, Bertram. 1938. *Arabia Felix: Across the Empty Quarter.* London: Reader's Union.

Thompson, Elizabeth. 2000. *Colonial Citizens: Republican Rights, Paternal Privilege, and Gender in French Syria and Lebanon.* New York: Columbia University Press.

Toomey, Christine. 2009. "Can Iran's Young Ring the Changes?" *New York Times Magazine.* 7 June.

Tozy, Mohamed. 1999. *Monarchie et Islam politique au Maroc.* Paris: Presses de la Fondation nationale des sciences politiques.

Tripp, Charles. 2006. *Islam and the Moral Economy: The Challenge of Capitalism.* Cambridge: Cambridge University Press.

Troutt Powell, E. M. 2003. *A Different Shade of Colonialism: Egypt, Great Britain, and the Mastery of the Sudan.* Berkeley: University of California Press.

Tuchman, Gaye. 2009. *Wannabe U: Inside the Corporate University.* Chicago: University of Chicago Press.

Tuğal, Cihan. 2006. "The Appeal of Islamic Politics: Ritual and Dialogue in a Poor District of Turkey." *Sociological Quarterly* 47: 245–273.

Turner, Victor Witter. 1967. *The Forest of Symbols: Aspects of Ndembu Ritual.* Ithaca, N.Y.: Cornell University Press.

———. 1969. *The Ritual Process: Structure and Anti-Structure.* Chicago: Aldine Publishing Co.

UNESCO. 2009. "Safeguarding Intangible Cultural Heritage."

Varisco, Daniel. 2005. *Islam Obscured: The Rhetoric of Anthropological Representation.* New York: Palgrave Macmillan.

Varzi, Roxanne. 2008. "Iran's Pieta: Motherhood, Sacrifice, and Film in the Aftermath of the Iran–Iraq War." *Feminist Review* 88: 1–13.

Vermeren, Pierre. 2002. *Histoire du Maroc depuis l'indépendance.* Paris: La Découverte.

Vertovec, Steven. 2002. "Islamophobia and Muslim Recognition in Britain." In *Muslims in the West: From Sojourners to Citizens,* ed. Yvonne Yazbeck Haddad, 19–35. Oxford: Oxford University Press.

Vigh, Henrik E. 2006. "Social Death and Violent Life Chances." In *Navigating Youth, Generating Adulthood: Social Becoming in an African Context,* ed. Catrine Christiansen, Mats Utas, and Henrik E. Vigh, 31–66. Stockholm: Uppsala.

Vinogradov, Amal. 1974. "Ethnicity, Cultural Discontinuity, and Power Brokers in Northern Iraq: The Case of the Shabak." *American Ethnologist* 1 (1): 207–218.

Vom Bruck, Gabrielle. 2005. *Islam, Memory, and Morality in Yemen: Ruling Families in Transition.* New York: Palgrave Macmillan.

Walters, Delores M. 1987. "Perceptions of Social Inequality in the Yemen Arab Republic." Ph.D. dissertation. New York University.

Waterbury, John. 1970. *Commander of the Faithful: The Moroccan Political Elite: A Study in Segmented Politics.* New York: Columbia University Press / London: Weidenfeld & Nicolson.

———. 1978. "La légitimation du pouvoir au Maghreb: tradition, protestation et répression." *Annuaire de l'Afrique du Nord* 16: 411–422.

Watson, Rubie. 1994. "Memory, History, and Opposition under State Socialism: An Introduction." In *Memory, History, and Opposition under State Socialism,* ed. Rubie Watson, 1–20. Santa Fe, N.M.: School of American Research Press.

Wehr, Hans. 1979. *A Dictionary of Modern Written Arabic (Arabic–English)*. Wiesbaden, Germany: Harrassowitz.

Weinberger, David. 2002. *Small Pieces Loosely Joined (A Unified Theory of the Web)*. Cambridge, Mass.: Perseus Publishing.

Weiner, Jerome B. 1979. "The Green March in Historical Perspective." *The Middle East Journal* 33 (1): 20–33.

Wheeler, Deborah. 2003. "The Internet and Youth Subculture in Kuwait." *Journal of Computer-Mediated Communication* 63 (2–3): 187–201.

———. 2006. *The Internet in the Middle East*. Syracuse, N.Y.: Syracuse University Press.

White, Jenny B. 1994. *Money Makes Us Relatives: Women's Labor in Urban Turkey*. Austin: University of Texas Press.

———. 2002. *Islamist Mobilization in Turkey: A Study in Vernacular Politics*. Seattle: University of Washington Press.

———. 2007. "The Ebbing Power of Turkey's Secularist Elite." *Current History* 104 (704): 427–433.

Wikan, Unni. 1991. *Behind the Veil in Arabia: Women in Oman*. Chicago: University of Chicago Press.

Wikipedia. 2011. "State of the Art." Accessed 24 October.

Wilder, Gary. 2005. *The French Imperial Nation-State: Négritude and Colonial Humanism Between the Two World Wars*. Chicago: University of Chicago Press.

Wilkinson, John. 1972. "The Origins of the Omani State." In *The Arabian Peninsula: Society and Politics*, ed. Derek Hopwood, 67–88. London: George Allen and Unwin.

———. 1977. *Water and Tribal Settlement in South-East Arabia: A Study of the Aflaj of Oman*. Oxford: Clarendon Press.

———. 1987. *The Imamate Tradition of Oman*. Cambridge: Cambridge University Press.

Williams, Paul. 2008. *Memorial Museums: The Global Rush to Commemorate Atrocities*. Oxford, U.K.: Berg.

Winder, R. Bayly. 1969. *Near Eastern Round Table 1967–68*. New York: Near Eastern Center, New York University.

———. 1987. "Four Decades of Middle Eastern Study." *Middle East Journal* 41 (1) (Winter): 40–63.

Winegar, Jessica. 2006. *Creative Reckonings: The Politics of Art and Culture in Contemporary Egypt*. Stanford: Stanford University Press.

Winter, Bronwyn. 2008. *Hijab and The Republic: Uncovering the French Headscarf*

Debate. Syracuse, N.Y.: Syracuse University Press.

Worth, Robert F. 2007. "Home on Holiday, the Lebanese Say, What Turmoil?" *The New York Times.* 24 December.

Xinhua News Agency. 1996. "Lebanon Has 2.25 Million Foreign Workers." 9 July.

Yacine-Titouh, Tassadit. 2001. *Chacal ou la ruse des dominés.* Paris: La Découverte.

Yamani, Mai. 2010. "Saudi Youth: The Illusion of Transnational Freedom." *Contemporary Arab Affairs* 3 (1) (January): 7–20.

Yankwich, Leon R. 1946–1947. "Some Characteristics of Mohammedan Law." *Southern California Law Review* 20 (4): 340–351.

Yata, Ali, and Jim Paul. 1977. "The Moroccan CP [Communist Party] and Sahara." *MERIP Reports* (56): 16–18.

Ye'or, Bat. 2005. *Eurabia: The Euro-Arab Axis.* Madison, N.J.: Fairleigh Dickinson University Press.

Yılmaz, Ihsan. 2005. "State, Law, Civil Society, and Islam in Contemporary Turkey." *Muslim World* 95 (3): 385–411.

Yovel, Jonathan. 2000. "What Is Contract Law 'About'? Speech Act Theory and a Critique of "Skeletal Promises." *Northwestern University Law Review* 94: 937–962.

Yuval-Davis, Nira. 2001. "Nationalism, Feminism, and Gender Relations." In *Understanding Nationalism,* ed. Montserrat Guibernau and John Hutchinson, 120–141. Cambridge: Polity Press.

Zartman, I. William. 1987. "King Hassan's New Morocco." In *The Political Economy of Morocco,* ed. I. William Zartman, 1–33. New York: Praeger.

Zemni, Sami, and Koenraad Bogaert. 2009. "Trade, Security, and Neoliberal Politics: Whither Arab Reform? Evidence from the Moroccan Case." *Journal of North African Studies* 14 (1): 91–107.

Zittrain, Jonathan and Benjamin Edelman. 2002. "Documentation of Internet Filtering in Saudi Arabia." Paper from the Harvard Law School Berkman Center for Internet and Society. 12 September. http://cyber.law.harvard .edu/filtering/saudiarabia/ (accessed 1 July 2012).

Zubaida, Sami. 1995. "Is there a Muslim Society? Ernest Gellner's Sociology of Islam." *Economy and Society* 24: 151–188.

Zulficar, Mona. 2008. "The Islamic Marriage Contract in Egypt." In *The Islamic Marriage Contract: Case Studies in Islamic Family Law,* ed. Asifa Quraishi and Frank E. Vogel, 231–274. Cambridge, Mass.: Harvard University Press.

Zunes, Stephen, and Jacob Mundy. 2010. *Western Sahara: War, Nationalism, and Conflict Irresolution.* Syracuse, N.Y.: Syracuse University Press.

CONTRIBUTORS

JON W. ANDERSON is Professor and Chair of Anthropology at the Catholic University of America and director of its Islamic World Studies program. He has done research on tribalism in Afghanistan, Islamic cosmology in Pakistan, and Internet pioneering in Jordan, Egypt, Syria, Saudi Arabia, and Qatar. He is author of *Arabizing the Internet* and co-editor of *New Media in the Muslim World: The Emerging Public Sphere* (IUP, 2003) and *Reformatting Politics: Information Technology and Global Civil Society.*

PAMELA CHRABIEH BADINE is Associate Research Scholar and Director of International Relations at the University of Montreal (CRCIPG), and a teaching fellow at Holy Spirit University, Kaslik (Lebanon). She has a doctorate in Sciences of Religions (University of Montreal). She is also an artist, blogger, and author of many publications.

DAWN CHATTY is University Professor of Anthropology and Forced Migration and Director of the Refugee Studies Centre, Department of International Development, Oxford University. She is the author of *Dispossession and Displacement in the Modern Middle East; Dispossession and Forced Migration in the Middle East and North Africa;* and *Deterritorialized Youth: Sahrawi and Afghan Refugees at the Margins of the Middle East.*

SUSANNE DAHLGREN is an Academy of Finland research fellow at the Helsinki Collegium for Advanced Studies. She is author of *Contesting Realities: The Public Sphere and Morality in Southern Yemen,* and numerous articles on Islam, law, morality, sexuality, and urban space.

LARA DEEB is Associate Professor of Anthropology at Scripps College. She is author of *An Enchanted Modern: Gender and Public Piety in Shi'i Lebanon*. She is a member of the editorial committee of *Middle East Report* and the editorial board of the *International Journal of Middle East Studies*.

SHERINE HAFEZ is Associate Professor of Women's Studies and Middle East and Islamic Studies at the University of California, Riverside. She is author of *The Terms of Empowerment: Islamic Women's Activism in Egypt* and *An Islam of Her Own: Reconsidering Religion and Secularism in Women's Islamic Movements*.

SONDRA HALE is Professor Emerita of Anthropology and Women's Studies and Interim Co-Director of the Center for Near Eastern Studies at the University of California, Los Angeles. She is a founding editor of *The Journal of Middle East Women's Studies*, author of *Gender Politics in Sudan*, and co-editor of *From Site to Vision: The Woman's Building in Contemporary Culture*.

CHRISTINE HEGEL-CANTARELLA is Assistant Professor of Anthropology at Western Connecticut State University. She contributed an essay to *Family Law in Islam: Divorce, Marriage and Women in the Muslim World* and has written on legal technologies and kinship in *Law, Culture, and the Humanities*.

CORTNEY L. HUGHES is Assistant Professor in the Department of Sociology and Anthropology at George Mason University. Her research interests are in medical anthropology, science and technology studies, feminist theory, Islam, and development. She has published articles in *Medical Anthropology Quarterly*, the *Journal of Telemedicine and e-Health*, and *Military Medicine* and through the UC Digital Library.

SUAD JOSEPH is Distinguished Professor of Anthropology and Women and Gender Studies and the founding director of the Middle East/South Asia Studies Program at the University of California, Davis. A past president of the Middle East Studies Association, she is general editor of the *Encyclopedia of Women and Islamic Cultures* and EWIC Online; editor of *Intimate Selving in Arab Families: Gender, Self, and Identity* and *Gender and Citizenship in the Middle East*; and co-editor of *Women and Power in the Middle East*.

CHARLOTTE KARAGUEUZIAN is a doctoral candidate in sociology at the École des Hautes Études en Sciences Sociales (EHESS), Paris. Her dissertation focuses on the rise of fine arts in the United Arab Emirates, for which she conducted a qualitative analysis of discourses of local artists, government, and merchants based in Abu Dhabi, Dubai, and Sharjah. She is a research associate at the Raoul-Dandurand Chair in Strategic and Diplomatic Studies at UQAM, University of Quebec in Montreal.

SEBASTIAN MAISEL is Associate Professor of Arabic and Middle East Studies at Grand Valley State University in Allendale, Michigan. His research focuses on social transformation among rural communities and minority groups, for which he conducted field work among the Bedouin tribes in Saudi Arabia, Yezidis in Syria and Iraq, and Dinka slave soldiers from Sudan. He is author of *The Customary Law of the Bedouins in Arabia* and co-author of *Saudi Arabia and the Gulf Arab States Today* and *The Kingdom of Saudi Arabia*.

NEFISSA NAGUIB is Professor of Social Anthropology at the University of Bergen, Norway. Her areas of research are faith-based activism, religious minorities, humanitarianism, gender, and the aesthetics and politics of water and food. As senior researcher at Chr. Michelsen Institute, she directs the Muslim Devotional Practices, Aesthetics, and Cultural Formation project and serves as the coordinator of the Cultures and Politics of Faith program. Among her publications are three co-edited volumes, *Movements of People in Time and Space; Water, Women and Memory: Recasting Lives in Palestine;* and *Interpreting Welfare and Relief in the Middle East.* She also co-produced the documentary *Women, War and Welfare in Jerusalem.*

SETENEY SHAMI is Program Director for Middle East and North Africa at the Social Science Research Council as well as Founding Director of the Arab Council for the Social Sciences (headquartered in Beirut, Lebanon). Her publications include an edited volume, *Publics, Politics, and Participation: Locating the Public Sphere in the Middle East and North Africa,* and articles in *Urban Imaginaries: Locating the Modern City; International Journal of Middle East Studies* and *Words in Motion: Towards a Global Lexicon.*

KIM SHIVELY is Associate Professor of Anthropology at Kutztown University of Pennsylvania, where she specializes in gender and religion in the Middle East. Her research has focused on interfaith dialogue efforts between Christians and Muslims in Turkey and the United States.

PAUL A. SILVERSTEIN is Associate Professor of Anthropology at Reed College. A 2008 Carnegie scholar, he is author of *Algeria in France: Transpolitics, Race, and Nation* (IUP, 2004) and co-editor (with Ussama Makdisi) of *Memory and Violence in the Middle East and North Africa* (IUP, 2006). He chairs the board of directors of the Middle East Research and Information Project (MERIP).

SUSAN SLYOMOVICS is Professor of Anthropology and Near Eastern Languages and Cultures at the University of California, Los Angeles. Among her works are *The Object of Memory: Arab and Jew Narrate the Palestinian Village* (winner of the Albert Hourani Book Award for best book in Middle East studies); *The Performance of Human Rights in Morocco; Clifford Geertz in Morocco* (edited); and *Waging War and Making Peace: The Anthropology of Reparations* (co-edited).

EMILIO SPADOLA is Assistant Professor of Anthropology at Colgate University. His research examines the social and subjective effects of Islam's mass mediation in urban Morocco. He is the author of *The Calls of Islam: Sufi Trance and Mass Mediation in Urban Morocco* (IUP, 2013).

JESSICA WINEGAR is Associate Professor of Anthropology at Northwestern University. She is the author of *Creative Reckonings: The Politics of Art and Culture in Contemporary Egypt,* which won the Albert Hourani Book Award for best book in Middle East studies. She serves on the editorial committee of *Middle East Report.*

INDEX

Abbas, Wael, 304, 306
Abd al-Aziz, King, 287, 293
'Abdali Sultanate, 229–230
Abdallah bin Abdulaziz, King, 288, 291
Abdellsalam, Shahnaz, 308
Abdulhamid, Ammar, 304, 309
Abdullah, Muhammad, 307–308
Abtal min al-Sahra (Heroes from the Desert) (al-Sudairi), 294
Abu-Ghraib, 95, 99
Abu-Lughod, Lila, 26, 38, 39; *Dramas of Nationhood*, 31–32; "Zones of Theory in the Anthropology of the Arab World," 18, 29–30, 33, 84
academia: conditions for Middle East–related issues, 80; fear, discourse of, 88–89; Palestine politics, political impact of, 81–82; tenure-track positions, 93–94. *See also* anthropologists, post 9/11
Academic Bill of Rights, 81
"Academic Freedom and Professional Responsibility after 9/11: A Handbook for Scholars and Teachers" (Task Force on Middle East Anthropology), 81, 92
Adams, John Quincy, 8
Adams, Robert M., 53
Aden, Crown Colony of, 228–232
Afghanistan, xiv, xvii, 27, 51–52
Agha-Soltan, Neda, 313, 315
Ahmadinejad, Mahmoud, 312, 313, 318

Ahmed, Leila, 253
Al Hilal P.V.O., 196–198
Al Rashid, Talal, 294, 296
Al-Ali, Nadje, 35
Alavi, Nasrin, 318
Alawite Sultanate, 261
al-Bidawi, Mohamed, 270, 273
Albright Institute of Archaeological Research, 52, 55
al-Dhuwaibi, Musaid, 296
Alexander, Catherine, 166
Algeria, xviii, 8, 262, 263; diaspora, 67, 72–74; French colonialism, 10, 14, 65, 67–68, 75, 77n3
Al-Ghazzawi, Razan, 308
al-Hithlain, Faisal, 296
Ali, Kamran, 34, 95
Ali El Himma, Faoud, 246
al-Omran, Ahmad, 307
al-Sudairi, Ahmad, 294
Amarji (A Heretic's Blog) (Abdulhamid), 304, 309
Amazigh activists. *See* Berber (Amazigh) activists
American Anthropological Association (AAA), xviii, 21n4, 79–80; Committee for Human Rights, 95, 98; Palestine politics and, 81–82, 95–98; post-9/11 anthropologists and, 95–101; resolutions, 80, 94, 95–99, 102n14
American Center of Oriental Research